Improving the Reading Program

Fifth Edition

Dorothy Albanese

Ph. D.

Improving the Reading Program

Fifth Edition

Delwyn Schubert
The California State University, Los Angeles

Theodore Torgerson
Emeritus, University of Wisconsin—Madison

wcb Wm. C. Brown Company Publishers
Dubuque, Iowa

Copyright © 1968, 1972. November 1976, 1981 by Wm. C. Brown Company Publishers

Library of Congress Catalog Card Number: 80-65712

ISBN 0–697–06186–8

Printed in the United States of America

Contents

Preface

The fifth edition of Improving the Reading Program continues to focus on the significance of educational and noneducational hazards to learning in the reading program. As in previous editions, the roles of prevention, diagnosis and mastery through the use of self-directed corrective material are highlighted. *Approximately 600 items pertaining to instructional material that is largely self-directed and self-corrective appear in chapters 12, 13 and 14.* Sources and prices are included. Chapters devoted to diagnosis, correction and the developmental program in reading have been extended and references have been updated.

The present edition introduces an extended glossary and a new chapter titled "Parents and the School." This chapter deals with the critically important role of parents in the home and in the school. It highlights vital resources existing in the home for child care and development and it describes specific ways in which parents can be of assistance to the school. The improvement of parent-teacher relationships is emphasized and examples of successful programs that have resulted in community-school cooperation are discussed and documented. The chapter is written in a manner that permits its being used with parents in the form of a newsletter.

Because of its practicality, *Improving the Reading Program* is popular with experienced teachers and beginning teachers who have spent little or no time in the classroom. Many teachers keep a copy of the volume on their desks so as to have finger-tip accessibility to recommended methods and materials that can meet the specific reading needs of children in their classroom. Written in a succinct style, *Improving the Reading Program* pinpoints the practical without sacrificing necessary theory.

Overview of Content and Organization

Tenets of Learning (Chapter 1)

Learning is the goal of all teaching.
Learning is inhibited when frustration and failure prevail.
Learning is enhanced when wholesome teacher-pupil-parent relationships prevail.
Learning is enhanced when parents provide wholesome incentives for learning.
Learning is maximized when the school provides adequately for individual differences.
The objective of the reading program is to teach all children to read at capacity level.
Reading problems are reduced to a minimum when hazards to learning are identified and corrected.
Reading problems are reduced to a minimum when a program of prevention is emphasized.
Teacher effectiveness in correcting reading problems is enhanced by use of self-directed material.

Hazards to Learning

Educational Hazards (Chapter 2)

Faulty practices in
Developmental reading
Diagnosis in reading
Correction in reading
Administrative policies

Noneducational Hazards (Chapter 3)

Impaired vision
Impaired hearing
Impaired speech
Impaired health
Neurological disorders
Mental immaturity
Emotional maladjustment
Cultural deprivation

Parents and the School (Chapter 4)

School involvement
Teacher-parent relationships
Parent-child relationships
School attendance
Respect for property
Good nutrition
Sleep and physical health
Good study environment
Parent-teaching pools
Television viewing

The Instructional Program In Reading

Developmental Program (Chapter 5)

Systematic instruction in the skills
Sequential development
Mastery of the skills
Prevention emphasized
Frustration level avoided
Diversified material utilized
Mastery of reading skills in the primary grades
Exploration of cultural needs

Interest and Motivation (Chapter 6)

Exploring interests
Law of effect
Paperbacks and comic books
Sustained silent reading
Games
Book reporting

Adapting Instruction to Meet Individual Needs (Chapter 7)

Grouping
Individualization
Instructional methods
Instructional material
Library

The Diagnostic Program (Chapter 8)

Discovers difficulties in
word recognition
word analysis
comprehension and rate
study skills
Explores reading expectancy
Identifies hazards to learning

The Diagnostic Process (Chapter 9)

Diagnosis identifies
problem readers
nature of the reading problem
severity of the problem
reading expectancy
hazards to learning
causal factors
correction needed

The Corrective Program (Chapter 10)

Corrects deficiencies in
sight vocabulary and word analysis
comprehension and study skills
dictionary skills
meaning vocabulary
technical vocabulary

The Corrective Material (Chapters 11 through 14)

Teacher-made and commercial
self-directive in nature
optimum in difficulty
varied in content and interest
tailored to meet individual needs

The Improvement Program in Reading (Chapter 15)

Qualified teachers of reading
In-service teacher training
Reading specialists and other consultants
Ample library facilities
Diversified instructional material
Professional library
Teacher research
Promotion based on achievement

1 Reading and the Learning Process

In spite of Postman's belief that reading is outdated in a technological society,[1] it remains literally true that the roads of knowledge are paved with printer's ink. Reading is a tool for mining the rich vein of man's recorded experience. Through reading, which in itself is a form of experiencing, we may live vicariously many lives. Through reading we can enter the minds of men and women in all walks of life. By expanding and extending our limited present into the broad past, reading enables us to gain insight into our cultural heritage and that of other people.

Reading is an important key to better citizenship. It is through reading that our citizens can become informed about local and national problems. The health of a democracy is dependent on an informed citizenry. And in the final analysis, it is public opinion that determines the course of our national destiny.

Illiteracy makes it difficult to function in a modern society in many ways. For example, reading directions on a bottle of aspirin requires tenth-grade reading ability; understanding income tax forms, ninth-grade reading ability; and insurance policies often are written on the twelfth-grade level.[2]

Thompson[3] found that 42 percent of his sample of 134 students were under-achieving readers. Paul Copperman, author of *The Literacy Hoax,** states that 20 percent of our young adults are functionally illiterate.[4] (Illiteracy is usually considered to be a reading level below fifth grade.) It has been found that 13 percent of all 17-year-olds are "unable to read a newspaper, fill out a job application or calculate change at the checkout counter."[5] A *Newsweek* estimate of the nation's adult illiteracy is 23 million.[6] Another report estimates that the following percentages of individuals over 16 could not fill out basic forms.[7]

*William Morrow and Company, 1978.

1. Three percent could not fill out a public-assistance form.
2. Seven percent could not make out the equivalent of an application for a Social Security number.
3. Eight percent failed in their attempt to complete an application for a driver's license.
4. Eleven percent were stumped by an application for a personal bank account.
5. Thirty-four percent could not fill out an application for medical aid.

Scores reported by the College Entrance Examination Board have been dropping for twelve consecutive years. The class of 1975 scored ten points lower in verbal skills than did the high school graduates of the preceding year. The average score was the lowest in two decades.[8]

Shocking facts like these impelled the late James E. Allen, Jr., former commissioner of education to spearhead a nationwide attack on reading deficiencies. On September 23, 1969, when addressing the National Association of State Boards of Education in Los Angeles, he stated:

> . . . I am herewith proclaiming my belief that we should immediately set for ourselves the goal of assuring that by the end of the 1970's the right to read shall be a reality for all—that no one shall be leaving our schools without the skill and the desire necessary to read to the full limits of his capability. J. E. Allen, "The Right to Read—Target for the 70's," *Journal of Reading* 13 (1969):95-101.

The goal set by the former United States commissioner of education charged the schools of America with full responsibility for eliminating reading deficiencies. (It must continue to be our goal in the 80's.) As an aid to understanding and achieving this goal, we set forth the following tenets which outline briefly the principles, conditions, and practices of the reading improvement program presented in this book. The program is clarified and suggestions for its implementation are provided in subsequent chapters.

1. Learning is the goal of all teaching.
   a. Teaching is an educational process and learning is the product.
   b. The chief aim of the school is to promote literacy.
   c. Illiteracy is rampant in the adult population.
   d. The reading skills provide the tools for learning.
   e. A preponderance of pupils in the schools suffer from reading disability.
2. Learning is inhibited when frustration and failure prevail.
   a. Tasks that are too difficult result in frustration and failure.
   b. Children resist learning when they do not succeed.
   c. Hazards to learning are inhibiting factors.

3. Learning is enhanced when wholesome teacher-pupil-parent relationships prevail.
   a. The learner must want to learn.
   b. The learner is motivated when optimum conditions for learning prevail.
   c. Cooperative efforts of teachers and parents are needed to provide optimum conditions for learning.
4. Learning is enhanced when parents provide wholesome incentives for learning.
   a. Pre-school education in the home arouses important incentives for learning.
   b. Appropriate experiential background for learning is an important responsibility of the home.
   c. Parental interest and supervision of home study insures more successful learning.
5. Learning is maximized when the school provides adequately for individual differences.
   a. Learning is facilitated when the child's favored mode of learning is promoted.
   b. Learning is enhanced when the teacher promotes a wholesome classroom environment.
   c. Learning becomes a challenging experience to children when they are made aware of their goals, when their interests are aroused, when appropriate incentives are applied, when their learning problems are corrected, and when they recognize their progress.
6. The objective of the reading program is to teach all children to read at capacity level.
   a. Nonreaders, disabled readers, underachievers, and dropouts are found in every school system.
   b. A diversified and challenging instructional program adjusted to individual needs must be provided.
   c. A child's reading program must consist of materials that are on an appropriate instructional level and are adapted to his/her learning needs.
   d. The atypical child will learn when his/her specific learning problems are discovered and a systematic individualized program of appropriate learning experiences is provided.

This book sets forth conditions and practices which are essential to successful learning. It delineates conditions essential to a flexible program of instruction designed to prevent, correct, and eliminate reading failure. It helps teachers to determine individual needs and to meet those needs with a minimum of time and effort. It clarifies the problem of how to modify group instruction to meet the needs of the retarded reader without using out-of-school time for individual tutoring. It resolves this question teachers raise. Do I dare neglect the bright children by giving extra time to the less able?

We recognize that in spite of the presence of many unwholesome conditions and inefficient instructional practices, from 50 to 60 percent of the pupils in the average school often attain a so-called normal status in reading. *This book describes an improvement program in reading which has as its objective the attainment of true reading potential for all pupils.*

Classroom teachers can streamline their corrective work by moving from individual tutoring into a program of individualized correction utilizing self-directed instructional material. When this is done, pupils can work independently to overcome their difficulties. The required high-level mastery of the basic reading skills of word recognition and word analysis can then be attained. Such mastery will give rise to independent fourth-grade readers, readers who can cope with the many new and unfamiliar words that are introduced at that level. We contend that a primary-grade program which ensures total mastery of the basic reading skills of word recognition and word analysis will preclude, in a large measure, later reading failures. Mastery of these basic skills provides a sound foundation for acquiring independent reading habits and the successful mastery of the vast hierarchy of new reading skills (using the dictionary, finding central thoughts of paragraphs, skimming, summarizing, and so on) which are developed at the fourth-grade level and beyond.

Another essential of reading improvement involves a carefully planned recreational reading program for all pupils. Daily fun reading permits individual choice of books and other reading material under teacher guidance. In order to find the right books for the right children, materials which vary widely in interest appeal and difficulty level must be provided. Pupils do not profit from books that are uninteresting or too difficult for them.

Parents can play an important role in making a reading program a success. In addition to providing a good home environment (proper nutrition, adequate sleep, love and acceptance, monitoring of TV and homework supervision, etc.), they should become actively involved with the school. It is widely recognized and accepted that teachers can't do everything. Parents and school must cooperate in the education of children.

SUMMARY

Problems in reading are problems in learning. Severe problems in reading resulting in illiteracy are of utmost concern in our schools. Pupils fail to learn when hazards to learning are not identified and corrected. No child can be forced to learn. The desire must come from within. Although teachers have the major responsibility of providing optimum learning conditions which give rise to intrinsic motivation, we are becoming increasingly aware of the responsibility of the home. Unless parents provide their children with a good home environment and do their utmost to cooperate with and support the school, teachers are markedly handicapped. Teachers cannot do the job alone.

PROBLEMS FOR ORAL AND WRITTEN DISCUSSION

1. Do you agree with the statement that "the roads of knowledge are paved with printer's ink?"
2. Why is prevention and early correction of reading difficulties important?
3. What can parents do to help the teacher?
4. Evaluate your instructional program in reading in terms of the nine tenets set forth in this chapter.

Notes

1. N. POSTMAN, "The Politics of Reading," *Harvard Educational Review* (May, 1970):244-252.
2. Kilty, Ted K., *The Readability of Commonly Encountered Materials.* Western Michigan University, Kalamazoo, Mich., 1976.
3. C. A. WOODBURY, "The Identification of Underachieving Readers," *Reading Teacher* (January 1963):218-223.
4. P. COPPERMAN, *Family Circle*, 3 March, 1979.
5. "Quest for Better Schools," *U.S. News and World Report*, 11 September, 1978.
6. "The Blight of Illiteracy," *Newsweek*, 8 November, 1978.
7. U.S. News and World Report, 19 August 1974.
8. "Schools Fail the Test," *Los Angeles Times*, 17 September 1975.

Selected Readings

BRUININKS, ROBERT; GLAMAN, GERTRUDE; and CLARK, CHARLOTTE. "Issues in Determining Prevalence of Reading Retardation," *Reading Teacher* 26 (November 1973):177-185.
HARRIS, ALBERT J. and EDWARD R. SIPAY, *How To Teach Reading.* New York: Longman, 1979, Unit 1.
McNEIL, JOHN D.; DONANT, LISBETH; and ALKIN, MARVIN. *How to Teach Reading Successfully.* Boston: Little, Brown and Co., 1980, ch. 1.
WILSON, RICHARD, and EINBECKER, POLLY. "Does Reading Ability Predict College Performance?" *Journal of Reading* 18 (December 1974):234-237.
WINKELJOHANN, ROSEMARY. *The Politics of Reading: Point-Counterpoint.* Newark, Del.: International Reading Association, 1973.

2 Educational Hazards That Inhibit Learning

"When I was a boy," writes an editorialist, "we all learned how to read. Of course, we didn't have to contend with those newfangled methods." Statements such as these are found daily in newspapers and magazines throughout the United States. They infer that a return to "the good old days" is the panacea for all educational ills.

Teachers do not share this opinion. Many of them would explain reading problems in terms of out-of-school hazards. They feel that poor readers are often the product of homes where the intellectual, physical, and emotional needs of children have been ignored. Parents, of course, admit no shortcomings and believe that the school alone is responsible for all reading problems. "If the teacher would devote more time to my child, she/he would be a better reader."

Needless to say, research shows that both home and school can contribute to reading failure; however, when the stigma of reading failure does fall on the school, an honest appraisal of the situation leads to the inevitable conclusion that only a small percentage of handicapped readers are products of schools where teachers did not give them sufficient attention. Most poor readers have received a lion's share of the teacher's time—time which likely as not included individual as well as group attention. How, then, was the school inefficient?

Many schools violate the principles and conditions of learning implied in the tenets listed in chapter 1 by promoting practices which tend to inhibit learning and produce problems in reading. The causes of reading disability are complex; usually a constellation of interacting factors is responsible. Although some of these factors are beyond the jurisdiction of the school, the latter still has an obligation to provide a compensating school environment. While we believe it is of fundamental importance to place emphasis on those factors over which the school has direct control, in this book we will also delineate hazards and causal factors of reading disability that stem from conditions inherent in the child and his out-of-school environment and give suggestions for their alleviation or correction. In this connection it should be pointed out that hazards may or may not be causal factors which deter learning. Individuals differ in their tolerance for particular hazards. Thus the potential effect of a specific hazard as a deterent to learning must be carefully considered in each case.

The remainder of this chapter is devoted to a discussion of educational hazards to learning which pertain to the (1) Developmental Program in Reading, (2) Diagnostic Program in Reading, (3) Corrective Program in Reading and, (4) Administrative Policies.

DEVELOPMENTAL PROGRAM IN READING

Beginning Formal Instruction in Reading Before a Child Has Attained Readiness

Reading readiness has been defined as "the level of maturity a child must reach before he can succeed in formal reading under normal instruction. A chronological age of six years and a minimum IQ of 100 is usually implied, with normal health, hearing, vision, etc."[1]

The problem of early reading instruction remains unsolved.[2] Some support it[3]; others [4,5] do not. They do not feel young children are sufficiently mature physically and emotionally to take formal reading instruction without undesirable side effects. The latter believe childhood is the time for many learnings that are needed before formal instruction in reading begins. Finally, they feel that premature introduction to reading might give rise to permanent antagonism or distaste for the reading process. (For a more detailed discussion of reading readiness see pages 83-87).

Accepting a Low Level of Mastery of Word Recognition in Primary Grades

The first step in learning to read involves mastering word perception. As children move through the primary grades, they should respond automatically and accurately to words appropriate to their grade placement. Any hesitation or delay is indicative of a low level of mastery. A 100 percent mastery of the current sight vocabulary should be a basic objective in the primary grades. Nothing is more fundamental to all reading skills than an adequate sight vocabulary. Brown and Loper concur in this belief when they state:

> A major concern of corrective instruction in reading is growth in word recognition. Although comprehension of reading material is the ultimate purpose of reading, there can be little hope that a student will ever be able to understand a passage unless he has sufficient word recognition skills to identify the printed words which make up the passage. It is not a question of whether word recognition or comprehension is more important; it is simply an understanding that written words cannot convey meaning to a student unless he is able to decipher them.

. . . Since beginning reading instruction is so largely concerned with the skills of word identification, it is not at all peculiar to find that most students who experience difficulty in reading in the first three grades do so because of poor abilities in the area of word recognition rather than comprehension. D. A. Brown and D. J. Loper, "Word Recognition in the Elementary School," *Corrective Reading in the Elementary Classroom* (Newark, Del.: International Reading Association, 1968), p. 91. (For a more detailed discussion of word recognition see chapter 12.)

Employing a Round-Robin Method of Teaching Oral Reading

Round-robin reading with a heterogeneous group is a pedagogically outdated as the dodo.[6] Unfortunately, there are some classrooms where this kind of archaic activity still persists.

Early research by Gilbert showed that children who followed silently what was being read aloud by another child made more fixations and regressions than when they read independently.[7] The poorer the oral reading, the worse were the follower's eye movements. As a result of his findings, Gilbert condemned the practice of "requiring silent readers to follow the oral reading of poor and mediocre readers."[8] We concur with Gilbert and wonder why more teachers haven't abided by his sage advice.

Failing to Develop Independent Reading Habits in All Pupils in the Primary Grades

One of the most difficult problems for the intermediate-grade teacher is to promote new reading skills in pupils who have failed to acquire independent reading habits. Achieving new goals in reading becomes extremely difficult if the basic sight vocabulary of the primary grades and the skills of word analysis have not been mastered. Continued sequential development of word-analysis skills, mastery of uncontrolled and technical vocabulary, and development of new study skills are all a part of normal growth in reading beyond the primary grades. When the basic sight vocabulary and the essentials of phonetic and structural analysis are taught in the primary grades to the point of mastery resulting in immediate recall, pupils will have acquired the tools that permit them to unlock new words with a minimum of hesitancy. Such pupils have acquired independent reading habits and are ready to pursue refinement and extension of these skills and to continue growth in meaning vocabulary and the study skills. Sequential developmental instruction resulting in a mastery of the reading skills appropriate to each grade level is the best prevention of later difficulties in reading.

Failing to Use Instructional Material Diversified in Difficulty and Content in Each Grade

Pupils in the average classroom above the primary grades usually reflect a range of five or more grades in reading ability, with the majority having instructional levels in reading either below or above their current grade placement. This wide disparity in achievement represents a diversity of individual reading difficulties and interests, and it demands instructional material that is diversified in content and difficulty. If frustration is to be avoided and inherent interests are to be challenged, basal readers on several grade levels are needed along with ample supplementary material. Teachers must be free to select widely from the textbook library as well as from the library of resource material that is available for supplementary and recreational reading. A teacher who discovers that the class average on an objective reading test is at the grade norm should recognize that both retardation and acceleration exist in the class. This means that the basal reader for the grade is usually too difficult for some pupils and too easy for others.

Methods that can be used in discovering the optimum instructional levels for retarded readers and the nature of their specific reading difficulties are discussed in subsequent chapters.

Requring Retarded Readers to Use Material on a Frustration Level of Difficulty

One cannot develop his biceps with weights that are too heavy to manipulate. By the same token, a child cannot improve his reading skill when books are too difficult. With books of optimum difficulty, however, practice becomes meaningful and improvement results. Relying on practice with materials of the grade at which a student is experiencing failure is largely a waste of time. When a pupil is asked to read material that is too difficult, he may fidget and squirm, become inattentive, frequently or continuously point with a finger, seem bored or lazy, or become mischievous. If he is actually forced to read material on the frustration level, a deepseated aversion to reading will usually develop.

The instructional level is the level at which a student should be taught.[9] Instructional material in reading should be sufficiently challenging to ensure progress, but not so difficult that frustration results. When a child is expected to work by himself without teacher assistance, easier reading material is needed. Suggestions for ascertaining a child's optimum instructional and independent or free reading levels are set forth in chapter 8.

Relying on Group Instruction to Meet
the Reading Needs of All Pupils

Undifferentiated group instruction, a common practice in the intermediate and upper grades, tends to be inefficient since all children do not thrive on the same educational diet. When instructional material is of optimum difficulty for the average reader, it is too difficult for some and too easy for others. What results? Poor readers invariably are stymied, while superior readers become bored because they are not challenged. As the superior readers stagnate, reading difficulties continue to accumulate for the disabled reader and resistance to instruction becomes increasingly acute. If this situation persists, all motivation, self-direction, and satisfaction in work well done wither away.

Undifferentiated group instruction also fails to take cognizance of factors that inhibit learning. In addition, resistance to learning which develops is treated frequently as a discipline problem rather than attitude and behavior to be understood and improved through proper guidance.

It is evident that undifferentiated group instruction provides but a partial answer to the multiplicity of learning problems facing the classroom teacher. Only when group practices are augmented by diagnosis and individualized corrective instruction can children's unique needs be met, and only then can effective learning be achieved. Ways to individualize instruction are discussed in chapters 7 and 10.

Failing to Promote a Balanced Program in Reading

Many reading programs fail to furnish a sufficient variety of materials. A well-balanced program should include several sets of basal readers on varying grade levels to provide systematic instruction in basic reading skills and the techniques of reading. Workbooks accompanying these readers are also needed to minimize the time-consuming activity of creating suitable follow-up work. Commercially made and teacher-made reading games and activities are valuable in making provision for pupils who need additional practice in word-recognition and word-analysis skills. A classroom library of books and magazines together with picture dictionaries should be found in all primary classrooms. Above the primary grades, reference books such as a world atlas and an almanac also have an important place. Other accessories needed to balance a reading program include filmstrips, slides, recordings, and films.

A functional reading program never overemphasizes one aspect of the reading process at the neglect of another. When it does, children's reading skills suffer. Too much emphasis on phonics, for example, tends to destroy interest in reading and results in low, laborious word calling. On the other hand, too little emphasis on phonics weakens word-attack skill and makes independent reading difficult. Other aspects of the reading program such as study-type reading versus recreational reading, oral reading versus silent reading, and independent reading versus group instruction also require a similar balance. It should be remembered that all readers must have their reading programs fit their individual needs.

If we wish all children to develop into well-rounded, independent readers with a lifetime interest in reading, constant vigilance must be given to both group and individual balancing of the reading program.

Failing to Motivate Children to Read Widely

It has been determined that the average American spends about 1.75 hours in daily reading.[10] Is there danger of our developing a generation of children who can read but will not? Are those who believe that we are in the twilight of the printed page alarmists or realists?[11]

Certainly, statistics show that we may be justified in being concerned. More money is spent in the United States each year for the repair of television sets (not for the purchase, mind you!) than is spent for new books. And what is particularly disconcerting is how we take many of the latest communicative gadgets as a matter of course. For example, when an elderly woman was offered a free plane ride recently she exclaimed, "No thank you. You won't catch me in one of those newfangled devices. I'm going to stay home and watch television just like the good Lord intended me to do."

It appears that teaching students how to read is not enough. Today's teachers must be aware of the need to inculcate children with a deep and abiding interest in reading. The ubiquitous query Why read? must be replaced by the more productive and forceful Let's read. (See ch. 6 for specific ways to motivate children to read.)

Assuming That Teaching Is the Goal of Education

Instruction is an educational process and learning is the product. Many teachers never evaluate their teaching in terms of learning or desirable changes in their pupils. These teachers are prone to say, "I do a good job of teaching. I work hard with my students—real hard. I have presented the required curricular content. What more can I do?"

Teaching does involve a generous expenditure of time and energy, but it is important that attention be devoted to what is appropriate. Teachers should consider themselves successful only when all the children with whom they work are progressing. This criterion of good teaching calls for continuous testing, diagnosing, teaching, testing, and more diagnosing. It calls for individualizing instruction in terms of pupils' levels of achievement, peculiar strengths and weaknesses, rates of learning, and learning potential. The answer, then, is not a need to work harder but to work more effectively.

When teachers can see students forging ahead in the acquisition of reading skills, when they can see interest sparkle, when they can see a noticeable improvement in scholarship, when these changes are taking place in the classroom, then, and then alone, can each teacher say with satisfaction, "I am doing a good job of teaching."

Assuming That Reading Can Be Taught Effectively as an Isolated Communicative Skill

A 12-year longitudinal study by Walter Loban has shown that reading, writing, speaking, and listening are related.[12] So it is not by accident that teachers' colleges invariably offer a basic methods course in the language arts rather than have prospective teachers take separate introductory courses in the teaching of reading, writing, listening, and speaking. The reason is that reading is not a skill that can be developed in isolation. Good teachers of reading capitalize on the relationships inherent in the language arts, all of which are means of social communication involving ideas, concepts, and emotions. Children express themselves through writing and speech, while they interpret the expressions of others through listening and reading.

The interrelationship of listening, speaking, reading, and writing is evident when one considers that lack of oral language stimulation in the home, delayed speech, impaired hearing, and speech defects often are associated with reading disability. Handicaps in the areas of listening and speaking are reflected in a child's writing and spelling.

It is probable that the world has known few successful writers who were not proficient readers. Many professional writers point out that they must read a great deal if they are to write. Similarly, a relationship exists between writing skill and oral speech. If what children write is poor the teacher should concentrate on oral language.

Buswell stresses the great similarity between speaking and reading in his definition of the reading process.

> Psychologically, the processes of speech and reading are quite similar, the difference being mainly in the sense avenues through which the verbal stimuli are received. . . . The essential difference between knowing how to understand oral speech is the substitution of visual perception of printed verbal symbols for the auditory impression of the same symbols when spoken. The thoughts expressed are the same, the vocabulary is the same, and the word order is the same. The new problem in reading is to learn to recognize the visual symbols with accuracy and reasonable speed. G. T. Buswell, "The Process of Reading," *Reading Teacher* (December 1959):108.

Dallman and associates make similar emphasis. "In reading we employ visual symbols to represent auditory symbols. The basic task in reading is therefore to establish in the mind of the reader automatic connections between specific sights and the sounds they represent."[13]

As a child gains proficiency in one communicative skill, all language skills benefit indirectly. This is reflected in high correlations between reading and spelling and reading and composition. The majority of poor readers are inaccurate spellers. By the same token, the child who reads little is not likely to write well. The language-experience approach, popularized by R. Van Allen, capitalizes on such interrelationships, the basic premise being, "What they can say, they can write, and what they can write, they can read."

Failing to Recognize That Mastery of Reading Skills Differs From Mastery of Information

Many teachers fail to recognize that learning of skills differs from learning information or developing concepts. Methods of instruction must differ in each instance. For example, information can be imparted orally by a teacher, but improving reading skills is something only the student can do through practice. It is a perfect example of learning through doing.

Demands on the learner are very exacting when skills are being learned. A pupil may acquire new information readily if he has an 80 percent mastery of previously related information, but an 80 percent mastery of the sight vocabulary by a given reader does not provide the readiness needed to succeed with the more complex comprehension skills and the more challenging vocabulary of subsequent material. Word-perception skill must entail at least a 95 percent mastery of the sight vocabulary before a student is ready to move into more difficult material.

Failing to Promote Wholesome Teacher-Pupil Relationships

Perhaps no condition for learning in the elementary school is more important than wholesome teacher-pupil relations. Glock states that "there is growing concern among educators to return to the concept of the basic importance of the pupil-teacher relationship."[14] The child who likes the teacher is the child who likes to learn. Strong emotions of insecurity, hate, fear, or resentment inhibit learning. Motivation must come from within rather than be imposed from without. Pupils resist learning if the teacher exhibits traits of unfairness, sarcasm, or ridicule. When teachers show partiality, when they are autocratic and disregard the rights and privileges of pupils, they destroy confidence, security, and social acceptance. As a result, learning is replaced by loss of interest, emotional tension, and disciplinary problems.

Mental health, a basic condition of learning, is best fostered in a classroom by a teacher who is warm and understanding, a teacher who has a genuine interest in children. These are teacher qualities that always have and always will have a magical effect in a learning situation.

Failing to Provide Special Instruction for Disadvantaged Children

The last several decades have brought awareness that children from impoverished homes are in need of special attention. These children have been referred to as underprivileged, deprived, disadvantaged, and the like, and they make their appearance in impoverished metropolitan areas, in Appalachia, and in other parts of the United States. They represent no one race or color, but are found among blacks, whites, Indians, Puerto Ricans, and Mexicans. Their parents have little or no interest in reading and do not provide an environment that is conducive to learning. Inadequate language experience is another handicap of the disadvantaged. An entirely different language may be spoken, or the language may be a dialect that diverges considerably from standard English. Syntax, too, is a major problem. The sentence structure to which disadvantaged children are exposed is at variance with that of sentences used by the teacher and employed in basal readers.

Although the language-experience approach is considered by many authorities to be an effective technique for teaching the disadvantaged child, research does not clearly demonstrate the superiority of any one method. It is most likely that the teacher who employs diversified approaches that are based on analysis of pupil needs is the one who will experience the greatest success in teaching reading to the disadvantaged.

Failing to Provide Appropriate Instruction for Children with Language Deficiencies

On January 2, 1974, a unanimous decision of the United States Supreme Court ordered the San Francisco Unified School District to provide special instruction to Chinese students not able to speak enough English to understand classroom proceedings. The court felt that Chinese-speaking pupils, though issued the same textbooks and instructed by the same teachers as English-speaking students, were "effectively foreclosed from any meaningful education." This decision meant that every public school system in the country that receives federal funds is obligated to set up remedial classes for non-English-speaking pupils.[15]

Although bilingualism in school children is not a new phenomenon in the United States, only in recent years has interest focused on non-English-speaking children, the culture from which they come, and the languages they speak upon entering school. There is no doubt that such children are tremendously handicapped in learning to read English. The problems encountered are multiple and involve vocabulary, concepts, syntax (sentence structure), and morphology (word formation). Therefore, traditional methods of teaching English-speaking children to read are not successful with non-English speakers.

Some children do not come from an environment in which an entirely different language is spoken, but rather come from one in which a dialect at variance with the standard dialects of American English is used. Because they are accustomed to different sounds and inflections, such children readily become confused when exposed to standard English. Shuy believes that teachers who work with these children should study the differences between black English and standard English.[16] This is especially true if it is decided that the children must be taught standard English before they learn to read or if it is decided that special reading material is needed that utilizes black English grammar.

Expecting a Low Level of Performance

There is reason to believe that teacher expectation may exert a powerful force on a child's intellectual performance. The teacher who believes a child is bright and expects high accomplishment is likely to have a stimulating effect on that child. By the same token, the teacher who believes that a child is dull and expects little or no accomplishment is likely not to be disappointed.

Studies with rats by Rosenthal and Fode and Rosenthal and Lawson led Rosenthal to hypothesize that teachers behave differently toward pupils whom they perceive as promising learners.[17, 18] Such behavior, he felt, results in pupils mirroring in their school performance teachers' expectations. To test this hypothesis, Rosenthal and Jacobson gave children an unfamiliar intelligence test for the supposed purpose of norming.[19] The elementary teachers involved were then given a list of randomly selected children who were designated academic "bloomers." The results? Significantly greater intellectual gains were shown in the bloomers than in other children. Rosenthal and Jacobson attributed the change in the bloomers to the created expectancies in the teachers' minds.

Although further research is needed, teachers must be aware of the fact that their own beliefs about a child can influence his conduct and performance.

DIAGNOSTIC PROGRAM IN READING

Failing to Detect Hazards to Learning

Nothing can be done to correct or minimize the undesirable effects of the many hazards to learning that may be operative unless they are detected. Teachers have a primary responsibility in this regard.

"I don't know exactly what it is," said a teacher, "but something is definitely wrong with that child." An examination by a physician revealed that the teacher who had made the foregoing statement was right. Something was wrong. The child had a visual impairment that had gone unnoticed for years. How could this be? Why didn't the child complain? Why hadn't his parents discovered the condition?

A child does not know that he is different from others. He supposes, for instance, that all children see fuzzy letters when reading or that everyone's eyes get tired after looking at books for a while.

Parents see their own child week after week, year after year, in more or less isolation. They become accustomed to his peculiarities. And because of this, they often are completely oblivious to aberrations which are readily evident to a teacher who works with several dozen children daily and has an opportunity to make comparisons. Teachers are in a unique position to detect hazards to learning.

Failing to Estimate the Potential of All Children

Teachers sometimes are prone to consider poor readers dull. "I do a good job of teaching," they say. "If a child doesn't learn, he's just dumb." The truth is that approximately 90 percent of all poor readers have an intelligence quotient (I.Q.) in excess of 80, with some reaching well into the 130s and above. In most cases, poor readers do have potential to do better.

It is unfortunate if teachers believe pupils are working up to capacity because distribution of reading and mental ability (M.A.) in a class are similar. Based on this premise, it is assumed that the poor reader is a slow learner. The school, they feel, is therefore absolved of any responsibility for improving the reading status of its pupils. Needless to say, intelligence test scores are often cited to bolster this contention.

Underestimating a poor reader's capabilities usually results in neglect of the child. This may prove disastrous to the individual and often results in a distinct loss to society. (For additional information see pages 53-56.)

Failing to Adequately Utilize Cumulative Records

Above the primary grades, all pupils will have attended school for three or more years. A number of teachers will have had extensive opportunity to observe, confer, and evaluate their growth in learning. Perhaps, too, certain physical, emotional, and intellectual problems impeding the success of normal progress will have been detected. All this information, together with the results of developmental and corrective programs, should be recorded on cumulative school records. When this responsibility is faithfully discharged by each teacher, a gold mine of useful information about each child can be readily available when needed. This is of particular value to new teachers at the beginning of a school year.

All teachers should study cumulative records very carefully at the beginning of each school year. They should add additional information to these records whenever anything of significance arises. The dividends resulting from this practice would be tremendous. The gap that too frequently exists because of the yearly break in continuity of instruction as a child moves from one teacher to another would disappear.

Failing to Provide a Systematic and Objective Testing Program

In terms of individual needs, both developmental and corrective instruction in reading assumes that these needs have been discovered through careful evaluation. Observation and informal testing are useful techniques to identify the more obvious problem cases. However, to evaluate an individual's reading problem more precisely, to determine its nature and severity, it becomes necessary to utilize objective tests of known validity and reliability (see Appendix C). Accuracy of evaluation is essential for a valid diagnosis on which an effective corrective program may be based.

A systematic objective testing program administered at least twice each year employing reliable survey tests will serve as an important method of identifying classroom problem readers, and test records will set forth their longitudinal development in reading. Diagnostic tests, both oral and silent, are needed to determine the nature of the disabled reader's problem. These tests are useful instruments to the teacher in spelling out the nature and extent of the corrective program needed. To be of greatest value and to be accessible to all teachers when needed, test data should be recorded in the cumulative record.

In summary, a systematic objective testing program alerts teachers to preventive needs, provides data for longitudinal records, suggests appropriate instructional levels, and enables them to chart individual corrective programs.

Assuming that Retardation Is Nonexistent When the Class Average on Standardized Reading Tests Reaches or Exceeds the Norm

Norms on achievement tests are averages of the performance of pupils in each of several grades throughout the nation. What is true of the country at large is not, however, always applicable to an individual grade or class. What is more, national norms do not constitute standards of excellence or even satisfactory achievement. Most students fail miserably to measure up to their full potential.

The teacher who consults norms is dealing with averages. It must not be overlooked that 50 percent of the scores fall below the norm. In a typical fourth grade, for example, approximately one-third of the children are reading on third-, second-, and even first-grade levels. By the same token, approximately one-third of the children in the average fourth grade are reading on fifth-, sixth-, and seventh-grade levels. It must be remembered that some of the accelerated pupils are retarded in terms of their potential.

These pupils have grade scores in reading which are substantially lower than their intelligence grade placement.

The teacher who accepts norms as the standard for her/his grade and expresses satisfaction with the result overlooks the retarded readers in her/his class who read on lower levels and are in dire need of corrective instruction. A teacher should convert individual scores on a standardized reading test to grade scores and group these scores in a way that highlights those children who are retarded one, two, three, or more years in their reading skills. She/he should make a similar tabulation of those who are accelerated. The teacher thus becomes aware of the retardation and acceleration in her/his grade. This gives a more realistic view of the problem to be faced in terms of the number of atypical readers in the class and the nature of their problems.

CORRECTIVE PROGRAM IN READING

Failing to Provide a Systematic Longitudinal Program of Developmental and Corrective Reading

In most elementary schools a child is assigned a new teacher each year. Teachers who wish to make maximum contribution to continued development of a new group of children must avail themselves of all pertinent information contained in previous school records. If new teachers do not study and profit from the developmental and corrective instruction provided by previous teachers, weeks and months will elapse before they are in a position to provide appropriate instruction. Thus valuable time is lost, student morale is impaired, and annual growth is hindered.

The school record should reveal a child's longitudinal progress in reading. Specifically, it should include the yearly instructional level, a description of the reading difficulties, the results of formal and informal methods of evaluation, and any corrective measures that were employed. Also included should be known hazards to learning and methods that were employed to alleviate them.

Cumulative records are often incomplete. Under these circumstances, interviews with parents and previous teachers should take place in an effort to augment school records. Children with learning problems must be challenged by new and more efficient methods and materials. Therefore, evaluation should seek to reveal the most appropriate instructional techniques to pursue. Uninterrupted growth in learning from year to year demands keeping and utilizing the results of past and current diagnostic and corrective practices.

Failing to Eliminate Individual Difficulties When They First Appear

A stitch in time saves nine. And so it is with reading disabilities. Often they are the product of accumulated neglected needs. Reading failures could be minimized if teachers would employ corrective measures whenever small problems were uncovered. Consider children such as these: Jim is absent for three weeks and misses instruction of short vowel sounds; Mary habitually makes mistakes involving little words such as *the* and *it;* Harry points at each word; Roger fails to group words into meaningful phrase units but plods along one word at a time.

Are the foregoing problems serious? Perhaps not in and by themselves, but as other difficulties arise and they begin to coalesce, a reading-disability case is born. It must be remembered that reading skill is dependent on a hierarchy of related and sequential skills. One difficulty leads to another. The child who has not mastered initial consonant sounds cannot be expected to cope with consonant blends; the child whose sight vocabulary is meager cannot read in thought units. Early diagnosis and immediate remediation are the only answers. Teachers who fail children in this regard are exposing them to certain reading failure.

The golden era for prevention is in the primary grades. In these grades the teacher should adopt a goal of complete mastery of reading skills taught at each level. This is the key to prevention. Introducing new and more difficult material to primary-grade children before they have mastered the current sight vocabulary ignores the first step in a program of prevention. This common practice results in a rapid accumulation of difficulties which cause loss of interest, absence of growth, lowered mastery, and ultimate failure.

Promoting a systematic program of prevention and mastery of the reading skills in the primary grades leads to the development of independent reading habits. This goal is attained when difficulties in word recognition and word analysis are detected and corrected.

Failing to Correct Individual Difficulties in Word Analysis in the Intermediate Grades

Children who have failed to acquire independent reading habits when they reach the intermediate grades are usually weak in word-analysis skills. Usually, too, they are reading below the fourth-grade level. They find it difficult to master the new skills needed to comprehend the texts that emphasize content material containing an uncontrolled and technical vocabulary. A diagnostic study of each retarded reader's mastery of a basic sight vocabulary and the primary-grade skills of word analysis is essential to an effective corrective program. Mastery of the skills in which there are deficiencies provides the background needed to become an independent reader.

The basic reading skills involved in word recognition and word analysis comprise a hierarchy of interrelated skills increasing in difficulty at each grade level. A partial mastery of these skills at any level will not permit the reader to succeed at subsequent levels. An independent reader, however, will have acquired automatic control over all the basic reading skills essential to his grade level.

Failing to Utilize Adequate and Appropriate Corrective Material

Reading difficulties are unique with each child. Three children in a class who are disabled in reading skills usually present three distinct problems in need of specific corrective material designed to alleviate the difficulties peculiar to each.

After a child's reading problem has been diagnosed, the teacher is ready to initiate correction. The material selected can make the difference between success and failure. It is essential, therefore, that instructional material should be appropriate in terms of the child's reading or instructional level, interests, and skills. Too often material is chosen simply because there happens to be much of it available or because it worked with another child who had trouble the year before. Material should be chosen to accomplish a specific purpose. Such material may be commercially prepared or may be evolved by the teacher. Sometimes, too, the child can actively participate in the construction and design of the material.

When materials are being designed, those of a self-directed nature should be given considerable emphasis. With disabled readers, group instruction often becomes inappropriate, and individual tutoring is impractical. The use of self-directed material enables each pupil to correct his difficulties at his own rate with a minimum of supervision from the teacher.

Self-directed materials—both commercial and teacher-made—designed to meet specific reading needs are described in chapters 12, 13, and 14.

ADMINISTRATIVE POLICIES

Failing to Demand Mastery As a Basis for Promotion

When automatic promotion is the policy of the school administration, reading disabilities flourish and illiteracy increases. Parents are deceived by passing grades that do not reveal the presence of their child's reading disability. Both parents and pupils are frequently unaware of a problem until the pupil reaches junior high school. Upon graduation from high school, a pupil with a reading disability usually joins the ranks of the functionally illiterate. In one large high school in an urban area 17% of the graduates were functionally illiterate.

The basic reading skills of word recognition and word analysis are taught in the primary grades. Unless pupils master these skills before exposure to the technical vocabulary of content subjects, frustration and ultimate failure will ensue. Only successful corrective and remedial instruction can salvage them. Dedicated and knowledgeable primary teachers can do much to prevent failures and retention. These teachers enable pupils to attain mastery by employing material at pupils' instructional and readiness levels and by discovering and correcting difficulties when they first appear. Automatic promotion without mastery compounds simple difficulties until they become severe problems that are destined to end in scholastic failure.

The problem of retention that results from requiring mastery of the reading skills is readily solved by an administration that provides the following: Dedicated teachers who are trained in teaching reading, reading specialists who can help the atypical learner, and summer school instruction for the more severely retarded.

Concerned parents are urging the school to return to basics and to impose mastery as a requirement for promotion. An example of the success of such demands can be found in the Greenville, Virginia County Schools.[20] Prior to 1971, Greenville County School children who were primarily Black, ranked in the lower third in every grade on state reading tests. In 1973, promotion based on achievement was introduced. As a result, the number of students who tested a year or more below grade level declined from 1,300 the first year to 276 the following year. Greenville's academic record rose from the bottom third in the nation to the top half. The percentage of high school seniors going to college increased from 45 percent to 89 percent.

Exposing Pupils to Difficult Content Materials Before They Have Achieved Independent Reading Habits

The skills of word analysis emphasized in grades two and three become the open sesame whereby children continue to acquire an extended sight vocabulary of new and unfamiliar words when they reach the fourth grade. This is evident when one learns that of the 2,000 words the average pupil can identify readily at this level, one-half of them are gained through the skills of word analysis. For example, one representative reading series presents 1,778 different words in its basal readers for the primary grades. Of these 1,778 different words, 863 are to be learned as a sight vocabulary and the remaining 915 through the skills of word analysis.

Fourth-grade pupils who are independent readers have acquired an introduction to dictionary usage. Their stock of sight words prepares them for recognizing and understanding almost all words except new technical ones. Pronunciation of unfamiliar words is accomplished independently through their knowledge of word analysis. The dictionary is of further assistance in arriving at the correct pronunciation of the most difficult words and provides an authoritative source for checking their meaning.

Students who have an adequate sight vocabulary and possess independence in word-analysis skills are ready to do recreational reading. They are eager to use these skills as tools in exploring new and interesting content. In guiding the reading growth of such pupils, teachers should shift instructional emphasis to comprehension skills since unfamiliar words and concepts are encountered more frequently by these students.

Fourth-grade pupils who lack mastery of word-perception skills cannot use reading as a tool in the content areas. Since the uncontrolled vocabulary they meet includes many words foreign to their own speaking and listening vocabularies, they readily become confused. Limitations of time make it extremely difficult for their teachers to help them overcome their deficiencies. The problem is further complicated by such pupils' resistance to corrective work involving lower-grade materials.

Students with I.Q.s between 70 and 80 are found in regular classrooms. If these slow learners are promoted to the fourth grade (a rigid grade standard of achievement is not tenable in such cases), teachers must continue to strive for high level of sight vocabulary mastery and word-analysis skill. The slow-learning child who is introduced to fourth-grade material before these foundational skills are well in hand will experience a hopeless sense of failure.

A basic cause of failure in reading in the intermediate grade stems from an administrative policy of promoting a child from the third grade into the fourth grade when his basic sight vocabulary is at a level of mastery of 90 percent or less. Teachers in the primary grades should strive for 95 percent mastery of word-recognition and word-attack skills. Similarly, intermediate-grade teachers should give retarded readers corrective work in these skills before moving into more difficult material. Reading progress would take place more rapidly and there would be considerably less failure if administrators encouraged teachers to adhere religiously to this basic principle.

Failing to Limit the Size of Classes

In a 1979 report titled "Meta-Analysis of Research on the Relationship of Class Size and Achievement," Gene Glass and Mary Lee Smith of the University of Colorado state that their research has "established clearly that reduced class size can be expected to produce increased academic achievement."[21] The report was based on an analysis of 80 studies on the topic, going back as far as 1900 and involving some 900,000 students of all ages and aptitudes. The most advanced and sophisticated methods of research integration ever applied to available data were used in the research.

A good school administrator knows that no teacher, regardless of how capable can do an adequate job of teaching with a classroom of forty or more children. A primary cause of reading failure could be eliminated if class size in the elementary school were limited to twenty-five children. Even smaller classes on the primary-grade level can prove trying since children in these grades have a short attention span and find it difficult to work independently.

A positive relationship exists between reading growth among students and provision for their individual needs. When classes are too large, it is a physical impossibility for a teacher to become well acquainted with the reading needs of all pupils. Students who develop difficulties go unheeded. And when they are brought to the attention of the teacher, she is so harassed by demands on her time that corrective work is not attempted. There is little doubt that large classes are fertile breeding grounds for poor readers.

Failing to Consider Competence in the Teaching of Reading When Hiring New Teachers

The problems of developmental and corrective reading found in the average classroom are numerous, diverse, and frequently very complicated. In order to recognize and resolve these problems, teachers must be competent, sympathetic observers of pupil behavior, and students of the psychology of learning. They must understand the reading process and be sensitive to the needs of a program which will prevent reading problems from arising or accumulating. They must be alert to optimum methods of learning and their application to individual needs. They must have achieved skill in analyzing reading problems and be adept at selecting techniques and materials involved in correction.

The foregoing understandings and skills may be acquired in accredited courses in the teaching of reading and in the related fields of psychology and child development. Preservice minimum standards set by the International Reading Association for classroom teachers in the field of reading consists of a bachelor's degree including a minimum of six semester hours in the teaching of reading.[22]

Administrators have the responsibility of requiring that these minimum standards be met by those teachers who are added to the teaching staff each year. Recommendations for a further improvement of the effectiveness of the existing staff of teachers is discussed in some detail in chapter 15.

Failing to Provide In-Service Education
for All Teachers in the Area of Reading

In-service training in reading is the primary responsibility of the administrator. Through a good in-service program, a staff of teachers who vary in training, experience, interest, and philosophy can develop into a concerted action unit. The in-service program takes many forms: It may involve individual consultation with a faculty member who has pupils in need of special reading help, or it may entail workshops, conferences, extension courses, and summer school courses in reading.

Teachers' meetings can be devoted to the subject of reading improvement. An administrator may also encourage department heads on the junior and senior high school levels to have subject matter teachers devote time to a discussion of reading and a sharing of effective methods and materials.

In-service programs are a boon to intermediate- and upper-grade teachers who have had little or no training in primary reading methods. These teachers feel frustrated in their attempt to provide correction for their severely retarded readers because they are unable to discover the nature or the extent of their reading difficulties. In some instances, intermediate- and upper-grade teachers place the blame on primary teachers by accusing them of not doing a thorough job of teaching. Passing the buck solves no problems and is not commendable professionally.

A superintendent is needed to coordinate the efforts of teachers by working with the principals whose schools are involved in reading improvement programs. For example, intermediate-grade teachers should know what reading instruction is given to boys and girls in the primary grades. Similarly, they need to know the exact nature of reading demands at the junior and senior high school levels. Insights such as these are provided by the alert administrator.

Failing to Provide Ample Material for Meeting the Wide Range of
Reading Ability and Interests in Each Classroom

The school budget is frequently a deterrent to the purchase of supplementary reading materials, both developmental and corrective. Administrators must be adamant, therefore, about the need for providing ample instructional materials for their school. Teachers should not be expected to make bricks without straw. Without a variety of materials on hand, they cannot begin to meet the diversified reading needs and levels within their classrooms. This diversification must encompass multilevel instructional materials including easy reading material with a high level of interest.

Failing to Interpret the School's Reading Program to the Public

Above all else, a good administrator must be a good public relations person. The administrator who fails to sell the lay public on the value of the school's reading problem will face taxpayers who are reluctant to support needed budgetary demands. Every effort should be made, therefore, to interpret to the public the corrective, remedial, and developmental reading programs of the school.

Because reading problems are often related to physical and emotional problems, the school administrator particularly needs to seek the cooperation of various medical and paramedical groups in the community. Included in these groups are psychiatrists, psychologists, neurologists, otologists, ophthalmologists, optometrists, pediatricians, and general practitioners.

These specialists can diagnose and treat children who are referred by the school. They can also provide the school with valuable information which enables teachers to be of maximum assistance to a handicapped child. Without such cooperation, teachers may unknowingly negate the efforts of the out-of-school specialist.

Failing to Provide a Well-Staffed and Well-Equipped School Library

Without a good librarian, no library can function well. It is the responsibility of school administrators to hire competent librarians for their school and not be satisfied with individuals who lack training and experience in library work.

A good school library needs funds if it is to acquire an ample supply of books, magazines, films, and recordings. Money must be found to purchase these materials. When money is not available, the administrator should investigate the possibility of getting financial support from the Parent-Teacher Association and other civic groups. Perhaps arrangements can be made with the local public library which will permit the school to borrow books and other reading materials when needed. Some school principals have encouraged librarians to avail themselves of the vast amount of free materials made available by commercial firms and government agencies.

The degree to which a library is used in a school is a valid index of the success of the school's reading program. An administrator should be alert to ways of increasing library usage, and can encourage and help the teachers avoid conflicts by having them schedule library periods at different times. Under no circumstances should the principal authorize the use of the library for study hall purposes. Such a practice often negatively conditions students to the library and raises havoc with the librarian's effectiveness.

Failing to Provide Optimum Classroom Lighting

It is evident that school administrators should be concerned about proper classroom lighting. At the Forty-Sixth Annual Convention of the California Optometric Association, Edmund F. Richardson stated that "we are ruining the health and vision of our youngsters because of poor lighting in improperly designed schoolrooms."[23] Richardson went on to say that schoolrooms not built for seeing properly give rise to an abnormally high incidence of visual difficulties, nutritional problems, chronic infections, posture faults, and chronic fatigue. To buttress his remarks, he cited research conducted by the Texas State Department of Health and the Texas Inter-Professional Commission on Child Development under the direction of Darell Harmon.

Although there is no consensus as to the exact amount of light a reader requires, some specialists recommend 50 foot candles in sight-saving class-rooms.[24] With this index in mind various areas of a classroom can be checked with a light meter to determine if sufficient light is present.

Allowing children to read while light is shining into their eyes is to be discouraged. Glare can be avoided by not having children face a window and by making sure the source of light is not too low. Positioning pupils' desks so that light from windows passes over their left shoulder if they are right-handed and over their right shoulder if they are left-handed is an excellent way to avoid unnecessary glare and also to minimize the possibility of shadows being cast on writing or reading materials.

Light-colored ceilings and walls are most effective reflectors of light. Ceilings and walls that are painted in darker colors are likely to absorb a sizable percentage of the light. Other suggestions that can prove helpful in eliminating undue brightness contrasts include the following:

When reading, a child's open book should not be more than three times as bright as the desk top on which it rests. Bright surfaces that are within the child's central visual field should not be more than three times brighter than his book. And, last, the source of light—whether a window or a lighting fixture—should not be more than twenty times as bright as the surfaces surrounding it.

John Ott, a photobiology researcher in the Department of Biology at the University of South Florida in Tampa, has made a study of the effects of fluorescent lighting on children.[25] Ott states that fluorescent lights give off soft X-rays similar to a color television set. In one experiment, all of the children in each of four classes of twenty-five children were exposed to ordinary fluorescent lights for a period of three months. Hidden time-lapse cameras filmed the children at their desks. It was shown that the children "fidgeted to an extreme degree, jumped up from their seats, flailed their arms and paid little attention to their teachers." At the end of the three months, the lighting in two of the classes was changed to full-spectrum, shielded lights. Soon, there was a marked improvement in the students' behavior and scholastic ability. "They were calmer, more relaxed and did better work."

Byron S. Tepper, associate professor of pathobiology at Johns Hopkins University School of Public Health in Baltimore, states that Ott's research shows that standard fluorescent lighting is a possible cause of hyperactivity in children.

SUMMARY

Learning is the goal of all teaching. Therefore, it is important that administrators and teachers be aware of any educational hazards that can inhibit learning. When hazards to learning do exist, they should be corrected or alleviated.

PROBLEMS FOR ORAL AND WRITTEN DISCUSSION

1. What educational hazards are frequently overlooked by teachers? Why?
2. Name two or more hazards to learning that you have corrected and describe the corrective measures you have taken.
3. Observe a class for thirty minutes and describe the hazards to learning you were able to identify.

Notes

1. D. G. SCHUBERT, *A Dictionary of Terms and Concepts In Reading*, 2nd. ed. (Springfield, Ill.: Charles C. Thomas, 1969), p. 258.
2. OLLILA, LLOYD, "Pros and Cons of Teaching Reading To Four- and Five-Year-Olds." In Robert C. Aukerman (Ed), *Some Persistent Questions on Beginning Reading*. Newark, Del.: International Reading Association, 1972):53-61.
3. DURKIN, DOLORES, *Children Who Read Early* (New York: Teachers College Press, 1966.
4. N. B. SMITH, "Shall We Teach Formal Reading in the Kindergarten?" *The Compass* (February 1964).
5. S. MOSKOWITZ, "When Should Reading Instruction Begin?" *IRA Conference Proceedings* (1963):218-222.
6. A. J. HARRIS and E. R. SIPAY, *How To Teach Reading*. (New York: Longman, 1979), p. 127.
7. L. C. GILBERT, "Effect on Silent Reading of Attempting to Follow Oral Reading," *Elementary School Journal* (April 1940):614-621.
8. Ibid., p. 621.

9. ALEXANDER, J. E. et al, *Teaching Reading*. (Boston: Little, Brown and Company, 1979), p. 361.
10. SHARON, A. T., What Do Adults Read: *Reading Research Quarterly*, 1973-74, 9, No. 2: 148-69.
11. D. H. RUSSELL, "Reading for Effective Personal Living," in *Readings in Reading*, eds. D. G. Schubert and T. L. Torgerson. (New York: Thomas Y. Crowell Co., 1968), pp. 3-10.
12. LOBAN, WALTER. *Language Development: Kindergarten Through Grade Twelve*. (Urbana, Ill.: National Council of the Teachers of English, 1976.)
13. M. DALLMANN, et al., *The Teaching of Reading*, 4th ed. (New York: Holt, Rinehart & Winston, 1974), p. 18.
14. M. D. GLOCK, "Is There A Pygmalion in the Classroom?" *Reading Teacher* (February 1972):405-408.
15. "Supreme Court Orders Special Instruction for Chinese Pupils," *Los Angeles Times*, 22 January 1974.
16. R. W. SHUY, "Speech Differences and Teaching Strategies: How Different Is Enough?" in *Language and Learning to Read*, eds. Richard E. Hodges and E. Hugh Rudorf (Boston: Houghton Mifflin Co., 1972).
17. R. ROSENTHAL and K. L. FODE, "The Effect of Experimental Bias on the Performance of the Albino Rat," *Behavioral Science* 8 (1963):183-189.
18. R. ROSENTHAL and R. LAWSON, "A Longitudinal Study of the Effects of Experimenter Bias on the Operant Learning of Laboratory Rats," *Journal of Psychiatric Research* 2 (1964):61-72.
19. R. ROSENTHAL and L. JACOBSON, *Pygmalion in the Classroom* (New York: Holt, Rinehart & Winston, 1968).
20. S. H. STAPLETON, "Where School Promotions Have To Be Earned," *Readers Digest*, September, 1978.
21. "900,000 Students Prove Small Classes Better," *CTA/NEA Action* (March 1979):11.
22. *IRA Bulletin of Minimum Standards for Professional Preparation in Reading for Classroom Teachers* (Newark, Del.: International Reading Association).
23. "Ill-Lighted Schoolrooms Held Menace to Pupils," *Los Angeles Times*, 16 June 1956.
24. TINKER, M. A. and McCULLOUGH, C. M., *Teaching Elementary Reading*. (New York: Appleton-Century-Crofts, 1968), p. 114.
25. "Fluorescent Lighting Can Cause Serious Behavior Problems," *National Enquirer*, 30 December 1973, p. 3.

Selected Readings

BARNARD, DOUGLAS P. and HETZEL, ROBERT W. "The Principal's Role in Reading Instruction," *The Reading Teacher* (January, 1976), pp. 386-388.
BOND, GUY, and TINKER, MILES. *Reading Difficulties: Their Diagnosis and Correction*. 3rd ed. New York: Appleton-Century-Crofts, 1973, chap. 6.
CARLSON, THORSTEN, *Administrators and Reading*. Newark, Del.: International Reading Association, 1973.
CUTTS, WARREN. "Does the Teacher Really Matter?" *Reading Teacher* (February 1975):449-452.
EKWALL, ELDON. *Diagnosis and Remediation of the Disabled Reader*. Boston: Allyn and Bacon, Inc., 1976, ch. 1.

FRY, EDWARD. *Reading Instruction for Classroom and Clinic.* New York: Mc-Graw-Hill Book Co., 1972, app. 14A.

GILLILAND, H. *A Practical Guide to Remedial Reading.* Columbus, Ohio: Charles E. Merrill Publishing Co., 1974, chap. 5.

HARRIS, ALBERT J., and SIPAY, EDWARD. *How to Increase Reading Ability.* 6th ed. New York: David McKay Co., 1975, chap. 12.

KARLIN, ROBERT. *Teaching Reading in High School.* 3rd ed. Indianapolis: Bobbs-Merrill, 1977, 315-320.

LUNDSTEEN, SARAH W. *Children Learn to Communicate.* Englewood Cliffs, New Jersey: Prentice-Hall, Inc., 1976, ch. 2.

OTTO, WAYNE, and SMITH, RICHARD, J. *Corrective and Remedial Teaching.* Boston: Houghton Mifflin Co., 1980, ch. 1.

ROBECK, MILDRED C. and WILSON, JOHN. *Psychology of Reading: Foundations of Instruction.* New York: John Wiley & Sons, Inc., 1974, 389-404.

RUPLEY, WILLIAM H. and TIMOTHY, BLAIR R., *Reading Diagnosis and Remediation.* (Chicago: Rand-McNally, 1979), pp. 57-61.

SCHELL, LEO, and BURNS, PAUL. *Remedial Reading.* 2nd ed. Boston: Allyn & Bacon, 1972, Pt. 2.

SCHUBERT, DELWYN, and TORGERSON, THEODORE. *Readings in Reading.* New York: Thomas Y. Crowell Co., 1968, sels. 12-14, 16, 70.

STAUFFER, RUSSELL G., ABRAMS, JULES C., and PIKULSKI, JOHN J. *Diagnosis, Correction, and Prevention of Reading Disabilities.* New York: Harper & Row, Publishers, 1978, ch. 14.

3 Noneducational Hazards to Learning

Noneducational hazards and educational hazards to learning differ largely in degree of control by the school. Teachers must be equally aware of the presence of both noneducational and educational hazards. While their responsibility for correcting educational hazards is assumed, their responsibility for noneducational hazards is largely limited to discovery of the hazards and referral to an appropriate specialist—nurse, school physician, psychologist, counselor and the like. The school, however, must be ready to provide an appropriate compensatory environment whenever possible. Parental interview and home visitation are largely the responsibility of specialists and are subject to the policies of the administration.

Noneducational problem areas may be categorized briefly as follows: visual, auditory, and speech defects; immaturity and sex differences; general health; dominance problems and neurological impairment; emotional maladjustment; home environment and intellectual development.

No one factor can be singled out to explain reading failure. While one cause or hazard may be of more consequence than another when an individual case is studied, several factors usually are involved. This is particularly true when series disability cases are encountered. The principle of multiple causation* has been stressed by many authorities in reading. One of the most thorough research studies corroborating the principle of multiple causation was done by Robinson.[1] Her investigation involved thirty cases of severe disability that were studied by a group of specialists. These included a psychiatrist, a psychologist, a pediatrician, a neurologist, an ophthalmologist, an otolaryngologist, a social worker, a speech pathologist, and an endocrinologist. Causal factors uncovered were categorized in order of frequency. The most frequent were visual difficulties and social problems, followed by emotional maladjustment, neurological difficulties, speech difficulties, school methods, auditory problems, endocrine disturbances, and general physical difficulty.

---

*In recent years some reading specialists have made reference to "Correlates of Reading Disability" rather than "Causes of Reading Disability." Their contention is that correlation can be readily demonstrated while causation is more difficult to determine.

It is estimated that about one-fourth to one-half of elementary children are in need of visual correction.[2] In a study of 52,000 school children, Hamilton found the mean percentage of those who manifested visual problems was 21.4, ranging from 4.2 at age four years to 36.7 at age 13 years and decreasing to 21.0 by age 17 years.[3]

On casual inspection one would expect to find a marked positive relationship between visual defects and reading skills because reading of printed symbols involves the eyes. But the literature is not conclusive. Some investigators find that visual defects contribute to reading failure while others do not. Why are not visual-reading relationships consistent?

Flax believes that poor research is the prime reason for inconsistent finding.[4] He feels that the majority of existing research studies are guilty of inherent deficiencies in research design which preclude the emergence of any meaningful relationships. Betts discusses a number of factors which investigators have not held constant: age of subjects, readiness to learn to read, and methods and quality of teaching.[5] Other factors which may explain the discrepancy of findings are lack of a universal definition of reading disability, differing methods of measuring visual deficiencies, and lack of agreement as to what constitutes a visual problem.

Errors of Refraction

There are many kinds of visual defects, some of which appear to have more etiological significance in connection with reading problems than others. Certain visual defects—errors of refraction—result from malformation of the eyeball. These include myopia, hyperopia, astigmatism, and aniseikonia. The myopic (nearsighted) eye has a posterior-anterior axis that is too long in relation to the focusing apparatus. As a consequence, the myope experiences difficulty when looking at distant objects (a blackboard, for example) because the image focuses in front of the retina. At near point, however, myopia if not too marked is an asset rather than a liability to efficient reading. Since the slightly nearsighted eye requires less accommodative effort to maintain proper focal distance when book reading, the viewer experiences little or no strain. A few of the investigators who report significantly higher percentages of myopia among good readers in comparison to unselected cases includes Eames, Farris, and Bartlett.[6-8]

The hyperopic (farsighted) eye has a posterior-anterior axis that is too short in relation to the focusing apparatus. According to Young and Leary, high degrees of hyperopia (three or four diopters) appear to be hereditary.[9] When both parents are highly hyperopic, the children tend to be highly hyperopic. When only one parent is highly hyperopic, the children tend to show a range from low to high hyperopia.

A small amount of farsightedness is often conducive to eagle-eye vision at far point. But the hyperope is likely to experience some difficulty at near point (when book reading, for example) because the image tends to focus behind the retina. This requires additional accommodative effort which can be fatiguing. Research by Eames, Robinson, Hulsman, and Walton and Schubert, support the contention that hyperopia is not compatible with good reading.[10-13]

Astigmatism is caused by unequal curvature of the surface of the cornea and/or the crystalline lens of the eye. The astigmatic individual experiences blurring because of these irregularities. Betts found astigmatism among many of his severe cases of reading disability and felt that the defect was one of the causes involved.[14] Eames, on the other hand, found a greater incidence of the defect among good readers than among unselected ones.[15] Many researchers report inability to differentiate groups of good and poor readers on the basis of astigmatism.[16-18] Several specialists have voiced the opinion that severe astigmatism might prove quite detrimental to efficient reading in individual cases. Romaine states, "It would seem most important to correct any marked degree of astigmatism."[19] Cleland, sharing the same view, states, ". . . in severe cases of astigmatism it was found to be closely allied with reading failure."[20] In a 1968 study involving induced astigmatism, Schubert and Walton state that astigmatism was a cause of eyestrain.[21] Blur and distortion, headaches, and adverse psychological effects were reported by the thirty subjects participating in the experiment. Since mild astigmatism, if uncorrected, can result in eyestrain, it was thought prudent to correct the defect whenever it was present.

Aniseikonia is a condition in which the images of the two eyes differ in size or shape, making fusion difficult and often resulting in headaches and other manifestations of discomfort. It is believed that differences in size or shape of retinal images exceeding 5 percent are serious. Individuals vary considerably, however, in their tolerance of this condition. Therefore, in some cases smaller discrepancies in the two images might cause difficulty. Research by Dearborn and Anderson led them to the conclusion that aniseikonia must be considered in about one-half the serious cases in reading.[22]

Fusion Difficulties

Normal binocular vision is dependent on proper alignment of the eyes. They must be focused accurately on the object of regard. When this occurs, the two retinal images which are transmitted simultaneously to the vision centers (occipital lobe) can be integrated into a single ocular image (fusion). Fusion problems vary in degree of severity. Mild, latent cases of muscular imbalance resulting in fusion difficulties are termed *phorias*.

The more extreme and manifest types of imbalance are termed *tropias*. Prefixes are employed to indicate the direction in which one eye turns or tends to turn in relation to the other. These are *exo-* (out), *eso-* (in), *hyper-* (up, and *hypo-* (down). When fusion is not complete, the subject experiences blurred imagery even though each eye individually (as in the case of aniseikonia) sustains a clear image. There are also cases of slow fusion which may prove a handicap in reading because very precise focusing is required. Some individuals overcome their fusion defects through sheer effort and experience, blurring only after prolonged use of the eyes when fatigue begins to develop. As a result of blurring, or possibly diplopia (seeing double), suppression may take place. The suppressed eye frequently weakens (becomes amblyopic) if continuous disuse is involved.

Numerous research studies have indicated that there is a positive relationship between reading difficulties and fusion irregularities. Statements regardng this relationship have been made by specialists in reading and vision. Romaine states, "In my opinion muscular imbalances themselves, more definitely than any other ocular defect, are a factor in poor reading."[23] In reference to reading clinic cases, Cleland says, "I sincerely believe that slow or sluggish fusion is the direct or indirect cause of more reading failures than the records show."[24] Park and Burri of the Northwestern University Medical School gave thorough ophthalmological examinations to 25 first- through eighth-grade children. The ocular defects which they felt were most closely related to poor reading were exophoria, esophoria, and fusion difficulties.[25] Of the many specialists who concur in the belief that fusion problems are of importance in connection with reading difficulties, a number of them believe that exophoria in particular is the principal offender. Park says, "Phorias are significant, especially exophoria for reading distance."[26] In comparing the eye movements of normal and exophoric students, Sabatini found that the latter showed greater divergent movements at the beginning of lines.[27] He felt that this resulted in greater reading fatigue and was a factor of considerable importance. Eames reports finding significantly greater incidence of exophoria among reading disability cases than among unselected ones.[28] In summarizing his study, Hulsman says that exophoria, along with hyperopia, ". . . seemed to be the eye defects most commonly found in poor readers."[29]

To overcome muscular imbalance and to help retarded readers many optometrists stress the value of orthoptic training or visual training.[30, 31] Medical eye specialists tend to minimize the value of orthoptics. Keogh reviewed the literaure and found that weak research design made available evidence as to the value of visual training inconclusive.[32]

The following news article tells a dramatic story of an eighth-grade student who was helped by orthoptic training.

MARK CAN READ

ROLLER COASTER
EYES ADJUSTED*

By Lorraine Bennett
Times Staff Writer

FOUNTAIN VALLEY — When Mark Umbriaco, an eighth grader at Fountain Valley Elementary School, tried to read a book last year, he had to lower his head onto his desk, cover his right eye and turn the words upside down.

He assumed the same posture when he attempted to write. His printing stretched across the page in a track as undulating as a roller coaster's.

Today Mark is reading at eighth grade level and holding his books and papers normally. He welcomes being called upon to read aloud in class (he used to cringe at the prospect) because now he can see the printed words.

He has developed a fondness for sports, particularly baseball, since he can see where the ball really is when it crosses the plate.

He is even exhibiting a flair for writing and has composed several themes and short stories of a mystery nature.

The change in Mark has been drastic, and happened only after his problem—a complex one having to do with visual perception—was corrected.

But the steps toward correction might never have been taken were it not for the persistence of a perceptive teacher who noticed Mark's symptoms and literally "bugged" his mother to take him to a specialist.

That is where educational therapist Pat King entered the picture. After meeting Mark and his brothers and sisters, she discovered to her astonishment that four of the Umbriaco family's six children were affected by perceptual problems.

Ms. King is a consultant in the mental health department of the Ross-Loos Medical Group, a family prepaid health care plan which is marking its 50th year of existence. Among its clients are the Los Angeles city schools.

"Mark came to me through his teacher and the school psychologist," Ms. King says. "He was having a lot of remedial instruction, but the school couldn't find out what was wrong."

She watched Mark read and thought his problem was visual. She sent him to an ophthalmologist who tested him and found he had slight astigatism, but pronounced his vision "within normal limits."

Ms. King wasn't satisfied, however, so she had Mark tested by an orthoptist. Orthoptics is the treatment of defective visual habits or defects

*Los Angeles Times, February 19, 1979. Reprinted by permission of the *Los Angeles Times.*

in binocular vision by reeducating the person in new habits through exercises and visual training.

"Mark had an imbalance in that his eyes weren't working together in convergence," Ms. King says in trying to simplify what obviously is not simple.

Last May Mark was reading at second grade level. He had been placed in special programs at school with little improvement. He read better with one eye covered. When he tried to look at print with both eyes, the letters became confused.

"He saw printed lines with a roller-coaster effect," says Ms. King. "He would read along and skip words.

"Now he has tested out in the 94th percentile for his age group in understanding vocabulary. He is reading at the eighth grade level. His visual acuity is fine and his vocabulary is good.

"Once his eyes connected the print with his brain, he just blossomed. His reading has grown about six years in eight months."

This "miracle" came about through weekly sessions with a therapist and diligent practice of orthoptic exercises.

Visual Immaturity

Of the various types of immaturity that relate to reading success or failure, there is strong evidence that visual immaturity is highly significant.[33-36] A sizable percentage of six- and seven-year-old children have eyes that have not had sufficient time to develop fully. Such eyes are likely to be so far-sighted that seeing objects like printed words on a page proves troublesome. Another problem stems from the inability of some children's eyes to work together as a team. When near-point binocular vision is not properly developed, a child sees printed words that are fuzzy and indistinct. According to Gesell, a child of five may have trouble adapting to a blackboard and in making adjustments from far to near and from near to far. Needless to say, conditions such as these do not augur well for reading success.[37]

The well-known optometrist and educator A. M. Skeffington advocates the use of convex spherical lenses in the first grade.[38] These "learning lenses," as he terms them, would protect the vision of young children and would make it easier for them to engage in near-point work.

Summary of Visual-Reading Relationships

In summarizing the findings regarding visual-reading relationships, the following conclusions seem warranted.

1. Many studies show that certain visual anomalies (e.g., exophoria and hyperopia) are found more often among retarded readers, but they also

show that among good readers there are children who suffer from exactly the same visual defects.

2. It is necessary to consider reading problems as a result of multiple causation if contradictions such a the preceding are to be explained. For example, the intelligence of a child as well as numerous other factors (physical or environmental) may make compensation for her/his defect possible or impossible.

3. Visual disorders may retard both good and poor readers so that comparison between groups does not give an accurate picture of the problem.

4. Findings based on group studies are not always applicable to individual cases.

5. Some visual defects like myopia may be conducive to good reading, while other defects like hyperopia or aniseikonia seem more detrimental to reading progress.

6. Lack of visual maturity rather than visual defect is a factor to consider in first-grade reading difficulty.

7. Although there is no consensus as to the exact relationship between the many specific defects of vision and the reading problem, authorities do agree that a thorough visual examination is an essential part of individual diagnosis.

8. To help ensure the possibility of children achieving their maximal efficiency in reading, it would seem wise to correct all possible visual anomalies.

EYE GLASSES AND VISUAL DEFECTS

How can one determine the visual condition of a child's eyes by scrutinizing his glasses? It can be done as follows: Hold the child's glasses before your sighting eye, approximately one foot away. Look through one lens at a spot on the wall. Continue to watch the spot while you move the lens vertically. If the spot moves with the movement of the lens, the lens is concave (a minus lens) and indicates myopia. If the spot at which you are looking moves in the opposite direction of the moving lens, the lens is convex (a plus lens) and indicates farsightedness. If the movement of the target viewed through the lens is very slow in comparison to the speed at which the lens is moved, then a stronger prescription, possibly a plus or minus 2.00 diopters or more, is involved. If the movement of the target is relatively fast, then the power of the lens is less, perhaps a half-diopter (0.50) or one diopter (1.00) lens. By moving the lens horizontally in front of the target it is possible to determine if astigmatism is involved. If the target moves faster or slower in one meridian than it does in another, then the two meridia differ in power, and one can be assured that the child is wearing glasses that correct for astigmatism. By repeating the procedure with the remaining lens, the teacher can determine whether the two eyes are equally astigmatic or different in that regard. These kinds of information are of value to the teacher who wishes to understand the visual status of a child.

EYE MOVEMENTS

In 1878, a Frenchman named Javal observed that an individual's eyes do not move smoothly along lines of print during reading, but make a number of starts and stops. These are called saccadic movements. Although the stops (fixations) last but one-fourth to one-half second, they are the pauses that inform. During these pauses the reader reacts to words and phrases. The number of fixations he makes depends upon the difficulty of the material and his knowledge of it, his purpose, the vocbulary encountered, and the format of the printed page. Dividing the words read by the number of fixations is an index of recognition span, the amount a reader sees per fixation. The average span of recognition according to Spache is 0.45 of a word in the first grade to 1.11 words in college.[39] This is much smaller than is generally realized.

If a reader's attention fluctuates or if he does not comprehend the text, his eyes may backtrack. These reverse movements of the eyes are called regressions. Most often, regressions serve a useful purpose. If, however, they become an unnecessary habit, they can impede reading speed.

The movement of the eyes from the end of one line to the beginning of another is called a return sweep. Unless muscular imbalances such as exophoria are present, the return sweep is accurate and quick, taking about one twenty-fifth of a second.

A camera for photographing eye movements, the ophthalmograph, was invented by Dodge in the early 1900s. A modern-day ophthalmograph, the Reading Eye II (Educational Development Laboratories; $2,397), is able to give an immediate readout of eye movements on graph paper. Careful study of eye-movement photographs makes it possible to detect far more than irregular fixation patterns and regressions. Eye coordination problems can also be studied.[40]

In an experiment in which they used nonlanguage materials to test inadequate readers, Griffin, Walton, and Ives found a higher incidence of inefficient saccadic eye movements, regressions, and skipping and omission of materials.[41] Nevertheless, most reading authorities regard oculomotor behavior as a reflection or a symptom of reading efficiency. Poor eye movements are not considered the cause of poor reading. The eyes are servants of the brain. When a reader is confused, it is mirrored in his eye-movement patterns. A poor reader, therefore, does not need eye-movement training to reduce the number of fixations he makes; he needs training to improve his word-recognition, phrasing, and comprehension skills.

Most hearing losses fall into two categories: perception (nerve) loss and conduction loss. The latter is a loss in loudness due to sound that is blocked in its transmission to the inner ear. Example of the causes for conduction losses are wax in the ear, otitis media damage, and otosclerosis. Nerve loss is the result of deterioration of or lesions within the structure of the inner ear. Vowel sounds can usually be heard when nerve loss is present, but many or all of the voiceless consonants are not heard. These include *f, h, th, p, t, sh,* and *ch.* Difficulties with voiced consonants also are likely. These involve *b, d, g, v, th, z, zh, j,* and *w.* Lastly, a nerve-deaf child tends to confuse nasal sounds such as *m, n,* and *ng.*

Since learning to read involves making visual auditory associations, the student having a hearing loss is readily confused and is at a distinct disadvantage.[42] He sees letters which he has been unable to hear and finds that words which sound the same to him have different letters in them. Embrey states that children with mild hearing loss are retarded in achievement by one-half to a full year.[43]

There is danger that the child who does not hear well may be regarded as mentally retarded. This may have a devastating and lasting effect on the child. According to Paparella (professor and chairman of otolaryngology at the University of Minnesota) the resulting emotional handicap is harder to treat than lack of hearing.[44]

The degree to which a given auditory loss impedes a child's progress in reading depends upon many factors, including the age at which the child suffered the loss, the extent and configuration of the loss, the extent of language development and comprehension prior to the loss, and the level of the child's intelligence. It should also be remembered that a constellation of factors is usually involved in reading retardation. A child with a marked visual problem, for example, would be more encumbered by a hearing loss than a child who had normal vision.

Children who cannot detect the presence of sound are said to lack *auditory acuity.* Some children, however, can hear the presence of sound, but have great difficulty discriminating between sounds that are similar. These children lack powers of *auditory discrimination.* They might find it impossible, for example, to hear the differences between the words *bat, bet, bit,* and *but.* Their inability to discern small differences between sounds is often manifest in their speech and spelling. Phonic training proves difficult, and word-recognition skill fails to develop at a normal rate. Some writers consider poor auditory discrimination an important cause of reading deficiency.[45] Ollila, Johnson, and Downing have opened a promising avenue to improving auditory discrimination by adapting the technique of a Russian psychologist, Ekonin, for making the phoneme a more concrete entity for young children.[46]

Children who speak a dialect such as black English or who speak another language are very likely to have problems in auditory discrimination. This is probably a result of their hearing sounds and words in the inflection of their native language or dialect.[47] A test such as the Wepman Test of Auditory Discrimination (Language Research Associates) is prejudicial to these children. Only when linguistic bias is eliminated from auditory tests do they perform satisfactorily. [48]

Spache states that poor auditory discrimination is often associated with pitch discrimination, recognition of auditory rhythms and beat, discrimination of tonal quality, timbre, and loudness.[49] If this is true, it would appear obvious that children with poor auditory discrimination would not show normal musical aptitude. The administration of the *Seashore Musical Aptitude Test* to such a group might prove interesting.

Regardless of causation, it would seem valuable to expose children with poor auditory discrimination to simple poems and nursery rhymes as well as to commercial games such a Consonant Lotto and Go Fish. Such exposure would bring to their attention both alliteration and rhyme and would motivate them to sharpen their auditory discrimination. Dallmann and associates suggest ways in which auditory discrimination can be developed during the prereading period by having such pupils follow these procedures:[50]

1. Think of words beginning with the same sound with which a given word begins.
2. Encircle each picture in a group, the name of which begins a certain sound.
3. Tell whether a sound given by the teacher is found at the beginning middle, or end of each of a group of words pronounced by the teacher.
4. Tell which pairs of words pronounced by the teacher begin with the same sound.
5. Tell which word in a list of words pronounced by the teacher begins with a different sound.
6. Tell which pair of words pronounced by the teacher ends in the same sound.
7. Tell which word in a list of words pronounced by the teacher ends with a different sound.
8. Tell which pair of words in a list of words rhyme.
9. Tell which word in a list of words does not rhyme.
10. Name words that rhyme.
11. Tell which pairs of individual sounds rhyme.
12. Make up rhymes.
13. Play the I Spy game. For example, I spy something that begins with the same sound as *Susan.*

14. Name objects in a picture that begin with the same sound as that is provided by the teacher.
15. Name objects in a picture that rhyme with a word provided by the teacher.
16. Supply words that will complete a two-line jingle.

Once the presence of a hearing defect is known, classroom teachers at all levels can take measures to minimize its effects. Some of these measures include the following:

1. Assign to the child a front seat which favors his better ear and give him a roving-seat privilege so that he may always move close to the source of sound.
2. Articulate clearly and at a moderate speed.
3. Liberally repeat oral directions.
4. Rephrase a question or statement if the child fails to understand.
5. Do not speak with your back to the child and give additional speech clues by letting him/her see your face in good light when you speak.
6. Try to keep the child within reasonable visual range so that she/he may read your lips easily.
7. Write directions being given orally on a small card or piece of paper and place it in front of the child.
8. Write new vocabulary words on the board and say them for the class so as to give the child a chance to see how these words look on the lips.
9. Incorporate all spelling words into sentences since many words look alike to the hard of hearing child.
10. Summarize the day's happenings periodically and provide the child with a preview of topics to be discussed the next day so that she/he may prepare for what is coming.

SPEECH

Speech development and reading ability are positively correlated. Children who have a limited vocabulary and find it difficult to express themselves in sentences are likely to experience reading difficulty. It should come as no surprise to learn that de Hirsch found high correlations between reading failure in the primary grades and several measures of language proficiency in kindergarten.[51]

Sometimes children with speech defects suffer from actual malformation of the speech organs. In most instances, however, the causal factors of the disorder are almost identical to those which give rise to reading problems. Emotional problems seem particularly potent as a cause of speech defects. This is especially true of stuttering. It must be remembered that children with a speech defect are often embarrassed when reading by real or imagined laughter from their classmates. In subsequent reading situations greater feelings of insecurity and a flooding of the emotions build up inside them. This in turn results in more articulatory difficulty, and a vicious circle is perpetuated.

Children with immature speech can be handicapped, too. Immature speech gives rise to embarrassment and can interfere with auditory discrimination and phonic analysis as well.

Children with speech problems should be referred to a speech specialist if possible. The teacher will want to do what is possible, however, to prevent the emotional difficulties that accompany speech defects from affecting reading. Scott and Thompson's book will prove valuable to the teacher who is unable to enlist the aid of a speech specialist.[52]

A child with a speech defect is likely to find phonic analysis difficult because of inability to sound individual phonemes. Patience is needed. The teacher should make a special effort to assist the child in word-attack skills.

MATURITY AND SEX DIFFERENCES

Superficially, seven- or eight-year-old children in a group look very much alike, but closer scrutiny soon reveals differences. Children enter every school grade showing wide disparities in mental, emotional, and physical maturities. The reasons for these variations are multiple. They involve inheritance, parental training, school environment, the child's chronological age, and sex. Although it is not fair to blame reading retardation on sex, it is a known fact that two and three times as many boys as girls have reading disabilities.

Some authors have tried to explain the difference in terms of hormones.[53] Criscuolo states that the development of girls' visual acuity and their fine motor skills are more advanced at early school age.[54] There is also a difference in the metabolic rate between the sexes. Since boys consume more oxygen and their energy output is greater, sedentary activity is affected. Dwyer[55] believes cultural factors are more important than biological factors in explaining sex differences. Apropos of this explanation is Sexton's contention that boys taught by female teachers are at a disadvantage. Perhaps this is why more girls than boys fail in Germany[56] where male teachers dominate the primary grades.

GENERAL HEALTH

Part of a teacher's detective work must concern children's general health. Research in reading has shown that to a degree the ancient Greeks were right in believing that a good body and good mind go hand in hand.

Eames compared 875 reading-failure students with 486 nonfailing students as to physical status and found that the reading-failure group exhibited 21.1 percent more frequency of disease than did the control group.

Physical malnutrition has been found prevalent among some groups of poor readers. In cataloging physical findings among 215 poor readers, Park classed a sizable percentage of them as suffering from disturbed nutrition. The seriousness of poor nutrition has been highlighted by Scrimshaw who states that an inadequate diet, especially one low in protein, can result in smaller brain size and damage to the central nervous system.[57]

Several investigators have found that endocrine disturbances and poor reading are related. Park reported that of 215 poor readers, 27 percent of them suffered from hypothyroidism, while 4 percent had hyperthyroidism.[58] Posner found hypothyroidism occurred frequently among reading disability cases he studied. When given thyroid extract, they showed great improvement in "understanding, remembering, and reading. Some gained one and one-half years in reading ability in one semester without any change in teaching methods. . . ."[59]

Allergic disorders of many types can have a variety of effects which may impede children's learning efficiency. Since allergens (substances causing allergies) can involve all sorts of things, many of which can be avoided, there is need for close cooperation between doctors and schools.

Freedom from disease, proper rest, and good nutrition give rise to the alertness and attention-sustaining power conducive to learning. Children who are ill are more likely to react phlegmatically to intellectual tasks or easily become irritable and tense when things do not go well. Many times, too, children who are ill miss out on basic reading instruction because of excessive absence. When such children do attend school, they often lack the zest and enthusiasm to profit from instruction.

Teachers should remain alert to the symptoms of poor health at all grade levels. They should be aware of symptoms indicative of underactivity of the thyroid gland, as well as overactivity.

DOMINANCE

The terms *dominance* and *laterality* refer to the consistent choice or superior functioning of one side of the body over the other. This is believed to result from a dominant cerebral hemisphere which is on the side opposite the preferred hand, eye, or foot.

Those who relate dominance to reading skill believe that not being completely one-sided in handedness, eyedness, and footedness constitutes a condition wholly or partially reponsible for reading disability.

A number of theories involving dominance have been evolved through the years to explain reading disability. Two of the better known are by Orton and Dearborn.

Orton believed that visual records, or engrams, found in the dominant hemisphere of the brain are used in making symbolic associations.[60] Engrams in the nondominant hemisphere, he reasoned, would be opposite in sign, or mirrored, in nature. Most often these mirrored engrams are elided or unused in the language function. When, however, an individual fails to develop consistent dominance, these latter engrams are evinced in the form of reversals. Since according to Orton the making of reversals was the foremost characteristic of the poor reader, he suggested the word *strephosymbolia,* meaning "twisted symbols," as a suitable label for the difficulty.

Dearborn believed that movements away from the center of the body are more easily made than those in the opposite direction.[61] The right-handed and right-eyed individual would find it easier, therefore, to write and read since both skills necessitate left-to-right progression. Left-handed individuals and those with a mixed or inconsistent preference for either side would be prone to make reversals and, in general, experience word-recognition confusion.

Another proponent of unilateral cortical control was Delacato. He stated, "Right-handed humans are one-sided, i.e., they are right-eyed, right-footed and right-handed, with the left cortical hemisphere controlling the organism."[62]

What Delacato and other theorists in this area fail to recognize is that *anatomically eye preference and handedness are unrelated.*[63, 64] Although the nerve fibers pass from each hand to the opposite hemisphere of the brain, *both hemispheres are involved in the control of each eye.*[65] When the nerve fibers from each retina pass through the optic chiasma, they decussate. Fibers from the nasal side of the retina pass onto the opposite hemisphere, while the others terminate on the same side. Crider found that individuals who were right-handed had retinas which were more sensitive on the right side.[66] Since the right hemisphere is involved in controlling the right side of the retinal field, one would expect such individuals to be left-handed. It is neurologically sound, it would seem, to be right-handed and left-eyed or vice versa. Ironically, this is a condition deplored by Dearborn, Orton, and Delacato.

Delacato's use of occlusion to change eyedness and his advocacy of the Stereo-Reader (a device designed to encourage suppression of vision in one eye which in itelf is considered by specialists in vision to be an unhealthy condition) would seem fruitless. As stated by Flax, "Since neither eye can send all of its incoming visual information to a single side of the brain, attempts to equate uniocular function with unilateral cortical dominance are incompatible. The success reported by Delacato must stem from factors other than visual dominance."[67]

Spache, a leading reading authority, states that reading disability cannot be cured or prevented by imposing one-sided motor preferences on an individual.[68] In reference to dominance tests, he says:

> The time spent in futile tests of these functions might better be devoted to discovering children whose perceptual-motor development is inadequate. These children exhibit problems of confusion in left-right orientation, in directionality, in form perception and spatial perception and in concepts of body image. Their lack of development results also in ocular inco-ordinations and lack of hand-eye co-ordination with consequent difficulties in reading and writing. George Spache, *Toward Better Reading* (Champaign, Ill. Garrard Publishing Co., 1963), p. 116.

Since 1960, a number of researchers have reported no significant relationships between dominance preferences or inconsistency and difficulties in reading. Among these are Balow and Balow, Beck, Belmont and Birch, Capobianco, and Coleman and Deutsch.[69-73]

In 1973, Coren and Kaplan gave an additional reason for discrepancies in the area of dominance.[74] Their research shows that ocular dominance is a multifaceted phenomenon in which three district types of dominance are involved. These are sighting, sensory, and acuity dominance. The existence of these three factors have even led some reviewers to doubt the validity of the entire concept of ocular dominance.[75]

Because we live in a right-handed society, left-handed children are subjected to many pressures and sometimes develop emotional problems which may account for confusion thought attributable to left-handedness per se. There have been instances, for example, where teachers and parents with misplaced zeal have tied a child's left hand behind his back so that he would be unable to use it.

Another frustration is that left-handed children often are forced to use desks designed for right-handers. Under these circumstances, writing proves a chore even though the children slant their papers in the appropriate direction. One elementary school principal has spent much time observing and studying left-handedness. He himself is sinistral. He believes left-handed children on the average write more slowly than right-handed children because left-handed children must push rather pull a pencil across the paper when writing from left to right. The latter, he contends, is easier.

In summary, the evidence that left-handedness or mixed dominance is directly involved in bringing about reading disability is insufficent to warrant such a conclusion. Dramatically new research approaches are needed before a definite relationship between laterality and reading disability can be established. Secondary conditions such as those described in the two foregoing paragraphs undoubtedly may contribute to a left-handed child's maladjustment and should not be overlooked.

NEUROLOGICAL IMPAIRMENT

There is no doubt that severe injury to the brain can cause loss of reading ability. For example, some individuals who are victims of an apoplectic stroke lose the ability to read. Dattner, Davis, and Smith tell of a fifty-year-old coast guard officer who lost his ability to read as the result of an accident.[76] The man was able to write, however, and showed no other loss in the area of language. This kind of aphasia is usually referred to as *word blindness,* or acquired alexia.

The man to whom use of the terms *word blindness* and *acquired alexia* is often attributed was the English ophthalmologist Hinshelwood.[77] Hinshelwood examined children who had not succeeded in learning how to read. Since the symptoms of these young nonreaders were similar to those who were victims of acquired alexia, he hypothecated the presence of a congenital variety of alexia. This was due, he said, to an abnormality of the angular and supramarginal gyri of the dominant hemisphere.[78]

Evidence that word blindness stems from an abnormality of a localized area of the brain (specifically the occipital lobe) is not conclusive. Hallgren feels that reading difficulty resulting from a localized lesion in the dominant hemisphere is exceedingly rare.[79] Goldstein views every mental performance as a dynamic process which involves the entire cortex.[80]

Gesell placed emphasis on minimal brain damage as a cause of reading disability and singled out birth injuries as frequently responsible.[81] In support of Gesell's views, several studies employing electroencephalography report that abnormal electroencephalograms appear in high concentration in children with reading disabilities.[82, 83] Other investigators do not share this opinion. Hartlage and Green state that an electroencephalogram does not prove helpful in indicating specific areas of academic deficiency.[84]

John E. Peters, chief of the Division of Child and Adolescent Psychiatry, University of Arkansas Medical Center, states that 5 to 10 percent of all children entering school are victims of a slight brain impairment syndrome which he calls minimal brain dysfunction (MBD). Peters says that most cases of mild MBD are noticed in the second half of the first grade and in the second grade because reading is the most important schoolwork of those grades.[85]

Contrary to the opinion of the foregoing theorists and researchers, many of the leading present-day reading specialists feel that there is too much concern over neurological impairment as a cause of reading disability. Bond and Tinker state, "It is likely that there is an overemphasis upon brain damage as a cause of reading disability.[86] Many children with severe reading disability show no neurological evidence of brain damage.[87]

Neurological Terminology

The terminology used to describe severely retarded readers, many of whom are thought to be neurologically impaired, is a matter of concern. For example, Herman employs the terms *congenital word blindness* and *congenital alexia*.[88] Spache is dubious about the use of these labels, stating, "The group is clearly identified in Dr. Herman's mind despite his recognition that there is not 'one symptom nor one straightforward objective finding on which to base the description.' "[89]

Similarly, Money, editor of a series of papers, uses the terms *specific reading disability* and *dyslexia* in referring to certain children.[90] Spache says the following about Money's designation of a group of readers as dyslexic:

> It is difficult for this reviewer to recognize clearly the small group of severely retarded readers who are assumed to be dyslexic. This is particularly true since, as repeated frequently in these papers, there is *not a single*, consistent symptom or reading behavior which distinguishes the syndrome called "specific reading disability," from among the clinical population of severely retarded readers. Perhaps it is naive to expect that a recognizable syndrome would be composed of a group of interrelated symptoms or behaviors which collectively have diagnostic significance and aid in differential diagnosis and treatment. Symptoms of dyslexia are mentioned by the dozens in these various papers, but no coherent or distinguishing syndrome appears. In fact, every symptom or behavior mentioned as characteristic of this "specific reading disability" has been observed in many retarded readers by this writer and other reading clinicians, who then, in naive ignorance of the incurability of the condition, proceeded to repair the retardation and restore the clients to apparent normalcy. We cannot help but wonder what the course of clinical reading would have been during the past three or four decades if this pessimistic theory had been offered earlier. George Spache, "Interesting Books for the Reading Teacher," *Reading Teacher* 18 (1964):239. Reprinted with permission of the author and the International Reading Association.

A number of other writers have expressed concern over the use of the word *dyslexia*. Adams states, "Its sound is noxious, its meaning is obscure, it has divided the efforts of honest men when collaboration would have been a better course.[91] In a similar vein, Dauzat writes, "The term has become so ambiguous, however, that educators as well as laymen have become confused."[92]

Allington gives six arguments against the phenomenon of labeling.[93]

1. Few of the labels have a single commonly accepted definition.
2. Labels do not communicate useful information.
3. Determining etiology is difficult, if not impossible.
4. Etiology does not matter.
5. Assigning some labels is beyond the professional scope of teachers.
6. The use of a label shifts the burden of failure to the child.

From the evidence available at the present time, it would seem prudent for teachers to be cautious about attributing reading disability to neurological impairment. They should be careful, too, about labeling a child *word blind*, or *dyslexic*. It is obvious that there is no consensus as to what is meant by such terms, and the application of an imposing label is not synonymous with diagnosis.

Causes of Neurological Impairment

The following are causes of neurological impairment with which reading specialists and teachers should be acquainted:

1. Familial neurological dysfunction
2. Congenital defects of the central nervous system
3. Complications of pregnancy
   a. German measles, mumps, virus pneumonia, scarlet fever, and encephalitis
   b. Rh incompatibility
   c. Toxemia
   d. Threatened abortion
4. Complications of birth or labor
   a. Caesarean section
   b. Premature birth
   c. Prolonged labor-breech presentation, high forceps delivery
   d. Dry birth
   e. Precipitous birth
   f. Improper use of anesthesia
   g. Asphyxia from various causes, for example, prolapse of the cord . (most of the foregoing in this group can result in oxygen deprivation)
5. Childhood diseases
   a. Encephalitis (particularly measles encephalitis)
   b. Meningitis
   c. High fever with delirium

6. Head injury involving unconsciousness (particularly before the age of three years)
7. Miscellaneous
   a. Poisons resulting in unconsciousness
   b. Burns involving large areas of the body surface
   c. Excessive crying or head-banging during the first year of life

HYPERACTIVITY

Some cases of reading disability demonstrate abnormality of the central nervous system which, it is assumed, is indicative of cerebral dysfunction. These children are compulsively responsive to stimuli and are, therefore, compulsively hyperative. The phenomenon has been given the medical name hyperkinesia, a term that is conducive to a certain amount of ambiguity.

Medical science has had success in treating hyperactive children with drugs such as Dexedrine, Ritalin, and Thorizine. In some manner which still is not completely understood, stimulants like the foregoing make the brain function better. The child behaves more normally and becomes less hyperactive.

Not all medical doctors believe in using drugs to treat hyperactive children. Dr. Sydney Walker III, a California M.D., refuses to prescribe stimulants for hyperactive children because he believes that they mask the causes of the difficulty without effecting a cure. Some of the causes he lists are: diabetes, hypoglycemia, glandular problems, brain lesions, pinworms and even hunger or tight underwear.[94]

Dr. Ben Feingold, M.D., believes that behavioral and psychological changes can take place in hyperactive children if synthetic foods and flavors are removed from the diet. He calls the diet he prescribes, the K-P diet, which is named after the Kaiser-Permanente Medical Center in San Francisco where he is chief emeritus of the department of allergy.[95] He describes the diet in detail in his book, *Why Your Child Is Hyperactive* (Random House, 1975).

EMOTIONAL MALADJUSTMENT

Pathological illness is not unknown among retarded readers. Some children complain of nausea when faced with a reading situation; others suffer pains, headaches, or dizziness. These psychosomatic manifestations are used by the child to escape or temporarily avoid a disagreeable situation.

Pathological illness is one of the many symptoms of personality maladjustments shown by poor readers. Gates has cataloged the symptoms manifested by one hundred cases of reading disability in the following way:

1. Nervous tensions and habits such as stuttering, nail biting, restlessness, insomnia, and pathological illness—ten cases;
2. Putting on a bold front as a defense reaction, loud talk, defiant conduct, sullenness—sixteen cases;
3. Retreat reactions such as withdrawal from ordinary association, joining outside gangs and truancy—fourteen cases;
4. Counterattack such as making mischief in school, playing practical jokes, thefts, destructiveness, cruelty, bullying—eighteen cases;
5. Withdrawing reactions including mind wandering and daydreaming—twenty-six cases;
6. Extreme self-consciousness, becoming easily injured, blushing, developing peculiar fads and frills and eccentricities, inferiority, feelings—thirty-five cases;
7. Give-up or submissive adjustments as shown by inattentiveness, indifference, apparent laziness—thirty-three cases. Arthur Gates, "Failure in Reading and Social Maladjustment," Journal of the National Education Association 25 (1963):205-206.

The full import of the relationship between emotional disturbances and reading problems is evident when one considers its frequency. Over three decades ago, Witty reported that about half the children coming to the psychoeducation clinic at Northwestern University suffered from "fears and anxieties so serious and so far-reaching that no program of re-education could possibly succeed which did not aim to re-establish self confidence and to remove anxieties."[96] Gates' estimate was still higher. He believed that seventy-five percent of poor readers show evidence of personality maladjustment.[97] More recently, Harris stated that close to 100 percent of the children seen in the Queens College Educational Clinic show some kind of emotional difficulty.[98]

Causal Factors

Many reading authorities concur in the belief that most of the emotional disturbance seen among disabled readers is a result of reading failure rather than the cause of it. The child who reads poorly not only feels inadequate because he knows he is not doing as well as his classmates, but also is often subjected to numerous social pressures. Teachers may unwittingly remark, "I don't think you'll ever learn" or "Why must you be so lazy?" Classmates do not hesitate to label him a dumbbell, and his parents may make home life intolerable by their unsympathetic reaction to his failure. Preston, for example, reports that parents of one hundred poor readers of normal intelligence called their children lazy, stupid, dumb, boob, dunce, simp, bonehead, big sissy, blockhead, fool, idiot, and feeble-minded.[99] Certainly it is not difficult to see why disabled readers become emotionally disturbed.

Although most disabled readers are emotionally disturbed because of their frustrations and failure, one must not overlook those children whose emotional difficulties came from other sources. For example, a child who is labeled lard, fats, slats, or bean pole because of physical stature is subjected to stress. Worse still is the emotional scarring suffered by the youngster born with crooked teeth, facial birthmarks, or strabismus. These conditions and many others can have an adverse effect on the emotional health of a child.

Those of us who have sat through a movie when the picture was out of focus can appreciate the emotional disturbance children with visual defects experience when they constantly have to contend with distorted images. On occasion, all of us have heard a defective sound track that proved intolerable after only a few minutes of unintelligibility. Think of what the auditorily impaired child experiences.

Endocrinologists tell us that hyperthyroidism is frequently manifest in nervousness and emotional instability. Similarly, it is not unusual to find irritability and irascibility accompanying brain damage. Certainly children suffering from undernourishment, lack of rest, chronic infection, and the like, find nothing in their poor health to improve their disposition and ability to learn.

Many emotionally disturbed children are victims of unfortunate home conditions. A child may be rejected because he was unwanted. Such a child may fail in reading as a means of securing attention from parents who otherwise are indifferent to him. On the other hand, a child may be the victim of oversolicitousness. Since busy teachers are not able to give undivided attention to a child who was babied and pampered, reading failure is inevitable. Certain children do not want to learn how to read since they realize that learning how to read is associated with growing up. The last thing they want to do is to grow up.

Youngsters who come from broken homes or homes in which dissension and inconsistent discipline are prevalent are in a perpetual state of emotional turmoil. Very often unwitting parents subject children to invidious comparisons. If a child is forced to compete with a superior sibling or neighborhood prodigy, he frequently develops feelings of inferiority resulting in a give-up or submissive attitude which spells defeat before he begins.

Because the home plays such an important role in the emotional life of children, teachers of emotionally unstable children will want to visit with parents. Once a possible cause, or causes, of the problem, is pinpointed, a teacher should not hesitate to talk to the parents about it. More often than not, parents will initiate changes if they believe their children will benefit.

Teachers, too, may be guilty of some of the same shortcomings characterizing parents. They may reject certain children or make unfavorable comparisons between brothers and sisters. Sarcastic remarks by the teacher such as "How can you be so stupid?" and "I don't know why I waste my time on you" may have traumatic effects on a child. An unpleasant teaching personality accompanied by uninspired teaching and the use of deadening drills has driven many children into maladjustment. Other children suffer maladjustment because they are forced into reading before they have the requisite readiness. Frustration and failure do not augur well for future mental health.

Emotional and Social Development

Teachers can help pupils develop emotionally and socially by using the following techniques:[100]

1. Using praise when deserved
2. Giving each child responsibilities
3. Minimizing competition among pupils
4. Encouraging self-reliance
5. Encouraging self-evaluation
6. Encouraging the development of special talents
7. Encouraging the expression of personal opinions
8. Providing children who are shy with opportunities to become increasingly involved in suitable activities
9. Helping children who are overaggressive take a rightful place in the social scene of the classroom
10. Having children appreciate the difference between license and liberty

Bibliotherapy

Simply stated, when a student solves a personal problem through reading, the process is called bibliotherapy. Shrodes provides a more detailed definition. She says that bibliotherapy is "A process of dynamic interaction between the personality of the reader and imaginative literature which may engage his emotions and free them for conscious and productive use."[101]

Bibliotherapy, like psychotherapy, involves three mechanisms: identification, catharsis, and insight. Of the three, identification is most important. A student encountering a character in a story or a book with whom she/he can identify is dependent on his/her experiences, attitudes, values, desires and needs. But when the reader does find a character who has problems and difficulties like his/her own, the mechanisms of catharsis and insight are likely to become operative.

According to Spache,[102] catharsis involves an emotional sharing of the feelings and motivations of the character in the book or story being read. Dependent on his/her experiences and emotional depth, the reader relives the conflicts and emotions of his/her alter-ego. Finally, insight occurs when the reader realizes that she/he can help himself/herself by adapting or copying the actions of the character who has problems that are comparable.

Teachers who recognize the importance of meeting the personality needs of their pupils will want to help students discover books for recreational reading in which they may meet a character facing a problem or situation similar to their own. Interest inventories, observations, interviews, and personal contact will enable a teacher to become acquainted with students and their personal problems. To find the right books for the right students, it will be helpful for the teacher to work closely with the librarian who is well acquainted with many books and their contents. It would also be valuable to consult Sharon Dreyer's *The Book Finder*, a guide to children's literature about the needs and problems of youth. The volume is published by the American Guidance Service, Incorporated, Circle Press, Minnesota.

IMPOVERISHED HOME

As early as 1933, Ladd reported that homes of lower socioeconomic status were associated with retarded readers.[103] A 1973 publication states that "practical literacy in the United States decreases in direct proportion to income."[104] Current research shows that reading retardation among culturally disadvantaged children, many of whom are from homes of low socioeconomic status, is massive. This is understandable. Since reading is a process of bringing meaning to the printed page, children need a good home environment, one that is experientially enriching. Disadvantaged children know no such home. Their home provides few, if any, stimulating experiences. Their parents do not read, and the language they hear is inadequate. They are not read to, they have no opportunity to take trips, to attend a nursery, or to go to summer camp. Children from a home such as this have not learned to think verbally and to express themselves with fluency. A command of oral language is basic to the initial and subsequent reading success of all children. Children with a good speaking and listening vocabulary are often also familiar with the syntax or sentence structure of the language. This is of inestimable value in helping them comprehend the printed word.

A number of unfavorable parent-child relationships (ambitious and dominating parents, overly solicitous parents, parents who reject the child or make invidious comparisons, etc.) which were discussed in connection with emotional maladjustment on pages 48 to 52 are also part of the total picture. Research by Stewart, Missildine, Seigler and Gynther, and many others, support the thesis that the emotional climate of the home has a pronounced effect on a child's academic success.[105-107]

INTELLECTUAL DEVELOPMENT

Thorndike regarded reading as a thinking process.[108] Consider the following: A child who reads well must be capable of sustaining attention, he must be able to remember what he has read, he must discern likenesses and differences, he must have a good meaning vocabulary, he must be able to follow a sequence of events and anticipate outcomes, he must be able to evaluate what he has read, and the like. There is little doubt that intelligence and reading are positively related.

According to Witty and Kopel, children who have I.Q.s under fifty are generally regarded as unable to learn how to read.[109] Those with I.Q.s between fifty and seventy are limited to fourth-grade achievement at best. Most readers, according to these same authors, "are sufficiently bright to read satisfactorily if appropriate and attainable goals are provided and if there is sound motivation."

Schools which abide by research findings often require a minimum mental age of six to six and one-half years for beginning reading. Of course, children with a much lower mental age can be taught to read when conditions are favorable. It is well known, however, that most children taught by an average teacher in an average classroom using conventional material need mental ages of six to six and one-half years if they are to prove successful in learning to read. Schools which base entrance solely on chronological age, therefore, expose many first-grade children to inevitable failure.

Although intelligence tests are not without error, intelligence quotients and mental ages derived from them have value if one bears in mind that a child's reading ability can be expected to approximate his intelligence only when all conditions are optimum. It must be recognized that intelligence test scores are influenced by a child's experiences, language development, and interest.

In their discussion of cognitive factors that are related to reading achievement, Harris and Sipay[110] state that the correlation between I.Q. and reading scores start as low to moderate (.40-.50) and then rise to about .70 by the fourth grade where they tend to remain.

The terms I.Q. and M.A. must not be used synonymously. I.Q., an index of brightness, refers to the rate of a child's mental development. M.A. indicates a child's degree of mental maturity in terms of his/her ability to reason, comprehend, remember, and so on. Therefore, a 14-year-old with a mental age of 12 years is comparable in reasoning power and understanding to a bright 10-year-old with a mental age of 12 even though their I.Q.s differ markedly.

Group Intelligence Tests

Group intelligence tests should be interpreted warily since many such tests above the third grade are heavily weighted with items involving reading. This means the intelligence quotient of a poor reader on a verbal intelligence test usually underestimates his true mental ability. It is therefore always important to secure a nonlanguage or performance I.Q. and M.A., along with verbal aspects of a poor reader's intelligence. When this is done, it is not rare to find that for poor readers most verbal I.Q.s are markedly below nonverbal I.Q.s This discrepancy has been widely reported in the educational literature. Records kept at the University of Wisconsin Reading Clinic, where the *California Test of Mental Maturity* was given to 266 intermediate-grade children who entered the clinic, revealed an average verbal I.Q. for this group of poor readers of 92 and an average nonverbal I.Q. of 99. Twenty-eight percent of the group had verbal I.Q.s of 100 and above, while 41 percent had nonverbal I.Q.s of 100 or above. Almost half (48 percent) had verbal I.Q.s that were five or more points below their nonverbal I.Q.s.

There are other reasons why group intelligence test scores may be invalid. Poor readers who have been exposed to years of failure often work at an intelligence test as they would any other school assignment; that is, they guess or do it in a very perfunctory way. Such a give-up or I-don't-care attitude may result in a low score. Then, too, there are many students who speak another language and have not had the opportunity to develop proficiency in the use of English. These students invariably are penalized.

Individual Intelligence Tests

A more valid measure of a retarded reader's intellectual capacity can be obtained by the school psychologist who administers an individual test of intelligence such as the *Stanford-Binet Test* or the *Wechsler Intelligence Scale for Children.*

Even with individual intelligence tests like the *Stanford-Binet Test* and *Wechsler Intelligence Scale for Children,* caution is still necessary. Bond and Tinker report that retarded readers do considerably poorer on the *Stanford-Binet Test* than do children of equal ability who have no reading problem.[111] Notwithstanding this indictment, many feel that the best measure of mental ability to be used with retarded readers is the *Stanford-Binet Test.*

Listening Comprehension Tests

Another avenue of appraisal open to the teacher is to read aloud for a child and then quiz him on what was heard. If the child can comprehend material at or above his reading grade level in difficulty, the teacher can be assured that the pupil has normal reading potential. However, the problem of the bilingual child must be given special consideration when listening comprehension is used as a criterion of reading potential. Commercial tests such as the *Durrell-Sullivan Reading Capacity Tests* (Harcourt Brace Jovanovich), *Spache's Diagnostic Reading Scales* (California Test Bureau), *Stroud-Hieronymus Primary Reading Profiles* (Houghton Mifflin), *Botel Reading Inventory* (Follett), and *Brown-Carlson Listening Comprehension Test* (Harcourt, Brace & World) use listening skill to ascertain a student's potential reading ability.

Mental Age and Beginning Reading

Minimum mental ages also have been set up for success in first-grade reading. Early researchers, Morphett and Washburne, believed that six to six years six months was optimum.[112] A few years later, Gates challenged these figures.[113] He contended that determination of an optimum mental age for beginning reading was difficult to arrive at because teachers vary in ability to meet individual differences. They also differ widely in the methods, procedures, and materials they employ.

Recent studies support the contention that no one mental age can be considered the criterion for beginning reading with all children. Although mental age is one of the major growth factors which contribute to success in beginning reading, it must be remembered that physical, emotional, and social growth are also important.

There is need for caution when using intelligence tests. Some of the reasons that are given by Strang are as follows.[114]

1. Intelligence tests measure the results of an interaction between a pupil's heredity and his environment. They do not measure an innate learning ability but represent developed ability. Malnutrition, lack of intellectual stimulation, and low reading achievement can affect intelligence test results adversely.

2. Intelligence tests show how an individual functioned at the time he took the test.
3. The scores an individual attains on an intelligence test fluctuate from test to test. Between the ages of three and ten years, I.Q. scores may change more than fifteen points. The reliability of intelligence tests is not high enough for individual diagnosis.
4. Intelligence tests may have a serious lack of validity, especially above the age of thirteen years.
5. Errors in interpretation may result if students' cultural background is not considered. Especially questionable is the suitability and validity of intelligence tests for black and other minority groups.
6. Language proficiency must be considered in interpreting intelligence tests. Students' cultural background and educational experiences must not be overlooked when interpreting test results. Children from non-English-speaking homes are likely to show retarded language development.
7. Practice and/or coaching may raise scores attained on intelligence tests.

SUMMARY

Noneducational hazards to learning are many and complex. Almost always a matrix of factors is involved. Teachers must be alert to any and all indications of the presence of factors inimical to learning. Areas of concern include visual and auditory problems, speech defects, neurological impairment, emotional and social maladjustment, limited intelligence and a poor home environment.

When hazards are detected they should be given immediate attention. In some instances provisions can be made within the classroom. For example, special seating arrangements can be provided for a nearsighted or auditorily impaired child. Warmth and special understanding can be given to the child who is emotionally disturbed. Bibliotherapy may be employed. In most cases school specialists should be alerted. Perhaps the school has a speech therapist, psychologist, or medical doctor who can render valuable assistance. When these measures are not sufficient, parents should be alerted and the assistance of out-of-school specialists solicited.

PROBLEMS FOR ORAL AND WRITTEN DISCUSSION

1. Discuss emotional maladjustment and its relationship to a reading disability.
2. Summarize and evaluate one or more of the references listed at the end of the chapter.

3. Describe the services a teacher could receive from a special teacher of reading, a school psychologist, an optometrist, a social worker.
4. Discuss the use of group intelligence tests by the classroom teacher in relation to reading.
5. Describe the compensatory school environment a teacher can provide for each of the noneducational hazards described in this chapter.
6. During the reading lesson Jane gets so sleepy she nods over her book. What are some possible reasons for her behavior?
7. Harold, a fourth-grade child with a high I.Q., anwers questions incorrectly and often seems to be daydreaming. What are some possible reasons for his behavior?
8. Visit several classrooms. Observe and record the manifestation of physical impairment you were able to identify.
9. What can a classroom teacher do to help the child who is having emotional difficulties?

Notes

1. HELEN ROBINSON, *Why Pupils Fail in Reading* (Chicago: University of Chicago Press, 1946).
2. M. DALLMAN et al., *The Teaching of Reading,* 4th ed. (New York: Holt, Rinehart & Winston, 1974), p. 22.
3. J. E. HAMILTON, "Vision Anomalies of School Children," *American Journal of Optometry and Physiological Optics* 51 (1974):482-486.
4. NATHAN FLAX, "Problems in Relating Visual Function to Reading Disorder," *American Journal of Optometry* 47 (1970):366-371.
5. Emmett A. Betts, "Visual Aids in Remedial Reading," *Educational Screen* 15 (1936):108-110.
6. Thomas Eames, "A Frequency Study of Physical Handicaps in Reading Disability and Unselected Groups," *Journal of Educational Research* 29 (1936):2.
7. L. P. FARRIS, "Visual Defects as Factors Influencing Achievement in Reading," *California Journal of Secondary Education* 10 (1934):51.
8. L. M. BARTLETT, "The Relation of Visual Defects to Reading Ability," Ph. D. dissertation, University of Michigan, 1954.
9. F. YOUNG and G. LEARY, "The Inheritance of Ocular Components," *American Journal of Optometry and Archives of American Academy of Optometry* 49 (1974):546-555.
10. THOMAS EAMES, "Comparison of Eye Conditions Among 1,000 Reading Failures, 500 Ophthalmic Patients and 150 Unselected Children," *American Journal of Ophthalmology* 31 (1948):717.
11. ROBINSON, *Why Pupils Fail,* p. 136.
12. H. L. HULSMAN, "Visual Factors in Reading with Implication for Teaching," *American Journal of Ophthalmology* 36 (1953):1585.
13. HOWARD WALTON and DELWYN SCHUBERT, "Effects of Induced Hyperopia," *American Journal of Optometry* 55 (1978):451-455.
14. EMMETT BETTS, *The Prevention and Correction of Reading Difficulties* (Evanston, Ill.: Row, Peterson & Co., 1936), p. 156.
15. EAMES, "A Frequency Study of Physical Handicaps," p. 3.

16. EAMES, "Comparison of Eye Conditions," pp. 713-717.
17. D. E. SWANSON and J. TIFFIN, "Betts' Physiological Approach to the Analysis of Reading Disabilities as Applied to the College Level," *Journal of Educational Research* 29 (1936):447-448.
18. PAUL WITTY and DAVID KOPEL, "Factors Associated with the Etiology of Reading Disability," *Journal of Educational Research* 29 (1936):449-459.
19. H. ROMAINE, "Reading Difficulties and Eye Defects," *Sight Saving Review* 19 (1949):98.
20. D. L. CLELAND, "Seeing and Reading," *American Journal of Optometry* 30 (1953):476.
21. DELWYN SCHUBERT and HOWARD WALTON, "Effects of Induced Astigmatism," *Reading Teacher* 21 (1968):547-551.
22. W. F. DEARBORN and I. H. ANDERSON, "Aniseikonia as Related to Disability in Reading," *Journal of Experimental Psychology* 23 (1938):559-577.
23. ROMAINE, "Reading Difficulties," p. 98.
24. CLELAND, "Seeing and Reading," p. 477.
25. G. E. PARK and C. BURRI, "The Relationship of Various Eye Conditions and Reading Achievement," *Journal of Educational Psychology* 34 (1943):290-299.
26. G. E. PARK, "Reading Difficulty (Dyslexia) from an Ophthalmic Point of View," *American Journal of Ophthalmology* 31 (1948):34.
27. R. W. SABATINI, "Behavior of Vision," *Optometric Weekly* 44 (1953): 1727.
28. THOMAS EAMES, "A Comparison of the Ocular Characteristics of Unselected and Reading Disability Groups," *Journal of Educational Research* 25 (1932):214.
29. HULSMAN, "Visual Factors in Reading," p. 1585.
30. I. J. PEISER, "Vision and Learning Disabilities," *Journal of the American Optometric Association* (February 1972):152-159.
31. W. L. SWANSON, "Optometric Vision Therapy—How Successful Is It in the Treatment of Learning Disorders?" *Journal of Learning Disabilities* (May 1972):285-290.
32. B. K. KEOGH, "Optometric Vision Training Programs for Children with Learning Disabilities: Review of Issues and Research," *Journal of Learning Disabilities* (April 1974):219-231.
33. LUELLA COLE, *The Improvement of Reading* (New York: Farrar & Rinehart, 1938), p. 282.
34. GEORGE BERNER and DOROTHY BERNER, "Reading Difficulties in Children," *Archives of Ophthalmology* 20 (1938):830.
35. GEORGE PARK and CLARA BURRI, "Eye Maturation and Reading Difficulties," *Journal of Educational Psychology* 34 (1943):538-539.
36. O. NUGENT and VIVIENNE ILG, "Newer Developments in Orthoptics with Reference to Reading Problems," *Archives of Physical Therapy* 22 (1941): 225-232.
37. A. GESELL, F. ILG, and G. E. BULLIS, *Vision: Its Development in Infant and Child* (New York: Paul B. Hoeber, 1948), p. 289.
38. A. M. SKEFFINGTON, "What 'Learning Lenses' Mean in the Beginning School Grades—and Why," *Optometric Weekly*, 6 September 1962.
39. GEORGE SPACHE, *Toward Better Reading* (Champaign, Ill.: Garrard Publishing Co., 1963), p. 111.

40. KENNETH M. AHRENDT and DONALD MOSEDALE, "Eye-Movement Photography and the Reading Process," *Journal of the Reading Specialist* (March 1971):149-158.
41. D. GRIFFIN, H. WALTON, and V. IVES, "Saccades as Related to Reading Disorders," *Journal of Learning Disabilities* 7 (May 1974):
42. DOROTHEA EWERS, "Relations Between Auditory Abilities and Reading Abilities," *Journal of Experimental Education* 18 (1950):239-262.
43. J. EMBREY, "A Study of the Effects of Mild Hearing Loss on Educational Achievement," Ph.D. dissertation, University of Tulsa, 1971.
44. "Early Uncovering of Deafness Aids Child," *Los Angeles Times*, 24 January 1973.
45. SPACHE, *Toward Better Reading*, p. 43.
46. L. OLLILA, T. JOHNSON, and J. DOWNING, "Adapting Russian Methods of Auditory Discrimination Training for English," *Elementary English* (November-December 1974):1135-1141, 1145.
47. William Labov and Paul Cohen, "Some Suggestions for Teaching Standard English to Speakers of Nonstandard and Urban Dialects," in Johanna S. DeStefano, ed. *Language Society, and Education: A Profile of Black English.* (Worthington, Ohio: Charles E. Jones, 1973): pp. 218-237.
48. DIANE BRYEN, "Speech-sound Discrimination Ability on Linguistically Unbiased Tests," *Exceptional Children* 42 (1976):195-202.
49. SPACHE, *Toward Better Reading*, p. 43.
50. M. DALLMANN et al., *The Teaching of Reading*, p. 77.
51. J. A. FIGUREL, ed., "Challenge and Experiment in Reading," *Proceedings of the International Reading Association,* 1962, p. 7.
52. LOUISE SCOTT and J. THOMPSON, *Talking Time* (Manchester, Mo.: McGraw-Hill Book Co., 1951).
53. GEORGE PARK et al., "Biologic Changes Associated with Dyslexia," *Archives of Pediatrics* 72 (1955):71-84.
54. NICHOLAS CRISCUOLO, "Sex Influences on Reading," *Reading Teacher* 21 (1968):762.
55. CAROL DWYER, "Sex Differences in Reading: An Evaluation of Current Theories," *Review of Educational Research* 43 (Fall, 1973):455-467.
56. PATRICIA C. SEXTON, *Education and Income* (New York: Viking Press, 1961).
57. NEVIN SCRIMSHAW, "Infant Malnutrition and Adult Learning," *Saturday Review*, 1968, pp. 64-66.
58. GEORGE PARK, "Dyslexia from a Physical Viewpoint," *Illinois Medical Journal* 97 (1950):31.
59. "Slow Thyroid Can Slow Child's Reading Ability," *Science News Letter* 68 (1955):8.
60. SAMUEL ORTON, *Reading, Writing and Speech Problems In Children* (New York: W. W. Norton & Co., 1937).
61. WALTER DEARBORN, "Structural Factors Which Condition Special Disability in Reading," *Proceedings of the American Association of Mental Deficiency* 38 (1933):266-283.
62. CARL DELACATO, *The Treatment and Prevention of Reading Problems* (Springfield, Ill., Charles C. Thomas, 1959), p. 6.
63. DELWYN SCHUBERT, *The Doctor Eyes the Poor Reader* (Springfield, Ill.: Charles C. Thomas, 1957), p. 24.

64. Lois Bing, "A Critical Analysis of the Literature on Certain Visual Functions Which Seem To Be Related to Reading Achievement," *Journal of The American Optometric Association* 22 (1951):454-463.
65. Blake Crider, "Ocular Dominance: Its Nature, Measurement and Development," Ph.D. dissertation, Western Reserve University, reported in *Why Pupils Fail in Reading* by H. Robinson (Chicago: University of Chicago Press, 1946), p. 42.
66. Ibid., p. 42.
67. Nathan Flax, "The Clinical Significance of Dominance," *American Journal of Optometry* 43 (1966):566-580.
68. Spache, *Toward Better Reading*, p. 117.
69. I. H. Balow and B. Balow, "Lateral Dominance and Reading Achievement in the Second Grade," *American Educational Research Journal* 1 (1964):139-143.
70. Harry Beck, "The Relationship of Symbol Reversals to Monocular and Binocular Vision," *Peabody Journal of Education* 38 (1960):137-142.
71. Lilian Belmont and H. G. Birch, "Lateral Awareness and Reading Disability," *Child Development* 36 (1965):57-71.
72. R. J. Capobianco, "Ocular-Manual Laterality and Reading in Adolescent Mental Retardates," *American Journal of Mental Deficiency* 70 (1966): 781-785.
73. R. I. Coleman and Cynthia P. Deutsch, "Lateral Dominance and Right-Left Discrimination: A Comparison of Normal and Retarded Readers," *Perceptual and Motor Skills* 19 (1964):43-50.
74. S. Coren and D. Kaplan, "Patterns of Ocular Dominance," *American Journal of Optometry and Archives of the American Academy of Optometry* 50 (1973):566-581.
75. Flax, "The Clinical Significance of Dominance," pp. 566-581.
76. Bernhart Dattner, Vernam Davis, and Charles Smith, "A Case of Subcortical Visual Verbal Agnosia," *Journal of Nervous and Mental Disorders* 116 (1952):808-811.
77. James Hinshelwood, *Congenital Word Blindness* (London: Lewis, 1917).
78. Ibid., p. 53.
79. Bertil Hallgren, *Specific Dyslexia* (Copenhagen, Denmark: Munksgaard, 1950), p. 53.
80. Kurt Goldstein, *Aftereffects of Brain Injuries in War* (New York: Grune & Stratton, 1942), p. 82.
81. Arnold Gesell and C. Amatruda, *Developmental Diagnosis: Normal and Abnormal Child Development* (New York: Hoeber Medical Books, 1947), p. 248.
82. J. Hughs, R. Leander, and G. Ketchum, "Electroencephalographic Study of Specific Reading Disabilities," *Electroencephalographic and Clinical Neurophysiology* 1 (1949):377-378.
83. Margaret Kennard, Ralph Rabinovitch, and Donald Wexler, "Abnormal Electroencephalogram," *Canadian Association Journal* 67 (1952): 332.
84. L. C. Hartlage and J. B. Green, "The EEG as a Predictor of Intellective and Academic Performance," *Journal of Learning Disabilities* 6 (1973): 239-242.
85. "Brain Impairment Found in Five to Ten Percent of School Children," *Los Angeles Times*, 30 January 1974.

86. GUY L. BOND and MILES A. TINKER. *Reading Difficulties: Their Diagnosis and Correction.* (New York: Appleton-Century-Crofts, 1973), p. 129.
87. T. T. S. INGRAM, A. W. MASON, and I. BLACKBURN, "A Retrospective Study of 82 Children with Reading Disability, *Developmental Medicine and Child Neurology* 12 (1970):271-281.
88. KNUD HERMAN, *Reading Disability: A Medical Study of Word-Blindness and Related Handicaps* (Springfield, Ill.: Charles C Thomas, 1961).
89. GEORGE SPACHE, "Interesting Books for the Reading Teacher," *Reading Teacher* 11 (1962):374.
90. JOHN MONEY, *Reading Disability: Progress and Research Needs in Dyslexia* (Baltimore: Johns Hopkins Press, 1962).
91. RICHARD B. ADAMS, "Dyslexia: A Discussion of Its Definition," a paper prepared for the Second Meeting of the Federal Government's Attack on Dyslexia (Washington, D. C.: Bureau of Research, U. S. Office of Education, 9 August 1967).
92. SAM V. DAUZAT, "Good Gosh! My Child Has Dyslexia," *Reading Teacher* 22 (1969):630-633.
93. R. ALLINGTON, "Sticks and Stones, but Will Names Ever Hurt Them?" *Reading Teacher* 28 (1975):364-369.
94. SYDNEY WALKER III, "The Drug-Hooked World of the Hyperactive Child," *Psychology Today* 8 (1974):43-48.
95. "A Therapy That's Too Simple," *Prevention* (October, 1978), p. 60.
96. PAUL WITTY and DAVID KOPEL, *Reading and the Educative Process* (Boston: Ginn & Co., 1939), p. 231.
97. ARTHUR GATES, "The Role of Personality Maladjustments in Reading Disability," *Journal of Genetic Psychology* 59 (1941):77-83.
98. ALBERT J. HARRIS, *How to Increase Reading Ability,* 6th ed. (New York: David McKay Co., 1975), p. 300.
99. MARY PRESTON, "The Reaction of Parents to Reading Failure," *Child Development* 10 (1939):173-179.
100. M. DALLMAN et al., The Teaching of Reading, p. 77.
101. CAROLINE SHRODES, "Bibliotherapy," *Reading Teacher* (October, 1955), p. 24.
102. GEORGE SPACHE, *Toward Better Reading* (Champaign, Ill.: Garrard Publishing Company, 1963), pp. 323-324.
103. MARGARET LADD, *The Relation of Social, Economic, and Personal Characteristics to Reading Disability* (New York: Bureau of Publications, Teachers College, Columbia University, 1933), p. 81.
104. "National Assessment of Educational Programs Newsletter," Sept. 1973.
105. ROBERT S. STEWART, "Personality Maladjustment and Reading Achievement," *American Journal of Orthopsychiatry* 20 (1950):415.
106. WHITNEY MISSILDINE, "The Emotional Background of 30 Children with Reading Disabilities with Emphasis Upon Its Coercive Elements," *Nervous Child* 5 (1946):271.
107. HAZEL SEIGLER and MALCOLM GYNTHER, "Reading Ability of Children and Family Harmony," *Journal of Developmental Reading* 4 (Autumn 1960):17-24.
108. EDWARD L. THORNDIKE, "Reading as Reasoning: A Study of Mistakes in Paragraph Reading," in *Readings in Reading,* eds. Delwyn G. Schubert and Theodore L. Torgerson (New York: Thomas Y. Crowell Co., 1968), pp. 47-57.
109. WITTY and KOPEL, *Reading and the Educative Process,* p. 228.

110. ALBERT J. HARRIS and EDWARD R. SIPAY, *How to Teach Reading*. (New York: Longman, 1978), p. 15.
111. GUY BOND and MILES TINKER, *Reading Difficulties: Their Diagnosis and Correction* (New York: Appleton-Century-Crofts, 1973), p. 98.
112. MABEL MORPHETT and C. WASHBURNE, "When Should Children Begin to Read?" in *Readings in Reading*, eds., Delwyn G. Schubert and Theodore L. Torgerson (New York: Thomas Y. Crowell Co., 1968), pp. 90-97.
113. ARTHUR GATES, "The Necessary Mental Age for Beginning Reading," in *Readings in Reading*, eds. Delwyn G. Schubert and Theodore L. Torgerson (New York: Thomas Y. Crowell Co., 1968), pp. 98-100.
114. RUTH STRANG, *Diagnostic Teaching of Reading*, 2nd ed. (New York: McGraw-Hill Book Co., 1969), pp. 216-218.

Selected Readings

BADER, LOIS A. *Reading Diagnosis and Remediation in Classroom and Clinic*. New York: Macmillan Publishing Co., Inc., 1980, ch. 3.

BURMEISTER, LOU E., *Reading Strategies for Middle and Secondary School Teachers*, 2nd ed. (Reading, Mass.: Addison-Wesley Publishing Company, 1978), pp. 19-22.

DERBY, CATHERINE, "Vision Problems and Reading Disability: A Dilemma for the Reading Specialist," *The Reading Teacher* (April 1979), 787-795.

EKWALL, ELDON E., *Diagnosis and Remediation of the Disabled Reader*. Boston: Allyn and Bacon, Inc., 1976, ch. 8.

GEARHEART, BILL R., *Teaching the Learning Disabled*. St. Louis: The C. V. Mosby Company, 1976), ch. 8.

HARRIS, ALBERT J., and SIPAY, EDWARD, *How To Increase Reading Ability*, 6th ed. (New York: David McKay Co., 1975), ch. 11.

HASLAM, ROBERT H. A. and VALLETUTTI, PETER J., *Medical Problems in the Classroom*. Baltimore: University Park Press, 1976.

Journal of American Optometric Association, May 1974 (entire issue is devoted to visual screening of children).

KARLIN, ROBERT, *Teaching Elementary Reading*, 3rd ed. (New York: Harcourt Brace Jovanovich, Inc., 1980), ch. 10.

KARLIN, ROBERT, *Teaching Reading in High School*, 3rd ed. (Indianapolis: Bobbs-Merrill Educational Publishing, 1977), ch. 11.

KENNEDY, EDDIE C., *Classroom Approaches to Remedial Reading*, 2nd ed., (Itasca, Ill.: F. E. Peacock Publishers, Inc., 1977), ch. 13.

KNIGHTS, R. M. and BAKKER, D. J., *The Neuropsychology of Learning Disorders*. (Baltimore: University Park Press, 1976).

OTTO, WAYNE, and SMITH, RICHARD, J. *Corrective and Remedial Teaching*. (Boston: Houghton Mifflin Co., 1980), ch. 1.

ROBECK, MILDRED, and WILSON, JOHN, *Psychology of Reading: Foundation of Instruction*, New York: John Wiley & Sons, 1974, chaps. 2, 6-8.

RUPLEY, WILLIAM H., and BLAIR, TIMOTHY R., *Reading Diagnosis and Remediation*. (Chicago: Rand-McNally, 1979), ch. 4.

SCHUBERT, DELWYN G. "What Every Teacher Should Know About Myopia," in Diane J. Sawyer (ed.), *Disabled Readers: Insight, Assessment, Instruction*. Newark, Delaware: International Reading Association, 1980.

SPACHE, GEORGE D., *Diagnosing and Correcting Reading Disabilities*. Boston: Allyn and Bacon, Inc., 1976, part II.

4 Parents and the School

Low achievement in the basic reading skills seems to prevail in most school systems throughout the country. Reading specialists have cited such factors as intelligence, impaired hearing, defective vision, glandular irregularities, neurological problems, emotional disturbance, and the like. Articles in popular magazines and national television programs concern themselves with curricular problems in the school, lack of teacher dedication, poverty, excessive television viewing, and parental indifference.

It is obvious that problems in learning are magnified when a child comes from a culturally different home in which a language other than English is spoken. However, that alone does not explain why some children resist learning and become behavior problems, truants, and juvenile delinquents. The authors contend that child study programs promoting cooperation between parents and teachers are helpful. Such programs would promote wholesome parent-child and teacher-pupil relationships and could do much to alleviate disciplinary and learning problems in our nation's schools. Incentives for learning would be aroused, and pupil achievement would show marked improvement.

Chapter 2 was devoted to teacher identification and correction of factors that inhibit learning in the child, the home, and the school. Noneducational hazards to learning were treated in some detail in chapter 3. This chapter sets forth the salient features of a program involving parental responsibilities that directly or indirectly are related to children's success in school.

The teacher has become a convenient scapegoat for the many problems plaguing America's young people. The teacher is expected to be the wonder worker who, in relatively short order, can transform boys and girls into the well-read, hard-working, and dedicated adults of tomorrow.

This chapter provides source material that may be used by the school in several ways to inform parents and/or the public of their role in the education of children. The material may be produced in whole or in part as a newsletter or a series of newsletters. The nature of the school's problem or problems will dictate the form and the extent to which the material may be used.

This is totally unrealistic. Without a good home environment, incentives for learning fail to materialize. As one writer states:

> One cannot expect to plant a seed in rocky, sandy soil, and have it blossom into a magnificent flower. Too many people have the mistaken notion that the school is the chief nurturing agent in a child's growth. For better or for worse, it is the home where a child receives the bulk of his emotional and intellectual nourishment. Teachers are in school to instruct, and the home is the place where the teaching must take root in the young person.[1]

There was a time when parents were encouraged to entrust their children to the school and not to interfere in any way. But today it is recognized that a good home and parental involvement in the school are basic to children's academic success.[2] Teachers can't teach everything. Parents and the school must work together to educate the child.*

Testing of students for "minimal competencies" has spread across the nation's schools. This is a matter of great concern to today's parents. Not only will students have to demonstrate mastery of basic skills at varying grade levels, but in many school systems students will have to pass examinations in reading in order to obtain a high school diploma.

SCHOOL INVOLVEMENT

Some parents may hesitate to become actively involved with their child's school. This is unfortunate because, in general, American education welcomes such involvement.[3]

A good way for a parent to get started is to create a school calendar at the beginning of the school year.[4] The dates of parent-teacher conferences, school programs, open houses, football games, school board meetings, and so on should be included.

To become acquainted with what is happening in the school, a parent should join the local parent/teacher organization. Better still, a parent can become a full-fledged partner in the education process by serving as a classroom volunteer. As part of the instructional team, she/he can arrange bulletin boards, rearrange materials on shelves, clean equipment, collect money, take attendance, read to children, listen to children read, construct reading games, help individual children under teacher supervision, and so on, thus permitting the teacher to focus on teaching tasks.[5]

---

*To help bring about cooperation between home and school, the Oakland, California, schools have been using an accountability contract, which is signed by the teacher, parent, and student. The contract pinpoints specific needs relevant to academic achievement, interest and motivation, attendance, citizenship, and homework. Copies of the contract are available at a cost of $2.00 by writing to the Oakland Unified School District, 1025 2nd Avenue, Oakland, California.

As a prelude to parent involvement, the school will want to interest parents in attending meetings or conferences. This isn't easy. Suggestions that may prove helpful include the following.[6]

1. An attractive invitation will stimulate the interest of parents. If coffee is to be served, an invitation in the shape of a coffee cup is appropriate.
2. To be certain that parents receive the invitation, include a portion that a parent must sign and have the child return it to school.
3. Other modes to contact parents include writing personal notes, mailing an invitation to each child's home, visiting the homes to extend an invitation, telephoning parents personally, and enlisting the support of parents already involved to perform such tasks as serving on telephone hospitality committees.
4. Special techniques may be needed for communicating with hard-to-reach parents. Personal visits inviting parents to a planned meeting could be made by teacher aides, social worker aides, or members of supportive groups. A colorful invitation should be left at each home, just in case parents forget.
5. If at all possible, scheduling both morning and afternoon meetings might enable more parents to attend.
6. Providing a baby-sitting service might make it possible for parents with preschool-aged children to attend. Mature sixth-grade students or teacher aides could look after the younger children in a separate room.

A school in East Los Angeles, Humphreys Avenue School, sends a letter to parents in both English and Spanish. (fig. 4.1) An attached page (fig. 4.2) gives parents the opportunity to choose the kinds of activities they would like to engage in as well as the time that is most convenient.

When parents arrive at the school, they sign their names to a classroom time sheet. At the end of the school year, a special party is given by the school principal and teachers for those parents who have volunteered as helpers. All parent participants are given a certificate of merit. Those who have made outstanding contributions in terms of time and effort, are given special recognition. This recognition takes the form of a gift or a plaque. According to the school's principal, Ada Mermer, the program has been a great success.

PARENTS AND SCHOOL CHANGE

A few parents may wish to become involved in school policy and curriculum making. School personnel in systems with open enrollment often encourage parent policy-making groups. Groups such as the parent advisory committee or advisory council function year-round and make recommendations to school personnel on a wide variety of matters.[7]

Dear Parents:

Are you interested in your child's future and the betterment of our community school systems and educational values?

To be actively involved, it is not enough to be just vocal! You must *Communicate* and *Participate.*

You are needed at school as a school volunteer in the Early Childhood Education program for children in grades Kgn. to 3rd. Our children and teachers will be happy with any help you can provide.

Please sign the tear-off and return it immediately with your child. We will contact you and give further information.

Voluntarily yours,

-------------------------------TEAR OFF----------------------------------

Name _____ Address _____

Child's Name _____ Room Number _____

Telephone Number _____

I will participate in the School Volunteer Program _____Yes _____ No.

The best time of the day to call me is _____ Morning _____ Afternoon

_____ Evening.

Figure 4.1 Humphreys Avenue School

I would like to:

_____ Assist in the classroom
_____ Work with small group of children
_____ Work with an individual child
_____ Work in the library
_____ Make posters and displays
_____ Type
_____ Prepare instructional materials for children
_____ Act as an interpreter for non-English-speaking children
              language: _____
_____ Help on the playground
_____ Use may special talent or training: _____ art _____ music
_____ woodwork _____ sewing _____ dance _____ gardening _____ cooking _____ science _____ other

NAME	ADDRESS	PHONE

Day or days I can help: ___ Mon. ___ Tues. ___ Wed. ___ Thurs. ___ Fri.

Hours I can help: Morning _____ Afternoon _____

At home_____ At school_____ Others_____

Figure 4.2

Parents who become convinced that the school is deficient—through a poor reading or mathematics program, for example—should band together with other parents who agree with them, and then as a group try to bring about the needed improvement. Many changes in school have been the result of parents who made it their business to do something about it.

Marburger[8] gives the following suggestions to parents who wish to affect school change.

Be well informed by: (1) asking for a written copy of any school policies or information you need; (2) finding out what really happens in school by asking the students involved; (3) seeking out those persons on the staff (teachers, custodians, aides, etc.) who are concerned about quality education and finding out from them what is going on in the school's classrooms; (4) visiting schools in other districts to find out what is happening; (5) being persistent and remembering that change takes time; and (6) organizing into a group of concerned parents and citizens.

After parents have organized into a group, Marburger[9] suggests that they: (1) identify problems and then concentrate on one that can be solved quickly; (2) decide what should be changed and when it should be changed; (3) decide how change is to be made and who will assume the responsibility for the tasks involved; and (4) work with the school staff.

If the parents get no support at the staff level, they should move up to the administration, including the board of education. If this proves fruitless, state officials or political leaders with influence should be contacted.

TEACHER-PARENT RELATIONSHIPS

Parents should establish a friendly relationship with their child's teacher or teachers. It is never desirable for a parent to engage in a heated argument with a teacher. Parents who alienate the teacher may find that their child suffers as a result.

During a parent-teacher conference, parents should let the teacher express his/her opinions, then ask questions and express their opinions. Finally, parent should determine what they can do to help their child overcome any problems. Concerted action between home and school can pay tremendous dividends.

If parents feel certain that an irreconcilable conflict exists between their child and his/her teacher, the school principal should be consulted.

PARENT-CHILD RELATIONSHIPS

Just as surely as plants need fresh air and sunshine, children need love and affection. Parents who neglect or reject their children will find that the resulting insecurity and lack of confidence spell failure in school at a later date. If, on the other hand, parents are overly solicitous, children may become so accustomed to being spoon-fed that first-grade teachers find it impossible to give them the attention to which they are accustomed. Again, these pupils are destined to a poor start in reading.

Parents who employ corporal punishment when a child does poorly in school will fill the child with seething emotions that block any and all attempts to improve. Other dont's for parents include bribing the child with money for getting good grades or denying television privileges because of failure to measure up to expectations.

Research studies show that there is a relationship between the quality of a child's self-concept and his achievement in reading. A healthy relationship between parents and child can do much to enhance a child's self-concept. In this connection, parents should do the following.

1. Respect the child as an individual, set realistic standards and expectations, and have faith in his/her capacity to succeed and grow.
2. Be hesitant about attempting to teach reading to your own child. Most parents are unable to establish the rapport necessary for effective learning to take place. What is more, they cannot control their frustration with their own child and, as a result, they lose emotional control and often do irreparable harm to the child's self-confidence. Particularly risky is the business of parents trying to teach their own preschooler to read.[10]
3. Resist the temptation to make invidious comparisons or foster rivalries. Measure the child against himself and not against another.
4. Avoid a dictatorial approach with emphasis on authority and obedience. Parents should deal with their child on the basis of mutual respect and take the view that if things can be explained and decided on jointly, there is no necessity to demand unquestioning obedience.
5. Design discipline procedures that are consistent and do not emphasize failure or entail severe corporal punishment that will fill the child with deep-seated resentments.
6. Recognize that praise of the positive and desirable is more effective in building self-esteem and molding behavior than criticisms that emphasize the negative or undesirable.
7. Protect your child from nurturing feelings of guilt. Feelings of guilt are incompatible with healthy self-concepts.

PARENTS AS MODELS

Parents can serve as models for their children not only because children are imitative but also because they are apt to view their fathers and mothers as people worthy of emulation. For example, parents who are careful about their speech are likely to have children who speak correctly.[11]

Because parents set examples for their children, it's not surprising to learn that research shows a relationship between the number of books in a home and the reading success of children. Parents who own books are usually readers, and the child who sees his parents do a lot of reading is more likely to look upon books as treasured possessions and reading as a worthwhile activity.

A young boy who was disinterested in reading had a father who spent most of his evenings watching television or playing cards. When it was learned that the boy emulated and admired his father, it was suggested that the father get an interesting book and read during the usual T.V. viewing and visiting hours. It worked. Within the short period of one week, father and son were seated in the living room, each enjoying a book.[12]

READING TO CHILDREN

Parents who read aloud to their children are able to share the excitement and joy of books, while their children see "those scratches on paper" become alive and meaningful. As questions arise and discussion follows, a rich background of vicarious experiences is built up for interpretive purposes at a later date. Reading aloud to children does a great deal to stimulate an interest in books, and it helps build a foundation for children's success in learning how to read.

SCHOOL ATTENDANCE

The history of disabled readers often includes excessive absence from school. When skills as basic to learning as reading are being taught, periods of absence may be one of the reasons for a child's general difficulties in school.

A week's absence for a child is like a month's absence for an adult. To assist the child who has fallen behind because of illness, parents should inquire about the school's provision for remedial intruction, home tutors, summer school, or other special help.

A child who is ill should be kept home for his/her own good and for the good of others. However, if a child is not ill, parents should be insistent about school attendance. Many children become adept at feigning illness when situations they consider unpleasant arise at school. If a child starts to develop school-morning stomachaches or headaches, parents should try to work with the teacher to solve the problem. In any event, it becomes very important for parents to learn how to differentiate between genuine illness and pseudo illness.

Dr. Herbert Hoffman,[13] director of the Hillside Psychological Guidance Center in New York gives the following tips to parents who are faced with the problem of deciding whether a child is ill or faking.

1. Ask the child to specifically describe his illness. Don't accept general complaints, such as "I feel terrible." General complaints of this kind are more likely fabrications than specific complaints, such as pains in the stomach, a sore throat, and so forth.
2. Observe the behavior of the child. The child who is comfortable in answering your questions and who looks you in the eye and speaks clearly when doing so is more likely telling the truth than the child who ignores your questions or appears uneasy with the conversation.
3. Test the appetite of the child. The child who is not tempted by his favorite foods is probably one who is genuinely ill.
4. Take into consideration the previous day's behavior. If the child was energetic and cheerful the day before and stayed up late to watch TV, the likelihood of his/her faking is greater than one who lacked spirit and went to bed early.
5. Check for physical behavior that matches the nature of the child's complaints. For example, a child who has a headache isn't likely to jump around, but should prefer sedentary activity. One who complains of feeling hot or having chills should be running a fever.
6. Suggest going to a doctor. Not infrequently the child who is fabricating illness shows a remarkable recovery when faced with the possibility of being examined by a physician.

RESPECT FOR PROPERTY

A child is not born with a respect for the property of others any more than one is born honest or dishonest. The most natural way for a child to gain a respect for what belongs to others is to be exposed from infancy to things that are "baby's" and things that are not "baby's." With the presence of brothers and sisters there are additional opportunities for children to learn what is and isn't theirs.

Parents who believe their child has taken someone's property should be firm about questioning him/her as to where the property came from. If it was stolen, it must be returned. The child must learn that stealing is something the parents will not condone. When the theft involves a place of business, it is desirable for a parent to accompany the child to the store. The parent can explain to the store's owner or salesman that the child took the property without paying and wants to return it.[14]

Since all behavior is caused, parents of a child who persists in stealing should seek help from a child guidance clinic or child psychologist. There is no simple answer as to why some children steal.[15] Perhaps the child needs more affection and approval. Perhaps there is a need for an allowance comparable to that of peers. In any event, it is important to uncover the causes of a child's persistent desire to take what doesn't belong to him/her.

GOOD NUTRITION

More and more attention is being given to the important of good nutrition in the physical and mental well-being of children. For example, some parents have employed the Feingold diet as a means of reducing hyperactivity in their children.[16] Schools provide students with a nutritious meal and have taken steps to ban the sale of junk foods. Parents can help by providing good nutrition for their children at home and by refusing to buy junk food.

After a night of rest during which the body has had no food, it is an absolute necessity for parents to provide their child with a good breakfast, preferably hot. The activities of the school day make heavy metabolic demands. If the body has not been refueled after a night's sleep, there is no reserve to draw upon. What is more, it is difficult to concentrate on a book when there is a deep, empty feeling in one's stomach.

SLEEP

According to the noted pediatrician, Dr. Benjamin Spock,[17] between the ages of 6 and 9, the average child requires 11 hours of sleep nightly. By the age of 12, the amount of sleep needed is 10 hours. Many children fail to get the sleep they need. It's not surprising that children who have been watching the late, late show on television is likely to find themselves in the lost, lost group at school.

PHYSICAL HEALTH

Reading clinics usually report a high incidence of physical defects among reading disability cases. It is essential that parents provide their children with physical examinations (annually, if possible) so that source of phyical difficulty can be detected and treated before it interferes with learning. It is especially important for parents to attend to their child's vision by making doubly sure that the specialist to whom they go is interested in near-point visual functions. Parents must realize that a 20/20 Snellen Chart rating does not mean freedom from visual defects.

EXPERIENTIAL BACKGROUND

Reading is a meaningful process that capitalizes on a child's background of experience. Unless children can bring proper meaning to printed symbols, they cannot understand what the author is trying to convey. Answering a child's questions; reading to the child; taking him/her on trips, picnics, boat rides, car rides, and so forth—all these things will add to the child's background of experience and will enlarge his/her speaking and listening vocabularies. Few things are more valuable to a child in a beginning reading situation.

GOOD STUDY ENVIRONMENT

The school can do a good job of instruction, but unless this instruction is accompanied by a certain amount of out-of-school practice it loses much of its effectiveness. The logical place for additional practice is in the home. Inescapably, it is up to the parents to make provisions for it.

A child needs a private place to work that is away from the family and all distracting influences. It is unrealistic to expect him/her to study or become engrossed in reading when family conversation or television viewing is taking place.

In addition to providing a place for practice, the home should furnish needed study materials, such as paper, pencils, and a dictionary. If possible, a desk should be purchased. Should a desk prove too expensive for the family budget, a card table or a large box might be provided. In any case, it is important for a child to have his own place to read and study and to store his materials.

HOMEWORK

David Hornbeck, Maryland's State Superintendent of Schools, doesn't believe that parents should do children's homework for them, "but it helps if you are willing to talk about an assignment or to look at it when it's completed."[18]

When a child is confused about his/her homework and asks for help, there would seem to be no harm in providing that help. But if a request to help with homework is almost a daily occurrence, or if the parent discovers that the child has no understanding of what the assignment is about, the teacher should be consulted. Should the teacher fail to straighten out the matter, the parent may have to assume the teacher's role. Rather than doing the homework for the child, parents should always try to get him/her to understand the work. In this way the child will move toward working independently, rather than being dependent on the parent for the answers.

Since parents often lack the patience needed to work with their own children, it may be advisable for them to seek the help of a friend, the college student next door, or a paid tutor. Sometimes, too, a parent-teaching pool can be formed.

Television is a major influence in children's lives. The average child watches television for 25 hours a week. By the time that same child graduates from high school, 11,000 hours will have been spent in school, but more than 22,000 hours will have been spent watching television.[19] According to Robert L. Stubblefield,[20] a child psychologist and medical doctor, excessive TV viewing can harm children emotionally. With young children, the symptoms indicative of danger are hyperactivity, poor appetite, sleeping difficulty, bad dreams, and refusal to play with other children. During early adolescence the symptoms associated with excessive TV watching include fantasy, isolation from boy-girl relationships, and avoidance of social activities.

When a child engages in excessive viewing of television, it is essential that parents set a limit on the amount of time allowed for that activity. Then, within the time decided on, a child should be given the privilege of selecting those programs he/she most wishes to see.

Too often, children wish to view television when they should be doing homework. Often, the best way for a parent to get a child to do homework without resentment when an "adult" show is appearing on TV is to set an example by turning off the set and engaging in other constructive activity. When older children complain that their friends are watching such-and-such a program, so "Why can't I?" resourceful parents should find out from each other what is permitted. If this is not done, there will be obvious difficulties.

A group of parents in Birmingham, Michigan, have been successful in weaning their children from television by coaxing rather than dragging them away from the set.[21] The Birmingham school district's "Alternatives to Television" program is highly thought of by all concerned—parents, teachers, and the children themselves. It began in early 1978.

The goal of the "Alternatives to Television" program was to cut in half the amount of time children spent watching TV. It sought to encourage youngsters to read and to engage in sports, hobbies, and other activities that they could enjoy by themselves or with their families. Eighteen months after its inception, Catherine Burns, president of the district's Council of Parent-Teacher Associations, said that informal indications pointed to an average 25 to 30 percent drop in TV viewing in some households.

The program listed five areas in which children could spend their free time in lieu of watching TV. These areas were sports, hobbies, family relations, academic pursuits, and social development. In addition to the suggested alternatives to television viewing, the program suggested that parents and children become critical viewers of all programs watched. It did not insist on junking the TV set.

According to Dr. Stubblefield,[22] parents should start early to get their children interested in active pursuits such as drawing, painting, making music, playing games, and doing chores around the house. Rewarding activities that build self-confidence and pique the curiosity are good antidotes for television viewing.

PARENT-TEACHING POOLS

While serving overseas in an administrative capacity with the United States Air Force Schools a number of years ago, one of the writers suggested to a group of concerned parents that they form a parent-teaching pool under the guidance of several interested teachers. This was done. Since the parents knew how very difficult it is to teach a loved one (emotional bonds stand in the way of instructional success, as in the case of husbands who try to teach their wives to drive a car), parents gave help on an exchange basis. For example, Captain Smith devoted 45 minutes twice a week to reading with Major Jones' son while Major Jones reciprocated by reading with the Captain's daughter. A number of wives were members of the pool, and they served in a similar capacity. The three teachers who volunteered their services met weekly with the parent-teaching pool. They answered questions; provided diagnostic insights; and furnished suitable books, materials, and reading games. In addition, they made a number of general suggestions, such as the following.

1. If you are right-handed, sit beside the child at his right. If you are left-handed, sit to the left of the child. This seating arrangement makes it easier to follow the reading and permits your taking notes without getting in the child's way.
2. If for any reason a book proves uninteresting or undesirable to the child, return it for another.
3. If the book selected proves too difficult (the child should know on sight at least 95 percent of the words and should be able to demonstrate a fair understanding of what is read), don't hesitate to return it for another.
4. If the child becomes impatient or restless, take a break or cut the session short.
5. When oral reading takes place, don't have the child do all the reading. Take turns.
6. Stop on occasions and discuss the story. Ask questions that will stimulate interest and involve him/her in the story. For example: What do you think will happen next? Do you think Jimmy should have gone into the cave when he knew it was dangerous? What would you have done?

7. Praise the child whenever it is deserved.
8. Be patient.
9. Keep a list of unknown words that seem important. Incorporate them into word games, such as Wordo or Word Rummy.
10. When the child encounters a word he doesn't know, try these approaches.
    a. Tell the child what the word is immediately. This is particularly advisable when the story is impelling and there is danger of destroying interest by too many breaks in its continuity.
    b. Encourage the child to skip the word and read the rest of the sentence. The context may provide the needed clues.
    c. Point to the word as it appeared elsewhere and ask what it was.
    d. Ask the child, "Do you know another word that begins the same way?" Although it is undesirable for a parent to teach phonics, it is safe and helpful to go this far, because the question may enable the child to provide a very valuable word recognition clue. That clue is the sound of the initial consonant or consonant blend.

The parent-teaching approach just described was very successful and the results reported were very gratifying. Teachers who were involved were enthusiastic and became convinced that parents can be of great help in a reading program if they work with children other than their own. By forming teaching pools through which a swap-a-child tutorial campaign can be initiated, parents can be of inestimable help to the children and teachers involved.

LETTER TO PARENTS
The following provides a summary of practical suggestions as to how parents can help their children become better readers.

1. Have your child receive an annual physical examination which gives particular attention to his vision, hearing, and general health. *Make sure the vision specialist to whom you go is interested in how well your child's eyes function at reading distance.* If you have a child about to enter first grade, a before-school visual examination is good insurance.
2. Should the teacher or nurse observe symptoms of problems that require referral to another medical specialist (neurologist, psychiatrist, endocrinologist, etc.) do your best to cooperate. The specialist may report that nothing is wrong, but it is unwise to take a chance when your child's welfare is at stake.
3. Make sure your child gets enough sleep and a hot breakfast in the morning. A youngster who is tired finds it difficult to remain alert in school; a child who is hungry finds concentration a chore.

4. Make sure your child develops good habits of school attendance. Keep him home only when justified. Remember, absence from school means that the work he misses is likely to impede progress.

5. Provide a healthy home atmosphere. A child is more likely to do poorly in reading when parents are inconsistent in discipline, when they reject a child or are overly solicitous or when they subject him to unfavorable comparisons with other children. As parents, it is important to build your child's confidence and feelings of self-worth. Give him plenty of love and accept him as an individual. Above all, do not resort to threats and bribes.

6. Enrich your child's language experiences by providing him with a rich background. Since reading involves bringing meaning to printed symbols, taking him on picnics, trips, and excursions and explaining the What, How and Why of situations or happenings proves invaluable.

7. Provide a comfortable and inviting atmosphere for reading at home. Set aside a period for reading to and with your child. If he wishes to share with you something he has read, take the time to listen. And that means giving your undivided attention. More is needed than an "uh-huh."

8. Set a good example. Actions speak louder than words. If you wish your child to develop a love of reading, you have to do a lot of reading yourself. Soon he will begin thinking, "Gee, Dad and Mom like to read. Reading must be fun. I want to do it, too."

9. Help your child develop the library habit. Take him to the neighborhood library and get to know the librarian. Perhaps she can show him around before she gives him his own library card.

10. Provide a place for whatever books your child acquires. Perhaps you can give him a special shelf in the family bookcase. Even a drawer in a dresser or the kitchen cupboard is better than no place at all. Having a place for his books and other reading material will help your child develop pride in his library and an interest in reading.

11. Buy books and magazines (*Boys' Life, Calling All Girls, Children's Digest*, etc.) for birthday gifts or any occasion. To ensure your child's reading for fun and pleasure, stick to purchases that are at or slightly under his reading grade level.

12. Help your child evolve a television-viewing schedule that will not interfere with his reading and schoolwork. Allowing him to choose with your help a select number of programs he wishes to view each week is a good democratic approach. In any event, an hour of television viewing daily should be sufficient. This means, of course, curtailing your own viewing of television on school nights. A child cannot concentrate on books when others are watching television.

13. Don't negate what is being done by the school. Get to know your child's teacher and find out what you can do to help. She may provide you with a list of books that have high interest appeal and are not too difficult. She may also recommend some reading game activities that are ideally suited to your child's needs. Many good books and reading games are available for purchase. They make fine birthday or Christmas gifts. But if your child has a severe reading problem, neither should be purchased without professional guidance.

14. Acquaint yourself with books that will help you understand the school's reading program or show you how to assist your child. Some recommendations follow:

BOOREAM, CURTIS et al. *Help Your Children Be Self-Confident.* Englewood Cliffs, N.J.: Prentice-Hall, 1979.

FRANK, JOSETTE. *Your Child's Reading Today.* rev. ed. New York: Doubleday, 1969.

GORDON, THOMAS. *Parent Effectiveness Training in Action.* New York: Wyden, Inc., 1976.

LARRICK, NANCY. *A Parent's Guide to Children's Reading.* New York: Bantam Books, 1975.

LOVE, HAROLD. *Parents Diagnose and Correct Reading Disabilities.* Springfield, Ill.: Charles C. Thomas, 1970.

MERGENTINE, CHARLOTTE. *You and Your Child's Reading.* New York: Harcourt Brace Jovanovich, 1963.

OXENFORD, VILMA. *Challenge to Parents: Improve Your Child's Reading.* Point Pleasant, N.J.: Point Press, 1977.

PICKERING, THOMAS. *Helping Children to Learn to Read.* New York: Chesford Inc., 1977.

SPARKMAN, BRANDON and SAUL, JANE. *Preparing Your Preschooler for Reading: A Book of Games.* Schocken Books, 1977.

15. If the school your child attends has no remedial specialist, avail yourself of a college or university reading clinic, should one be in the community. Reading clinics often have a team of specialists who can diagnose your child's reading problem and provide him with proper instruction. Sometimes, too, remedial reading specialists are available outside the school, but choosing a good one is not a simple matter. Reading specialists vary greatly in background. If possible, select one who has had experience and training in a college or university reading clinic. And most important, make sure the individual is the kind of person capable of establishing a good relationship with your child. Whether your child likes or hates his reading lesson is largely dependent on whether he likes his teacher.

16. Accept your child as an individual and resist the temptation to compare him with a brother, a sister, or anyone else. Encourage him to compete with himself.

17. Tutoring your own child is not recommended. As a parent you are emotionally involved, and it is almost impossible to sustain the patience that is needed in a learning situation. Although there is no danger in furnishing your child with a word when he is stymied, it would be hazardous to attempt formal reading instruction involving phonics. Most parents lack not only the patience needed to teach word-attack skills, but also the knowledge.

Notes

.1 JOHN A. CLEMONS, "Students' Minds Need Nourishment at Home," *Los Angeles Times*, 14 October 1978.

2. CAROLYN WARNER, "Parents Are the Key," *U. S. News & World Report*, 12 September 1977, p. 34.

3. SANDRA ANSELMO, "Parent Involvement in the Schools," *Clearing House* (March 1977):297-99.

4. "How To Help Your Kids in School," *Better Homes and Gardens* (November 1977):18.

5. GEORGIA SCRIVEN, "Teachers Working with Parents in Schools," *Peabody Journal of Education* (October 1975):53-55.

6. "How to Get Parents to Attend the Meeting," *Parent Participation*, Elementary and Secondary Education Act, Tile I, Milwaukee, Wisconsin, Public Schools.

7. CARL MARBURGER, "How Parents Can Affect School Change," *Family Weekly*, 15 October 1978.

9. Ibid.

10. J. L. HYMES, "Early Reading Is Risky Business," *Grade Teacher* 88 (1965): 90-91.

11. MILES A. TINKER, and CONSTANCE M. McCULLOUGH, *Teaching Elementary Reading*, 3d ed. (New York: Appleton-Century-Crofts, 1968), p. 402.

12. ALBERT J. HARRIS and EDWARD R. SIPAY, *How to Increase Reading Ability* (New York: David McKay Company, 1975), p. 542.

13. *National Enquirer*, 10 October 1978.

14. BENJAMIN SPOCK, *Baby and Child Care* (New York: Simon and Schuster, 1976), pp. 359-60.

15. DOREEN J. CROFT, *Parents and Teachers* (Belmont, Calif.: Wadsworth Publishing Company, 1979, p. 148.

16. RUTH SABO, "The Feingold Families Are on the March," *Prevention* (September, 1976).

17. SPOCK, *Baby and Child Care*, pp. 359-60.

18. MAYA PINES, "You Can Help Your Children Learn," *Readers Digest* (January 1979):101.

19. NANCY LARRICK, *A Teacher's Guide to Children's Books* (Columbus, Ohio: Bobbs-Merrill Company, 1960).

20. ROBERT L. STUBBLEFIELD, "The Lure of Television—Ways to Unplug Your Kids," *U. S. News and World Report*, 12 September 1977, p. 24.
21. *Manitowoc Chronical*, 9 September 1979.
22. STUBBLEFIELD, "The Lure of Television," p. 24.

Selected Readings

CRISCUOLO, NICHOLAS P., "Activities That Help Involve Parents in Reading," *The Reading Teacher* (January 1979):417-19.

FISKE, EDWARD B., "Schools—versus Television," *Parents* (January, 1980), pp. 55-58.

GRANOWSKY, ALVIN; MIDDLETON, FRANCES; and MUMFORD, JANICE, "Parents as Partners in Education," *The Reading Teacher* (April 1979):826-30.

LOSEN, STUART M. and DIAMENT, BERT, *Parent Conferences in Schools: Procedure for Developing Effective Partnership.* Boston: Allyn and Bacon, 1978.

MANGRUN, C. T. and FORGAN, H. W., *Developing Competencies in Teaching Reading.* Boston: Little, Brown and Company, 1979, Chap. 18.

NEDLER, SHARI E. and McAFEE, ORALIE D., *Working with Parents.* Belmont, Calif.: Wadsworth Publishing Company, 1979.

RUPLEY, W. H. and BLAIR, T. R., *Reading Diagnosis and Remediation.* Chicago: Rand McNally College Publishing Company, 1979, pp. 351-55.

WYNN, SAMMYE J., "Involving Parents in the Reading Program" in *Teaching Reading.* Boston: Little, Brown and Company, 1979, Chap. 18.

ZINTZ, MILES V., *The Reading Process.* Dubuque, Ia.: Wm. C. Brown Company Publishers, 1975, Chap. 7.

5 The Developmental Program in Reading

A number of authors have written about developmental reading,[1,2] but a clear-cut definition of the term *developmental reading* is difficult to find. It is not easy to define something that has as many facets as developmental reading. A brief definition by Schubert is as follows:

> Reading instruction designed to develop systematically the skills and abilities considered essential at each grade level; at the junior and senior high school levels it may involve giving all students one or more courses in reading or giving all students reading instruction in every subject matter area. D. G. Schubert, *A Dictionary of Terms and Concepts in Reading*, 2nd ed. (Springfield, Ill.: Charles C Thomas, 1968), p. 263.

Inherent in the foregoing definition is the assumption that all children should develop flexible reading habits that will enable them to read at their maximum potential. Since students vary in ability and rate of learning, a developmental program inescapably includes diagnosis and correction or remediation.

Corrective reading entails "remedial activities carried on by a regular classroom teacher within the framework of regular class instruction."[3] Corrective reading is ordinarily provided for those who have mild difficulties and may involve one pupil, a group of pupils, or the entire class.

Remedial reading instruction consists of "activities taking place outside the framework of class instruction, usually conducted by a special teacher of reading."[4] Since pupils falling into this category are generally those who experience more severe difficulty in reading, the remedial specialist would more likely employ an individual approach to their problems.

In practice, there is considerable overlap between "corrective reading" and "remedial reading." The types of problems and kinds of instruction may differ only in location because they are more likely to differ in degree than in kind.

Bond and Tinker contend that there is a type of retardation which relates either to corrective reading or to remedial reading.[5] They would have classroom teachers deal with those pupils whose problems coincide with their classification of "general retardation." Such pupils have a diagnostic profile which reveals no significant high or low points. Pupils who show "specific retardation" are more likely, according to Bond and Tinker, to be given help by the remedial or special teacher. Such pupils have a diagnostic profile which reveals definite high or low points.

Categorizing pupils is not quite as simple as Bond and Tinker contend. When does "general retardation" become "specific retardation"? Often, it is a matter of opinion as to how a child should be categorized. Problem readers do not fit neatly into two discrete types.

BASIC ELEMENTS OF A DEVELOPMENTAL PROGRAM IN READING

1. Reading is not a subject but a process that cuts across the entire curriculum. All teachers regardless of grade level or subject are teachers of reading.
2. The developmental program requires cooperation among all persons involved in pupils' growth. Parents, teachers, counselors, psychologists, medical specialists, and the like, must work together as a team.
3. Reading continues throughout the educational life of the individual. It starts during the preschool years and continues into high school and college. Many individuals continue to develop their reading skills throughout their adult life.
4. The developmental program involves the whole child. It must take cognizance of all skills, attitudes, and personal, social, and intellectual factors that are directly or indirectly related to learning and the reading process.
5. The developmental program should capitalize on the interrelationships between reading and other communicative skills. It must not treat reading as an isolated activity.
6. The developmental program should employ a variety of methods and approaches to learning, at all times striving to meet the needs of the learner in the most efficient way.
7. The developmental program should employ a vast variety of materials that are designed to meet the needs of the learner in terms of his interests and abilities.
8. The developmental program must strive to develop independent readers who are capable of reading critically.
9. The developmental program must strive to develop independent readers who, throughout their lives, will use reading both as a learning tool and as a recreational activity.
10. The developmental program must strive to help all students reach their maximum reading potential. In this regard, it must take particular cognizance of the culturally disadvantaged and must provide appropriate correction to meet the needs of this group.

11. The developmental program entails continuous evaluation of pupils so that prevention and correction can be given immediately to those experiencing difficulties.
12. The developmental program involves a structured and logical sequence of instruction in the basic reading skills.

THE PRESCHOOL PERIOD

A child is on the road to reading just as soon as he begins to distinguish similarities and differences in the world about him. A baby's excitement when he sees his mother's face, his parents' joy when he listens to their speech, the thrill of baby's first words—all these things are steps leading to the day when printed symbols representing auditory symbol will become meaningful to the child.

As a child develops ability in communication and language skills, both speaking and listening, readiness for beginning reading is enhanced. Since reading is a language experience, whatever the child learns through listening and speaking (sounds, words, inflections, language structure, etc.) will help him/her turn visual symbols into meaningful communication.

There is little doubt that a child's early experiences with printed matter have an influence on his altitude toward books and reading during her/his early school years. Monroe and Rogers believe that as early as one year a child may give books and magazines attention as objects to be mouthed, manipulated, and dropped.

> A year-old infant spends many happy moments of the day in his playpen tearing out magazine pages, crumpling, mouthing, stamping them with his feet until he has surrounded with a litter of shredded paper. During such activity he may give momentary attention to a portion of a picture attracted primarily by its brightness. Marion Monroe and Beatrice Rogers, *Foundations for Reading* (Chicago: Scott, Foresman & Co., 1964), p. 6.

According to Monroe and Rogers, a child from twelve months to fifteen months of age realizes that books contain pages to be turned and that pictures resemble familiar objects.[6] From fifteen months to eighteen months, he begins to appreciate that books are to be taken care of and that pictures represent both familiar and unfamiliar objects. From eighteen months to twenty-four months, the child learns to turn pages without tearing them. He also recognizes the front and back of a book and that pictures have a top and a bottom. At this age the child derives more and more pleasure from books. He attends to adults who tell stories about the pictures in books, and he begins to appreciate that the language used relates to specific pictures and that one picture leads to another. Gradually, true awareness and appreciation of reading develops.

The child's accelerated linguistic development during this period is fundamental to his preparation for reading. Dallmann and associates state, "Never in all the later years of his life will the child even dimly approximate the stupendous growth in power of oral communication that he has made in his first five or six years."[7]

It is evident from the foregoing discussion that parents who have a profound effect on children's language development have a responsibility that cannot be minimized.

READING IN THE PRIMARY GRADES

Reading Readiness

Reading readiness for beginning reading is a multifaceted concept involving factors such as a child's mental maturity, chronological age, sex, linguistic maturity, emotional and social maturity, experiential background, interest in books, powers of visual and auditory discrimination, dominance, and general health.

Although reading readiness is of great significance at the first-grade level, it is not a concept that should be limited to beginning reading. This was pointed out by Cole as early as 1938. She wrote:

> Readiness to read is usually thought of as a problem met only in the first grade. On the contrary, it reappears whenever a pupil starts a new level of work. One should therefore investigate a given individual for his readiness to read at the first grade, the fourth, the seventh, the ninth, and at his entrance o college. In each of these grades the pupil meets new types of reading matter; his work will inevitably be below the necessary level of achievement if he is not ready before he starts. L. Cole, *The Improvement of Reading* (New York: Farrar & Rinehart, 1938), p. 281.

The number of years and months a child has lived does not tell us with any degree of assurance the amount and quality of his experiential background, how much native ability or intellectual maturity he possesses, his powers of visual and auditory discrimination, and his emotional and social maturity. Other factors relating to the instructional program itself (specifically, the degree to which it provides for individual differences) are responsible for reading success or failure in the first grade. We cannot, therefore, consider a child's sixth or seventh birthday as optimum to initial reading instruction.[8, 9]

Unfortunately, many parents feel their children are ready to read as soon as they reach school age. Parents are often so ambitious for their children that they will initiate instruction at home at very young ages. Newspaper advertisements and books have added fuel to the fire by advocating the formal teaching of reading to children at two, three, or four years of age.

Piaget, according to Furth, believes that young children's internal motivation is dampened by early reading instruction. Average five-to-nine-year-old children are not likely to engage their intellectual powers when they read. "Neither the process of reading itself nor the comprehension of its easy content can be considered an activity well suited to developing the mind of the young child."[10]

Of all the factors related to readiness, a child's mental level is by far the most important. In 1931, a carefully controlled study by Washburne and Morphett led them to the conclusion that a mental age of six to six and one-half years was essential for success in beginning reading.[11] In 1962, a study by Roche provided evidence indicating that children who are not ready for reading profit from being given appropriate readiness experiences and that any delay resulting from such training does not affect their later school progress. Durkin[12], in contrast to some of her earlier views, found no lasting advantage to early reading. Unfortunately, many schools are introducing formal reading instruction in kindergarten, and others have urged that reading instruction be given to two-, three-, and four-year-old children. Sipay, with tongue in cheek, has written an entertaining article suggesting that instruction be given prenatally.[13]

Most reading specialists agree that there is a substantial correlation between mental age and success in beginning reading. But as pointed out by Gates, one cannot set a specific minimum mental age for beginning reading.[14] Too many factors are involved. As reported by researchers studying the teaching of reading in Denver kindergartens, some mature and capable children are ready to read at four or five years of age.[15] The majority are not. Forcing a child into reading prematurely can result in an antipathy for reading. Since delaying initial reading instruction does not appear to be harmful, it would seem better for schools to err on the side of waiting too long to introduce reading than to err on the side of introducing reading too soon.

Kindergarten Experience

A good kindergarten experience is of inestimable value to children who might otherwise lack readiness for beginning reading.[16] In a study by Fast it was shown that there is a definite relationship between attending kindergarten and reading progress in the first grade.[17] Children who have had the benefit of kindergarten experiences are better able to sustain attention, follow directions, and adjust to group situations in the primary grades. Such training is particularly vital to children who come from homes that have failed to provide needed verbal stimulation and an appropriate background of experience. Culturally deprived children fall into this category. They may be wise in the ways of street gangs, but beyond this, their cultural horizons come to an abrupt halt. What, then, is more fundamental to a program in reading for this group than the filling in of experiential gaps? If the home has failed to provide the stimulation needed to develop the background requisite to successful reading, the school must do the job—and the earlier this can be done the better. Some of the ways to accomplish the task are as follows:

1. Take pupils on trips and excursions to places of interest.
2. Give experience with concrete objects.
3. Expose pupils to lively bulletin boards and other displays.
4. Label objects.
5. Have pupils make picture collections.
6. Use marionette and puppet shows and other dramatic activities.
7. Expose pupils to choice movies and television shows.
8. Use filmstrips, slides, and charts.
9. Familiarize pupils with picture dictionaries and illustrated books.
10. Have the pupils guess rhyming words and repeat words and experiences.
11. Read choice selections orally.
12. Discuss experiences and stimulate informal conversation.
13. Use oral directions.

Knowledge of Letter Names

Because several research studies report a substantial correlation between knowledge of letter names and reading success,[18, 19] the question arises, Should the names of the letters be taught as part of a reading-readiness program? It should be remembered that *correlation* and *causation* are not synonymous terms. The fact that children who know their letters are likely to succeed in early reading is more likely a reflection of the higher socioeconomic status of homes that encourage this kind of learning. Although knowledge of letter names may not play a strong causative role in early reading success, it does make teaching easier and should be taught. If, for example, children confuse the word *book* with *look*, the teacher can say, "This word is *book*, not *look*. It begins with a *b*, not with an *l*." Knowing letter names is also involved in spelling and phonics instruction. And it is interesting to note that certain letters of the alphabet—*l*, *f*, and *s*, for example—contain the sounds of the letters in their names.

Perceptual Motor Training

Teachers working with culturally disadvantaged children should make extensive use of experience charts, capitalizing on the children's oral communication. Use also can be made of the Peabody Language Development Kit and the Ginn Language Kit. To enhance visual and auditory perception the *Michigan Successive Discrimination Listening Program* (Ann Arbor Publishers) and the *Frostig Program for the Development of Visual Perception* (Consulting Psychologists Press) may prove valuable. The latter material, however, should be used with reservation. A study by Rosen indicates that perceptual training with the Frostig material contributes very little to reading achievement. The following is an abstract of the Rosen study:

> To investigate the effects, if any, of perceptual training upon selected measures of reading achievement in first grade, 12 experimental classrooms of first-grade pupils, randomly selected, received a 29-day adaptation of the Frostig Program for the Development of Visual Perception, while 13 control classes added comparable time to the regular reading instructional program. Analysis of the data revealed statistically significant differences between the treatment groups in most of the post-perceptual capabilities, favoring the experimental groups, without concommitant effects on reading criterion measures. While the total score from the Frostig Developmental Test of Visual Perception appeared to have a strong predictive function regarding first grade reading, the training of visual perception subskills did not appear to have a significant effect on reading ability at the end of the first-grade year. Additional findings are reported that strongly suggest the need for further research. C. L. Rosen, "An Investigation of Perceptual Training and Reading Achievement in the First Grade," *American Journal of Optometry* 45 (1968):322-332.

In support of the Rosen study, Balow evaluates research in this area by stating, "Fully consistent with most of the other experimental investigations reported in the professional literature is the finding that the application of Frostig work sheets for development of visual perception did not produce particular change in reading skills."[20]

Although some forms of immaturity such as myelination of nerve fibers require time, and time alone, teachers need not sit back and wait for readiness to develop. Difficulty with fine muscle tasks may be associated with learning problems.[21] To help immature children develop the motor skills that underlie perceptual ability, teachers will want to acquaint themselves with the unique approaches described by Kephart, and Getman and Kane.[22-23] However, Balow has commented as follows about weaknesses in motor and perceptual skills:

> While motor and perceptual skills weaknesses are frequently found in learning disabled pupils, there is great likelihood that these are most often simply concomitants wtihout causal relevance; thus the argument cannot depend upon assumed etiologies for learning disabilities. . . . No experimental study conforming to accepted tenets of research design has been found that demonstrates special effectiveness for any of the physical, motor, or perceptual programs claimed to be useful in the prevention or correction of reading or other learning disabilities. Bruce Balow, "Perceptual-Motor Activities in the Treatment of Severe Reading Disability," *Reading Teacher* (March 1971):523.

In summarizing research of visual-perceptual motor activities related to reading achievement, Cygan concludes ". . . the studies showed that visual-perceptual motor training was no more beneficial to reading improvement than standard remedial reading techniques.[24]

In a similar vein, Hammill, Goodman, and Wiederholt state:

We have little doubt that any interested person who reads the efficacy literature will conclude that the value of perceptual training, especially those programs often used in schools, has not been clearly established. If he concludes that such training lacks solid support, he may begin to question the purchase of attractively packaged materials which some companies offer teachers along with unsubstantiated claims concerning their merits, the practice of providing perceptual-motor training to all school children in the name of readiness training, and the assumption that a lack of perceptual-motor adequacy causes a considerable amount of academic failure. D. Hammill, L. Goodman, and J. Weiderholt, "Visual Motor Processes: Can We Train Them?" *Reading Teacher* (February 1974):469-478.

Readiness Workbooks

Readiness workbooks are still recommended by many teachers, but they no longer enjoy the universal favor they did at one time. Readiness workbooks have been severely criticized as being of limited value in contributing to children's reading readiness. Durrell and Nicholson state, "Although the lessons of the reading readiness books may develop desirable abilities such as language fluency, motor skills and attention to nonword form and sounds, it is doubtful that they contribute greatly to reading readiness."[25]

In a similar vein Spache states that "despite the widespread dependence upon readiness workbooks, here has been extremely little research demonstrating their supposed values."[26] Fry and Emmer concluded from an experimental study of readiness workbooks and teachers' manuals that such materials "did not offer much help for most of the first graders and, in fact, tended to hurt reading achievement when used with the whole class."[27]

Immature children can be the bane of a first-grade teacher's existence. It is difficult, if not impossible, to teach reading to children who cannot give sustained attention, cannot get along with others in group situations, cry easily, have temper tantrums, and cannot and will not remain seated.

Better schools of today employ sensitive screening procedures to detect children who lack the requisite readiness for reading. Informal day-by-day observations by kindergarten and first-grade teachers, combined with reading readiness and intelligence tests, yield valuable data in determining a child's readiness for reading.

Phonics

Everyone agrees that phonics (phonics and related terms are defined in Appendix B) should be emphasized in the primary grades. However, there is disagreement as to how early this instruction should begin and the emphasis it should receive. In 1937, Dolch and Bloomster correlated mental age with the ability to apply phonic principles.[28] They concluded that a mental age of seven years was minimal to phonic success.

The influence of the Dolch-Bloomster research was widespread. For many years basal readers placed major emphasis on phonics in the second and third grades, minimizing it in the first grade. Today, however, the situation is somewhat different. Many reading specialists are favoring early introduction of phonics. Chall, for example, reviewed research from 1912 to 1965 and concluded that intensive decoding (identifying the relationship between the letters of the alphabet and the sounds in words) was responsible for early success in reading.

The publication of Chall's book in 1967 resulted in a heated debate between those authorities who supported her research and conclusions and those who felt that it had minimal value because in arriving at conclusions she failed to differentiate good research from poor research.[29] Nevertheless, the increased amount of intensive phonics and linguistic materials that was published indicated renewed interest in decoding.

Synthetic and Analytic Phonics

Phonic methods fall into two categories: synthetic and analytic. Synthetic phonics involves building up words from their parts; analytic phonics (sometimes called intrinsic phonics) involves discovering natural sound units within words. Many of today's reading specialists and teachers employ a combination of the two approaches.

Synthetic phonics is begun by teaching a child a large number of letter sounds and other isolated phonetic elements. After these are mastered, the child is expected to sound out words by recognizing and blending the parts in a left-to-right manner.

The greatest weakness of letter-by-letter sounding is that the extraneous *schwa* sound is appended to voiced sounds and, often, to voiceless sounds as well. Thus the word *man* becomes *muh-a-nuh*. To circumvent this problem of unwanted distortion, some reading specialists recommend sounding the initial consonant and the vowel following it as a single unit. By employing this suggestion, the word *man* now becomes *ma-nuh*.

Synthetic phonics has other disadvantages. Drill on isolated sounds is uninteresting and can easily dampen a child's enthusiasm for reading. It must be recognized, also, that *l, st, cl, ed,* and so forth, are meaningless to a child and are unrelated to his listening and speaking vocabularies.

Analytic phonics uses meaningful words that are presented as wholes. The child does not learn to sound isolated elements of words. Intead, he is led to identify the elements in whole words. He is encouraged to use letter substitution techniques. For example, if the child encounters a new word such as *rake,* he may reason as follows: It begins like *run* and ends like *take.* Why, it must be *rake.*

Analytic phonics is preferred by most reading authorities. Although there is no experimental proof of the superiority of analytic phonics, the following advantages seem apparent.[30]

1. The whole-word approach capitalizes on children's interest in words.
2. The whole-word approach enables children to discover letter sounds by themselves. Because of this, they are more likely to understand and use what they learn in reading situations.
3. Blending problems are avoided.
4. The whole-word approach results in practice in "reading through" words. This is the skill needed when a child encounters new words in contextual setting.
5. The analytic method is conducive to learning words so that they are likely to become familiar sight words.

Phonic Sequence

Teachers are interested in the sequence in which children should learn phonic elements. In 1948, Dolch recommended the following order:[31]

1. Single-consonant sounds
2. Consonant blends and digraphs
3. Short vowel sounds
4. Long vowel sounds
5. Final *e* rule
6. Double vowels
7. Diphthongs
8. Soft *c* and *g*
9. Number of syllables in a word
10. Dividing words into syllables

More recently, Spache recommended a phonics syllabus that is similar to the early one proposed by Dolch.[32] The order is as follows:

1. Simple consonants
2. Harder consonants
3. Consonant blends and digraphs
4. Short vowel sounds
5. Long vowel sounds
6. Silent letters
7. Vowel digraphs (double vowels)
8. Vowel diphthongs
9. Vowels with *r*
10. Phonograms

Burmeister compared the findings of seven studies that were designed to investigate scientifically the value of commonly found structural analysis and accent generalizations. Although the research studies reviewed showed variations in sampling, methods of selection, dictionary sources considered authoritative, definitions of short and/or long vowels, and ways of determining usefulness, Burmeister through careful analysis was able to dichotomize the generalizations as "especially useful" and "of limited usefulness."

Especially Useful Generalizations*

Consonant Sounds

1. *C* followed by *e, i,* or *y* sounds soft; otherwise *c* is hard (omit *ch*). For example: certain, city, cycle; attic, cat, clip; success.
2. *G* followed by *e, i,* or *y* sounds soft; otherwise, *g* is hard (omit *gh*). For example: gell, agile, gypsy; gone, flag, grope; suggest.
3. *Ch* is usually pronounced as it is in *kitchen,* not like *sh* as in *machine.*
4. When a word ends in *ck,* it has the same sound as in *look.*
5. When *ght* occurs in a word, *gh* is silent. For example: thought, night, right.
6. When two of the same consonants are side by side, only one is heard.

Vowel Sounds

1. If the only vowel letter is at the end of the word, the letter usually stands for a long sound (one-syllable words only). For example: be, he, she, go.
2. When a consonant-plus-*y* are the final letters in a one-syllable word, the *y* has the long *i* sound; in a polysyllabic word, the *y* has a short *i* (long *e*) sound. For example: my, by, cry, baby, dignity.
3. A single vowel in a closed syllable has a short sound, except that it may be modified in words in which the vowel is followed by an *r*. For example: club, dress, at, car, pumpkin, virgin.
4. The *r* gives the preceding vowel a sound that is neither long nor short (single or double vowels). For example: car, care, far, fair, fare.
5. In digraphs, when the following double-vowel combinations occur together, the first is usually long and the second is silent: *ai, ay, ea, ee, oa,* and *ow* (note that *ea* may also have a short *e* sound, and *ow* may have an *ou* sound). For example: main, pay; eat, bread; see, oat; sparrow, how.
6. In diphthongs (blends), the following double-vowel combinations usually blend: *au, aw, ou, oi, oy,* and *oo* (*oo* has two common sounds). For example: auto, awful, house, coin, boy, book, rooster.
7. *Io* and *ia* after *c, t,* and *s* help to make a consonant sound. For example: vicious, partial, musician, vision, attention, ocean.

Syllabication

1. Every single vowel or vowel combination means a syllable (except a final *e* in a vowel-consonant-*e* ending).
2. Divide between a prefix and a root (takes precedence over phonic syllabication generalizations).

*Adapted from Lou E. Burmeister, "Usefulness of Phonic Generalizations," *Reading Teacher* (January 1968):349-356, 360. Used with permission of the author and the International Reading Association.

3. Divide between two roots.
4. Usually divide between a root and a suffix (takes precedence over phonic syllabication generalizations).
5. When two vowel sounds are separated by two consonants, divide between the consonants, but consider *ch, sh, ph,* and *th* to be single consonants (takes precedence over phonic syllabication generalizations). For example: as/sist, con/vey, bun/ny, Hous/ton, rus/tic.
6. When two vowel sounds are separated by one consonant, divide either before or after the consonant, giving preference to dividing before the consonant, and consider *ch, sh, ph,* and *th* to be single consonants. For example: a/lone, se/lect, a/shame, Ja/pan, so/ber, com/et, hon/est, ev/er, ag/ile, gen/er/al.
7. When words end in consonant-*l-e,* divide before the consonant. For example: bat/tle, tre/ble.

Accent

1. In most two-syllable words, the first syllable is accented.
   a. When there are two like consonant letters within a word, the syllable before the consonant is usually accented: be'gin'ner, let'ter.
   b. In inflected or derived forms of words, the accent usually falls on or within the root word, and therefore, if *a, in, re, ex, de,* or *be* is the first syllable in a word, it is usually unaccented. For example: box'es; retie'.

Generalizations of Limited Usefulness

1. The vowel in an open syllable has a long sound.
2. The letter *a* has the same sound (/ô/) when followed by *e, w,* and *u.*
3. When there are two vowels, one of which is final *e,* the vowel is long and the *e* is silent.
4. In many two- and three-syllable words, the final *e* lengthens the sound of the vowel in the last syllable.
5. When a word ends in vowel-consonant-*e,* the vowel is long and the *e* is silent.
6. When two vowels occur together, the first is long and the second is silent.
7. If the first vowel sound in a word is followed by a single consonant, that consonant usually begins the second syllable.
8. When two sounds are separated by one consonant, divide before the consonant, but consider *ph, ch, sh,* and *th* to be single consonants.

There are those authorities who attribute all reading failure to a lack of phonic training. By the same token, there are other authorities who attribute reading failure to overemphasis on phonics. To attribute all reading failure to too little or too much phonics is unrealistic. The reasons why children do poorly in reading are multiple. Lack of phonic skill could at best be only one of the factors contributing to a child's disability.

Structural Analysis

A knowledge of phonics is very helpful in structural analysis. However, structural analysis involves the discernment of larger, more meaningful units (morphemes) than phonics, which deals with phonograms (a letter or letters representing speech sounds) and their matching phonemes (units of sound). Included in structural analysis are inflectional endings, compound words, roots, syllables, prefixes, and suffixes. By studying the structure of unknown words pupils may note the following:

1. Variant endings based on common roots

look	looking	looked
talk	talking	talked
wash	washes	washed

2. Compound words consisting of two familiar words

sunshine	milkman	sometimes

3. Root words to which prefixes have been added

unhappy	export	recount

4. Root words to which suffixes have been added

blackness	dangerous	sinful

5. Root words to which both prefixes and suffixes have been added

unkindly	distrustful	repayable

Current basal reader series introduce all of the foregoing structural units in the primary grades. During the intermediate grades, pupils' knowledge is extended as additional prefixes, suffixes, and roots are taught. Syllabication, introduced at the third-grade level, becomes increasingly valuable as a method of word analysis in the intermediate and upper grades. In spite of this fact, a number of reading authorities are dubious about the teaching of syllabication rules. Spache questions their values and cites a number of studies to corroborate his opinion.[33] Deighton, for example, advocates teaching only three principles: (1) each syllable has a vowel sound, (2) prefixes are separate syllables, and (3) doubled consonants may be split.[34] Too many other rules, he says, are of doubtful value because of exceptions. Zuck gives several reasons why the teaching of syllabication rules is questionable. These are as follows: (1) the rules for dividing words correctly at the end of a line are too numerous and complex, (2) the rules taught to help a child read are too few and have too many exceptions, (3) the rules for spelling can apply only after a child knows how to spell the word, and (4) the rules are based upon the written word and fail to consider differences between written syllables and spoken syllables.[35]

Oral Reading

At the time of the Pilgrims, reading was synonymous with reading the Bible, and this meant reading aloud. Few people could read, and those who were able to do so were expected to share the contents of The Good Book with others. It was common practice, for example, to find families gathered around the dinner table each evening while father read aloud from the Bible. Under these circumstances, it is understandable why schools stressed oral reading.

There were complaints about the practice of oral reading, but they were few and far between. In 1838, Horace Mann pointed out that there was too much emphasis on pronouncing words and that children "do not understand the meaning of the words they read. . . ."[36] In the early 1900s Huey registered a similar complaint.[37] And in the 1920s, Judd and Buswell called for a change in reading instruction which would shift emphasis from oral reading to silent reading.[38] The pendulum finally did begin to swing it. It swung so far, in fact, that in many schools oral reading was minimized to the degree that inaccurate word recognition and poor spelling resulted.

Today oral reading usually receives the basic emphasis in a developmental reading program for the primary grades and with older retarded students who are reading on a primary level. At the intermediate grade level, emphasis shifts to silent reading, with oral reading remaining a useful tool in diagnosing strengths and weaknesses in word recognition, word analysis, and independent reading habits (oral reading as a diagnostic tool is discussed on pages 178-181).

Round-Robin Reading

Very few children benefit from round-robin reading. When proficient readers are obliged to follow the slow, halting reading of a disabled reader (most often the former will have read ahead on their own and finished the selection before others are halfway through), they understandably find the reading lesson an unbearable chore. It is quite conceivable, too, that they might acquire some of the bad habits to which they have been exposed. For example, Durkin feels it is likely that oral reading by one child fosters subvocalization in the silent reading of those who follow what is being read.[39] When the proficient reader is called upon to read aloud, he/she covers the material with such ease and fluency that the deficient readers in the room are quickly lost. Round-robin reading has other disadvantages.

As poor readers stumble and stutter their way through their oral reading, embarrassment and misery know no bounds. Often the class is critical and unkind. Even the teacher may share a similar attitude. As a result, poor readers develop emotional problems, and reading becomes a source of aversion.

Values of Oral Reading

Most children enjoy reading orally and do profit from the experience. Some of the benefits of oral reading are these:

1. Oral reading helps in the removal of speech defects that may stem from the presence of another language in the home or from a culturally deprived background.
2. Oral reading before a group helps a shy child gain self-confidence and poise.
3. Oral reading gives the child practice in oral communication which can result in improved conversational skill.
4. Oral reading provides the teacher with opportunities to diagnose reading problems and to evaluate reading progress.
5. Oral reading provides opportunities for dramatizing stories and results in increased motivation.

Oral Versus Silent Reading

Although there are similarities between oral and silent reading, there are also differences between the two processes which have important implications. Some of these differences are the following:

1. Oral reading requires vocalization; silent reading does not.
2. Oral reading is characterized by more fixations and regressions than silent reading.
3. Oral reading results in a narrower span of recognition.
4. Oral reading narrows the anticipation span.

Oral Reading Instruction

Teachers who wish to improve their oral reading instruction will find the following suggestions helpful:

1. Provide children with a model of good oral reading. This can be done by having them listen to radio and television programs, to commercial or teacher-made recordings of exemplary readers, or to the teacher's reading.
2. Give children opportunities to read material silently before reading it aloud.
3. Minimize round-robin reading activity and substitute meaningful reading before an audience. This can be accomplished in a number of ways.
   a. Children can turn a story into a play by reading aloud suitable parts.
   b. Children can read aloud sections from a story as others act out what they have heard.
   c. Children can stimulate a radio or television program (the latter can be done by having children illustrate parts of a story or play with

pictures or slides) by reading before a microphone over station READ.

d. Children can read in proper sequence numbered parts of a story that has been cut and divided. It is advisable to mount tthe story on oaktag before cutting it into parts.

e. Children can read aloud announcements, directions, or instructions before the group or class.

f. Children can provide general information relating to a topic or subject under consideration by reading aloud before the group or class.

g. Children can read poetry or poetic prose in unison or in groups or by parts. Choral reading of this kind has many values.

(1) It develops a feeling of belongingness and helps build self-confidence among shy children.

(2) It teaches cooperation because the children participating must work together if the speaking choir is to produce results that are pleasing.

(3) It motivates children to improve the quality of their speech.

(4) It enhances children's appreciation of poetry.

4. Emphasize oral reading as an act of interpretation. Recognize that the ability to pronounce words is only incidental to the main purpose of reading aloud, which is to interpret to the listener ideas, information, feelings, and action which is in printed form.[40]

Oral Reading and the Tape Recorder

The tape recorder is a very valuable device for improving children's oral reading and should not be overlooked by the teacher. Some of the advantages of using the tape recorder are as follows:

1. The teacher who records the oral reading of children can rehear the recording and analyze carefully the kinds of errors made.

2. When pupils are given an opportunity to hear themselves, they are likely to become aware of their own weaknesses.

3. The use of a tape recorder motivates better oral reading.

4. Tapes are easily stored and do not wear out readily. They can be used and reused.

5. Sections of tape can be replayed whenever the teacher wishes to emphasize a point illustrated by the reading.

In writing about the value of the tape recorder, Strang, McCullough, and Traxler make the following observation:

. . . (it) can be used to record book discussions, dramatic interpretations of books, reactions to newspaper or magazine articles, and the like. The playback of such recordings helps the students evaluate their organization of ideas, their reasoning, and the effectiveness of dramatic presentations or arguments. Interest in reading is contagious through a well-presented recorded discussion which is sent to other classes or schools, the interest can spread. Ruth Strang, Constance McCullough, and Arthur Traxler, *The Improvement of Reading* (New York: McGraw-Hill Book Co., 1961), p. 421.

Evaluating Oral Reading

Teachers who wish to evaluate children's oral reading can employ standardized tests (see Appendix C) or they can make an informal appraisal. The latter can take place when the reader is sharing interesting material on his/her independent reading level with an audience. The reader should be well prepared and always should be permitted to preread the selection silently.

When evaluating a child's performance, Tinker and McCullough[41] recommend using an oral reading checklist. Parts A and B of the checklist which appears on page 217 may be used for oral reading assessments. A shorthand system for recording specific kinds of errors can be found on page 180.

Word Recognition

To become a proficient reader, a child has to acquire a large reservoir of sight words. These are words which the child recognizes instantly rather than through delayed recall. If too much time and energy are expended on analyzing words through phonic and structural analysis, the reader's comprehension suffers. Every effort must be made to assist children in developing a visual memory of words.

Teachers who are concerned about which words should become part of a child's sight vocabulary will want to familiarize themselves with word lists such as those compiled by Dolch in the 1930's as well as more up-to-date lists. (See pages 181-183 for additional information.)

The amount of repetition required to have a word become part of a child's sight vocabulary varies tremendously. Some pupils are able to recall words with a minimum of practice. Others fail to recognize words even though they have been exposed to them many times. At one time, Arthur Gates said that twenty to forty repetitions are necessary before mastery takes place. Other things being equal, the highly intelligent child adds new words to his sight vocabulary more rapidly than a dull child. But many factors unrelated to intelligence have a bearing on the speed of sight vocabulary development. For example, a pupil may be unable to see words clearly or may have difficulty retaining a visual image long enough to ensure retention. Then, too, words are easier to learn if they are meaningful and familiar to the child through everyday conversation, if they have distinctive shapes or features, if they have a high imagery component, and if they are emotionally pleasing. In the case of the latter, a child may learn to recognize the word *cookie* after one repetition, but the word *where* may require weeks of repetition before he responds to it correctly.

Whole-Word Method

Gates who advocated the whole-word method set forth a number of principles to observe in developing wordform perception in children.[42] Some of the techniques involved include the following:

1. Inducing pupils to react actively and vigorously to word forms.
2. Providing guidance in discovering the most significant features of printed words.
3. Displaying words in many different forms.
4. Avoiding the introduction of too many words in a single lesson.
5. Helping pupils utilize a variety of clues.
6. Helping pupils see and use those parts of words which are most helpful for word recognition.
7. Encouraging pupils to try different ways to analyzing words instead of repeating the same word.
8. Comparing new words with other words. Such comparisons should involve words which have been previously encountered.

When the whole-word method which Gates advocated is employed, it is essential that the teacher make sure children are looking at the specific word being identified. Too often they are looking at the teacher for help and do not have their eyes on the word when it is being pronounced. Getting children to attend to the details of a word is also important. Durkin believes that one good way of doing this "is to have them name, spell, and rename a word, once it has been identified."[43] Although an able reader should not employ spelling as a means of identifying a word, the neophyte benefits by spelling a word he is trying to learn because it forces him to attend to the letters that make it up.

Wolpert found that when presented out of context high-imagery words were learned significantly more easily than low-imagery words.[44] Therefore, when presenting a new vocabulary prior to a reading activity, teachers should be guided by the following suggestions:

1. Provide additional practice for low-imagery words.
2. Introduce low-imagery words in context.
3. Develop higher-imagery values for words having low-imagery value by emphasizing them orally in a rich contextual setting prior to presentation in written form.

When a child experiences sight vocabulary problems, he/she is in distress. An immediate halt should be called. A child should not be exposed to more difficult readers until he/she can demonstrate at least a 95 percent mastery of the words listed in back of his present reader. Daily and weekly evaluations of word mastery are essential. The teacher can help a child acquire this mastery by giving him/her other books and materials of parallel difficulty and by employing suitable individualized corrective procedures. If a child is exposed to a new and more difficult reader before he/she has acquired the requisite sight vocabulary, his/her reading ceases to be meaningful and enjoyable. Independent reading habits and skills become an unattainable goal.

Basal readers in the primary grades contain a controlled vocabulary based on the spoken and hearing vocabularies of children in these grades. Investigations reveal that six-year-old children who do not have a language handicap have a speaking vocabulary of at least three to five thousand words. A first-grade reader containing a vocabulary of a thousand words or less, therefore, does not present a problem in comprehension to the vast majority of children. In this connection, it is significant that problems of comprehension which seem apparent when children read orally or silently are usually nonexistent when the same material is read aloud to the children by the teacher. In the lower grades problems of comprehension during silent and oral reading usually are the result of inadequate sight vocabulary coupled with inability to attack new words.

It is true that a few stories entail settings that may be foreign to the experiential background of some pupils. When these stories are involved, a resourceful teacher provides appropriate learning experiences. By taking pupils on field trips, by using pictures, films, and the like, and by employing oral discussion, the teacher can furnish the orientation needed.

Kinesthetic Method

When pupils experience great difficulty in remembering words, the kinesthetic method which was devised by Grace M. Fernald and Helen B. Keller in 1921, should be tried. The method is based on tracing and writing and includes a language-experience component. Visual, auditory, and motor senses are involved. Any number of highly respected reading authorities have vouched for the method's effectiveness. In referring to the kinesthetic method and Dr. Fernald, Dr. Russell Stauffer of the University of Delaware states: "To the best of my knowledge no other technique has been introduced that could supplant hers."[45]

The following is an adaptation of the method as it appears in Grace Fernald's book, *Remedial Techniques in Basic School Subjects*, (New York: American Book, 1943). Teachers wishing to employ the kinesthetic method would find it profitable to consult the original source.

Explain to the child that we have a new way of learning words and that many bright people who have had the same difficulty as she/he have learned easily by this method. Let him/her select any words he/she wants to learn. Teach the words in this manner.

1. Teacher writes the word in manuscript with crayola.
2. Child traces the word with his finger and says each part of the word as he traces it.
3. Child writes the word without looking at the copy and then compares his effort with the copy.
4. If he has made an error, he continues to trace the copy until he can write it correctly.

After the child has learned several words in this manner and has discovered that he can learn, he begins to write stories about any subject he chooses. The following procedure is used:

1. The child asks the teacher to write any word which he needs in his story.
2. He learns the word by tracing it and saying the parts as he does so.
3. He writes the word first on scrap paper and then in his story.
4. He files the word.
5. Teacher types the story.
6. The child reads the story to the teacher or to the group.

Cautions to the teacher:

1. Be sure that the child always writes the word in the story without looking at the copy.
2. Be sure that the child's finger actually touches the paper as he traces the word.
3. The word should always be written as a unit and should never be patched up by erasing or substituting.
4. Emphasize success. Call attention to the new words which he has learned.

A child who begins to learn to read by the kinesthetic method will need to learn words by tracing for only a limited period. He may be expected to pass through the four following stages:

1. Tracing stage (average tracing stage is about two months).
2. Learns new words by simply looking at the word in script and saying it over to himself and then writing it. He should say the word as he writes it.
3. Child learns directly from the printed word without having it written for him. He begins to want to read from books. He is allowed to read

as much and whatever he wishes. He is told words he does not know. After he has finished a story, he goes over the new words and writes them. The teacher should check the words later to see that they have been retained.

4. He soon begins to make out new words from words he already knows. He glances over a paragraph and notes all the words which he does not recognize. He sounds these words and then reads the paragraph.

Methods of Teaching Beginning Reading

There is no one best method for teaching beginning reading. However, one method may have some features that are more effective with certain children. Among the programs used are language experience, linguistics, alphabet approaches, words in color, individualized reading, and basal reading approach.

Language-Experience Method

The language-experience approach is based on the interrelationship and interdependence between listening, speaking, writing, and reading. It had its beginning in 1862 when Leo Tolstoy introduced reading to young pupils enrolled in his school as Yasnaya Polyana by asking them to read their own compositions. As Van Allen, the chief proponent of the approach, phrased it:[46]

> What I can think about, I can talk about.
> What I can say, I can write.
> What I can write, I can read.
> I can read what I write and what other people can write for me to read.

The language-experience approach which is recommended for use with the disadvantaged,[47] does not separate reading instruction from the development of listening, speaking, and writing skills. Therefore it is possible to capitalize on children's background of experience in developing instructional materials. From the very beginning, children are encouraged to express themselves orally while working with various media—paint, clay, drawing, and the like. Initially, the teacher records thoughts as dictated by the child. After reading their own stories, children move naturally into reading other children's stories. The teacher works with individual children and with small groups of children. Soon they express a desire to write their own stories. This is encouraged by the teacher who gives all the help needed. The stories (some may be very short) are illustrated and are bound together into a book. Sometimes several students contribute materials which become books devoted to topics such as airplanes, pets, and summer vacations. Books become everyone's reading property.

Stauffer and Spache have written about the limitations of the language-experience approach.[48, 49] Some of the limitatitons discussed by Spache are as follows. (1) Continuing the language-experience approach beyond the primary grades may retard a child's reading development. (2) There is doubt regarding children's ability to make a transition from reading their own language to reading the language of others. (3) Since children's listening, speaking, writing, and reading vocabularies vary in size and depth, there is some doubt as to the truth of the assumption "What I can think about, I can talk about. What I say, I can write. What I can write, I can read." (4) Organizational problems are significant: How do teachers record and evaluate the various materials used? How do teachers measure and evaluate the development of children's reading skills? What checklists of reading skills do teachers use? (5) Many educational experiments refute the assumption inherent in the language-experience approach that incidental learning of skills is equal to or superior to direct or planned presentation.

Linguistics

Linguists are concerned with grapheme-phoneme relationships. They believe that children find meaning when they learn to associate sounds (phonemes) with appropriately matched printed symbols (graphemes). Learning to read consists of responding to patterns of letters. In other words, reading is a matter of turning graphic symbols into speech sounds.

The ideas of the late Leonard Bloomfield, an outstanding linguist, were published in 1961.[50] It was Bloomfield's belief that teachers should begin reading instruction by teaching the sounds of the letters in the alphabet, both uppercase and lowercase. In his book *Let's Read*, initial reading experiences exclude English words that are not phonetic, that is, those for which the grapheme-phoneme relationship is unreliable. Later, as the child develops competence, words that represent inconsistencies in the English writing system are introduced. In Part I of *Let's Read*, words that fit a consonant-vowel-consonant pattern are found: *man, pin, but,* and so on. These evolve into lists of words. In the case of *man*, the list becomes *man, ran, fan, van*. Accompanying *pin*, the words which appear are *bin, din, fin, kin*. Simple sentences employing learned words are provided: A man ran a tan van. In Part II of *Let's Read*, consonant blends are introduced. Subsequent parts and lessons are devoted to carefully planned modifications of a sequential nature. As instruction continues, meaningful usage of words that have been learned changes from short sentences to paragraphs, and paragraphs eventually become stories which are eight to ten pages in length. In contrast to other reading programs, the Linguistic program does not include the use of pictures as an aid to word recognition or reading comprehension.

There are a number of basal reading series using a linguistics approach including the following: *Basic Reading Series* by Goldberg and Rasmussen

(Science Research Associates), *Merrill Linguistics Readers* by Fries and others (Charles E. Merrill), *Miami Linguistics Readers* (D. C. Heath), *Structural Reading Series* by Stern (L. W. Singer), and *Linguistic Readers* by Smith, Stratemeyer et al, (Benziger Corp.), and the *Palo-Alto Program* (Harcourt).

In commenting on reading series based on linguistic principles which have been introduced since 1961, Harris has stated the following:

> They have in common agreement that "decoding" or translating the printed forms into spoken equivalents is the first and most important goal of a reading program. Most of them also agree on using whole words and the principle of minimal variation, rather than a synthetic sounding-blending procedure. . . . Just as with programs in other approaches, no two linguistic series agree very closely on details. A. J. Harris, *How to Increase Reading Ability*, 6th ed. (New York: David McKay Co., 1975), p. 63.

The study of linguistics often seems difficult because of the many unfamiliar terms such as grapheme, morpheme, phoneme, etc. Some of these terms which were selected from the glossary (App. B) are listed below:

Intonation: The rise and fall of the pitch of the voice during speech.

Juncture: A pause in the flow of oral language caused either by a catch in the breath or a breath stoppage.

Morpheme: A unit of language that conveys meaning.

Morphology: The study of the forms of language, particularly those used in declension, conjugation, and word building.

Phonemics: The science of phonemic systems concerned with identification and description of the phonemes of a language.

Phonics: The study of sound-letter relationships in reading and the use of this knowledge in recognizing and pronouncing words.

Phonology: The history and theory of changes in speech sound.

Pitch: The quality of auditory sensitivity interpreted by an individual as high or low; the result of frequency of vibration.

Semantics: The study of word meanings.

Stress: The degree of loudness with which a phoneme is uttered.

Syntax: The branch of grammar dealing with sentence structure and the arrangement of words as elements in a sentence to show their relationship.

Alphabet Approaches

It should be common knowledge that inconsistencies in English spelling complicate the reading process. English might be classed paradoxically as an unphonetic phonetic language. It has twenty-six letters to represent some forty-four sounds. And three of the twenty-six letters—*c*, *q*, and *x*— have little or no value.

According to Hildreth, of the three hundred fifty commonest words in the English language, fewer than two hundred can be written as they sound: for example, *again, always, before, where,* and so forth.[51] Approximately one-third of all the words in an unabridged dictionary have one or more silent letters in them. Is it any wonder that there have been attempts to develop and promote a phonetically regular alphabet? Benjamin Franklin proposed one. In more recent years George Bernard Shaw strongly advocated a more "fonetic" approach to spelling because of the time and trouble it would save. It was he who humorously pointed out that the word *fish* could be spelled "ghoti." His reasoning was as follows: The letters *gh* have the sound of an *f* in the word *enough,* the vowel *o* has a short-*i* sound in the word *women,* and the letters *ti* sound like the consonant digraph *sh* in the word *nation.*

Initial Teaching Alphabet

The alphabetic scheme that has had the largest following was introduced in Great Britain during the early 1960s by James Pitman. Initially, it was referred to as the Augmented Roman Alphabet (ARA). Later, the name was changed to Initial Teaching Alphabet (ITA).

ITA recognizes forty-four phonemes in the English language, and it provides one symbol for each of these sounds. To minimize confusion between capital and lowercase letters such as *B* and *b* it employs capitals that are enlarged versions of lowercase letters. With the exception of *q* and *x* (these letters are completely eliminated), the beginning reader of ITA is introduced to only lowercase letters of our alphabet plus twenty augmentations. Primarily, the augmentations involve two conventional letters that have been linked together, with most of the changes occurring in the bottom or middle parts. Since the tops of letters provide more clues to recognition than the lower parts, reading ITA does not prove very difficult. As soon as children have learned the sounds of the forty-four symbols, they are on their way. There is no silent-*e* rule to remember or no double-vowel rule to apply. Rules or generalizations are not needed.

In a study reported by Downing, British children exposed to ITA were significantly better readers after two years than children who were taught by exposure to traditional orthography.[52] The ITA groups learned to read more easily, they were better spellers, and they were more creative and fluent in their writing. In a later report, Downing and Rose pointed out the following advantages of ITA: it lightens the load of learning to read, it requires fewer whole-word representations to be learned, and it simplifies spelling and reduces the complexity of phonic symbols.[53] Hilaire and Thompson reported that children participating in their ITA study "conceptualized stories better, developed more imaginative story lines and showed more original and flexible use of the words they selected."[54] For those who are concerned about the undesirable effects of ITA on reading development at later stages, Downing[55] has reported that the Bullock Commission found no such adverse effects.

Cutts, who was not convinced of the merits of ITA, pointed to several factors that make appraisal of its validity doubtful: not knowing the long-range effects of ITA, the role of the Hawthorne effect in ITA experiments, difficulties some children may have in making a transition from ITA to traditional orthography, and the fact that studies show that the importance of an early start in reading is not particularly advantageous.[56]

Words in Color

Words in Color, designed by Gattengo, uses a color scheme (thirty-nine different colors are involved) to represent forty-seven different sounds, twenty of which are vowel sounds and the remainder, consonant sounds.[57]

Diacritical Marking System

Edward Fry evolved a marking scheme to help in the pronunciation of graphemes. His Diacritical Marking System (DMS) is felt to be superior to the ITA because of greater consistency in phoneme-grapheme relationships. Also, transfer problems are minimized. Fry's system uses letters found on a standard typewriter so that basic orthography is retained. In 1964, Fry compared ITA with two basal approaches, both identical except for his diacritical marking system which was employed with one of them. No significant differences in reading were found among the three first-grade groups involved in the experiment.[58]

Individualized Reading

Individualized reading is based on the concepts evolved by Willard C. Olson. These include self-seeking behavior, self-selection, and self-pacing.[59] Olson contends that children have an inherent maturational drive and pattern of development which enable them to select wisely materials suited to their needs, interests, and maturational level. As children proceed at their own rate with materials and instruction provided by the teacher, pacing is achieved.

The following outline provides a brief description of some of the more important aspects of individualized reading.

1. The teacher secures a wide variety of reading materials. These materials vary in level of difficulty and in interest appeal. Trade books, basal readers, newspapers, pamphlets, magazines, and reference books may be included.
2. Children choose what they want to read.
3. The teacher holds individual conferences with the children. During the conference (the time involved usually is five to ten minutes), the teacher discusses with the child the material being read. By having the pupil read aloud, the teacher is able to note reading errors. Phonic principles are taught, and comprehension is checked by previously

prepared questions. Some teachers suggest other books to be read in an effort to help the child's reading progress.

4. The teacher and the child keep detailed records. For the teacher these may include things such as the date, the name of the book being read, the particular page involved, and the like.
5. Special needs and interest groupings are utilized. All groups are temporary and are dissolved when they have served their function.
6. Evaluation is made in terms of quantity and quality of the books read. Attitudinal changes about books and reading are considered. Standardized tests are not used very extensively.

Those who are enthusiastic about individualized reading contend that it has the following advantages. (1) Children read more and their interests are given consideration. (2) The teacher discovers the needs of each child and provides a reading skills program designed to meet those needs. (3) The plan is equally successful with classes of differing size and with classes having children of differing abilities. (4) Parents as well as their children are pleased with the plan.[60]

Sartain lists certain dangers in the approach, including the following.[61] (1) There is a lack of opportunity for teaching new words and concepts needed before reading is begun. (2) Teaching a systematic and complete program of skills and identifying individual difficulties are hardly possible when the teacher has only a few working minutes weekly with each child. (3) Skills taught for short periods and not systematically reviewed may lack permanence. (4) Limited group interaction lessens the opportunity for critical thinking and literary appreciation. (5) Slow-learning pupils who do not respond to independent work become restless and waste their time. (6) Working with individuals rather than with groups of children with similar needs is inefficient timewise. (7) Conscientious teachers are frustrated by individual conference demands, while careless teachers are provided with no direction.

Basal Readers

The basal reader program is the most widely used approach to the teaching of reading in the United States. Recent surveys reveal that the basal reader is used in more than 90 percent of the schools. In general, basal readers are designed for grades one through six, although some have been developed for the secondary school. The typical series starts with a readiness book, a preprimer, a primer, and a first reader. At the second- and third-grade levels, two texts a year are provided. At grade four and beyond, one text a year is furnished. Workbooks accompany each textbook. A teacher's manual and additional supplementary materials such as filmstrips and recordings are available.

Basal programs provide a logical and sequential development of material that seeks to achieve mastery of basic reading skills. Strict vocabulary control, especially at the primary level, is adhered to. As a result, the language of basal readers has been considered colorless, boring, and unduly repetitious. Humorous stories of the "look, look, look" and "see, see, see" variety are widely circulated.

Using basal readers and workbooks in a stereotyped manner fails to meet individual differences present within a classroom. But even if used intelligently (many teachers admit that they never bother reading the teacher's manual), one cannot expect basal readers that are limited to one grade level to prove effective with all pupils in the class. Special methods and special supplementary materials are also needed in a sound reading program.

Because of their wide acceptance, it is interesting and valuable to learn exactly how schools employ basal readers. In a questionnaire study titled "How Are Basal Readers Used?" Ralph Staiger found that of the 474 schools responding, roughly half were using a single series of readers.[62] About 17 percent were varying their procedures, so it was doubtful if a one-series plan was being used. Two series of readers were used cobasally by 20 percent of the schools, 5.7 percent used three series cobasally, and 5.1 percent used more than three series.

Workbooks accompanying basal readers were used widely. According to Staiger, of those schools employing a single basal, 91.4 percent of them used workbooks, while only 76.3 percent of schools employing cobasals and 49.0 percent of schools employing tribasals used workbooks.

In a presentation at the 1971 International Reading Association (IRA) convention in Atlantic City, Harris described the most recent trends in basal readers.[63] These include increased emphasis on decoding in beginning reading, less stress on literal comprehension with more emphasis on critical and creative reading, interest in behavioral objectives, richer vocabularies, and greater emphasis on critical and interpretive reading and study skills. The content of basal readers shows a trend toward multiethnic and multicultural materials. More nonfiction is provided at the intermediate grade levels, and workbooks are being replaced by skills practice.

Some of the most widely used basal reading programs are those of Allyn & Bacon, American Book Company, Ginn & Company, Harper & Row, Holt, Rinehart & Winston, J. B. Lippincott Company, Macmillan Company, and Scott, Foresman & Company.

According to Spache, those who support the basal reading program (most reading specialists do) agree on advantages such as the following.[64] Basal reading series provide systematic guidance in the development of reading skills; use materials based on children's interests and common experiences; offer a program greatly superior to what most teachers could create; give techniques and provide materials for determining initial reading readiness and for proceeding step-by-step through easy stages; use a basic or core vocabulary essential to beginning or subequent reading; provide materials carefully scaled in difficulty and sequentially arranged to facilitate learning; use material that is exemplary in terms of typography, format, and physical readability; and include a variety of different kinds of reading experiences—recreational and work-study reading, poetry and prose, factual and fictional, and so on—that extend children's ideas and knowledge in many areas.

Spache and various writers he quotes mention the following limitations of the basal reader approach.[65] Basal reading series fail to inform teachers of the true purposes of the reading readiness program; they offer readiness training materials that are of doubtful validity; they contain many stories that are uninteresting; they fail to prepare children for reading in the content fields; they have workbooks of questionable value; they are too restrictive in their control of vocabulary. Other limitations, according to Sartain, are a result of teacher misuse.[66] For example, all children are expected to read the same stories at the same rate; the reading program is limited to one series of basal readers; whole groups of children are expected to follow in their books while individual pupils read aloud; teachers fail to utilize the skills program of the teacher's manual to meet children's varying needs.

READING IN THE INTERMEDIATE GRADES

The intermediate grades are those in which previously learned skills are refined and improved. Word-analysis skills become more automatized, and the pupil is given systematic instruction in the use of the dictionary. The latter is particularly important in helping students develop their meaning vocabulary. It should be pointed out, however, that the pupil who reaches the intermediate grades without a mastery of basic skills in word recognition and word analysis is not prepared to cope with the technical vocabulary of content field reading.

During this period more and more expository or factual reading is encountered (reading for knowledge becomes increasingly important), and many comprehension skills are consolidated or added to the pupil's repertoire: anticipating outcomes; following directions; reading for different purposes; spotting central thoughts of paragraphs; remembering important details; outlining; summarizing; reading graphs, charts, and tables; and locating information.

In the fourth, fifth, and sixth years in school, very rapid growth takes place in the rate of comprehension and the extension of reading interests. Witty and Kopel report that the amount and variety of reading activity of typical boys and girls reach their peak at twelve or thirteen years.[67]

Strang, McCullough and Traxler indicate that the intermediate grades are good ones in which to teach techniques of locating information such as using card catalogs, tables of contents, indexes, headings, and italics.

> . . . After learning to locate sources of information, the pupil is ready to begin examining them for accuracy, authenticity, and relevancy. He takes useful notes, organizes the facts, and writes a readable report which he presents in an interesting way. It is here that he receives instruction in the special skills of reading maps, graphs, and tables. Ruth Strang, Constance McCullough, and Arthur Traxler, *The Improvement of Reading*, 4th ed. (New York: McGraw-Hill Book Co., 1967), p. 127.

READING IN THE CONTENT FIELDS

Intermediate and upper-grade pupils find reading subject matter text-books more difficult than storybook reading. The reasons for this are (1) lack of a technical vocabulary and needed background of experience may stand in the way of comprehension, (2) limited mastery of the skills of word analysis, and (3) lack of a definite purpose in reading.

The field of mathematics includes such unusual words as *cone, root,* and *integer*. The reader of scientific material encounters *watt, spectrum,* and *oxidation.* Not knowing one of these key words and not having in mind the concepts involved can make comprehension of a sentence or paragraph rather difficult. It is important, therefore, that all subject matter teachers assume the responsibility of helping pupils learn new words basic to understanding the subject.

There are instances when students are familiar with certain technical words when they hear them. But if they have not mastered the skills of word analysis (for example, knowing how to break a word into syllables or being able to interpret diacritical markings in the dictionary), the words remain unknown to them until someone pronounces them. If not given this kind of assistance, such pupils are quickly inundated and frustrated by the numerous polysyllabic words encountered in content field reading.

Good readers of content field material vary the way they read according to the purpose for which they are reading. For example, reading technical material requires a slow, meticulous rate, while reading an exciting short story permits faster reading. A student reads a laboratory manual for the purpose of following directions and reads a problem in mathematics to discover what facts are given that will facilitate solving it. Different types of materials require different mental approaches as well as various reading rates. Pupils need guidance in learning how to adjust to the purpose for which they are reading.

Mathematics

Everyone knows that when reading mathematical materials, one must read slowly and exactly. It has been estimated that 16 specialized reading-study skills are needed.[68] A problem in mathematics seldom contains a great deal of superflous or unnecessary information. Fast or cursory reading is likely to result in confusion and many mistakes and should be discouraged.

In solving a written problem the reader should go through a number of steps. First, read the problem quickly to learn what it is about. During a second reading, locate exactly what is being asked. Just what is the problem? Is it the cost of a dozen eggs or the number of fifteen-cent stamps that can be purchased with a given amount of money? Once the reader knows what he is supposed to find out, he then reads the problem again, looking for relevant details which will provide the facts needed to solve it. When he is completely familiar with the facts, he works out an answer. Finally, he rereads the problem a last time to check the answer and to make doubly sure the solution is complete.

Science

Science, like mathematics, makes reading demands on pupils that are similar in many respects. Pupils must read carefully and give full attention to details. Rereading is often necessary because the material is too difficult to be understood in one reading.

The technical vocabulary of science is heavy. During the assignment period, the science teacher should introduce pertinent words by writing them on the chalkboard. Each word should be pronounced so that pupils will become acquainted with the spoken word as well as with the printed symbol. Familiarizing students with the technical vocabulary of science is time well spent. Only when pupils understand scientific terminology can they begin to understand scientific language patterns.

In addition to a technical vocabulary, equations, formulas, graphs, diagrams, and drawings frequently appear. Since understanding and mastery of these are essential, the wise teacher takes time to discuss and clarify them.

The pages of science books are often filled with sentences and paragraphs that are heavily ladened with facts, many of which are beyond the child's realm of experience. Through the use of visual aids (especially motion pictures), discussion, and demonstration, a teacher can help build a background of experience which will make comprehension of the text easier.

Social Studies

Although the difficulty level of social studies books may be decreasing,[69] the volume of reading required in the social studies area makes heavy demands on students. Efficient reading in this area involves emphasis on informational reading. Some of the specific skills entailed include finding central thoughts of paragraphs, locating related details, detecting a sequence of events, discerning cause-and-effect relationships, reading graphs and charts, and map-reading ability.

The intelligent reader of social studies is in need of a broad general vocabulary. He also needs to be acquainted with various technical vocabularies: politics, government, religion, sociology, law, and so forth.

When reading social studies material, there is a need to react critically to what is read. The reader must be sensitive to the presence of propaganda and should not hesitate to compare the viewpoints of several authors before accepting what is read as true. He must decide if statements are facts or opinions and must become acquainted with sources which generally are thought to be reliable.

If pupils are to become discerning citizens and intelligent voters of the future, teachers of social studies must assume the responsibilities of teaching needed reading skills.

Reading Skills

Context Clues

As stated by Hildreth, "inferring the meaning of a word from what went before, and deliberately reading ahead for clues to meaning, is an essential technique for word recognition."[70]

Because of its importance to word recognition, practice in utilizing context clues begins very early. Continued instruction and constant practice during the primary grades and beyond result in continuous improvement of the skill. Klein, Klein, and Bertino point out the difficulties many fourth-grade pupils experience with context clues.[71]

Children who read a great deal learn many words by using context clues. Typically, the following occurs when a child encounters an unknown word. He tries phonics and structural analysis to arrive at a pronunciation. If the result is unfamiliar to his learning vocabulary, he guesses at the word from the context and moves on. By the end of the fourth grade, the average reader becomes quite adept at helping himself through a combination of context clues and sounding. And if he is unhappy with the tentative pronunciation or supported meaning of a word, he may consult a dictionary.

Dictionary Usage

Although picture dictionaries are introduced in the primary grades, formal dictionary training is reserved for the intermediate grades. Once pupils know how to use this important tool, they have acquired true independence in word attack. They then have a source for assistance in the pronunciation, spelling, and meaning of words. Unfortunately, many readers have a distinct aversion for the dictionary. This antipathy is undoubtedly an outgrowth of their lack of skill in using it. In any event, it is necessary for teachers to exercise all of their ingenuity when trying to instruct students in dictionary usage.

Subskills essential to locating words, pronouncing them, and defining them are as follows:

1. Location Skills
   a. Knowing alphabetical sequence
   b. Determining what letters precede and follow a given letter
   c. Alphabetizing words according to their beginning letters
   d. Alphabetizing words according to beginning two- and three-letter patterns
   e. Using guide words intelligently
   f. Knowing the value of thumb indexes
   g. Learning to open a dictionary that lacks thumb indexes at a point near the word
2. Pronunciation Skills
   a. Using key words to interpret diacritical markings
   b. Recognizing syllables
   c. Understanding and interpreting primary and secondary accent marks
   d. Understanding and appreciating tthe *schwa* sound
   e. Reading phonetic spelling
3. Definition Skills
   a. Realizing that a word may have multiple meanings
   b. Comprehending definitions provided
   c. Choosing from several definitions given the one that gives the best explanation of the meaning of the unknown word

Comprehension

A study entitled "Reading as Reasoning" was published in 1917. The author, Edward L. Thorndike, considered reading to be a thinking process. Although reading specialists gave relatively little emphasis to this concept prior to 1950, many reading texts currently in use devote space to it.[72, 73]

Evidence that calling words is not reading was provided by Smith in relating the case of a fifth-grade boy reading the Gettysburg Address. Parenthetical interpolations indicate what the pupil was thinking when trying to make the words meaningful.

Fourscore (a score is what we have after a baseball game is played) and seven years ago our fathers (this must mean our own and our stepfathers) brought forth on this continent (that's North America, we had that in social studies) a new nation (that's America or the U.S.A. I think) conceived (I wonder what that means) in liberty (that's what a sailor gets) and dedicated (that's what they did to the building on the corner) . . . N. B. Smith, "Reading: Concept Development," *Education* (May 1950):540-558.

It is obvious that reading is more than a process of eye movements and word-recognition skill. Reading is more than "barking at the print." Proper meaning must be brought to printed symbols to ensure their understanding and enhance interpretation. Too often students lack the concepts needed to make words live. The ability to call words accurately does not mean in itself that a student comprehends the material. One third grader read beautifully before the class, but when asked to tell in his own words what he had just read, he hesitated a few moments and said, "Gee, I guess I wasn't listening to myself."

Reading comprehension, the goal of reading instruction, is usually conceived of as tri-leveled: literal reading, inferential reading, and critical reading. These may be thought of as understanding what the author says, understanding what the author means, and evaluating what the author said. As one sage stated it, "reading the lines, reading between the lines, and reading beyond the lines."

Reading comprehension should involve more than getting the meaning of a story or selection. Thinking should be encouraged. And with thinking comes inferential and critical reading. For example, a child may read a story about elephants. He compares what he has read with what he has actually observed elephants do at the zoo. Or, she/he may compare two stories about elephants to see if they agree or disagree in the facts presented. This is critical reading, the kind of thoughtful reading that teachers should endeavor to develop in their pupils. (See pages 313-314 for specific suggestions relating to critical reading.) It is begun in the primary grades but receives greater emphasis at the intermediate level.

The kinds of questions which are asked by teachers have an important bearing on the quality of a child's comprehension of what is read. Guszak reports that 56 percent of all reading questions studied were the recall type, while 13 percent involved recognition.[74] In other words about 70 percent of all questions asked dealt with literal understanding. Only 6 percent of the questions involved interpretation, and 15 percent were at a problem-solving level.

Teachers should not exclusively employ such questions as, "In what grade was the boy? Where did the boy go? Did the story take place in the morning or afternoon?" Rather, they should ask such questions as these: "What would be a good title for this story? Did the story make you happy or sad? Why? What would you have done if you were Jim?" As stated by an experienced elementary teacher, "Never ask a question which you can answer yourself." By this was meant that the answer will be individually determined by each child's experiences, attitudes and opinions. Ultimately, children should learn to formulate their own questions and guide their own thinking so that they no longer need the teacher.[75]

Teachers who feel they need detailed assistance in evolving thought-provoking questions should read the book by Norris Sanders, *Classroom Questions: What Kinds?* (Harper & Row), 1966.

Research by Wiesendanger and Wollenberg[76] has shown that the use of questions prior to the reading of a selection adversely effects children's reading comprehension. Apparently, pupils who are provided with questions fail to formulate their own purposes for reading and thus lower their overall comprehension of a reading passage. In spite of this finding, countless children who use basal readers (about 90%)are regularly exposed to prequestioning activities as a means of increasing comprehension.

Comprehending and interpreting what is read depends on concepts acquired through past experiences. These may be direct or vicarious. Early sensory experiences—tasting, touching, smelling, hearing, seeing—are basic and fundamental. Later, listening to the radio, watching television, traveling, and hearing the conversation of older people increase the tempo of concept development. Children who have been denied these kinds of experiences not only find it difficult to comprehend written language, but are also unable to comprehend spoken language. Since the understanding of spoken language is basic to reading the language, these children should be given instruction in oral language. In some instances children's experiential backgrounds are so meager that reading-comprehension problems cannot be solved through more instruction. The solution lies in their acquiring more experience. One must not forget that reading involves bringing meaning *to* the page more than it involves getting meaning *from* the page.

Comprehension assumes varying roles at different reading levels. In the primary grades it is highly correlated with a child's sight vocabulary. The written material to which beginning readers are exposed keeps within the average child's background of experience. In addition, it is expressed in familiar words and employs a sentence structure that the child can comprehend in spoken language. In the intermediate grades, reading comprehension correlates more highly with intelligence and is more of a problem since the reading material encountered becomes more complicated and is likely to go beyond what the child can comprehend in spoken language.

Understanding the meaning of individual words is requisite to meaningful reading. Mastery of a technical vocabulary is often synonymous with concept development. Studies show that many textbooks are loaded with unnecessary technical words.[77] If the reader does not know the meaning of words used by an author, she/he cannot comprehend the author's thoughts.

The ability to group words into units of thought rather than reading word-by-word is another requisite to reading comprehension. For example, the sentence The boy / hit the ball / over the fence contains three thought units. Proficiency in perceiving thought units leads naturally to sentence comprehension. And when a pupil learns to discern the difference between topical sentences and those which provide examples, details, or support the main idea, he/she is comprehending paragraphs. Skills of these kinds require greater emphasis in the intermediate grades than in the primary grades.

Other comprehension skills that are important to develop or expand during the intermediate grades include (1) reading to follow more complex directions, (2) reading to remember, (3) reading to anticipate outcomes, (4) learning to outline, (5) learning to summarize, and (6) critical reading.

Study-type Reading

Since study-type reading begins to have importance during the intermediate grades, many teachers introduce the survey, question, read, recite, review (SQ3R) method of study. The method was evolved by Francis Robinson several decades ago and has proved particularly effective in aiding comprehension and retention.[78] A simplified version of Robinson's SQ3R method of study follows.

Survey: Have the pupil read quickly all the headings in the chapter or article to see the big points that are to be developed. This survey should not take more than two or three minutes. Darkened paragraph headings, italicized headings, pictures, graphs, and summary statements should receive attention. This orientation will help the pupil organize ideas as he reads them later.

Question: Now have the pupil begin to work. Tell him to turn the first heading into a question. This can be done by using *what, why, where, when,* or *how*. The question will arouse curiosity and increase comprehension. It will bring to mind information already known and will help him understand the section more quickly. Most important, the question will make important points stand out while explanatory details will be recognized as such. Turning a heading into a question should be done immediately when reading the heading.

Read: The pupil now reads to find the answer or answers to the question. This is not a passive plowing along but an *active* search for answers.

Recite: This is the most important step in the SQ3R Method. The pupil now looks away from the book and briefly recites the answer in his own words. If he cannot do this, he glances at the book again. A second attempt is made to recite. He continues to read and recite as long as necessary. An excellent way to do this reciting from memory is to have the pupil jot down under the written-out questions cue phrases in outline form.

When the pupil is satisfied he knows what he has read, he repeats steps two, three, and four on each succeeding headed section. That is, he turns the next heading into a question, reads to answer that question, and then recites the answer by jotting down cue phrases in outline form. Reading is continued this way until the lesson is completed.

Review: When the lesson has thus been read through, the pupil looks over his notes to get a bird's-eye view of the lesson and checks his memory again by quickly reciting the subpoints under each heading. He can do this by covering up his notes and trying to recall the main points and by covering the main points while he tries to recall the subpoints under them.

Speed of Reading

It is definitely an advantage to get desired information from books quickly and efficiently. By the time the average student has reached the fourth grade, articulation during silent reading is minimal, phrasing ability has improved, and silent readng may be as much as twice the speed of oral reading. Spache[79] states, "If given proper instruction, children show proportionately more growth in speed of reading at about the fourth grade than during any other period in their schooling." It is evident that special emphasis on reading speed at this time can pay dividends.

Teachers who are interested in increasing the reading speed of intermediate-grade students should keep in mind the following points.

1. Reading speed without comprehension is not reading. The most adequate definition of reading speed is *rate of comprehension.*
2. Rapid, average, or slow readers who comprehend poorly should not be pressured to read more rapidly. With all poor comprehenders, major emphasis should be given to training that stresses accurate reading.
3. Slow readers who comprehend well are the most likely candidates to profit from increased emphasis on speed.
4. Flexibility in reading rate is more important than speed per se. Good students vary their reading speed in accordance with their purposes and the difficulty of the reading material.
5. Mechanical devices are not needed to improve students' rate of comprehension.

Teachers may give periodic tests of an informal nature to encourage students to develop acceptable reading rates for different kinds of material.

READING IN THE UPPER GRADES

Junior high school students face heavy reading demands, a great deal of which is centered around assignments which students are expected to complete independently. The reading is not easy. Specialized nomenclature is encountered in different subject matter areas accompanied by more involved sentence and paragraph structure. Many secondary teachers assume that their students can analyze words, read interpretively and critically, and study effectively. The truth, however, that reading deficiencies are all too prevalent.

A report by Donovan in 1955 showed that almost one-quarter of 45,000 New York City freshman and sophomore high school students were reading two to five or more years below grade.[80] In terms of mental ability, 42.3 percent were reading below their potential.

What can be done? Some secondary schools have reading specialists who offer developmental reading courses for all students regardless of their reading status. Other schools provide developmental or remedial courses which can be taken by students as an elective. English teachers frequently are asked to assume the responsibility of teaching reading even though they have little background and/or interest in the area. Ideally, all subject matter teachers should be involved in the reading program since reading skills differ in science, history, mathematics, and other subjects. Few high schools have developed a well-coordinated, concerted approach.

Study Skills

Upper-grade students are expected to study independently a number of hours each week, but few of them receive instruction from their teachers that proves helpful. Students who are exposed to study-skills instruction often fail to employ it properly, either because they were not given sufficient practice or because they find a haphazard approach easier to use.

Since reading at the junior and senior high school levels is not taught as a separate subject, content field teachers must assume additional responsibility in giving students how-to-study tips. For example, getting-to-know-your-textbook sessions can prove very profitable in bringing to students' attention ways in which their textbooks can help them study. The following questions are offered as a guide.

Knowing Your Textbook
1. What is the title of your text and when was it published?
2. Why is the date of publication important?
3. What can you learn about the author?
4. What does the author tell you about the features of the book which will help you in your studies?
5. If the book has a glossary or an appendix, how will they help you in your studies?
   a. How does a glossary differ from a dictionary?
   b. What type of material is found in an appendix and how does it help you?

6. Does the author furnish study helps to aid you in comprehending the book?
   a. Are there questions at the beginning or end of each chapter?
   b. Is there an introductory statement at the beginning of each chapter?
   c. Are summaries or conclusions provided at the end of each chapter?
   d. Does the author list additional references which you might consult?
   e. Are division or section headings set forth clearly in boldface or italicized type?

SQ3R Method

Students in the upper grades need to become acquainted or reacquainted with Robinson's SQ3R method of study. It is a very efficient and effective method which can be used in studying practically any subject. Students who use the method will find that their comprehension and retention of studied material markedly improves. Gruber reported enthusiastically about results of a program which introduced the SQ3R method to one hundred forty-three seventh- and eighth-grade students, as follows:

> Students who previously rarely attempted an assignment now tried their hardest to win bookmarks. The most rewarding aspect of all, however, came when the so-called failures finally achieved in reading and could display their achievement with all the other Super Stars. Students with low past reading performances were now able to read well enough to pass a quiz with 80 percent accuracy. . . . Paulette Gruber, "Junior High Boasts Super Stars," *Journal of Reading* (May 1973):600-603.

Because of its positive effects on scholarship, subject matter teachers should take time to incorporate the SQ3R method into their particular area of specialization. (See pages 114-115.)

Skimming

Skimming, which is also the first step of the SQ3R method of study, should be given special attention because it is a valuable skill for streamlining reading. There are two types of skimming: one is skimming to get a general impression of a selection, and the other is skimming to locate a specific bit of information.

When skimming for a general impression, the reader gets a bird's-eye view of the material by reading headings, first and last sentences of paragraphs, pictures, graphs, diagrams, and summaries or conclusions. It is this type of skimming a student uses when there is not sufficient time to read an article or chapter conscientiously. Skimming may also be used when the title of a selection suggests that a student possesses a considerable amount of advance information about the material and that it will contain little that is new.

In skimming to locate a specific piece of information (called scanning by some reading specialists), the student lets the eyes travel down the page without actually reading, stopping once or twice on each line of type. By looking at the white space between the lines rather than at the lines themselves, a sudent can spread attention more evenly throughout the field of vision. Thus, with the proper mind set, the student is able to locate quickly the precise fact or bit of information he is seeking.

Outlining

Pupils who learn to outline (initial instruction begins in the intermediate grades) have mastered the technique of locating main ideas and related details. This means, of course, that comprehension is taking place—and comprehension is the crux of the reading process.

Good outliners are invariably good comprehenders, but not all good comprehenders are able to outline. Since planned exercises in outlining are needed, every subject matter teacher has the responsibility of improving reading through teaching students to outline.

Teachers should use the blackboard for outlining several pages from a class textbook to furnish students with a good example of what should be done. In this connection, students should become familiar with the following lettering and numbering system: Roman numbers (I, II, III . . .) for the highest-order headings, capital letters (A, B, C, . . .) for the second order, Arabic numerals (1, 2, 3, . . .) for the third order, and lowercase letters (a, b, c, . . .) for the fourth order. If additional orders are needed, parentheses can be used to enclose Arabic numerals, for example, (1), for the next order, and parentheses can enclose lowercase letters, for example, (a), for a still lower order. Accompanying this lettering and numbering system with consistent indention results in a nicely structured outline.

It is important to point out to students that they need more than one item under any subdivision. For example, should there be a "1," there also should be a "2." Should only one item exist, subordination of the point involved is unnecessary.

Note Taking

Outlining skill provides the needed organizational training to take notes more efficiently when one reads or listens to a speech. Taking notes when reading, of course, is quite different from taking notes during a speech. With the former, students can take their time, but when lecture notes are taken, time is of the essence. Students must remain very attentive and critical and must learn to record ideas clearly and succinctly. Students will find the following points helpful in developing note-taking skill during lectures:

1. Take notes in your own words whenever possible. You will remember and understand better by not writing verbatim the words of the lecturer.

2. If you miss an important point, speak to the lecturer at the end of the period. Perhaps, too, a fellow student might be consulted for the needed information.
3. Write as legibly as circumstances permit and look at your notes before they become too cold. If too much time does not pass, you more likely will be able to decipher your hieroglyphics. What is more, additional points you were unable to record may occur to you, and these can be incorporated into the outline.
4. If you have time, it is very desirable to rewrite and reorganize your notes. Use a colored pencil or pen to highlight certain important points.
5. Review your notes with regularity.

Summarizing

The ability to express in brief the essential ideas of a lengthy selection is a valuable study skill. Several subskills are involved in learning to summarize.

Pupils who have learned how to locate the main ideas of paragraphs have mastered the skill that is most basic to writing good summaries. Another skill that is important is the ability to put information in sequential order. Last, pupils must be able to put the writer's statements into their own words as succinctly as possible. This means deleting unnecessary adjectives, adverbs, and other padding words that contribute little to the thought of a selection.

Pupils will find summarizing a chapter or lengthy selection somewhat easier if they outline the material first. Then, after checking the outline and using it as a guide, they can write briefly a series of paragraphs summarizing the material.

SUMMARY

A developmental reading program begins at birth and continues throughout the life of an individual. Parents and teachers both have important roles to play in preventing reading problems. An effective program of developmental reading must encompass such factors as readiness, mastery of the reading skills, appropriate instructional level, diversification of instructional material, prevention, motivation, diagnosis of reading problems, and individualized correction. Mastery of the reading skills and development of independent reading habits in the primary grades are the indispensable goals to be sought. A number of approaches to instruction, including such methods as linguistics, language experience, Initial Teaching Alphabet, and individualized reading, are in various stages of experimentation. The most widely accepted method involves the use of basal readers. Although proficiency in silent reading is an ultimate goal of reading instruction, teachers should not overlook the value and place of oral reading. As a pupil encounters more and more expository reading material, it is important that content field teachers—science, history, mathematics, and so on—assume responsibility for teaching reading skills peculiar to their area of specialization. Dictionary skill and the use of the SQ3R method of study are invaluable in content areas. In addition, mastery of study skills such as outlining, note taking, and summarizing can do much to enhance a student's learning efficiency.

PROBLEMS FOR ORAL AND WRITTEN DISCUSSION

1. Describe a program of reading readiness in the first grade, indicating the use of tests, teacher judgments, and other criteria.
2. Describe your use of experience charts in the first grade.
3. Describe your use of basal readers, indicating strengths and weaknesses of materials used.
4. Summarize and evaluate the content of the manual accompanying a series of basal readers.
5. Outline a program of phonics you would use in the primary grades, indicating emphasis and materials.
6. Discuss prevention in the reading program, indicating its importance and methods of attainment.
7. Discuss the importance of acquiring independent reading habits in the primary grades and its impact on learning and promotion.
8. How can a special teacher of remedial reading or other specialist help the classroom teacher with reading problems?
9. What new reading skills must be developed in the intermediate grades?
10. Why is a knowledge of primary reading methods and materials important for intermediate- and upper-grade teachers of reading?
11. What study skills must be mastered by pupils in the intermediate and . upper grades?
12. Outline a program for developing meaning vocabulary.
13. Describe and evaluate the use of workbooks in reading for a particular grade.
14. Discuss the importance of recreational reading, indicating materials and methods of promotion.
15. Determine the rate of oral and silent reading at each grade level by consulting the norms appearing in reading test manuals.

Notes

1. Lou E. Burmeister, *Reading Strategies for Middle and Secondary School Teacher*, 2nd ed. (Reading, Mass.: Addison-Wesley Publishing Company, 1978), p. 352.

2. ROBERT KARLIN, *Teaching Reading in High School*, 3rd ed. (Indianapolis: Bobbs-Merrill Educational Publishing, 1977), pp. 21, 39.
3. DELWYN G. SCHUBERT, *A Dictionary of Terms and Concepts in Reading*, 2nd ed. (Springfield, Ill.: Charles C. Thomas, Publisher, 1968), pp. 262-263.
4. Ibid., 268-269.
5. GUY L. BOND and MILES A. TINKER, *Reading Difficulties: Their Diagnosis and Correction*, 3rd ed. (New York: Appleton-Century-Crofts, 1973), ch. 4.
6. MARION MONROE and BEATRICE ROGERS, *Foundations for Reading* (Chicago: Scott, Foresman & Co., 1964), p. 6.
7. MARTHA DALLMAN et al, *The Teaching of Reading*, 4th ed. (New York: ?
8. I. H. ANDERSON et al., "Age of Learning to Read and Its Relation to Sex, Intelligence and Reading Achievement in the Sixth Grade," *Journal of Educational Research* (February 1956):447-453.
9. R. S. HAMPLEMAN, "A Study of the Comparative Reading Achievements of Early and Late School Starters," *Elementary English* (May 1959):331-334.
10. H. G. FURTH, *Piaget for Teachers* (Englewood Cliffs, N. J.: Prentice-Hall, 1970), p. 4.
11. MABEL MORPHETT and CARLTON WASHBURNE, "When Should Children Begin to Read?" in *Readings in Reading*, eds. Delwyn G. Schubert and Theodore L. Torgerson (New York: Thomas Y. Crowell Co., 1968), pp. 90-97.
12. DOLORES DURKIN, *The Teaching of Reading*, 2nd ed. (Boston: Allyn & Bacon, 1974), chap. 7.
13. EDWARD R. SIPAY, "The Effect of Prenatal Instruction on Reading Achievement," *Elementary English* (April 1965):431-432.
14. ARTHUR I. GATES, "The Necessary Mental Age for Beginning Reading," in *Readings in Reading*, eds. Delwyn G. Schubert and Theodore L. Torgerson (New York: Thomas Y. Crowell Co., 1968), pp. 98-100.
15. J. E. Brzeinski, "Beginning Reading in Denver," *Reading Teacher* (October 1964):16-21.
16. M. C. ALMY, *Children's Epxerience Prior to First Grade and Success in Beginning Reading*, Contributions to Education, no. 954 (New York: Bureau of Publications, Teachers College, Columbia University, 1949).
17. R. FAST, "Kindergarten Training and Grade I Reading," *Journal of Educational Psychology* (January 1947):52-57.
18. JAY S. SAMUELS, "The Effect of Letter-Name Knowledge on Learning to Read," *American Educational Research Journal* (Winter 1972):65-74.
19. DIANE CHISHULM and JUNE D. KNAFLE, "Letter Name Knowledge as a Prerequisite to Learning to Read," *Reading Improvement*, (Spring, 1978):2-7.
20. BRUCE BALOW, "Perceptual-Motor Activities in the Treatment of Severe Reading Disability," *Reading Teacher* (March 1971):521.
21. WILLIAM H. RUPLEY and TIMOTHY R. BLAIR, *Reading Diagnosis and Remediation* (Chicago: Rand McNally, 1979), p. 316.
22. NEWELL C. KEPHART, *The Slow Learner in the Classroom* (Columbus, Ohio: Charles E. Merrill, 1960).
23. G. N. GETMAN and ELMER KANE, *The Physiology of Readiness* (Minneapolis, Minn.: P.A.S.S., Inc., 1964).
24. WALTER F. CYGAN, "Research in Visual-Perceptual-Motor Activities Related to Reading Achievement," *Optometric Weekly*, 29 August 1974, pp. 796-803.
25. DONALD D. DURNELL and ALICE K. NICHOLSON, "Preschool and Kind Experience," in *Readings in Reading*, ed. Delwyn Schubert (New York: Thomas Y. Crowell, Co., 1968), pp. 122-123.

26. George D. Spache and Evelyn B. Spache, *Reading in the Elementary School*, 3rd ed. (Boston: Allyn & Bacon, 1973), pp. 91-92.
27. Edward Fry and Sara Emmer, "Are Reading Readiness Materials Necessary in First Grade?" *Reading Teacher* (March 1972):567.
28. Edward Dolch and M. Bloomster, "Phonic Readiness," *Elementary School Journal* 38 (1937):201-295.
29. Jeanne Chall, *Learning to Read: The Great Debate* (New York: McGraw-Hill Book Co., 1967).
30. Gertrude Hildreth, *Teaching Reading* (New York: Henry Holt & Co., 1958), pp. 341-342.
31. Edward Dolch, *Problems in Reading* (Champaign, Ill.: Garrard Press, 1948).
32. Spache and Spache, *Reading in Elementary School*, p. 470.
33. Spache and Spache, *Reading in Elementary School*, p. 491.
34. Lee Deighton, *Vocabulary Development in the Classroom* (New York: Bureau of Publications, Teachers College, Columbia University, 1959).
35. L. V. Zuck, "Some Questions About the Teaching of Syllabication Rules," *Reading Teacher* (March 1974):583-588.
36. Horace Mann, *Second Annual Report Covering the Year 1838 to the Board of Education, Massachusetts* (Boston: Dutton & Wentworth, State Printer, 1839), p. 40.
37. Edmund Huey, *The Psychology and Pedagogy of Reading* (New York: Macmillan Co., 1908), p. 10.
38. Charles H. Judd and Guy T. Buswell, *Silent Reading: A Study of the Various Types*, Supplementary Educational Monographs, no. 76. (Chicago: University of Chicago Press, 1922).
39. Dolores Durkin, *Teaching Them To Read* (Boston: Allyn & Bacon, 1974), p. 88.
40. Sterl A. Artley, "Oral Reading as a Communication Process," *Reading Teacher* (October 1972):46-51.
41. Miles A. Tinker and Constance M. McCullough, *Teaching Elementary Reading*, (New York: Appleton-Century-Crofts, 1968):232-233.
42. Arthur Gates, *The Improvement of Reading* (New York: Macmillan Co., 1947), chap. 9.
43. Dolores Durkin, *Teaching Them To Read* (Boston: Allyn & Bacon, 1974), p. 201.
44. Edward M. Wolpert, "Length, Imagery Values and Word Recognition," *Reading Teacher* (November 1972):180-186.
45. Russell G. Stauffer, Jules C. Abrams, and John J. Pikulski, *Diagnosis, Correction, and Prevention of Reading Difficulties.* (New York: Harper & Row, Publishers, 1978), ch. 11.
46. R. Van Allen, "Three Approaches to Teaching Reading," *Challenge and Experiment in Reading*, International Reading Association Conference Proceedings, vol. 7 (1962):153-156.
47. Ricardo Garcia, "Mexican-Americans Learn Through Language Experience," *Reading Teacher* (December, 1974):301-305.
48. Russell G. Stauffer, "The Language-Experience Approach," in *First Grade Reading Programs*, ed. James F. Kerfoot, Perspectives in Reading, no. 5 (Newark, Del.: International Reading Association, 1965).
49. Spache and Spache, *Reading in Elementary School*, pp. 252-254.
50. Leonard Bloomfield and Clarence L. Barnhart, *Let's Read: A Linguistic Approach* (Detroit: Wayne State University Press, 1961).

51. HILDRETH, *Teaching Reading*, p. 162.
52. JOHN DOWNING, "The I.T.A. (Initial Teaching Alphabet) Reading Experiment," *Reading Teacher* (November 1964):105-110.
53. JOHN DOWNING and IVAN ROSE, "The Value of ITA: We're Enthusiastic," in *Readings in Reading*, eds. Delwyn Schubert and Theodore Torgerson (New York: Thomas Y. Crowell Co., 1968), pp. 506-508.
54. PHILIP G. HILAIRE and LOUIS THOMPSON, "ITA: A Review and Assessment," *Occasional Papers*, Oakland Schools, Pontiac, Michigan.
55. JOHN DOWNING, "The Bullock Commission's Judgment of I.T.A.," *Reading Teacher* (January, 1976):379-382.
56. WARREN G. CUTTS, "The Value of ITA: It's Too Soon to Know Definitely," in *Readings in Reading*, eds. Delwyn Schubert and Theodore Torgerson (New York: Thomas Y. Crowell Co., 1968), pp. 508-510.
57. CALEB GATTENGO, *Words in Color* (New York: Xerox Educational Division).
58. EDWARD FRY, "A Diacritical Marking System to Aid Beginning Reading Instruction," *Elementary English* 41 (1964):15-17.
59. WILLARD C. OLSON, *Child Development* (Boston: D. C. Heath & Co., 1949).
60. HARRY W. SARTAIN, "Individual Reading—An Evaluation," in *Readings in Reading*, eds. Delwyn Schubert and Theodore Torgerson (New York: Thomas Y. Crowell Co., 1968), pp. 517-523.
61. Ibid., p. 520.
62. RALPH STAIGER, "How Are Basal Readers Used?" in *Readings in Reading*, eds. Delwyn Schubert and Theodore Torgerson (New York: Thomas Y. Crowell Co., 1968), pp. 302-306.
63. ALBERT J. HARRIS, "New Dimensions in Basal Readers," *Reading Teacher* (January 1972):310-315.
64. SPACHE and SPACHE, *Reading in Elementary School*, p. 163.
65. Ibid., pp. 93-103.
66. SARTAIN, "Individualized Reading," p. 519.
67. PAUL WITTY and DAVID KOPEL, *Reading and the Educative Process* (New York: Ginn & Co., 1939), p. 27.
68. RICHARD A. EARLE, *Teaching Reading and Mathematics*. Newark, Del.: International Reading Association, 1976.
69. ROGER E. JOHNSON, "The Reading Level of Elementary Social Studies Textbooks Is Going Down," *Reading Teacher* (May, 1977):901-906.
70. HILDRETH, *Teaching Reading*, p. 155.
71. HELEN A. KLEIN, GARY KLEIN, and MARY BERTINO, "Utilization of Context for Word Identification Decisions in Children," *Journal of Experimental Child Psychology* (February, 1974):79-86.
72. COLDEN GARLAND, *Developing Competence in Teaching Reading*. (Dubuque, Iowa: Wm. C. Brown Company Publishers, 1978), ch. 5.
73. CHARLES T. MANGRUM and HARRY W. FORGAN, *Developing Competencies in Teaching Reading*. (Columbus, Ohio: Charles E. Merrill Publishing Company, 1979), ch. 5.
74. FRANK GUSZACK, "Teacher Questioning and Reading," *Reading Teacher* (December 1967):229.
75. HARRY SINGER, "Active Comprehension: From Answering to Asking Questions," *Reading Teacher* (May, 1978):901-907.
76. KATHERINE D. WIESENDANGER and JOHAN P. WOLLENBERG, "Pre-questioning Inhibits Third Graders' Reading Comprehension," *Reading Teacher* (May, 1978):892-895.

77. EDGAR DALE and TAHER RAZIK, *Bibliography of Vocabulary Studies,* 5th ed. (Columbus, Ohio: Ohio State University Press, 1973.)
78. FRANCIS ROBINSON, *Effective Study* (New York: Harper & Brothers, 1946), p. 28.
79. GEORGE SPACHE, *Toward Better Reading.* (Champaign, Ill.: The Garrard Press, 1963):247.
80. BERNARD E. DONOVAN, *Survey of Reading Abilities of Pupils Entering the Academic High Schools in September 1955* (New York: Board of Education, 1955), pp. 1-3.

Selected Readings

BAGFORD, JACK, *Instructional Competence in Reading.* Columbus, Ohio: Charles E. Merrill Publishing Co., 1975.

CUNNINGHAM, PATRICIA M.; SHARON V. ARTHUR; and JAMES W. CUNNINGHAM, *Classroom Reading Instruction.* Lexington, Mass.: D. C. Heath and Company, 1977.

DURKIN, DOLORES, *Teaching Young Children to Read.* 2nd ed. Boston: Allyn and Bacon, Inc., 1976.

GARLAND, COLDEN, *Developing Competence in Teaching Reading.* Dubuque, Iowa: Wm. C. Brown Company Publishers, 1978.

GRIESE, ARNOLD A, *Do You Read Me?* Santa Monica, Calif.: Goodyear Publishing Company, Inc., 1977.

HARRIS, LARRY A. and SMITH, CARL B. *Reading Instruction.* 2nd ed. New York: Holt, Rinehart and Winston, 1976, chaps. 4, 5.

HEILMAN, ARTHUR W. *Principles and Practices of Teaching Reading.* 4th ed. Columbus, Ohio: Charles E. Merrill Publishing Company, 1977.

KARLIN, ROBERT, *Teaching Elementary Reading,* 3rd ed. (New York: Harcourt Brace Jovanovich, Inc., 1980)

MANGRUM, CHARLES T. and FORGAN, HARRY W. *Developing Competencies in Teaching Reading.* Columbus, Ohio: Charles E. Merrill Publishing Company, 1979.

MCNEIL, JOHN D.; DONANT, LISBETH; and ALKIN, MARVIN. *How to Teach Reading Successfully.* Boston: Little, Brown and Co., 1980, chs. 4, 5, 6, 7.

MILLER, WILMA. *Elementary Reading Today.* 2nd ed. New York: Holt, Rinehart and Winston, 1977).

OLLILA, LLOYD, O. *The Kindergarten Child and Reading.* Newark, Del.: International Reading Association, 1977.

OTTO, WAYNE, and SMITH, RICHARD J. *Corrective and Remedial Teaching.* Boston: Houghton Mifflin Co., 1980, ch. 6.

SMITH, BROOKS E.; GOODMAN, KENNETH S.; and MEREDITH, ROBERT. *Language and Thinking in School.* 2nd ed. New York: Holt, Rinehart and Winston, 1976, chap. 7.

WEAVER, CONSTANCE, *Psycholinguistics and Reading: From Process to Practice.* Cambridge: Winthrop Publishers, Inc., 1980.

ZINTZ, MILES V. *The Reading Process.* 2nd ed. Dubuque, Iowa: Wm. C. Brown Company Publishers, 1975, chaps. 9-12.

6 Interest and Motivation

Motivating forces that channel attention and energize action stem from interests. As stated by one student, "When I am reading something I'm really interested in, someone could fire a cannon and I don't think I'd know it." A good teacher capitalizes on interests to stimulate reading. For example, a child who would rather draw pictures than read was pleased when his teacher said, "Doesn't Jim draw beautifully? Perhaps he would like to draw a picture that would tell us about this next story." Needless to say, by giving Jim recognition for his drawing skills, the teacher was able to help Jim improve his reading. It should be noted here that many of the techniques suggested in chapter 10 in the discussion of Principles Underlying Corrective Instruction (especially items 3 to 5, 10, 13 to 16, 19, and 20) are basic to motivation.

Belloni and Johgsma[1] found that low-achieving, seventh-grade students comprehended material better when they considered it highly interesting. Students also were able to transcend their frustration levels when reading materials were highly interesting. Even cloze performance increased markedly when low-interest passages were compared with high-interest passages.

Although teachers can find many studies that do an excellent job of furnishing them with a knowledge of the general trends of children's interests, they find no rule of thumb for determining the exact interests of specific children.[2-4] This requires detective work, the most fruitful of which involves observation, interviews, and interest inventories.

As early as 1938, Witty and Kopel published interest inventories which have many items that are still valid and useful.[5] Teachers may wish to become acquainted with interest inventories and questionnaires provided in current professional books on reading such as those by Bond and Tinker, Harris, and Strang.[6-8] Some teachers have been successful in evolving their own interest inventories.

Teachers have often wished they could administer "motivation pills" to their pupils. But it is doubtful that a solution to the problem of motivation will ever take capsulated form. What proves effective for one pupil may not work with another. A technique used by teacher X may be ineffectual when tried by teacher Y. Although there is no panacea, the following suggestions and guidelines may prove helpful in interesting pupils in reading.

CAPITALIZE ON THE LAW OF EFFECT

When reading materials are chosen that broaden or coincide with a pupil's interests and needs, the pupil is likely to accept reading as worthwhile and self-motivation results. "I want to learn more about this," he says to himself, "because I can use it." Helpful, too, are parents of pupils who are policemen, firemen, doctors, lawyers and the like. They can be invited to talk to pupils about ways in which reading helped them in their work.

Motivation that is generated when a child reads books in which he is interested is intrinsic in nature. The reward is in the reading. When the incentive is irrelevant to the process of reading-good grades, gold stars, prizes, special privileges-extrinsic motivation is involved. It must be recognized that extrinsic motivation isn't all bad. Although the satisfactions are not derived from the intrinsic values of reading, nevertheless, in being indirectly attached to these outcomes, they often promote reading.

ISSUE ATTRACTIVE CERTIFICATES FOR READING

An effective form of extrinsic motivation centers around designing colorful certificates for book reading which bear the names of the recipients. These certificates can be counter-signed by the teacher, the school principal, or anyone else whom the pupils admire. Differently colored paper, ribbons or seals may be used to designate the number of books read and the particular level of merit attained. As in the case of other forms of extrinsic motivation, pupils working for a certificate hopefully will discover that reading is an enjoyable activity that carries its own reward.

TAKE ADVANTAGE OF SOCIAL MOTIVATION

Social motives can greatly influence a pupil's behavior and can be used to good advantage by an alert teacher. For example, encouraging children to form a book club can be a stimulant to reading interest. Pupils who become members of the club can be scheduled to meet during the school day or after school. Time can be devoted to reviewing books, dramatizing books, or holding book fairs.

READ ALOUD TO PUPILS

To stimulate an interest in reading, teachers should take the opportunity to read aloud to their pupils. Pupils of all ages enjoy being read to. Even if the material read is somewhat over the heads of pupils, the enthusiasm of the teacher will generate interest.

A teacher may read aloud an exciting incident from one book, a humorous selection from another, a beautiful description from a third, or perhaps an exciting build-up for a mystery. When she/he places such books on the library table and says, "I'll just leave these here in case you would like to read them," one can be sure that pupils will scramble to check them out for leisure reading.

AVOID MATERIAL THAT IS TOO DIFFICULT

Pupils become discouraged when books are introduced that are too difficult or too lengthy. It should be noted that reading test scores often coincide with instructional or frustration levels rather than with a child's level for independent reading.

PROVIDE PUPILS WITH A KNOWLEDGE OF RESULTS

Progress charts can be designed by pupils to provide dramatic evidence of growth in vocabulary development, comprehension, number of books read, and the like. Self-competition should be encouraged. Placing progress charts on bulletin boards leads to group competition. Children may develop feelings of inferiority and defeatism if they are exposed to overwhelming group competition.

EMPLOY GAMES

Pupils with reading problems need to engage in a great deal of repetitive activity. To keep repetition interesting, games can be employed. Enthusiasm for games usually runs high and if they are used with circumspection, they can be a real asset to the teacher who is trying to motivate poor readers. The reader is referred to pages 291-292 for a more detailed discussion of the place of reading games in the reading program.

CHOOSE MATERIALS THAT HAVE APPEAL

According to Kohl, many highly interesting and motivating materials that are instructional boons to teachers are encountered in everyday life.[9] Black students in a poor community high school would profit from television guides, gospel song handbooks, soul food cookbooks, price lists from different stores, top record lists, radio schedules, political handbills, Black Panther newspapers, how-to books, greeting cards, labels on different kinds of packages, driver's manuals, road maps, record jackets, catalog collections, and wilderness survival manuals. Teachers in a Chicano bilingual elementary or junior high school would find that the following materials have instructional value: telephone books, television guides, cookbooks in

Spanish and English, minibike repair manuals, how-to manuals, games such as checkers and chess with instructions included, bilingual menus, and collections of old tickets to athletic events.

EMPLOY PAPERBACKS

Paperbacks have many advantages. They are inexpensive and, unlike hardcover books, are not associated as readily with study, examinations, and other unpleasantries. Since they are not bulky, they can be slipped into a purse or pocket for ready accessibility whenever opportunities for reading are present.

In a controlled study at the elementary school level, Lowery and Grafft concluded that the use of paperback books brought about significant increase in the number of pleasant or positive attitudes the groups studied had toward reading and a decrease in the number of negative attitudes.[10]

Another experiment employing paperbacks was initiated with sophomores at the Lincoln High School in Manitowoc, Wisconsin. The students were given a chance to read paperbacks in class two to three hours a week. They were subjected to no lectures, no discussion, no tests, no homework, and no book reports. The paperbacks included quality novels, plays, biographies, and collections of essays and poems. In one semester, slow readers completed twenty books, and fast readers completed fifty books. At the end of the experiment, the two hundred eight-six sophomores involved reacted enthusiastically. Most of them stated that it was the best way to study literature.

One ingenious teacher used paperbacks in connection with the initiation of a familiarization period for twenty nonreaders. Attractive paperbacks were distributed, and after each two-minute interval, a whistle was blown. The blowing of the whistle was a signal for the pupils to exchange paperbacks. After it had been blown three or four times, several students gave the teacher unfriendly looks (they had already found a book they wished to read). But the whistle blowing continued until the class period ended. At that point, the teacher informed the students that the paperbacks with which they had become familiar were available for checkout. Within a few minutes all paperbacks disappeared.

Teachers who wish to locate appealing paperbacks for their pupils should send for free annotated catalogs such as the following:

Bantam Pathfinder Editions for Young People. Bantam Books, Inc., Educational Division, 271 Madison Ave., New York, N.Y. 10016

Bantam Books—Junior and Senior High Schools. Bantam Books, New York, N.Y. 10019

Berkley Highland School Catalog. Kable News Co., 777 Third Ave., New York, N.Y. 10017

Collier Paperbacks for Children. Collier Books, 200G Brown St., Riverside, N.J. 08075

Complete Guide to Tempo Books. Select Magazines, 229 Park Avenue, South, New York, N.Y. 10003

Dell Paperbacks for K-6 Schools, 245 E. 47th St., New York, N.Y. 10017

Educational Paperbacks—Junior and Senior High Schools. Simon & Schuster, Inc., Educational and Library Department, 1 W. 39th St., New York, N.Y. 10018

Elementary Paperback Catalog. E & R Development Co., Vandalia Rd., Jacksonville, Ill. 62650

New Readers Press Catalog. New Readers Press, Box 131, Syracuse, N.Y. 13210

Paperback Books for Grades K-6. Sundance Paperback Distributors, Littleton, Mass. 01460

Paperback Classroom Libraries and Learning Units. Educational Reading Service, 320 Rt. 17, Mahwan, N.J. 07430

Paperback Classroom Libraries and Learning Units. Educational Reading Service, E. 64 Midland Ave., Paramus, N.J. 07652

Paperbacks for Junior and Senior High Schools. Dell Publishing Co., 750 Third Ave., New York, N.Y. 10017

Readers' Choice Catalog. Scholastic Book Services, Scholastic Magazines, 904 Sylvan Ave., Englewood Cliffs, N.J. 07632; also, 5675 Sunol Blvd., Pleasanton, Calif. 94566

LOOK FOR RIF

Reading is Fundamental (RIF) is a non-profit national organization dedicated to motivating children to read. It attempts to create the desire to read among children at an early age by showing them that reading is fun.

Volunteers go to schools and libraries, tell stories, talk about books, and allow each child to pick a book to keep from an attractive assortment of colorful paperbacks. After four visits to a classroom during the year, each child has the beginning of a library and often a lifelong reading habit.

Funds to buy books are raised by member contributions, workshops, bookfairs, etc., and publishers usually offer a generous discount price. Recently a program has been enacted by the Federal Government to match funds raised by local volunteers throughout the country, which means twice as many books will get into the hands of twice as many children.

Branches of RIF are found in many parts of the United States. There may be one in your area.

USE COMIC BOOKS

Comic books are perennially popular with pupils of practically all ages. An unbelievable 20 million comic books are sold monthy in the United States. Ever since Paul A. Witty taught men to read during World War II with "Private Pete" comic books, many reading specialists have suggested using them in reading classes. A fine article by Swain[11] provides 20 suggestions for reading and language arts activities using comic books or comic strips. Some of the skills she covers include alphabetizing, finding main ideas, reading for details, following directions, predicting outcomes, and critical reading.

Pendulum Press series *Now Age Illustrated Comics* with a reading level of 3.5 to 4.5 are excellent. The series embraces twenty-four titles (for example, *Black Beauty, Call of the Wild, Dracula, Dr. Jekyll and Mr. Hyde, Tom Sawyer*) and are accompanied by exercise materials designed to help the student develop important language skills (Pendulum Press; $1.45 each).

A high school teacher in Phoenix, Arizona, has used comic books for needed motivation. His students were surprised when he distributed twenty-five comic books to the class. A work sheet accompanying each comic book asked students about the title, characters, plot, conflicts, and symbols. Also included were probing questions such as Did you make any discoveries about life and people? Did you learn any facts new to you? Did you get any ideas or new concepts which had never occurred to you before? The program proved so successful that the problem of motivating students to read independently virtually disappeared.[12]

Some of the reasons why comic books are effective as motivators have been provided by Alongi.[13] Comic book characters are perfectly dressed in the very latest teenage styles. They use slang phrases and expletives of everyday speech rather than standard English. Emotions are clearly indicated through the use of facial expressions, boldface type, blocked and colored punctuation marks, and floating symbols. The stories seem sophisticated to youngsters even though they appear trite and predictable to grown-ups. Preposterous situations are treated as real, and righteous revenge resolves many book situations. The art work is filled with color, action, and semirealistic caricatures of human figures.

GIVE DAILY OPPORTUNITIES FOR FUN READING

Fun reading frequently results in laughter which is important in a child's life. Some reading-laughing time should be part of the daily reading schedule. Perhaps the teacher reads aloud a funny story. Since the teacher should provide a good example, she/he takes the opportunity to laugh along with the children. Rowell[14], a strong advocate of making reading fun says, "A hearty laugh benefits the lungs and clears the respiratory system.

It also provides a healthy emotional outlet, discharges superfluous energy, combats boredom, and alleviates social pressures."

INTRODUCE SUSTAINED SILENT READING

Sustained Silent Reading (SSR), which originated with Lyman C. Hunt of the University of Vermont, has proved successful in motivating students of all ages to read silently for relatively long periods of time. It may be used profitably to supplant a part of any student's reading program. According to McCracken, the following six rules should be adhered to rigidly when SSR is introduced.[15]

1. Each student must read silently.
2. The teacher reads something that interests him/her and brooks absolutely no interruption while reading.
3. Each student selects one book, one magazine, or one newspaper. Changing of reading material is not permitted.
4. A timer is used (an alarm clock or cooking timer is recommended). The timer is placed so that students cannot see how much time has elapsed. When the timer rings (starting with five to ten minutes is desirable) the teacher says, "Fine. You have sustained your silent reading for _____ minutes. If you wish, continue reading." The next day the timer is advanced so it almost reaches the sustained reading time of the first student who stopped reading.
5. No reports are given and no records are kept. Initially, reports or records are likely to discourage reluctant readers. Later on, after the habit of sustained silent reading has been established (usually the second week), the teacher can begin to encourage responses of different kinds.
6. Begin with large groups of students such as an entire class. Difficulties sometimes arise when groups of 10 or fewer are involved because students are likely to comment or request help.

A Los Angeles elementary school which introduced SSR in the manner described reported that an overwhelming number of students and classroom teachers were enjoying it. The school's report of an evaluative study of SSR included the following comments from teachers:

> For the first time children wanted to take their books with them on a field trip. They share their books in class.
>
> With these few minutes a day, a difference can be seen in the children's interest in reading.
>
> Reading for a continuous period is often something the children have not experienced before.
>
> This is the first time some children have read a book completely.

Many children have only read prescribed materials. Free choice gives them the opportunity to develop likes and dislikes, exposes them to ideas, and expands their vocabulary and experiences.

Students often ask to have the silent reading extended so they may better enjoy a special book.

This is probably the only time the children see others reading except for their reading groups.

This is a very worthwhile project.

It has a calming influence and helps teach the value and enjoyment of reading.

Teachers who are language arts orientated will be interested in High Intensity Practice. Marvin Oliver has added Sustained Silent Writing (SSW) and Self-selective Activities (SSA) to SSR. He refers to this series of language activities as High Intensity Practice (HIP). HIP is described in detail in Oliver's publication *Making Readers of Everyone* (Dubuque, Iowa: Kendall/Hunt Publishing Company, 1976).

AVOID STEREOTYPED BOOK REPORTS

Stereotyped laboriously detailed book reports destroy reading interest. Imaginative teachers are capable of devising book-reporting procedures that are both enjoyable and motivational. For example, a California teacher has great success employing a bimonthly book-court session which she describes as follows:

> We hold court session in our room every other Friday. The court consists of a judge, a defendant (the person who is making the book report), and a jury, consisting of class members who also have read the book being reported on.
>
> The defendant who is seated to the left of the judge is sworn in with his hand on a dictionary. After he is sworn in, the judge asks some leading questions about events in the story, about the characters, etc. During this examination, the judge and defendant are very serious. When the questioning is concluded, the jury decides whether the defendant has read and understood the book, or was trying to bluff. If the jury decides he was just bluffing, the judge sentences him to read the book and to appear in court in two weeks to report on it again.
>
> "Next case!" The gavel bangs on the desk, and a new defendant and a new jury take their places for the next book report. All is done in good spirit, and no one becomes angry. As a matter of fact, the children love this form of book reporting and look forward to it avidly. Leah Rawson, Grendel School, Azusa, California.

Another teacher had book reports take the form of a Tell-the-Truth panel. This is based on the television show bearing the same name. A moderator introduces three students who are seated behind a table as numbers one, two, and three. The title and the author of the book in question are then introduced by the moderator. Class members ask questions of the panel members by addressing them by number. Each member is supposed to pretend he has read the book, or conversely, each member can fabricate vague replies so that the class wonders if anyone has read the book. After a few minutes of questioning, the moderator asks the class to decide, by a show of hands, who is the real reader of the book. The person who really read the book then stands and gives the rest of his report.

Many students enjoy supplementing the reading of a book by writing a follow-up story of their own. Other students can be encouraged to write a letter to the author of the book read. If the letter to the author is addressed in care of the publisher, an answer is very often assured. (It is important, however, not to write to authors who are no longer living.) The author's reply can be posted on the bulletin board for all to see.

Students who are artistically inclined should be encouraged to design posters or book jackets as a form of book reporting. Other pupils can model clay figures or dress dolls in costumes to depict characters in stories. Teachers who wish to familiarize themselves with some of the countless ways for a child to report on a book will want to read G. Peterson's "Fifty-eight Ways to Make a Book Report" which appeared in the September 1974 issue of *Teacher*.

It is evident that book reports can be used to motivate and stimulate pupils to read. They need not incur negative reaction. If handled properly, book reporting can be a rewarding experience serving to interest all students in the joys of reading.

GIVE THE UNUSUAL A TRY

Teachers and others have had success in motivating children to read by employing original and ingenious approaches such as the following.

A Salt Lake City elementary-school teacher got children to read by using a bathtub. She bought an old cast-iron tub in a secondhand store, painted it orange, and added some pillows. It became the reading corner. Children loved to sit in it, but they had to obey the rules: Three in a tub and keep reading!

An Upland, California, teacher motivated his remedial readers during silent reading by having them use a stopwatch and graph paper. Each student was instructed to start the stopwatch when he began reading and to stop it when he wanted to take a break or when he had finished. At the end of the period, the student entered the time spent in actual reading on the graph. The technique was reported to be very successful.[16]

In Hawthorne, California[17], Wally Amos, originator of the famous Amos chocolate chip cookies, agreed to an ingenious idea. If the neighborhood children would read books from the local Holly Park community library, he would provide free cookies. Initial financing of the program was provided by the local Imperial Bank.

Every two weeks, a child could qualify for a half-pound bag of cookies by reading four books at his/her educational level, and by filling in a questionnaire designed to ascertain whether the books had been read. According to librarian, Dennis Martin, 1,245 bags of cookies were distributed during the twelve-week program. "Our circulation of young people's books doubled."

A California State University graduate student told of an approach she used. "I taught third grade in Salinas, California, a community where the rodeo was a major annual event. With the help of a local cowboy, we had a unit on branding cattle. With the assistance of the cowboy, each child developed his own personal brand. Then during the year each time a child read a book he "branded a calf." The goal was to see how many cattle would be branded by rodeo time, which came at the end of the school year."

A teacher known to one of the authors had students in his ninth-grade English class write on the subject, "The Most Exciting Thing That Has Ever Happened To Me." The teacher checked the papers for errors in spelling and grammar, after which they were returned to their authors. Revised copies were then given to a senior typing class which cut stencils for mimeographing purposes. As soon as combined papers came out in booklet form, students in the class read with an eagerness never before encountered. Interest in the publication spread like an infectious virus. Soon copies of "The Most Exciting Thing That Ever Happened To Me" were circulating throughout the school. The project not only was an overwhelming success that stimulated an interest in reading, but it gave the self-concepts of the authors a badly needed boost.

Another teacher used score sheets from a local bowling alley to record the results of reading tests consisting of ten questions. Ten questions answered correctly constituted a strike; ten questions correct after a second try netted a spare. After ten frames a reading bowling score was tabulated.

Students enjoy developing their reading skills when a local newspaper is used as a teaching resource. A high school reading teacher in Fontana, California, reported unanimous student agreement that the use of the newspaper was a most enjoyable way of refining their reading skills. Teachers who are interested in using the newspaper for constructing their own materials will want to read Nancy Whisler's fine article, "The Newspaper: Resource for Teaching Study Skills."[18] Another source of valuable information can be found in a newsletter titled "Teaching with Newspapers."[19]

An experiment aimed at encouraging youngsters to read was tried in Philadelphia. Programs were shown on closed-circuit television while the children followed the action in printed scripts handed out beforehand. Later, lessons were based on the scripts. According to associate superintendent Michael Marcase, the results were amazing. Students who had fallen asleep during reading instruction clamored to read aloud from scripts. Some developed a strong interest in writing and asked to be admitted to typing classes so that they could write their own scripts.[20]

To motivate content reading, Sartain suggests utilizing a purposeful project involvement approach.

> It is necessary to first observe carefully what is important in the everyday lives of the young people with whom you work. Observe their behaviors and listen to their conversations to determine their major frustrations, their strongest desires, their peer values, their social activities, and their family concerns. Consider what these young people would be doing with their time if they were not required to attend school. Then make a list of projects which can be carried out in school to satisfy some of their social, recreational, and other self-fulfillment needs as growing human beings. Harry Sartain, "Content Reading— They'll Like It," *Journal of Reading* (October 1973):47-51.

Sartain suggests a number of specific projects in the areas of English, social studies, mathematics, science, and fine and applied arts.

Two San Diego teachers described several techniques they found successful in motivating seventh-grade students to improve their reading ability.[21] These involved having students assume the role of imparting information to others by becoming teachers, assigning offbeat improvisations such as imaginary ball throwing or rope pulling, an incentive point system involving rewards such as a field trip to Sea World or the choice of several paperbacks, and development of a class newspaper which the students entitled *What You See Is What You Get.*

DON'T FORGET PARENTAL COOPERATION

Teachers will have more success in interesting their pupils in reading if they have the cooperation of parents. The attitude of parents toward reading and the role they assume in making reading an essential part of a child's life is of utmost importance. Parents should be encouraged to set a good example by reading in the presence of their children. A family reading hour once or twice a week is an excellent stimulant to reading. Parents who have the means should buy suitable children's books and subscribe to children's magazines. They can accompany their children to the local library and help them become acquainted with the librarian and library facilities. Providing a place for their children's books, a place they can call their own, is another motivational plus. (See chapter 4 for many additional suggestions.)

SUMMARY

One of the basic problems in teaching reading in today's schools is lack of student motivation. Although motivating students to want to read is not a simple mater, general guidelines and suggestions that apply to a majority of students can be offered. These include capitalizing on students' interests, reading aloud to pupils, avoiding material that is too difficult, providing students with a knowledge of their accomplishments, employing reading games, using paperbacks and comic books, introducing Sustained Silent Reading (SSR), using ingenious book reporting procedures, and seeking parental cooperation.

PROBLEMS FOR ORAL AND WRITTEN DISCUSSION

1. How are interests and motivation interrelated?
2. How can a teacher discover a student's interests? How can she/he use this information?
3. How do intrinsic and extrinsic methods of motivation differ?
4. Why is motivation an important factor in the instructional program?
5. How can parents foster incentives to learn in their children?

Notes

1. LORETTA F. BELLONI and EUGENE A. JONGSMA, "The Effects of Interest on Reading Comprehension of Low-Achieving Students," *Journal of Reading* (November, 1978):106-109.
2. GEORGE NORVELL, *The Reading Interests of Young People* (Boston: D. C. Heath & Co., 1950).
3. HERBERT RUDMAN, "The Informational Needs and Reading Interests of Children in Grades IV Through VIII," *Elementary School Journal* 55 (1955):502-512.
4. ROBERT THORNDIKE, *Interests* (New York: Bureau of Publications, Teachers College, Columbia University, 1941).
5. PAUL WITTY and DAVID KOPEL, *Reading and the Educative Process* (New York: Ginn & Co., 1939).
6. GUY BOND and MILES TINKER, *Reading Difficulties: Their Diagnosis and Correction*, 3rd ed. (New York: Appleton-Century-Crofts, 1973).
7. ALBERT J. HARRIS, *How to Increase Reading Ability*, 6th ed. (New York: David McKay Co., 1975).
8. RUTH STRANG, *Diagnostic Teaching of Reading* (New York: McGraw-Hill Book Co., 1964).
9. HERBERT KOHL, *Reading, How To* (New York: E. P. Dutton & Co., 1973), pp. 86-88.
10. L. F. LOWERY and W. GRAFFT, "Paperbacks and Reading Attitudes," *Reading Teacher* (April 1968):618-623.
11. EMMA H. SWAIN, "Using Comic Books to Teach Reading and Language Arts," *Journal of Reading, December,* 1978, pp. 353-358.
12. JOHN HAIRE, "Comic Book in Class?" *Journal of Reading* (December 1973): 237.
13. CONSTANCE ALONGI, "Response to Kay Haugaard: Comic Books Revisited," *Reading Teacher* (May 1974):801-803.
14. ELIZABETH ROWELL, "Is Reading Fun"? *The New England Reading Association Journal* Vol. 12, No. 1, 1978:50-51.

15. ROBERT A. MCCRACKEN, "Initiating Sustained Silent Reading," *Journal of Reading* (May 1971):521-524.
16. ALLAN RHODES, "Stopwatch Reading," *Journal of Reading* (January 1975): 327.
17. *Los Angeles Times*, July 11, 1978.
18. NANCY WHISLER, "The Newspaper: Resource for Teaching Study Skills," *Reading Teacher* (April 1972):652-656.
19. *Teaching with Newspapers*, Vol. 1, No. 2. A newsletter published by the American Newspaper Publishers Association Foundation. The Newspaper Center, Box 17407, Dulles International Airport, Washington, D. C. 20041.
20. *TV Guide*, 4 August 1973.
21. CONSTANCE BAER and LINDA FISCHER, "Let Me Read: Five Techniques That Worked for Us," *Journal of Reading* (December 1972):227-235.

Selected Readings

CRISCUOLO, NICHOLAS P., "Effective Approaches for Motivating Children To Read," *Reading Teacher* (February, 1979):543-546.

HARRIS, ALBERT J. and SIPAY, EDWARD R. *How to Increase Reading Ability*. 6th ed. New York: David McKay Co., 1975, chap. 13, part II.

HARRIS, ALBERT J. and SIPAY, EDWARD R. *How to Teach Reading*. New York: Longman, 1979, Unit 10.

HEILMAN, ARTHUR W. *Principles and Practices of Teaching Reading*. 4th ed. Columbus, Ohio: Charles E. Merrill Publishing Co., 1977, pp. 70-73.

KENNEDY, EDDIE. *Classroom Approaches to Remedial Reading*. Itasca, Ill.: F. E. Peacock Publishers, 1971, chap. 9.

ZINTZ, MILES V. *The Reading Process*. Dubuque, Iowa: Wm. C. Brown Company Publishers, 1975, pp. 30-33.

7　Adapting Instruction to Meet Individual Needs*

NECESSITY FOR ADAPTING INSTRUCTION TO MEET INDIVIDUAL NEEDS

A veteran fourth-grade teacher who was given a third-grade assignment complained, "I'm a fourth-grade teacher; I can't teach third grade." Little did this teacher realize that she had been teaching third grade, and second grade, and fifth grade, and several other grades. The fact that children are in the fourth grade bears little relationship to their reading skill. It merely means that they have attended school for a period of more than three full years. Within a given grade, children vary greatly in their reading level, and the amount of overlap from one grade to the next is marked.

A simple way to determine the range of reading achievement in a typical classroom is to multiply the median chronological age of the students by two-thirds.[1] For example, a seventh-grade class with a median age of 12.2 years would have a range of reading achievement from third to eleventh grade.

EARLY ATTEMPTS AT INDIVIDUALIZATION

As early as 1888, a Pueblo, Colorado educator, Preston Search, pointed out the need for individualizing instruction. Some thirty-five years later, the Twenty-Fourth Yearbook of the National Society for the Study of Education stated that it was necessary for teachers to study the needs of their pupils if reading instruction were to develop desirable attitudes, habits, and skills.[2] Early attempts at individualization along these lines were described in the Twenty-Fourth Yearbook. Included were the Winnetka

---

*For many years, children with emotional, intellectual and physical defects received their instruction in segregated classrooms. The practice has been considered by some to be contrary to the goal of having these children eventually function in the mainstream of society. Mainstreaming brings exceptional children into classrooms with their nonexceptional peers. Here they receive instruction in reading, spelling, science, arithmetic, and social studies. Teachers involved in mainstreaming will find that many of the suggestions in this chapter will help them meet the needs of exceptional children.

and Dalton plans which permitted children to work toward mastery of skills at their own rate while the teacher acted as a helper. Interestingly, a number of aspects of the teacher's role were quite similar to those assigned teachers who engage in the more recently proposed Individualized Reading as described by Lazar and Veatch.[3, 4]

One of the earliest strategies used to cope with individual differences involved retention and acceleration. Children who could not keep up with their class were forced to repeat the grade, and children who showed varying degrees of precocity skipped one or more grades. Research by Caswell showed that the former practice did not have the desired effect of stimulating laggards who were likely to end up dropouts or to prove discipline problems.[5]

MEETING NEEDS OF ATYPICAL CHILDREN

Today's teachers face a number of children in their classrooms who have unique instructional needs. Among these are culturally disadvantaged learners, bilingual learners, slow learners, and gifted learners. The first part of this chapter highlights the characteristics of these children and the implications for their reading instruction.

Culturally Disadvantaged Learners

Culturally disadvantaged children frequently come from homes in which standard English is not spoken, reading of stories does not take place, trips and excursions are not provided, and books and newspapers are absent. The words *culturally disadvantaged* are likely to bring to mind blacks and Puerto Ricans in big city ghettos. But far greater numbers are included: American Indians living on reservations, white Appalachians, and a vast group of Spanish Americans in the Southwest United States also fall into the same category. It is important to be aware of the fact that cultural deprivation does not apply exclusively to minority groups. Even children in the homes of wealthy Caucasian parents can be culturally disadvantaged.

The terms *culturally disadvantaged* and *culturally deprived* have been subjected to criticism as being derogatory of those described. Other terms equally objectionable are widely used. These include *culturally different* and *economically disadvantaged.* Finding desirable terms to describe these people may be commendable, but in the meantime something has to be done to alleviate the problem. Every year the incidence of cultural deprivation increases. Estimates run as high as one deprived child for every two enrolled in the schools of the fourteen largest cities in the United States. This is a matter of great concern for teachers because teaching reading to culturally deprived children is quite different from teaching reading to culturally advantaged children. Middle-class children as a whole do well in school, and retarded reading among gifted children is frequently over-looked because they are likely to score above the norm on reading tests. But the disadvantaged child is destined to experience failure from the very beginning.

The seriousness of the problem of the culturally disadvantaged is mirrored in the amount of federal concern and involvement that has taken place. Operation Head Start was begun in 1965 and was designed to give children a "head start" by lessening the readiness handicap with which disadvantaged children enter school. Because of encouraging results, Project Follow Through was initiated in 1967. A comparable program for economically deprived junior and senior high school students who demonstrated potential took the form of Project Upward Bound.

In spite of the large amount of federal money spent on innovative pre-school programs for educationally handicapped pupils, appraisals have been rather disappointing. Pupils in the inner city still achieve well below national averages. Teachers can only hope that at some time in the future the right combination of preschool enrichment and improved elementary program will reduce the incidence of reading retardation among the disadvantaged population.

Teachers who are trying to improve the reading ability of the culturally disadvantaged should keep in mind these facts about culturally disadvantaged children:

1. They have a meager background of experience and are retarded in conceptual development.
2. They possess negative or weak self-concept relevant to functioning in school.
3. They come from homes that have not internalized many of the customs, values, and elements of the majority-group culture.
4. They have limited or unrealistic aspirations.
5. They tend to have an excess of health and physical problems.
6. They are likely to consider doing well in school "sissy stuff" and are in need of strong motivational approaches.
7. They are deficient in speech and language development (this is an especially important factor if bilingualism or inner-city dialects are involved).
8. They are deficient in visual and auditory perception.
9. They are, from the first year of school, likely to fall behind in reading until they are a year or more below grade level by the intermediate grades.
10. They are likely to read two or three years below grade by the time they reach the secondary schools.

Poor auditory discrimination is a serious impediment to the language development of the culturally disadvantaged. Unfortunately, auditory discrimination does not respond to training as easily as visual discrimination.[6] Feldman and Deutsch report accomplishing very little in their attempts to improve the auditory discrimination of Negro children who were reading disability cases.[7] It has been found, however, that when linguistically unbiased tests are used, there are no significant differences in auditory discrimination among white and black children.[8]

Another major impediment for disadvantaged children is the nature of their background of experience. Many of these experiences are foreign to the teacher and to the program of the school. The teacher as a member of the middle class often assumes that children possess certain basic information. For example, if the word *napkin* is mentioned, the teacher is surprised to learn that few of the children have any idea of what a napkin is. In fact, some of the children may not know the difference between a fork and a spoon. It is estimated that 33 percent of all general learning takes place from birth to age six years.[9]

The language of educationally disadvantaged children is generally informal and restricted. Their vocabulary is small, and words are pronounced in a way that makes it difficult for an "outsider" to understand. By the same token, the formal and more complex speech of the teacher is not understood by these children.

Helping the disadvantaged build a vocabulary requires a special technique. The teacher must build a bridge between the child's primary language and that of the school. How this is done is crucial. The you-must-not-say-that approach is not the answer since it forces students to reject their nonstandard primary language. Riessman has stated:

> One's primary language, because it is primary, is not to be denied lightly, for it is, in very basic ways, one's own self. Asking the disadvantaged child to suppress the language he brings to the learning situation is equivalent to demanding that he suppress his identity, and all the defenses that go with it. . . . Frank Riessman and Frank Alberts, "Digging the Man's Language," *Saturday Review*, 17 September 1966, p. 80.

Riessman suggests the Dialect Game. The teacher takes a word she has heard students use—*cool*, for example. She asks them to explain its meaning in their language. They may reply with "You play it cool" and "When the cops are coming you cool it." The teacher then asks how the same things might be said on the radio or television. Replies may include words such as *calm, casual,* and *collected.* Students react enthusiastically to this approach.

It is evident that the successful teacher of the culturally disadvantaged builds on what pupils bring to the learning situation rather than take something away from them. When a first-grade pupil refers to a dog as "bow-wow," the teacher says, "Yes, this is a dog. Dogs say 'bow-wow,'" rather than, "No, this is not a 'bow-wow,' it is a dog."

Dallmann and associates make the following suggestions to teachers who wish to initiate a program for working with culturally disadvantaged children.[10]

1. Try to understand him.
2. Consider his assets and not only his deficits.
3. Guard against expecting too little from him.
4. Start where he is and build on what he already knows.
5. Have an interest in the whole child rather than a limited interest in his reading achievement.
6. Develop in the child the realization that being different is not the same as being inferior.
7. Guard the child's right to love his home regardless of its cultural deprivation.
8. Read all you can about working with underprivileged children.

It is important for teachers to realize that reading materials found in many schools are completely foreign to culturally disadvantaged children. They care little about Dick and Jane and the little red hen. What interests them are stories that relate to their own experiences and background. Needless to say, many teachers have found the language-experience approach helpful in this regard. Other teachers have had success with commercial materials designed to meet the needs of the culturally disadvantaged. Among these are: *Skyline Series* (McGraw-Hill Book Co.), *Chandler Language-Experience Readers* (Chandler Publishing Co.), *Bank Street Readers* (Macmillan Co.), *Lift Off to Reading* (Science Research Associates), *Reading in High Gear* (Science Research Associates), and the *Miami Linguistic Readers* (D. C. Heath & Co.). *Reading in High Gear* is written for junior and senior high school students; *Lift Off to Reading* and the *Miami Linguistic Readers* are designed for younger children.

A number of writers have described programs designed to meet the reading needs of the disadvantaged child.

In discussing a successful reading program for ghetto children in Kansas City, Missouri, Samuels and Dahl recommend strong academic leadership, high expectation for student achievement, additional personnel (teachers and aides), behavior modification via rewards with tokens, individualized instruction, and good classroom atmosphere characterized by order, sense of purpose, relative quiet, and pleasure in learning.[11]

Hunt, Serling, and Theriault believe in providing an environment for the inner city child that includes opportunity for exploration, manipulation, and speech.[12] The Title I program for primary children at the Woodrow Wilson School in Trenton, New Jersey, is partially based on Piaget's thesis that reading and thinking are synonymous and that the latter is best developed through play. As a result, a visitor to the learning center might see children engaged in reading activities along with cooking, craft work, and play with sand or clay. Other facets of the program give consideration to building each child's self-esteem by accepting his language and using his words for beginning reading stories, giving large amounts of positive reinforcement for desirable behavior, and selecting experience stories, phonics materials, and reading games that meet individual needs. A very favorable teacher-child ratio is maintained so that children in the learning center can receive individual attention when necessary.

Following is a list of professional publications that are of value to teachers of the culturally disadvantaged:

BEREITER, CARL, and SIEGFRIED ENGLEMANN. *Teaching Disadvantaged Children in the Preschool.* Englewood Cliffs, N.J.: Prentice-Hall, Inc., 1966.

BRODERICK, DOROTHY. *The Image of the Black in Children's Fiction.* Ann Arbor, Mich.: R. R. Bowker Order Department, 1973.

BURLING, ROBBINS. *English in Black and White.* New York: Holt, Rinehart & Winston, 1973.

DeSTEFANO, JOHANNA, ed. *Language, Society and Education: A Profile of Black English.* Worthington, Ohio: Charles A. Jones, 1973.

FROST, JOE L., and GLENN R. HAWKES. *The Disadvantaged Child: Issues and Innovations.* Boston: Houghton Mifflin Co., 1966.

GOWAN, JOHN C., and GEORGE D. DEMOS, eds. *The Disadvantaged and Potential Dropout.* Springfield, Ill.: Charles C. Thomas, 1966.

HORN, THOMAS. *Reading for the Disadvantaged: Problems of Linguistically Different Learners.* Newark, Del.: International Reading Association, 1970.

LORETAN, JOSEPH O., and SHEELEY UMANS. *Teaching the Disadvantaged.* New York: Teachers College Press, Columbia University, 1966.

PASSOW, A. HARRY. *Reaching the Disadvantaged Learner.* New York: Teachers College Press, Columbia University, 1970.

RIESSMAN, FRANK. *The Culturally Deprived Child.* New York: Harper & Row, 1962.

SEITZ, VICTORIA. *Social Class and Ethnic Group Differences in Learning to Read,* International Reading Association, 1977.

SMITH, B. CARL. *Parents and Reading.* Newark, Del.: International Reading Association, 1971.

SPACHE, GEORGE D. *Good Reading for the Disadvantaged Reader*. Champaign, Ill.: Garrard Publishing Co., 1975.

STROM, ROBERT D. *Teaching in the Slum School*. Columbus, Ohio: Charles E. Merrill Publishing Co., 1965.

TABA, HILDA, and DEBORAH ELKINS. *Teaching Strategies for the Culturally Disadvantaged*. Skokie, Ill.: Rand McNally & Co., 1966.

THONIS, ELEANOR W. *Teaching Reading to Non-English Speakers*. New York: Macmillan Co., 1970.

WEBSTER, S. W., ed. *The Disadvantaged Learner: Knowing, Understanding, Educating*. San Francisco: Chandler Publishing Co., 1966.

ZINTZ, MILES. *Education Across Cultures*. Dubuque, Ia.: Kendall/Hunt Publishing Co., 1969.

Bilingual Learners

Providing for the education of bilingual children is a matter of great concern in our society. A recent article in a large metropolitan newspaper reports that almost two million Mexican-Americans now in public schools will become dropouts with no skills and only marginal abilities in reading, arithmetic, and writing.[13] Bilingualism is prevalent in our large metropolitan areas, in the rural areas of the Middle West and South, in the five southwestern states, and in Hawaii. In some areas bilinguals constitute all or nearly all of the school population, as in Puerto Rican districts in New York City and Chicano (Mexican-American) sections in cities of the Southwest, and the Chinatown areas of New York City, San Francisco, and Los Angeles. Understandably, there is an increasing need for school principals and teachers who are bilingual.

When the term *bilingualism* is used, there is frequently a vagueness of meaning attached to it. Some people think of a bilingual as an equilingual, a person who can perform proficiently in all aspects of two languages. However, when the term *bilingualism* is used in its broadest sense, it is considered without qualification as to the degree of difference between the two languages or systems known; it is immaterial whether the two systems are "languages," dialects of the same language," or "varieties of the same dialect." Thus, a bilingual's achievement may be limited to one aspect of a language, dialect, or variety of a dialect, such as understanding, speaking, reading, writing, or he may have varying degrees of ability in all these aspects. Actually, bilingualism and monolingualism can be thought of as opposite extremes of a continuum, with a continuum for each aspect of language, dialect, or variety of a dialect.[14] Many children come to the classroom with a set of values and background of experience radically different from that of the average American child. To teach these children successfully, teachers must be cognizant of these differences and must above all else seek to understand without disparagement those ideas, values, and practices different from their own.

Special Needs of the Bilingual Child*

There are a number of special needs and learning problems which teachers of bilingual children must be aware of if they are to guide them effectively towards successful school achievement.

Cultural Values

It is especially important that teachers of bilingual children develop sensitivities to the cultural values of the children whom they teach. As Miles Zintz so aptly states, "Too many teachers are inadequately prepared to understand or accept these dissimilar cultural values. Teachers come from homes where the drive for success and achievement has been internalized early, where 'work for work's sake' is rewarded, and where time and energy are spent building for the future."[15]

Language

Before the bilingual child can learn to read English, he must be able to understand it and speak it effectively. Teachers too frequently push the child into reading before he can understand English well and speak it fluently. It is no wonder the bilingual child then encounters difficulty and eventual failure in learning to read and thus develops a negative attitude toward reading. The following are possible language needs of bilingual children which must be developed before they are taught to read.

Experiential-Conceptual-Informational Background

Many bilingual children often fail to understand what they read in the school situation, both because they lack vital firsthand experiences necessary to expand their fund of concepts and general information and also because they have experienced the life adventures of their own particular culture, which are not represented in the school texts.

Reading ability is negatively affected by a meager background of experience, concepts, and general information. Although the child may be able to recognize words on the printed page, they will be meaningless nonsense if he does not know what concepts they represent. Thus, the teacher of bilingual children must be certain to provide them with an educational program which will provide them with a variety of experiences and the remediation essential to help them acquire meaningful concepts from these experiences.

Auditory Discrimination

Because the bilingual child has been exposed to a system of speech sounds which is at considerable variance with the standard regional dialects of

*Most of the material in this section is excerpted from unpublished manuscript by Dr. Doris Ching, professor of education at California State University, Los Angeles.

American English, he may have difficulty in comprehending the speech of others and may pronounce English words incorrectly in his own speech. The results of a study by Tireman of the vocabulary of Spanish-speaking children showed that phonetic interference caused by differences in the phonemic structure of English and Spanish was cause for many errors in pronunciation and meaning of English words.[16] For example, when the word being tested was *hit*, the child would give the long *e* sound to the short *i* sound. This response then sounded like *heat*, and the child would speak of the "heat of the stove" when using the word in a sentence.

Auditory discrimination ability correlates significantly with success in learning to read as a child must be familiar with speech sounds before he can master the symbols that are used to represent them on the printed page. Inadequately developed auditory discrimination undoubtedly accounts for much of the difficulty that bilingual children experience with phonics in learning to read.

Syntax

The syntactical structure with which the bilingual child is familiar is frequently quite at variance with that which he hears or tries to read in school. Both the word order and degree of complexity of the sentences in the textbooks and which the teacher uses in the classroom are likely to overwhelm the child. In order to help the child acquire the patterns of speech of the English language, the teacher must provide the child many opportunities to hear and use English in various situations, such as listening to stories, singing songs, memorizing poems or lines from plays, participating in choral reading.[17]

Slow Learners

In regular classrooms children whose intelligence quotient falls in the seventies and eighties present a special problem for the classroom teacher. To be of greatest help to such children, teachers must take into consideration the following factors.

1. Although the mental maturity of slow learners lags behind their chronological age, they have emotional and social needs that are like those of other children. Each wants to be accepted as a person as well as a child in need of instruction.
2. Slow learners have a poor self-concept. If they are going to succeed in reaching their full potential, special attention must be given to improving their self-image.
3. Slow learners have strengths and weaknesses like all of us. The successful teacher of slow learner must help such children discover and develop their strengths as well as assist them with their weaknesses.

4. Slow learners have interests which are only slightly less mature than normal children of the same age. Their interests are definitely more mature than the interests of younger children of the same mental level.
5. The level of achievement at maturity of slow learners is limited to approximately the fourth grade through the eighth grade.

Teachers planning a reading program for slow learners should observe the following principles:

1. Provide a warm and friendly learning atmosphere and have confidence that the slow learner can improve.
2. Proceed slowly and uniformly.
3. Keep tasks to be learned brief and simple.
4. Provide greater repetition of tasks to be learned.
5. Provide as much individualized help as possible.
6. Emphasize facts of the what-when-where variety.
7. Employ concrete materials and direct experiences, minimizing emphasis on abstractions.
8. Include liberal amounts of praise and use extrinsic rewards to reinforce success.
9. Employ progress charts which provide visible evidence of successful learning.
10. Use a variety of teaching methods.
11. In teaching new words, give special emphasis to the kinesthetic method which uses all sense avenues.
12. Secure help from the school librarian in seeking out material on lower reading levels which coincides with the content covered in social studies, science, English, and other content areas.

Gifted Learners

Intellectually gifted students are in need of guidance in reading, also. A reading program for gifted learners should be designed to develop and expand their interests and tastes and provides enriched experiences. Such a program should include the following tenets:

1. Give freedom of library use and provide opportunities for self-selection of books.
2. Impose no grade ceiling on students' book choices as long as they can read them.
3. Encourage independent research.
4. Instruct students in good study habits and skills (the SQ3R method would be especially valuable).

5. Make available to the student an adult dictionary, a thesaurus, and encyclopedias.
6. Encourage biographical reading so that students will be influenced by accomplishments of outstanding people.
7. Provide instruction in library skills such as use of reference materials, how to locate sources of information, and how to find data about important persons.
8. Help students develop an interest in areas such as semantics and etymology (word origins).
9. Provide training in listening skills.
10. Emphasize *how*-and-*why* questions that are designed to stimulate critical thinking and critical reading (this minimizes the tendency to accept everything on authority).
11. Do not bore students with instruction not needed.
12. Do not give unnecessary drill beyond the attainment of mastery.
13. Provide special assignments which permit students to move ahead at their own pace.
14. Help students achieve a balance in daily activities—reading, television viewing, socializing, rest, and family time.

The foregoing points are predicated on the contention that if gifted students are to measure up to their full potential and make a true contribution to society they must develop the ability to discipline themselves and to expand their educational horizons.

WAYS TO ADAPT INSTRUCTION TO MEET INDIVIDUAL NEEDS

Grouping Strategies

Grouping has been a much used and sometimes misused approach to meeting the diverse reading needs of pupils. Grouping refers to organization of the class to reduce heterogeneity and to facilitate instruction. It is not an instructional procedure. Grouping in and of itself does not result in more effective learning.

Through the years various grouping plans have been proposed. These plans fall into two categories: interclass grouping and intraclass grouping.

Interclass, or administrative, grouping is designed to make teaching easier by reducing the range of ability within classes.

During the late 1950s, an interclass grouping plan used in Joplin, Missouri, received wide publicity. Under the plan, fourth, fifth, and sixth grade children are divided into groups according to reading test scores and teacher judgment. When the reading period arrives, all children leave their homeroom and report to their reading room where they are instructed by a teacher at their grade level.

The Joplin Plan used reading test scores as a criterion for grouping. But according to Clymer, many criteria have been applied to achieve homogeneity. Among these are intelligence, chronological age, sex, achievement, and interest or vocational goal.[18] Unfortunately, studies have shown that homogeneous grouping does not accomplish a great deal. Hollingshead found that ability grouping did not substantially reduce the range of achievement in reading within the group.[19]

Studies such as these give credence to the recommendation of Wilson and Ribovich.[20] They recommend "open grouping." During "open grouping" children meet with their regularly assigned reading group. However, during independent reading they may participate in any group session. To encourage movement among groups, children are informed daily as to what will be happening in each reading group.

It seems obvious that selecting individuals on the basis of one criterion does not ensure similarity in other respects. For example, several readers may have almost identical reading test scores and yet differ tremendously in reading comprehension or specific word-attack skills. Similarly, students who have almost identical sight vocabularies may not be at all comparable in reading speed or level of comprehension. Homogeneity in one respect or trait cannot eliminate individual differences in other respects or traits.

Grouping homogeneously by one or more traits is ineffective in improving learning if not accompanied by instructional material of appropriate difficulty and use of special methods. On the other hand, it is apparent that learning can be enhanced by providing diversified material and appropriate instructional techniques to homogeneous groups.

To the classroom teacher, intraclass grouping is an economical way to individualize instruction. Various types of grouping within the classroom have been identified. These are achievement grouping, research grouping, interest grouping, special-needs grouping, team grouping, and tutorial grouping.

The efficient teacher is adept at employing several kinds of grouping in a flexible manner, employing one kind today and a different kind tomorrow. On occasions, several kinds of grouping may take place simultaneously: achievement, research or interest, special needs, team, and tutorial.

Achievement Grouping

Grouping by reading level is common practice. Customarily, three groups are organized, but there are times when a teacher may wish to divide a class into two groups: those who can read normally for the grade and those who cannot. For an average class, Harris suggests placing two-thirds of the class in the upper group and one-third in the lower group.[21] This kind of grouping, he feels, is best for the teacher who is learning the technique. Later, as the teacher gains experience, the number of groups can be increased.

Since there is a greater spread in reading ability in the intermediate grades than there is in the primary grades, one would expect to find fifth- and sixth-grade teachers employing four or five groups rather than the traditional three. But quite to the contrary, very often there is less grouping at these levels. Are intermediate-grade teachers less interested than primary teachers in meeting individual reading needs?

Teachers who employ ability grouping should exercise care in naming their reading groups. Designations such as bluebirds, robins, and sparrows or oaks, willows, and saplings are likely to dampen the enthusiasm of many children. Also, teachers should be cautious of their demeanor. Too often they are animated when working with their top group, somewhat somber with the middle group, and downright depressing with the low group.

Ability grouping need not be limited to the elementary grades. It can be employed very profitably at the junior and senior high school levels. For example, when studying the short story, an English teacher can assign poor readers a simple short story; average readers, one of medium difficulty; and able readers, a difficult one. Likewise, ability grouping might find application in a social studies, or even a science, class.

Research or Interest Grouping

When a group of children have a common interest or wish to find answers to a common problem, opportunities for interest and research grouping are present. With the help of the librarian, the teacher can provide an array of appropriate reading material on several levels of difficulty. Good readers brush elbows with poor readers. The group is held together by a common interest or problem. Later, when a report is made to the class, all pupils have an opportunity to contribute, regardless of their reading level. Research and interest groupings have the advantage of not stigmatizing the students involved.

Special-Needs Grouping

Very often a teacher discovers that several pupils have a weakness in common. If, for example, a sixth-grade teacher finds that a half-dozen pupils cannot break polysyllabic words into syllables, she can bring them together to play a suitably designed syllable game and have them receive special instruction in the principles of syllabication. As soon as the pupils develop the needed skill, the group is disbanded.

If used judiciously, special-needs grouping can be extremely helpful in reducing the need for remedial reading since the classroom teacher can correct students' difficulties just as soon as they appear.

Team Grouping

As the saying goes, two heads are better than one. So when two pupils have a common interest or need, they can be encouraged to work together. What they cannot accomplish individually, they may be able to do as a team. To facilitate this kind of grouping, sociometric techniques may be used.

Teachers who employ team grouping will find the following advice helpful.

To be successful a team must have a definite job to do and know exactly what is expected. Requiring a concrete result—such as a written report or filled-in blanks—and a reasonable but not too generous time limit will hold the partners down to business. They must discover that teamwork is a privilege that can be lost through horseplay. Ruth Strang, Constance McCullough, and Arthur Traxler, *The Improvement of Reading*, 4th ed. (New York: McGraw-Hill Book Co., 1967), p. 50.

Tutorial Grouping

When one student knows a skill and another does not, the teacher can assign the two students to work together. As with team grouping, the teacher may wish to use the sociogram to minimize personality clashes.

Because there is a strong desire on the part of a student to please his peers, tutorial grouping is likely to pay dividends. But what about the helper? How does he benefit? The following quotation answers this question:

As teachers all know, one understands better the things he has had to teach. Martin reinforces his learnings by teaching them. He will spend a large part of his life explaining his ideas to other people. If education is preparation for life, he can learn how to get along with different kinds of people. So Martin's teaching benefits him while it releases the teacher for other instructional tasks which only he can perform. Ruth Strang, Constance McCullough, and Arthur Traxler, *The Improvement of Reading*, 4th ed. (New York: McGraw-Hill Book Co., 1967), p. 50.

Some schools have experienced success with cross-age tutoring. For example, the Dana Hills High School in California initiated a summer program in which forty-one elementary school pupils with specific problems in reading and other areas were individually tutored by forty-one high school students five mornings for six weeks. After a daily period of individualized instruction lasting two hours, each session was brought to a close with a half hour of recreation on the athletic field. The high school students involved went through a five-day training session before being assigned a pupil. Tutors were carefully chosen to correctly match their charges because it was felt that a basis for a relationship was needed if pairing was to be successful. For example, a little girl with no father at home was assigned an older boy as an instructor. Common interests such as surfing, animals, sports, or camping were also considered when assignments were made.[22]

Multilevel Unit Approach

According to Heilman certain subject matter areas lend themselves to a multilevel unitary teaching procedure.[23] Consider, for example, a high school instructor who is teaching a unit on the short story. Instead of all students being required to read the same short story, students are allowed to choose from a large number of short stories the particular ones that coincide with their interest and level of reading skill.

A social science teacher who is introducing a unit on the Civil War would begin a multilevel approach by exposing students to a large collection of relevant material. Included would be textbooks that vary in difficulty, trade books of all kinds, newspaper and magazine articles, pamphlets, and even encyclopedias. After an exploratory stage during which students would decide on suitable activities, the class starts studying various aspects of the topic. Students might work individually or in groups. While this takes place, the teacher moves about giving help and making suggestions. As individual students or groups of students finish their work, they contribute their reports in a pooling and sharing period. The exchange of information may be by tape recording, panel of experts, quiz games, bulletin-board displays, debates, and the more formal committee report.

Differentiated Questioning and Assignments

Many teachers of content subjects are addicted to the single textbook approach. Not only is this true in junior and senior high schools but also in the intermediate grades one finds teachers employing a single textbook in content areas while using basal, cobasal, and supplementary textbooks for teaching reading.

One way a teacher can provide for individual differences while making the single-textbook approach more tolerable is to employ differentiated questioning. Assuming students can read the textbook, a teacher can ask poorer readers to respond to factual questions of the what-when-where variety. Better readers can be exposed to why-how questions which involve varying degrees of critical thinking. Interpretation of material on different levels of difficulty can also be encouraged. In this connection, Ruth Strang has said the following:

> . . . [that while a teacher may] be content to have Helen enjoy a given story as a simple boy-meets-girl romance, he will expect Betty to discover its deeper social significance, perhaps in relation to an understanding of some adolescent problem. The teacher may induce Tony, who rejects the story as a whole, to

improve his oral reading by taking part in a dramatization of a single scene that appeals to him. Ruth Strang, Meeting Individual Differences in Reading, in Supplementary Educational Monograph no. 94, "Effective Use of Classroom Organization in Meeting Individual Differences" (Chicago: University of Chicago Press, 1964).

Because poor readers are likely to read more slowly and laboriously than good readers, a teacher may allow some students to skip parts of an assignment. On other occasions, parts of the textbook may not be assigned because it is too difficult for poor readers to comprehend. There is no doubt that skillful teachers who know their students' strengths and weaknesses can adapt assignments to individuals by means of differentiated questions and assignments.

Learning Centers*

Some teachers implement individually prescribed instruction by utilizing learning-center activities. These learning centers provide a variety of opportunities for all children to reinforce their reading skills. An elementary teacher is not only responsible for teaching the basic skills of reading. She/he should create a classroom environment wherein these skills can be strengthened and applied. Learning centers do much to help teachers meet this responsibility.

The typical learning center involves a cluster of categorized activities in a table-and-chairs setting. Activities vary. Some of the many possible learning centers may include the following.

1. Listening Center
2. Library Center
3. Dictionary Center
4. Oral Language Center
5. Phonics Center
6. Poetry Center
7. Reading in Content Area
8. Classification Center (Classify books according to humor, adventure, mystery, biography, etc.)
9. Writing Center
10. Programmed Reading Center
11. Game Center—Teacher-made and Commercial
12. Spelling Center

Children who have particular weaknesses are assigned learning-center activities which are designed to help overcome their deficiencies. They

*Parts of the material in this section are excerpted from an unpublished manuscript by Ruth Levine, Supervisor of Reading, in Downey, California.

work individually, in pairs, or possibly in small groups and can secure help from the teacher whenever it becomes necessary.

Two important factors must be considered in planning an effective reading program for children: (1) Their attention span is short; (2) They need opportunities to alternate quiet work-type activities with those that involve movement and interaction with other children. Since learning centers can accommodate only very small groups of children, a high degree of individualization of instruction can be accomplished and standards for good work and study habits can be built. In the learning center approach, children are active participants during the entire reading period and are highly stimulated and motivated since all activities have great appeal for them. As small groups of children work together in a productive, exhilarating classroom atmosphere, they learn to think independently and to solve problems by considering alternatives and making choices. Finally, the self-esteem of each pupil is nurtured in this activity oriented reading program since all children are assured daily success and encouragement in some, if not all, of their reading and reading related experiences.

Teachers who wish to develop learning centers in their classrooms will find the self-directed and self-corrective material described in chapters 12, 13, and 14 of inestimable value.

Contract Learning

As Wilson and Gambrell state, "contracting is one good way to individualize instruction."[24] Contract learning may be used to foster many types of learning. Grayce Ransom, a reading specialist at the University of Southern California, has employed it to further children's skill development in reading.[25] Students are party to contracts that are usually binding for a period of one week. After students agree to "do the following work this week," they then encircle on the contract the particular skills on which they wish to concentrate. These are categorized as phonic skills (initial sounds, endings sounds, short vowels, etc.), structural skills (compounds, prefixes, suffixes, etc.), and comprehension skills (sequence, main ideas, following directions, etc.). A final category is devoted to voluntary reading commitments (stories I will read, articles I will read, and books I will read.)[26] Ransom reports that students react enthusiastically to contract learning. They especially like having the opportunity to make their own choices of skills on which they will work.

Ruth Levine, reading specialist in Downey, California, designed the following contract form.

Contract Reading

This agreement is entered into between _____ ,
hereafter referred to as Student; and _____ ,
hereafter referred to as Teacher.

Upon entering into this contract, student does hereby agree to read
_____ and perform

Name of Book

_____ as required

Contract Number

at the end of Readings. Teacher reserves the right to ask Student to perform
such activities at any predetermined place, such as classroom, auditorium,
or library. Student does further agree to perform activity on the date designated previously by him/her.

This agreement entered into this _____ day of _____ ,

_____ .

_____   _____

Teacher   Student

Teacher-Made Tape Recordings

Children needing help with a basic sight vocabulary or word analysis skills
can listen to their teacher's recorded voice while they read the same materials silently. Questions pertaining to the comprehension or evaluation of
a selection also can be recorded. If an individual pupil is involved rather
than a group, headphones can be provided to minimize disturbance.

A typical recording by a teacher that is designed to give a pupil practice
in recognition of initial consonants is as follows: "This is a test to see if you
can hear the first letter in a word and the letter it stands for. I shall pronounce two words which begin with the same letter. You are to find the
letter sound and circle it. Now look at row one. My words are *wagon* and
window. Think of the letter *wagon* and *window* begin with. Find that letter in row one and circle it. You should have circled *w*." The teacher continues with other word pairs: 2. girl gate; 3. lion leaf; 4. etc.

"You will correct your own paper to see how well you have done. If you
do not have the correct letter circled, place an X on the wrong answer and
circle the correct letter. 1. wagon and window begin with a *w*; 2. girl and
gate begin with a *g*; 3. etc.

"Place the number of correct answers in the upper right-hand corner of
your paper. This is the end of your lesson."

Team Teaching

Team teaching provides opportunities for individualization of reading instruction by releasing one teacher for student conferences and for more
individualized attention. Two teachers can discuss individual students and
their problems. This often results in insight and a course of action which

might have escaped them had they worked individually. Another advantage of a team approach is the fact that one teacher may be able to establish rapport with students with whom the other has experienced failure.

School and Classroom Libraries

Everyone recognizes that a reading program stressing individualization must make available to pupils a wide selection of reading materials. According to Hildreth, "every school with two hundred or more pupils should have a central library and library service."[27] Another well-known authority states, "The school library and its subsidiary classroom libraries provide the hub of a sound reading instruction program."[28] Unfortunately, more than three-quarters of the elementary schools in America have no libraries.[29] And the situation is no better on the secondary level. It is estimated that more than ten million American students attend secondary school without libraries.[30]

The teacher who wishes to build a good classroom library should select in cooperation with the school librarian a minimum of seventy-five books of varying interest and difficulty. After a few weeks the books may be changed. This is in keeping with the dynamic, expanding nature of pupils' reading interests.

It is very important that the appearance of the reading center be conducive to reading. If reading is done in pleasant surroundings, a positive form of conditioning will result, beneficial to reading activity. Children enjoy reading in a spot that has attractively arranged flowers, colorful pictures on the walls, and bright curtains.

To simplify children's finding books and to give the library corner an air of orderliness, a labeling system should be employed. Harris suggests classifying books for this purpose under a few broad headings such a Make Believe, People and Places, Real Life Stories, Animals, and the like.[31]

SUMMARY

The well-known fact that children vary greatly in reading achievement has concerned educators since the 1880s. Early attempts at individualization were described in the Twenty-Fourth Yearbook of the National Society for the Study of Education. Administrative grouping (interclass grouping) has been employed to reduce the range of ability within classes. Teacher grouping (intraclass grouping) has been used to individualize instruction. Based on Willard Olson's principles of self-interest, self-selection, and pacing, individualized reading has been promulgated as a solution to the problem of meeting children's reading requirements. Multilevel materials, both commercial and teacher-made, have been increasingly popular as a means of realizing the goals of individually prescribed instruction. Teachers who adhere to a single-textbook approach can help provide for individual differences by differentiating their questions and assignments. Other approaches that have been used to meet individual reading needs include learning-center activities, contract learning, teacher-made tape recordings, and team teaching. Basic to the success of any and all reading programs stressing individualization are classroom libraries and central libraries that make available to students a wide variety of reading materials. When programs are planned to meet individual reading needs, special attention must be given to culturally disadvantaged, bilingual, retarded, and gifted children.

PROBLEMS FOR ORAL AND WRITTEN DISCUSSION

1. What does individualization attempt to accomplish?
2. Discuss the pros-and-cons of grouping.
3. Discuss the advantages and the limitations of one of the instructional methods.
4. How may the classroom teacher utilize the school library?

Notes

1. Lou E. Burmeister, *Reading Strategies for Secondary School Teachers* (Menlo Park, Calif.: Addison-Wesley Publishing Company, Inc., 1974), p. 9.
2. National Society for the Study of Education, *Twenty-Fourth Yearbook,* part 2, "Report of the National Committee on Reading." (Bloomington, Ill.: Public School Publishing Co., 1925).
3. May Lazar, *A Practical Guide to Individualized Reading,* Bureau of Educational Research Publication no. 40 (New York: Board of Education, City of New York, 1960).
4. Jeannette Veatch, *Individualizing Your Reading Program.* (New York: G. P. Putnam's Sons, 1959).
5. Hollis Caswell, "Non-Promotion in the Elementary School," *Elementary School Journal* 33 (1933):644-647.
6. George D. Spache, et al., "A Longitudinal First Grade Readiness Program," *Reading Teacher* (May 1966):580-584.
7. Shirley C. Feldmann and Cynthia P. Deutsch, *A Study of the Effectiveness of Training for Retarded Readers in Auditory Perception Skills Underlying Reading,* U.S.O.E. Title VII Project 1127 (New York: Institute for Developmental Studies, Department of Psychiatry, New York Medical College, 1965).
8. Diane N. Bryen, "Speech-sound Discrimination Ability on Linguistically Unbiased Tests, *Exceptional Children* (January 1976):195-201.
9. Hulda Grobman, "Accountability for What?" *Nation's Schools* (May 1972):65-68.
10. Martha Dallman et al., *The Teaching of Reading,* 4th ed. (New York: Holt, Rinehart & Winston, 1974), p. 470.

11. S. Jay Samuels and Patricia Rawerts Dahl, "Ghetto Children Can Learn to Read—A Personal Report," *Reading Teacher* (October 1973):22-24.

12. B. C. Hunt, L. Serling, and E. M. Theriault, "Teaching Reading in an Innercity School: A Program That Works," *Reading Teacher* (October 1973):25-28.

13. *Los Angeles Times*, 7 May 1975.

14. Uriel Weinrich, *Languages in Contact: Findings and Problems* (New York: Publication of Linguistic Circle of New York, 1953), pp. 1-2.

15. Miles Zintz, *The Reading Process: The Teacher and the Learner* (Dubuque, Iowa: William C. Brown Co., 1970), p. 326.

16. Lloyd Tireman, "A Study of Fourth Grade Reading Vocabulary of Native Spanish-Speaking Children," *Elementary School Journal* 46 (1945):223-227.

17. Thomas Edwards, "Learning Problems in Cultural Deprivation," in *Reading and Inquiry*, 1965 Convention Proceedings (Newark, Del.: International Reading Association, 1965), pp. 256-261.

18. Theodore Clymer, "Criteria for Grouping for Reading Instruction," *Proceedings of the Annual Conference on Reading*, vol. 21 (Chicago: University of Chicago Press, 1959).

19. Arthur Hollingshead, *An Evaluation of the Use of Certain Educational and Mental Measurements for Purposes of Classification*, Contribution to Education, no. 302, Bureau of Publications.

20. Robert M. Wilson, and Jerilyn K. Ribovich, "Ability Grouping? Stop and Reconsider," *Reading World*, December, 1973, pp. 84-91.

21. Albert J. Harris and Edward R. Sipay, *How to Increase Reading Ability*, 6th ed. (New York: David McKay Co., 1975), p. 111.

22. *Los Angeles Times*, 20 July 1973.

23. Arthur W. Heilman, *Principles and Practices of Teaching Reading*, 4th ed. (Columbus, Ohio: Charles E. Merrill Publishing Company, 1977), pp. 299-305.

24. R. Wilson and L. Gambrell, "Contracting—One Way to Individualize," *Elementary English* (March 1973):427-429, 444.

25. Ransom, Grayce A., *Preparing to Teach Reading*, (Boston: Little, Brown and Company, Inc., 1978), pp. 101-104.

26. Lecture delivered at the 1973 reading conference at California State University, Los Angeles.

27. Gertrude Hildreth, *Teaching Reading* (New York: Henry Holt & Co., 1958), p. 540.

28. Russell G. Stauffer, "The Dimension of Sound Reading Instruction," *The New England Reading Association Journal*, (September, 1978), pp. 27-37.

29. American Association of School Librarians, *Standards for School Library Programs* (Chicago: American Library Association, 1960), p. 5.

30. *The School Facilities for Independent Study in the Secondary School* (New York: Educational Facilities Laboratories, 1963), foreword.

31. Albert J. Harris, *How to Increase Reading Ability*, 6th ed. (New York: David McKay Co., 1975), pp. 528.

Selected Readings

DALLMAN, MARTHA, et al. *The Teaching of Reading.* 4th ed. New York: Holt, Rinehart & Winston, 1974, chap. 13.

DURKIN, DOLORES. *Teach Them to Read,* 2nd ed. Boston: Allyn & Bacon, 1974, chap. 3.

GARLAND, COLDEN. *Developing Competencies in Teaching Reading.* Dubuque, Iowa: Wm. C. Brown Company, Publishers, 1978, chap. 7.

HEILMAN, ARTHUR W. *Principles and Practices of Teaching Reading,* 4th ed. Columbus, Ohio, 1977, chaps. 9, 11.

LAPP, DIANE, and FLOOD, JAMES. *Teaching Reading to Every Child.* New York: Macmillan Publishing Company, Inc., 1978, chap. 13.

KARLIN, ROBERT, *Teaching Elementary Reading,* 3rd ed. (New York: Harcourt Brace Jovanovich, Inc., 1980), ch. 3.

MAY, FRANK B., and ELIOT, SUSAN B. *To Help Children Read.* Columbus, Ohio: Charles E. Merrill Publishing Company, 1978, chap. 10.

McNEIL, JOHN D.; DONANT, LISBETH; and ALKIN, MARVIN. *How to Teach Reading Successfully.* Boston: Little, Brown and Co., 1980, ch. 9.

SCHWARTZ, JUDY I., "Teaching Reading to the Hearing Impaired Child," in Diane J. Sawyer (ed.), *Disabled Readers: Insight, Assessment, Instruction.* Newark, Delaware: International Reading Association, 1980.

SMITH, BROOKS E.; GOODMAN, KENNETH S.; and MEREDITH, ROBERT. *Language and Thinking in School.* 2nd ed. New York: Holt, Rinehart and Winston, 1976, chap. 3.

SMITH, JAMES A. *Creative Teaching of Reading in the Elementary School.* 2nd ed. Boston: Allyn & Bacon, 1975, chap. 3.

8 Diagnosis in the Instructional Program

THE IMPORTANCE OF DIAGNOSIS

Reading diagnosis has been defined as follows:

> A scientific analysis and description of a reading disability designed: (a) to identify the nature of the difficulty such as reading errors, faulty reading habits, and level of the reading competence; (b) to locate underlying causal factors, and (c) to prescribe corrective or remedial treatment. The process encompasses both formal and informal techniques involving interviews, observations, oral reading, silent reading, and intelligence tests along with an assessment of personal and environmental factors conditioning learning. Delwyn Schubert, *A Dictionary of Terms and Concepts in Reading*, 2nd ed. (Springfield, Ill.: Charles C Thomas, 1968).

The major purpose of a reading diagnosis is to gather data and acquire insights which will be helpful in planning an effective corrective program. Without diagnosis a teacher can make only hit-or-miss decisions regarding materials and procedures that should be used with a reading problem case.

Effective treatment is impossible without diagnosis. When someone visits a physician and complains of chills and muscular aches, he isn't plunged into a tub of ice water to break his fever or given rubbing liniment to assuage his pain. A physician knows too well that the elimination of symptoms does not cure a disease. If he finds a syndrome that indicates bacterial invasion, antibiotics may be prescribed to attack the infection at its source and thereby restore good health.

A perusal of the literature on reading reveals that all too often corrective work in reading parallels the ice-water and rubbing-liniment analogy. Methods, techniques, and gadgets are used which are primarily concerned with manifestations of symptoms rather than amelioration of causal factors.

Although many authorities feel that diagnosis should precede prescription, it is not necessary to delay corrective work until absolutely all data about a child's problem are collected. Diagnosis and corrective procedures should be combined. As instruction continues and more testing and observation take place, the teacher gains additional insights into the problem. Diagnosis does not end until correction is completed.

When the elementary teacher in a typical school meets a new class, she can expect that 10 to 25 percent of the pupils will be retarded one or more years in reading. If the school is located in a culturally depressed area, the retarded group may exceed 50 percent of the class. The reading problems in this instance not only become more numerous but more severe because the children involved are often from bilingual and/or culturally deprived homes which have provided them with meager intellectual stimulation and limited cultural experiences. The children have known nothing but failure, and they no longer have a zest for learning.

Identifying retarded readers, determining the nature and severity of their problems, and locating causal factors and specific reading difficulties become the paramount problems for every elementary school teacher at the beginning of the school year. Appropriate developmental and corrective work cannot be planned for the ensuing year without the information gained from an efficient diagnostic program.

Some of the many questions that can be answered in a reading diagnosis are as follows:

1. What educational and/or noneducational hazards are involved?
2. What is the nature of the pupil's reading problem? Do the difficulties encompass faulty word recognition, faulty word analysis, or faulty comprehension?
3. What faulty reading habits has the pupil acquired, and what specific reading skills and abilities has he failed to master?
4. What are the pupil's oral- and silent-reading grade levels?
5. Is the difficulty of the present developmental material on the pupil's frustration level, instructional level, or independent reading level?
6. What grade level of difficulty is recommended for developmental in-instruction?
7. What is the pupil's present independent reading level?
8. What is the pupil's potential reading level?
9. What sequence of corrective instruction seems advisable?
10. What reading level should the pupil seek to attain this year?

Many of the foregoing questions can be answered by employing silent and oral reading tests. These tests (particularly the latter) will demonstrate objectively what deficiencies in the basic reading skills have led many pupils into scholastic doldrums. In order to eliminate the individual difficulties indicated by a detailed diagnosis, individualized self-directed corrective instruction should be provided.

NATURE AND EXTENT OF A READING DIAGNOSIS

It's almost axiomatic that the more a teacher knows about a child and his reading problem, the more likely he will be able to help the child overcome his difficulties. But a teacher must stop data-gathering at some point. Where and when he or she stops will depend on a number of factors: the diagnostic equipment and materials available, the teacher's background of experience and training, the severity of the problem, and the amount of time at the teacher's disposal. The latter often is the primary factor that limits the depth of a teacher's diagnosis. The teacher's chief means of gathering information involves the following: cumulative records, observation, interviews with teachers and parents, informal testing, reading inventories, screening tests, and reading test scores. It also becomes important to recognize when a child's reading problem is sufficiently complicated and severe to warrant referral to a reading specialist. It is unfair to expect a classroom teacher (even an exceptionally capable classroom teacher) to do advanced diagnostic and remedial work when she or he has not had the requisite academic preparation.

Reading specialists, because of their training and smaller student load, are able to delve more profoundly into a child's reading problem. Not only are reading specialists interested in cataloging the symptoms of reading disability, but they are also concerned with uncovering the etiological or causal factors of the disorder. In addition to diagnostic approaches used by the classroom teacher, therefore, reading specialists employ individual intelligence and personality tests, in-depth diagnostic reading tests, and additional physical screening tests. This often involves a case-study approach.

PRINCIPLES OF DIAGNOSIS

Classroom teachers as well as reading specialists can profit from the following principles of diagnosis:

1. Diagnosis is continuous. It does not stop until reading disability ceases to exist.
2. Standardized tests do not determine instructional or independent reading levels. Most often a frustration level is represented.
3. Reading test scores are not valid indicators of achievement or potential unless a child has put forth his best efforts. Therefore, the child should be free from undue tension in the testing situation. Rapport is essential.
4. Test scores are not sacrosanct. They are not fixed and immutable. They are measures of status attained and must not be considered unerring indicators of future performance.

5. Causal factors of reading disability do not operate in isolation. Although there may be a primary cause, a constellation of causes is usually involved. Therefore, each cause must be interpreted and evaluated as part of the total pattern.
6. The diagnostic process should be as objective and scientific as possible. Diagnostic prejudice (the tendency to attribute all reading disability to a pet cause or causes) should be avoided.
7. When causality of reading disability is being considered, a team approach is desirable. Specialists in differing areas—social worker, speech correctionist, school psychologist, psychiatrist, endocrinologist, optometrist, otolaryngologist, neurologist, and others—are likely to discern cause-and-effect relationships which escape the generalist.
8. A syndrome or pattern of symptoms is more important in diagnosis than isolated symptoms.
9. Data must be analyzed and evaluated so as to establish cause-and-effect relationships. Care must be exercised. Symptoms can easily be confused with causes; causes can be confused with symptoms.
10. An early diagnosis has greater value than a belated one. It can do much to prevent reading difficulties from becoming serious, and it can help children avoid failure and personality maladjustment.

INFORMAL TOOLS AND PROCEDURES

Cumulative Records

A vast amount of valuable information can be gleaned from cumulative records. Routinely, cumulative records should be studied by all classroom teachers at the beginning of the school year. When a child is given remedial help, teachers should avail themselves of existing school records. Questions that may be answered by consulting them are as follows: What was the nature of the difficulty when it first manifested itself? What was the age and grade of the child at that time? What corrective work was provided? Does the child have a history of frequent absences? Has the child attended a number of different schools? What is the nature of his achievement record? What are the results of past and current standardized achievement tests? What intelligence test scores are available? Do data on the child's past and present physical status indicate the presence of any defects that are significant? Are there anecdotal records that might prove helpful in understanding the child's problem?

Observation

As an impartial observer, a classroom teacher can readily identify many reading problems. A retarded reader is often disinterested in reading and cannot, even if he tries, do the reading required. The child may read in a slow, halting manner and demonstrate a limited sight vocabulary. He fails to understand what he reads, and when he encounters an unfamiliar word, he does not know how to analyze it and pronounce it.

Through observation, a teacher may detect habits which are detrimental to a child's reading. These include lip movements and subvocalization during silent reading, unnecessary head movements, and finger pointing. By observing a reader's eyes during silent reading, the teacher may learn about eye-movement patterns, span of recognition, regressive tendencies, and other reading idiosyncrasies that interfere with reading efficiency.

During silent reading periods, the teacher can answer a number of important questions about a pupil's reading. Does he seem to enjoy reading? Does he appear to be able to use reference books? What seem to be his reading preferences? Can he read for long periods without losing interest?

One of the ways to learn about a pupil's interests is through observation. What does he like to talk about? What does he do when he has free time? Does he draw? If so, what does he draw? A child who draws airplanes, for example, may find books such as *Sabre Jet Ace* or *Pilot Jack Knight* interesting reading.

To improve the reliability and validity of observations, Carter and McGinnis offer suggestions such as the following:[1] study all school records (teacher reports, test information, physical report), family history, and academic history; establish rapport with the child observed; have a flexible and original approach—one that can be modified; develop hypotheses implicitly, use your intuitive powers, substantiate hypotheses by observation of the pupil in different settings; do not infer too much, be explicit, stick to facts and simple interpretation whenever possible, judgments should be tentative and not too technical and profound; be aware that individuals and surroundings change, don't assume an individual's responses will be the same in all situations; recognize that physical, psychological, and environmental factors are involved; observed facts are valid and reliable to the degree that the observer is aware of his own prejudices, preconceptions, and emotional bias.

Perceptive, impartial observers depend on a rich background of information and experience. Without an adequate background and experience observers would not know what to look for, nor would they appreciate the significance of what they observe. Since the psychology of reading problems embraces many fields, some knowledge of ophthalmology, otology, neurology, endocrinology, psychology, pediatrics, and education is needed. The more observers can learn about reading and its related areas, the better they will perform in their role as observer.

Classroom teachers and reading specialists who are sensitive to significant symptoms of overt pupil behavior in the areas of hearing, vision, health, social and emotional behavior, and speech can readily identify pupils who require special attention or are in need of referral. The use of the inventories suggested in this chapter will alert teachers to many symptoms of learning problems and will provide a record of systematic observational data. Intelligent use of these inventories will serve to make observation more objective and impartial.

Behavior Inventories

The following inventories will prove valuable to observing teachers who wish to relate specific symptoms of difficulty to areas of concern.*

Subjective Factors Affecting Pupil Behavior

Home Environment

PARENTAL RELATIONSHIP
1. Parents are incompatible
2. Parents quarrel
3. Broken home
4. One or more relatives live in the home

CHILD TRAINING
1. Parents disagree on methods of child training
2. Parents dominate the child
3. Parents are inconsistent in disciplining the child
4. Parents are too severe in their discipline
5. Parents are overindulgent or oversolicitous
6. Parents are neglectful
7. Child's spending money is inadequate or excessive
8. Child has no home duties or responsibilities
9. Child's food habits are undesirable
10. Child's rest is inadequate
11. Child's moral and ethical training is inadequate

PARENT-CHILD RELATIONSHIP
1. Parents reject the child.
2. Father seems unconcerned about the child's problem
3. Father seems unconcerned about the child's future
4. Father disapproves of the child's choice of a career
5. Father shows no concern for the child's education
6. Mother seems unconcerned about the child's problem
7. Mother seems unconcerned about the child's future ·
8. Mother disapproves of the child's choice of a career
9. Mother shows no concern for the child's education

*All inventories and forms appearing in this book may be reproduced by teachers for their own use.

1. Children are quarrelsome in the home
2. Child is jealous of a sibling
3. Child is an only child
4. Child has too few contacts with other children

SOCIOECONOMICS STATUS

1. Parents do not speak English
2. Parents have few if any cultural interests
3. Parents do not read to the children
4. Parents do not use a public library
5. There are no worthwhile books or magazines in the home
6. There are no books for children in the home
7. Father tends to be shiftless
8. Mother tends to be shiftless
9. Family is insecure economically
10. Home is inadequate

COMMUNITY

1. Neighborhood is undesirable
2. Companions are undesirable
3. Playgrounds are lacking or unsupervised
4. Home-community relationship is unwholesome

Hearing

ACUITY

1. Questions must be repeated
2. Imitates other pupils
3. Seems confused
4. Daydreams
5. Faulty speech
6. Unintelligible speech
7. Speaks in a monotone
8. Voice abnormally loud or soft
9. Symbolic gestures in lieu of words
10. Language handicap
11. Strained expression on face when listening
12. Ignores verbal directions
13. Reads lips
14. Tilting or turning head as if to favor better ear
15. Cupping a hand behind the ear
16. Blank expression on face

1. Spells of dizziness
2. Noises in the ears
3. Excess of wax in ears
4. Discharge from ears
5. Earaches or mastoid pains
6. Previous middle-ear problems

Vision

1. Squints when reading from or looking at the blackboard
2. Excessive blinking, scowling, or facial distortion when reading at near point
3. Holds book too close to eyes
4. Holds head too close to desk
5. Confuses words and letters
6. Tilts head to one side
7. Closes or covers one eye when reading
8. Irritability evidenced when reading
9. Has inflamed, swollen eyelids
10. Has inflamed eyeballs
11. Has discharge from eyes
12. Pain in and about eyes
13. Pain in the back of the neck
14. Has headaches after reading, seeing a movie, or viewing television
15. Eyes sensitive to light
16. Eyes tire when reading
17. Unwilling to wear glasses prescribed
18. One eye turns in (squint)
19. Eyes tremble or twitch
20. Frequent rubbing of the eyes
21. Watering of the eyes with close work
22. Dizziness or nausea after much close work

Observable Pupil Behavior Symptomatic of Underlying Problems When Frequently Displayed

Physical Development

1. Obese, overweight
2. Thin, underweight
3. Excessive height
4. Retarded stature

Health

1. Mouth breather
2. Frequent severe colds
3. Frequent sore throat
4. Chronic cough
5. Poor teeth
6. Sore gums
7. Swollen or enlarged neck glands
8. Dry, scaly skin
9. Protruding eyeballs
10. Frequent itching
11. Blank spells
12. Fainting spells
13. Frequent headaches
14. Persistent pain
15. Nervous mannerisms, tics
16. Puffiness of eyes and face
17. Swollen hands or feet
18. Sallow complexion
19. Flushing of the skin
20. Listless, tired
21. Falls asleep in school
22. Frequent absence due to illness

Neurological

1. Awkwardness, clumsiness, or poor coordination when walking, running, or writing
2. Difficulties in sucking and swallowing
3. Delayed speech or articulation difficulties
4. Paralysis or weakness of the extremities
5. Abnormalities of the head
6. Persistent headaches
7. Convulsive seizures or lapses in consciousness
8. Overactivity and concentration difficulties

Social and Emotional Behavior

AGGRESSIVE

1. Angers easily
2. Temper tantrums
3. Uncooperative
4. Sex irregularities
5. Uncontrolled bladder or bowels
6. Enuresis (bed-wetting)

7. Truancy, unexcused absences
8. Cheats
9. Resents correction
10. Destructive
11. Overcritical of others
12. Irresponsible
13. Impudent, defiant
14. Quarrelsome
15. Cruel to animals
16. Irritable
17. Belligerent, bossy
18. Bully
19. Vindictive
20. Steals
21. Dishonest, untruthful
22. Marked change in personality
23. Negativistic

RECESSIVE
1. Runs away from home
2. Seeks attention
3. Overconscientious
4. Emotionally inadequate
5. Overexuberant
6. Whiner
7. Pessimistic
8. Suspicious
9. Plays alone
10. Avoids others, unfriendly
11. Shunned by others
12. Overreligious
13. Daydreams, preoccupied
14. Plays with younger children
15. Physical coward
16. Selfish
17. Feigns illness
18. Too submissive
19. Depressed
20. Overdependent
21. Sullen
22. Nervous tensions, tics
23. Bites fingernails
24. Fearful, timid, shy

25. Worries
26. Jealous
27. Cries easily

Speech

VOCAL

1. Remains silent because of speech handicap
2. Speaks too loudly
3. Has to be reminded frequently to speak louder
4. Quality of voice annoying
5. Voice lacks variety
6. Inflections of voice are tiresomely repetitious
7. Voice suggests a person of different age or sex

ARTICULATORY

1. Speaks too slowly
2. Speaks too rapidly
3. Omits or slides over sounds
4. Adds superfluous words
5. Difficult to understand pronunciation of certain words
6. Clumsy speech
7. Speech requires undue effort
8. Speech is accompanied by distractive movements of the lips or tongue

RHYTHMIC

1. Speech blocked at times
2. Speech blocked by stopping the air flow
3. Speech blocked by restricting movements of the tongue or lips
4. Repeats certain sounds unnecessarily
5. Distractive movements of head, face, or hands during speech block

LINGUISTIC

1. Shows difficulty in understanding simple oral directions
2. Although words are clear, difficult to understand the meaning of thought
3. Resorts to signs and gestures to express wants
4. Has difficulty in recognizing simple words when spelled orally

Children who are identified by inventories as having a physical or speech problem should be brought to the attention of the proper specialist. The school nurse or doctor, the psychologist, and the speech specialist can be helpful with such cases.

A school psychologist may be of assistance with children who have been identified as emotional and social behavior problems. Teachers can help by employing an anecdotal method. By concentrating on a pupil's problem and recording his behavior in situations as they arise, the teacher gains an insight into the pupil's attitudes, feelings, and conflicts. Insight and understanding make it possible for the teacher to apply proper therapy. A series of objective behavior descriptions which reveal the pupil's manner of adjusting to others and to problem situations in general will provide valuable information to the school psychologist as well.

Interviews

Most teachers and reading specialists find the interview or conference a simple and direct approach which can provide information useful in the diagnosis and treatment of a disabled reader.

Interviews may serve a variety of purposes: to acquaint the interviewer with the subject and his reading problem, to produce pertinent information, to disclose developmental aspects of the problem, and to permit cooperative planning between the interviewer and the pupil for a program of correction. Frequently, answers that a pupil has given to questions on a reading test or any other test can be verified or enlarged upon during an interview. The interview is particularly useful in helping the teacher or reading specialist to secure developmental history, beginning with the onset of the problem, which may reveal the causes of the pupil's present reading difficulty.

The skilled interviewer gives the subject full opportunity to relate his experiences and express his feelings. It is advisable to avoid as many direct questions as possible and to elicit information through conversation in which the interviewer tells the story about himself, his problems, his successes, and his failures. Pertinent facts to be gained will depend upon the function of the interview, the subject's age, and the nature of the problems. The interviewer must be kind, sympathetic, and very adept at placing the subject at ease, at eliciting pertinent data, at recognizing whether or not the responses are genuine, and at evaluating the importance of the information gained. Throughout the interview he must be alert to significant behavior on the part of the subject.

The present status of the child can be understood best in the light of his developmental history. The sum of his experiences in and out of school is largely responsible for his present status and must be evaluated so that the teacher can locate the causes of his reading problem. When and where did the symptoms of his difficulty first appear? What environmental factors which could be considered causal were present at that time? Are these factors still present? Has the child been living in an environment conducive to normal physical, emotional, and social development? What therapeutic measures have already been attempted by parents and teachers? How can the human relationships which the child experiences be measured and evaluated? These are some of the important problems to be considered.

The influence of the home on the adjustment of a child cannot be over-emphasized. The experiences gained during the preschool period, the most formative years, result in well-developed modes of adjustment and well-defined levels of emotional and social maturity. The child comes to school with an acquired personality and a pattern of habits which encourage learning, if normal, but retard learning if the development has been unwholesome. If he is socially and emotionally immature, the child has not acquired the habit of following directions, a sense of responsibility, nor the cooperation and concentration necessary for learning to read in a formal school environment. Extreme negativism and emotionality likewise are hazards to a successful reading experience. Maladjustment in the home reappears in the school and interferes with all learning. In these cases, the home and school must cooperate in planning a program of home and school responsibilities for the pupil.

Interest Inventories

Interest inventories, which are available in a number of professional books, are valuable for gathering information about a student's activities and interests. After looking over professional inventories some teachers feel that they would like to evolve their own inventories more suited to the kinds of pupils with whom they work. We encourage and recommend this practice and have seen a number of fine teacher-made interest inventories.

Readiness Tests and Checklists

Besides intelligence tests, kindergarten or first-grade teachers find that reading readiness tests are helpful in deciding whether children are ready for formal instruction in beginning reading. They are also of value to teachers of children who have failed beginning reading.

Although there is some overlap between intelligence tests and reading readiness tests, the latter focus attention on items that are dependent to some degree on training and are less likely, therefore, to be measures of aptitude or learning potential. They include items such as letter discrimination and word matching, selecting an appropriate picture from several presented, remembering a story, detecting rhyming words, and writing one's name.

Some representative readiness tests are the *Clymer-Barrett Prereading Battery* (Personnel Press), *Gates-MacGintie Reading Readiness Tests*

(Bureau of Publications, Teachers College), *Harrison-Stroud Reading Readiness Test* (Houghton Mifflin), *Lee-Clark Reading Readiness Test* (California Test Bureau), and the *Metropolitan Readiness Test* (Harcourt Brace Jovanovich). Appendix C provides additional information on reading readiness tests.

Combining intelligence test data with what has been learned from a reading readiness test and informal observation gives the teacher a fairly broad basis for determining readiness of a given child. To objectify informal observation a checklist such as the following is recommended.

	Evaluation of Factor Involved				

Vision
Acuity at near point	1	2	3	4	5
Acuity at far point	1	2	3	4	5
Binocular skill	1	2	3	4	5
Eye-hand coordination	1	2	3	4	5
Directional sense	1	2	3	4	5

Hearing
Auditory acuity	1	2	3	4	5
Auditory discrimination	1	2	3	4	5
Clarity of enunciation	1	2	3	4	5

Speech
Absence of baby talk	1	2	3	4	5
Absence of a lisp	1	2	3	4	5
Absence of stuttering	1	2	3	4	5
Overall clarity of speech	1	2	3	4	5

General Health
Absence of fatigue	1	2	3	4	5
Well-nourished body	1	2	3	4	5
Bodily coordination	1	2	3	4	5
Freedom from physical defects	1	2	3	4	5

Social and Emotional Status
Leadership ability	1	2	3	4	5
Ability to work with others	1	2	3	4	5
Ability to carry on independently	1	2	3	4	5
Absence of infantile behavior	1	2	3	4	5
Feelings of security	1	2	3	4	5

Home Environment

Quality of English spoken in home 1 2 3 4 5
Parental interest in books 1 2 3 4 5
Parental sharing of books with child 1 2 3 4 5
Parental harmony 1 2 3 4 5
Parental agreement on disciplinary measures 1 2 3 4 5
Parental acceptance 1 2 3 4 5
Travel opportunities 1 2 3 4 5

Language Skill

Listening skill 1 2 3 4 5
Speaking vocabulary 1 2 3 4 5
Use of complete sentences 1 2 3 4 5
Ability to tell a story 1 2 3 4 5

Intelligence

Ability to recognize relationships 1 2 3 4 5
Ability to think sequentially 1 2 3 4 5
Ability to memorize with ease 1 2 3 4 5
Ability to sustain attention 1 2 3 4 5
Ability to make good judgments 1 2 3 4 5

Informal Reading Inventory

An informal reading inventory is a nonstandardized measuring instrument that provides a means whereby a teacher can evaluate a child's reading as he reads aloud materials on different levels of difficulty. It is composed of a number of paragraphs that are graded according to difficulty and accompanied by a series of comprehension questions. By administering an informal reading inventory a teacher can determine the level at which a child can read independently, the level at which the child needs instructional aid, the level at which he encounters failure and frustration, and the child's hearing comprehension level.

As a child reads materials that vary in difficulty, the teacher can learn much about his strengths and weaknesses. The teacher can pinpoint the specific kinds of errors that characterize the child's reading and can note detrimental habits such as skipping, reversing, and repeating words. Analysis of this kind enables the teacher to provide a suitable instructional program.

Knowing the difficulty level of reading material which a pupil can read without any special help is of great value to a teacher. Much of the work a child does in school must be carried out by him independently. If the material presented is too difficult, the pupil fails and cannot be expected to develop an interest in reading, nor can he develop a high standard of performance.

Instructional material that is too easy results in little or no intellectual stimulation. By the same token, instructional material that is too difficult not only proves intellectually stultifying, but also develops a distaste for learning in the pupil.

If teachers are to read aloud to pupils or engage them in other kinds of listening activity, it is important for them to know the pupils' listening comprehension level.

Teachers who wish to locate the right book for a child's independent, instructional, or listening comprehension level should be aware of the specific criteria to be applied in determining them.

Although the lines of separation between the following levels are not always distinct, teachers should keep in mind that when doubt arises it usually is wise to provide a book that is at an easier level. Children will be inclined to read more widely and will develop a more favorable attitude toward books if they encounter fewer difficulties.

Independent Reading Level: This is the highest reading level at which a child can read easily and fluently, without help, with few word-recognition errors and very good comprehension and retention. Word-recognition errors do not exceed more than one per 100 words of running text and comprehension scores are 90 percent or higher. It is the level of optimum difficulty for recreational reading material.

Instructional Reading Level: This is the highest level at which a child reads satisfactorily, provided he receives teacher preparation and supervision. Word-recognition errors do not exceed more than 5 per 100 words of running text, and comprehension scores are 75 percent or above. It is the level of optimum difficulty for textbook reading.

Frustration Reading Level: This is the lowest level at which a child's reading skills break down. Fluency disappears, word-recognition errors are common, comprehension is defective, retention is poor, and evidence of emotional tension and discomfort is manifest. Word-recognition errors exceed 10 per 100 words of running text, and comprehension scores are 50 percent or below. It is the level that usually reflects the difficulty of textbooks used by retarded readers.

Listening Comprehension Level: This is the highest level at which a child can comprehend 75 percent of what is read aloud to him. This level can serve as an index of the child's capacity for reading achievement.

What kind of material should be used in an informal reading inventory? Betts suggests the following:

. . . any type of material, especially when the level of reading ability can be ascertained. To be most helpful, however, the inventory should be made with materials used in classroom reading activities. When an approximation of general level of reading achievement is needed, a well-graded series of basal readers is probably appropriate. Emmett Betts, *Foundations of Reading Instruction* (New York: American Book Co., 1957), p. 454.

Betts feels that the use of a basal series for the purpose of making a reading inventory has three advantages: (1) at least one basal series can be found in most classrooms; (2) some attention to readability has been given by the authors and publishers; (3) because some control has been exercised over vocabulary, it is often possible to observe pupil application of word recognition skills a second time with a word that has been missed.[2]

The steps in giving an individual reading inventory have been described by Strang, McCullough, and Traxler.[3] These authors suggest that the teacher begin by deciding on a series of graded paragraphs which may be obtained from an unfamiliar basal reader series or may be specially written for the students being tested. Each paragraph should be mounted on a separate card. When working with the student, the teacher begins by asking a few friendly questions about his interests and reading habits. Then a word-recognition test such as the *Wide Range Achievement Test* should be given. The results from this test indicate the level at which the student should begin to read orally. (It is desirable that a pupil begin with a paragraph on the highest level at which he can pronounce without error all the words.) As the pupil reads, the teacher records the errors made. When comprehension questions are asked, the teacher notes whether the pupil answers briefly or at length, whether he does so in his own words or uses the words of the book, and whether he embellishes what the author said. After the first oral reading, the teacher should let the student read silently, then reread orally, and note any improvement. The student continues to read the graded series of paragraphs until he reaches his frustration level. The teacher then reads aloud a paragraph on the same level of difficulty and asks the same kinds of questions about it. The teacher continues reading to the student until his frustration level of listening is reached. This information is a valuable index of reading potential. Finally, the teacher records the student's independent, instructional, and frustration levels and checks evidences of poor phrasing, comprehension, vocalization, and methods of word attack. He makes notes on other significant indications of reading ability, attitudes, and interests. Such information is valuable to the teacher in planning a corrective program based on a pupil's individual needs.

Beyond the third grade level, an informal silent reading assessment is often desirable since most children begin to read faster silently than orally at that time. Starting with material on the previously determined independent level, the child's silent reading should be timed, tested, and coninued upward until comprehension reaches 50 percent. Comparisons can then be made between silent and oral reading rates and comprehension.

No informal reading inventory is included in this volume. Teachers who wish to use already prepared inventories or material lending itself to constructing an inventory will find the following list of value. Teachers will not wish to overlook some of the fine informal inventories that accompany basal readers.

ARONOW, MIRIAM S., and WRIGHTSTONE, J. W. *The Informal Appraisal of Reading Abilities.* Educational Research Bulletin No. 10, May 1949. New York: Board of Education of the City of New York.

BETTS, EMMETT A., and WELCH, CAROLYN. *Informal Reading Inventory.* New York: American Book Co., 1964.

BOTEL, MORTON. *Botel Reading Inventory.* Chicago: Follett Publishing Co., 1961.

EKWALL, ELDON. *Reading Inventory.* Boston: Allyn and Bacon, 1979.

GOODMAN, YETTA, and BURKE, CAROLYN. *Reading Miscue Inventory.* New York: Macmillan Co., 1972.

Group Informal Reading Inventory. Language Arts Supplement ·to Suggestions for the Teaching of Reading. Philadelphia, Pa.: Curriculum Office.

JACOBS, DONALD and SEARFOSS, LYNDON. *Diagnostic Reading Inventory,* 2nd ed. Dubuque, Iowa: Kendall/Hunt Publishing Co., 1978.

JOHNS, JERRY L. *Basic Reading Inventory.* Dubuque, Iowa: Kendall/Hunt Publishing Co., 1978.

JOHNSON, MARJORIE S., and KRESS, ROY A. *Informal Reading Inventories.* Newark, Del.: International Reading Association, 1965.

MCCRACKEN, ROBERT A. "The Development and Validation of the Standard Reading Inventory for the Individual Appraisal of Reading and Performance in Grades One Through Six." *Improvement of Reading Through Classroom Practice.* Proceedings of the IRA Annual Convention, 9 (1964):310-313.

Macmillan Reader Placement Test. New York: Macmillan Co., 1967.

SILVAROLI, NICHOLAS J. *Classroom Reading Inventory,* 2nd ed. Dubuque, Iowa: Wm. C. Brown Co. Publishers, 1977.

SMITH, EDWIN; GUICE, BILLY; and CHEEK, MARTHA. "Informal Reading Inventory for the Content Areas: Science and Mathematics." *Elementary English* (May 1972):569-666.

SMITH, NILA B. *Graded Selections for Informal Reading: Diagnosis for Grades 1 Through 3.* New York: New York University Press, 1959.

SMITH, NILA B. *Graded Selections for Informal Reading: Diagnosis for Grades 4 Through 6.* New York: New York University Press, 1963.

SPACHE, GEORGE. *The Diagnostic Reading Scales.* New York: McGraw-Hill Book Co., 1963.

Filling in blanks at random as in silent reading tests of the recognition type is not possible when a pupil is given an oral reading test. Guessing or bluffing is quickly discerned, and the teacher is able to detect faulty habits and to locate specific difficulties in word recognition and word analysis.

Information particularly relevant to analysis of each pupil's weaknesses in word-recognition and word-analysis skills can be obtained through the child's oral reading performance.

1. What is the size of his sight vocabulary?
   a. Does he skip words?
   b. Does he add words?
   c. Does he substitute words?
   d. Does he repeat words?
   e. Does he reverse words?
   f. Does he read word by word?
   g. Does he point to words?
   h. Does he lose his place?
2. Does he know the names of the consonants and their sounds?
3. Does he know the sounds of common blends and consonant digraphs?
4. Does he know the long and short sounds of the vowels? of the diphthongs?
5. Is he aware of any generalizations or so-called rules pertaining to vowel sounds?
6. Does he utilize context clues?
7. Can he blend parts of a word into a whole?
8. Does he recognize common prefixes and suffixes?
9. Is he aware of word roots?
10. Does he recognize compound words?
11. Does he know that a word has as many syllables as it has vowel sounds?
12. Does he apply the principles of syllabication?
13. Does he apply common accent generalizations?

Other faulty habits which can be uncovered through an analysis of a pupil's oral reading performance include disregard for punctuation, unnecessary head and body movements, and vocal and articulatory problems.

Unlike silent reading tests, oral reading tests must be administered individually. From ten to twenty minutes is usually ample time for administration. Commonly used oral reading tests include the *Gray Test* (Bobbs-Merrill Co.) and *Gilmore Test* (Harcourt Brace Jovanovich).

Most standardized oral reading tests are similar to the *Gilmore Oral Reading Test*. The 1968 revision of the test has four forms and consists of ten paragraphs of increasing difficulty which range from preprimer to high school. A child taking the test reads from a booklet of heavy cardboard in which single paragraphs appear on individual pages. In a separate booklet, the examiner records the errors made according to the code described. He also records reading time in seconds and the answers to the five comprehension questions following each paragraph. A manual provides directions for errors, norms for accuracy, comprehension, and rate of reading. Although designed for pupils in grades one through eight, it can be employed most profitably with disabled readers in high school.

The teacher who uses an oral reading test soon becomes adept at employing a shorthand system for recording reading errors. A code such as the following (*Gilmore Oral Reading Test*) can prove valuable when making assessments of a pupil's reading needs through informal reading tests. Teachers have many opportunities for informally evaluating children's oral reading in the classroom. It is especially valuable to have each child come to the teacher's desk for several minutes of oral reading while the rest of the class is preoccupied. Material read by the child should be done on sight rather than accompanied by preparatory silent reading. The latter could very easily conceal the kinds of problems which the teacher wishes to know about.

Through the use of a tape recorder, teachers will learn how to score an oral reading test objectively. Teachers can get practice and become proficient in objectively scoring oral reading tests by listening in peace and quiet to tape recordings of children who have taken such tests. Several teachers should listen to the same recorded performance. When teachers agree as to errors made, they have acquired the necessary objectivity in their scoring. An individual record sheet will enable the teacher to record errors made by the pupil as he reads. After the scoring has been completed, the significant errors should be entered on a reading checklist (see fig. 8.1 in chapter 9).

Miscues

Because of the writings and research of Kenneth Goodman,[4] *miscue* rather than the word *error* is frequently being used to indicate a deviation from what is an expected response during reading. This has significance in planning a corrective program because a study of miscues can reveal a reader's strategies in trying to attack words and comprehend written language.

Miscue analysis involves a cataloguing of graphic, syntactic, and semantic information gleaned from students' oral reading. The analysis helps the

TABLE 7.1
Code for Recording Reading Errors

Type of Error	Rule for Marking	Examples
Substitutions A sensible or real word substituted for the word in the paragraph.	Write in substituted word.	black The boy is back of the girl. girl See the girls.
Mispronunciations A nonsense word which may be produced by (1) false accentuation; (2) wrong pronunciation of vowels or consonants; or (3) omission, addition, or insertion of one or more letters.	Write word in phonetically (if time permits) or draw a line through the word.	sĭm'-bŏl-ĭk (1) symbolic (or) ~~symbolic~~ blĕs'-fool (2) blissful (or) ~~blissful~~ blĕnt (3) bent (or) ~~bent~~
Words Pronounced by Examiner A word on which the subject hesitates for 5 seconds. (The word is then pronounced by the examiner.)	Make two checks above word pronounced.	It is a fascinating (✓✓ above "fascinating") story.
Disregard of Punctuation Failure to observe punctuation.	Mark punctuation disregarded with an "x."	Jack, my brother, is in (x above comma after "brother") the navy.
Insertions (including additions) A word (or words) inserted at the beginning, middle, or end of a sentence or line of test.	Write in inserted word or words.	the The dog and ∧ cat are fighting.
Hesitations A pause of at least 2 seconds before pronouncing a word.	Make a check above the word on which hesitation occurs.	It is a fascinating (✓ above "fascinating") story.
Repetitions A word, part of a word, or group of words repeated.	Draw a wavy line beneath word (words) repeated.	He thought he saw a (wavy line under "He thought") whale.
Omissions One or more words omitted. (If a complete line is omitted, this is counted as one omission error.)	Encircle the word (or words) omitted.	Mother does all (of) her work with great care.

Gilmore Oral Reading Test. Manual of Directions. Copyright 1952 by Harcourt, Brace & World, Inc., New York. All rights reserved. Reprinted by permission.

teacher answer questions such as the following: Does there appear to be graphic similarity between the miscue and the actual word? Is the miscue a reflection of the child's dialect? What is the degree of similarity between the miscue and the actual word sound? Are the miscue and the actual word grammatically the same? Is the miscue corrected? Is the miscue acceptable grammatically and/or semantically? Does the miscue change the meaning?

WORD RECOGNITION

Teachers may acquire information about a child's sight vocabulary and word-attack skill by the use of informal tests. Selecting the fifteenth or twentieth word from several representative pages from an unfamiliar reader or textbook provides a useful word-recognition test. When this is done, two copies should be prepared. One is placed before the child and the other is used by the teacher for recording responses. A small card can be employed to expose words tachistoscopically. When a child misses a word that has been flashed, it can be presented a second time without any time limit. Such a procedure will give the teacher a useful insight into a child's word-analysis skill. Mastery is indicated when a pupil responds immediately; lack of mastery is indicated when a pupil shows delayed recall. Usually, a flash recognition vocabulary of 95 percent indicates an adequate sight vocabulary for fluent reading.

Word lists are helpful in bringing to teachers' attention words that should be learned by children when encountered in reading. But children should not be required to learn words from a word list. A felt need is more likely to arise when words are encountered in contextual settings. Teachers who wish to use already prepared word lists will find the following of value.

BELINA, TOM. *Pacemaker Core Vocabulary*. Belmont, California: Fearon Pitman Publishers, Inc., 1975. A list of 1,021 words recognized in isolation by junior high students reading at the third grade level.

BOTEL, MORTON. *Bucks County 1,185 Common Words. How to Teach Reading*. Chicago: Follett Publishing Co., 1959, pp. 103-113. A list of 41 preprimer words, 67 primer words, 124 first-grade words, 359 second-grade words, and 594 third-grade words.

CARROLL, JOHN B., et al. *American Heritage Word Frequency Book*. New York: Houghton Mifflin and American Heritage, 1971. A list of 85,000 words drawn from school materials in grades three through eight. The words were selected from content-area tests, readers, and supplementary materials. Based on frequency, it was found that five common words ("the, of, a, and," and "to") made up 17.5 percent of all words at these levels.

DAVIES, PETER et al. *The American Heritage Word Frequency Book.* Boston: Houghton Mifflin Co., 1972. A list of words based on a survey of classrooms (grades three through nine) involving standard school subjects. Public, independent, and parochial schools are represented.

DOLCH, EDWARD W. "A Basic Sight Vocabulary." *The Elementary School Journal* 36 (1936):456-460. A list of 220 words said to make up more than 50 percent of the running words in elementary school reading materials. Printed cards useful in teaching these words are available from Garrard Publishing Co., Champaign, Ill.

DOLCH, EDWARD D. *Ninety-Five Nouns Common to the Three Word Lists.* A list of nouns common to three first-grade vocabulary lists. Picture word cards for teaching these are available from Garrard Publishing Co., Champaign, Ill., 1941.

DURR, WILLIAM K. "Computer Study of High Frequency Words in Popular Trade Journals." *Reading Teacher* 27 (1973):37-42. A list of 188 words appearing most frequently in eighty popular trade journals.

DURREL, DONALD. *Improving Reading Instruction.* New York: World Book Co., 1956, pp. 367-392. A list of words according to intermediate grade levels: fourth, fifth, sixth.

FRY, EDWARD. "Teaching a Basic Reading Vocabulary." *Elementary English* 37 (1960):38-42. A list of 100 first-grade words, 100 second-grade words, and 100 third-grade words.

GATES, ARTHUR. *A Reading Vocabulary for the Primary Grades.* New York: Bureau of Publications, Teachers College, Columbia University, 1935. A list of 1,811 words, arranged in three levels of 500 words each and supplementary list of 311 words.

HARRIS, ALBERT J. and JACOBSON, MILTON D. "Basic Vocabulary for Beginning Reading," *Reading Teacher* (January 1973):392-395. *Harris-Jacobson Core List.* A list based on the vocabulary in grades one through six of sixteen basal reader series widely used in 1970.

JOHNSON, DALE D. "The Dolch List Reexamined," *Reading Teacher* (February 1971):449-457. A list of 220 words which according to the author are more commonly used by children today than those on the Dolch Basic Sight Vocabulary List.

KEARNEY, NOLAN C. "An Analysis of the Vocabulary of First Grade Reading Material," *Journal of Educational Research* 43 (1950):481-493. A list of the 441 most common words found in 121 preprimers, primers, and first readers.

KNIPP, HELEN. *Basic Vocabulary Phrases and Sentences for Early Reading Instruction.* Meadville, Pa.: Mast/Keystone View Co., 1952.

KRANTZ, L. L. *The Author's Word List for Primary Grades.* Minneapolis, Minn.: Curriculum Research Co., 1945. A graded list of words based on the study of vocabulary of 84 preprimers, 69 primers, 84 first readers, 85 second readers, and 47 third readers.

MOE, ALDEN. *High Frequency Words.* Saint Paul, Minn.: Ambassador Publishing Co. One hundred words comprising 53 percent of the more than 100,000 words found in 110 widely used trade books for grades 1 and 2. Also, 100 High Frequency Nouns used in the same books.

OTTO, WAYNE, and CHESTER, ROBERT. "Sight Words for Beginning Readers," *Journal of Educational Research* (July-August, 1972):435-443. *Great Atlantic and Pacific Sight Word List.* A list based on *The American Heritage Word Frequency List involving* 500 words that had the highest frequency on the third-grade level.

RINSLAND, HENRY. *A Basic Vocabulary of Elementary School Children.* New York: Macmillan Co., 1945. A list of 14,571 words which is based upon words used in writing by children in grades 1-8.

STONE, DAVID R., and BARTSCHI, VILDA. "A Basic Word List from Basal Readers." *Elementary English* 40 (1963):420-427. A composite list, based on the words introduced in five of the most widely used basal reading series together with the Dolch and Fry lists.

STONE, CLARENCE. *Word Lists by Reading Levels.* New York: Webster/McGraw-Hill Book Co., 1950. A list of 100 preprimer words, 225 primer words, 455 first-reader words, 1,101 second-reader words, and 1,916 third-reader words.

THORNDIKE, EDWARD L. *A Teachers Wordbook of 30,000 Words.* New York: Bureau of Publications, Teachers College, Columbia University, 1944. A list based on a count of 10,000,000 words from both adult and children's books. Each word is categorized with a symbol denoting the thousand in which it belongs. Words in the first 5,000 are designated as first half or second half of the thousand.

WALKER, CHARLES. "High Frequency Word List for Grades 3 Through 9," *Reading Teacher* (April, 1979). A listing of 1,000 words of high frequency of occurrence in both voluntary and assigned reading in grades 3 through 9 in the United States.

CLOZE TESTING

Wilson Taylor originated the cloze procedure and found a high correlation (0.76) between results of the cloze test and scores on a multiple-choice test made on the same passage. Since then Rankin and Bormuth have carried out more research on the validity and reliability of the cloze procedure as a measure of the comprehension ability of a student and the comprehension difficulty of the material read.[5, 6]

To construct a cloze test, delete every fifth word from a typed passage of approximately 250 to 300 words in length. Deletions begin with the second sentence, and all blanks representing words that have been deleted should be of uniform length. Selections chosen for developing a cloze test may be drawn from a basal reader series. The pupil who is being tested begins with a selection two grades below his estimated reading level and stops with a selection two grades above his estimated reading level. When scoring the test, the examiner gives credit for only those words which exactly match the deleted words. This is done to insure objectivity.

A percentage score of the number of spaces filled in correctly is used in arriving at the reader's level of comprehension. Usually, more than 57 percent correct is indicative of an independent or recreational reading level. Percentages between 44 to 57 indicate the student's instructional level. Percentages below 44 are equated with the frustration level.

CRITERION-REFERENCED ASSESSMENTS AND BEHAVIORAL OBJECTIVES

Criterion-referenced tests, in contrast to norm-referenced tests, involve no percentiles, stanines, or grade-level scores. These tests do not compare an individual's performance with that of others. Instead, they determine whether a pupil has mastered a specific goal or has measured up to a given standard of performance.[7] Behavioral objectives provide the standards of performance and constitute a basis for criterion-referenced assessment.

In the area of reading, behavioral objectives are specific goals that have been expressed in behavioral terms. Some examples of behavioral objectives are as follows:

1. The pupil is able to alphabetize a list of ten words, each of which begins with a different first letter.
2. The pupil is able to locate the main idea of a paragragh.
3. The pupil is able to differentiate synonyms from antonyms.

It should be noted that the behavior of each objective is observable. Hence, verbs such as *compare, list, state, show,* and the like, are employed. However, expressing educational goals in terms of behavioral objectives has advantages and disadvantages.[8] Some of the advantages of employing behavioral objectives include: (1) clarification of purposes for both teachers and pupils, (2) breaking of broad content or curriculum areas into more manageable bits, (3) feasibility of handling a sequence and/or hierarchical arrangement of content, (4) facilitation of evaluation, (5) improvement in the organization and selection of materials, (6) assistance given teacher training, and (7) clarification of the role of research and planning in education.

Some of the disadvantages of employing behavioral objectives include: (1) the recognition that schooling involves more than content mastery, (2) the fact that some individuals organize content in ways differing from the usual sequenced objectives, (3) the possibility of overemphasis on skills at the expense of generalizations, interpretations, and application, (4) the fact that some areas are not amenable to a behavioral approach, (5) the possibility that the realities of the classroom may not be stated through objectives, and the fact that unexpected results may be as important as the intended results.

A natural outcome of criterion-referenced tests and the use of behavioral objectives has been increased interest and emphasis on accountability. Teachers, many people feel, should be held responsible for what they teach. Proponents of this idea reason that teachers should be held accountable for their product just as businessmen are held accountable for their products. On the other hand, there has been considerable criticism of criterion-referenced tests. According to Durkin, "the negative reaction with the most relevance to reading is probably the one that has warned that such tests will exaggerate the importance of what is observable and easily measured."[9] It is felt that more important things such as a favorable attitude toward reading might be overlooked.

USING AND ADMINISTERING TESTS

If teachers have questions about a standardized test, they should consult Buros's *Mental Measurements Yearbook*.[10] Information relevant to the validity, reliability, and usability of a test very likely can be found in this book. After consulting the volume, teachers can decide if the test in question is suitable for their needs.

When a teacher selects a standardized test, there are a number of things to consider. First, it is important to match a reading test to the age-grade level of the pupils involved. If this is not done, the norms automatically are invalidated. An example of this is the administration of an elementary test to a high school student. Although much could be learned about the student, the age scores derived from the test would not be applicable. Second, a test should not be selected if it fails to measure skills that are a matter of concern. For example, a reading speed test should not be chosen for a pupil who is deficient in word analysis. Third, it is essential that a classroom teacher not select clinical tests which she is not trained to administer or interpret.

Tests should be administered under optimum conditions. Noisy rooms, crowded rooms, and overly warm or cold rooms are not conducive to obtaining valid test scores. When tests are given, it is essential that the administrator adhere rigidly to the standardized directions. If the administrator of a test feels that a child did more poorly than he was capable of doing, the administrator should give the pupil another form of the test under more favorable circumstances. But repeating directions, giving extra assistance, or allowing additional time are strictly taboo unless the test manual specifies that such things may be done. The demeanor of the administrator is also important. A relaxed but businesslike manner is preferable to an authoritative and commanding approach likely to frighten students.

THE IMPORTANCE OF SILENT READING TESTS

Some teachers see no need for silent reading tests because they assume that an analysis of oral reading errors or miscues indicates exactly what is happening during silent reading. Research does show a definite correlation between oral reading errors and silent reading comprehension in grades 1 and 2.[11] But in the third grade and at levels beyond the third grade there is a marked decrease in this relationship. According to Newman[12] more is needed than oral reading test data. Silent reading assessments are essential if reading behavior is to be understood.

SILENT READING TESTS: SURVEY

Most silent reading survey tests provide a meaning vocabulary score and a comprehension score and are helpful in determining the level at which pupils can read. Although most of these tests have a working time of only thirty to forty-five minutes and enable a teacher to locate retarded readers quickly, they do have limitations.

A teacher must recognize that a child's reading level as indicated by a silent reading survey test is often an overestimate of his instructional level. Silent reading tests are group tests and are usually of the recognition type. They permit pupils to guess, which often results in grade scores, especially for retarded readers, that average one grade or more above their effective reading level. For example, a sixth-grade boy could recognize only two or three words on sight. His word-analysis skill was nonexistent. Yet, on a standardized silent reading test for the intermediate grades, he achieved a 2.7 grade score. Investigation revealed that this had been accomplished by filling in blanks at random.

When silent reading tests of the survey type are employed, one must not assume that several pupils in a given grade share the same difficulties because they received the same low score on the test. Further study will show that these pupils usually do not suffer from the same reading handicaps. The reading grade score on a silent reading test is based on the total correct responses. Each pupil has his own constellation of strengths and weaknesses of which an effective corrective program must take cognizance and be designed to meet. For example, in the skills of word analysis some pupils may be weak in beginning sounds and blends, while others need help with vowel sounds and the principles of syllabication. Seldom do pupils in a class have identical weaknesses in many of the basic reading skills.

Most survey tests provide grade norms which the teacher may use as a rough measure of a child's reading level. Other norms frequently found include age norms and percentile norms. When a comparison is made between intelligence and reading, it is advisable to use age rather than grade scores. A descriptive list of silent reading tests appears in Appendix C.

SILENT READING TESTS: DIAGNOSTIC

Group diagnostic silent reading tests are more analytical than survey tests since they provide measures of such silent reading abilities as noting important details, discovering central thoughts, following directions, using reference skills, summarizing, outlining, organizing and reading maps, graphs, and charts.

Although most group diagnostic reading tests do not provide sufficient information regarding sight-vocabulary deficiency and word-analysis skill, several tests are very helpful in these respects.

The *Silent Reading Diagnostic Tests* (Bond, Balow, and Hoyt; Rand McNally & Co.) are especially valuable because they can be administered and interpreted by a classroom teacher who has not had special training in clinical reading. The tests can be used with pupils of any age who read at second- through sixth-grade levels. Junior and senior high school teachers may use the tests even though they measure skills usually taught in the elementary school. By employing the tests, teachers can learn a great deal about a pupil's word-recognition vocabulary and word-attack skills. The following description of eight subtests involved give an understanding of what kinds of information the *Silent Reading Diagnostic Test* yield.

Test I: Words in Isolation: This test has fifty-four items. Each consists of a picture accompanied by five words. The child selects a word that describes a picture. The test reveals not only reading vocabulary, but also visual habits in recognizing words.

Test II: Words in Context: This test consists of thirty items, each of which involves a child's choosing one of five words to complete a sentence.

Test III: Visual-Structural Analysis: This test is designed to test knowledge of word structure. It consists of thirty affixed words which contain common prefixes and suffixes. The child is asked to choose the root word.

Test IV: Syllabication: This test has thirty items and measures ability to separate words into syllables. It tests a pupil's knowledge of six rules of syllabication.

Test V: Word Synthesis: This test consists of eight paragraphs and thirty comprehension questions. In each paragraph, hyphens are used to separate common blends, syllables, or affixes from the remainder of words. Unless the child can blend the hyphenated words, the paragraphs cannot be understood.

Test VI: Beginning Sounds: This test consists of thirty items which require a child's choosing one of four word elements pronounced by the examiner. Most of the test involves initial blends and digraphs.

Test VII: Ending Sounds: This test consists of thirty items, each of which requires a child to choose from four word endings the one which ends the stimulus word pronounced by the examiner.

Scores obtained from the foregoinng subtests can be transferred to a graphic profile to facilitate interpretation.

Another group test that assesses pupils' decoding skills is the *Doren Diagnostic Reading Test of Word Recognition Skills* (American Guidance Service). This test consists of eleven subtests:

1. Letter recognition
2. Beginning sounds
3. Whole word recognition
4. Words within words
5. Speech consonants
6. Ending sounds
7. Blending
8. Rhyming
9. Vowels
10. Sight words
11. Discriminate guessing

As with the *Silent Reading Diagnostic Tests*, results from the *Doren Test* can be used to provide a profile which will help highlight a pupil's areas of strengths and weaknesses. The only deterrent to using the test is its length. Nearly three hours are needed to administer the test.

Another group reading test which provides diagnostic data relevant to sight vocabulary and word analysis is the *McCullough Word Analysis Test*.

IN-DEPTH TESTING

Several individually administered tests of a more detailed nature are available when such data are needed. One such test is the *Diagnostic Reading Scales* by George Spache. These scales provide the examiner with a wide range of diagnostic information.

The first unit of the *Diagnostic Reading Scales* is devoted to three word lists designed to test a pupil's skills at word recognition and analysis and to determine the level of reading passages to which he should be introduced. According to the author, these reading passages (they number twenty-two and are of graduated difficulty) simulate the type and range of material that might be found in classroom reading assignments at levels ranging from mid-first grade to eighth grade. The materials include narrative, expository, and descriptive selections from the natural and physical sciences, social sciences, and children's literature. The passages yield three levels for each pupil. These are the intructional level, the independent level, and the potential level. The latter is determined by ascertaining the auding level.

The battery closes with six supplementary phonic tests which furnish information about a child's knowledge of consonant sounds, vowel sounds, consonant blends, common syllables, blends, and letter sounds.

We have employed the foregoing test in a reading clinic setting with excellent results. Other tests which merit attention include the *Durrell Analysis of Reading Difficulty* and the *Gates-McKillop Reading Diagnostic Test*.

DIAGNOSING DIFFICULTIES IN COMPREHENSION AND THE STUDY SKILLS

Reading is more than "barking at the print." Reading is a meaningful process. Because this is true, the child who fails to bring proper meaning to printed symbols and fails to comprehend what the writer wishes to convey is not reading.

While comprehension is the all-important goal at all grade levels, generally it is not a problem to the average primary grade child. The narrative material used by authors of basal readers at this level employs well-controlled vocabularies which carefully stay within the average child's background of experience. Consequently, understanding the printed page becomes little more than blending sight and sound. Once primary grade children have learned to associate familiar sounds with the new and unfamiliar written symbols on the printed page, they are able to understand the story the author wishes to convey. It is obvious, then, that a mastery of the basic reading skills is the "open sesame" to comprehension for most children in the primary grades. Since, however, there is a natural tendency on the part of children to accept what appears in print as sacrosanct, there is always a need for teachers to stimulate children to react critically to what has been read.

Any weakness in the basic reading skills is evidenced quickly in the fourth grade and beyond. Expository materials are encountered and vocabulary burdens increase with alarming rapidity at these levels. The child whose basic sight vocabulary and word-analysis skills are below par is soon in over his head. Not only is he troubled by high-frequency words which he should have mastered long ago, but he is bewildered by technical words in arithmetic such as *minuend, subtrahend,* and *quotient,* and technical words in geography such as *latitude, longitude,* and *doldrums.* As the number of unknown words increases, comprehension is impossible and mastery of the unknown symbols proves an overwhelming task because of their prevalence.

Evaluating a child's competence in the basic reading skills is an important first step in dealing with comprehension problems in the intermediate and upper grades. Too often teachers expend time and energy on trying to develop high-level comprehension skills when attention should first be devoted to building a basic sight vocabulary and to teaching independence in basic word-attack skills.

Pupils who comprehend material read to them by the teacher but who fail to comprehend when reading silently are often handicapped by basic reading skill deficiencies. Formal and informal listening tests, therefore, prove valuable in diagnosis. Further corroboration or verification of sight-vocabulary and word-attack deficiencies that are needed can be had by employing formal and informal oral reading tests.

Word Meaning

In intermediate and upper grades, word meaning becomes an important factor in comprehension since students encounter many aurally unfamiliar words at these levels. When a student lacks a good meaning vocabulary, sentence comprehension and paragraph comprehension become difficult because of the many gaps in the continuity of the reading process. It is essential, therefore, to measure the size of a student's meaning vocabulary and to evaluate his ability to use the dictionary when diagnosing comprehension problems. Fortunately, most silent reading tests, both survey and diagnostic, include sections that are devoted to meaning vocabulary.

When a pupil's meaning vocabulary is meager, a teacher will find it profitable to inventory his background of experience. It will be found that some children are products of an environment that has provided little or no cultural stimulation. If this is true, the school has the responsibility of giving the kinds of direct and indirect experiences needed to compensate for such impoverishment.

Sentence Comprehension

When complete thoughts are expressed, the shortest basic unit is the sentence. The disabled reader who learns to understand sentence can move directly into paragraph comprehension.

A great deal more than meaning vocabulary is involved in sentence comprehension. Many poor readers can call all the words in a sentence and, seemingly, know the meaning of each word, but the overall meaning or concept of the sentence escapes them. Such a difficulty may stem from inability to group words into meaningful thought units. Consider, for example, how difficult it is to comprehend the following sentence.

/It was a long/   /time after the/   /big fight had/   /taken place by/ /the roadside./

Words go together to make thought units. The child who has not sensed the inherent rhythm within the language structure struggles vainly for meaning. How much easier and more meaningful the sentence becomes when the words are grouped into logical phrases.

/It was/   /a long time/   /after the big fight/   /had taken place/ /by the roadside./

The simplest way to check phrasing ability is to ask a pupil to read aloud. Does he group the words into intelligent phrases? Are there slight pauses in the right places?

Another impediment to sentence comprehension which can be detected by having a child read aloud is his inattention to punctuation. Ignoring commas can result in immediate confusion of sentence sense. Consider, for example, the following:

Jim, too, saw two of them.
Bill said to him, "Today, we shall go to the movies."

Paragraph Comprehension

"The whole is more than the sum of its parts." A disabled reader often is inclined to consider each sentence in isolation from the rest of the sentences in a paragraph. He fails to connect all sentences into a unified whole. He sees the trees but misses the forest.

In order to comprehend a paragraph as a unified whole, it is necessary for the reader to spot the main or central idea of the paragraph. Once he knows what the general idea of the paragraph is, related details fall into place.

Fortunately, most silent reading tests devote sections to paragraph comprehension, enabling teachers to determine if pupils have weaknesses in this regard.

As was true with difficulty in sentence comprehension, inattention to punctuation must be considered a possible cause of poor paragraph comprehension. Ignoring periods, question marks, semicolons, and colons will result in running together the thoughts of sentences. A pupil's tendency to ignore these landmarks, which an author employs to emphasize the ideas he has organized into a paragraph, can be readily detected by having a pupil read aloud.

Summarizing

Three skills are basic to a pupil's skill in summarizing what he has read. These are the ability to locate main ideas, the ability to give proper sequence to these ideas, and the ability to write succinctly.

Hartig has emphasized the value of writing abstracts and summaries in connection with the improvement of reading, as follows:

> Perhaps any writing activity has some value for the improvement of reading skill since the act of writing itself develops general language ability. But one particular form of writing—the writing of abstracts or summaries of written essays, book chapters or articles—seems particularly likely to develop reading comprehension abilities. This would seem to be true because such writing involves the most rigorous kind of thinking about basic comprehension factors such as author's purpose, central ideas, main points, methods of support and development, and the like. H. Hartig, "A Writing Approach to Reading Comprehension," *Reading Improvement* (Winter 1967):33.

Critical Reading

We live in a democracy where it is essential for pupils to discern truth from falsehood and good from evil. Unfortunately, many pupils fail to realize that there is a need to evaluate what they read. They are too prone to accept anything and everything in print as infallible. The statement I know it is true because I read it, is a familiar refrain.

Two important factors which are associated with a pupil's ability to read critically are intelligence and experiential background.

Children of superior intelligence are more likely to react critically to what they read than children of average or below average intelligence. Although the relationship between intelligence and critical reading is positive, a high intelligence quotient does not assure high performance in critical reading. Even the very bright have weaknesses in this regard.

Children who have a reservoir of rich experiences are in a better position to evaluate what is read than are children whose background of experiences is meager. Critical thinking is difficult when one possesses an inadequate frame of reference.

When a pupil reads, understands, and then sanctions material containing contradictions, questionable opinions, or improbable situations which should be obvious, a need for instruction in critical reading exists. Chapter 13 provides a number of practical suggestions for helping students develop critical reading ability.

Concentration

Some students suffer comprehension difficulties because of mind-wandering tendencies. They read words and lines of print but find on turning a page that although their eyes were going through the mechanical process of reading their minds were playing hide-and-go-seek. This inability to concentrate makes comprehension difficult, and efforts should be made to uncover causes of the problem.

Visual difficulties, poor general health, and emotional disturbances are frequently responsible for concentration problems. Other factors that should be investigated when causal factors are probed include difficulty of the material being read, reader interest, lighting, and the presence of distracting influences in the study environment.

Retention

Since many reading comprehension tests are tests of retention, a pupil's ability to remember what he has read has a direct bearing on his comprehension test score.[13]

Although some disabled readers can remember material they do not understand, the opposite is often true. Problem readers show little retention for what has been read. Although it is infrequent, we have encountered children who could not tell in their own words the thought of simple sentences just read.

When a disabled reader is forced to read material that is too difficult, poor retention is understandable. But when the reading material is relatively simple, why should retention be poor? Some children become victims of an unfortunate kind of conditioning brought about by teachers who consistently ask factual questions immediately after silent reading takes place. When this occurs year after year, it is not surprising to find that children expect and wait to be pumped for information. Means of correcting this situation are treated on pages 314-315.

Following Directions

Standardized reading tests frequently have a section devoted to following directions. There is a very good reason for this. We live in a gadget-filled world. The ability to understand and follow directions is essential to our efficient use of the latest modern conveniences. Manuals of all kinds containing printed directions are available to the housewife, auto mechanic, radio technician, and numerous other specialists who are part of our modern-day world. The inability to follow printed directions leads to frustration and costly errors.

The results of an inability to follow directions may be amusing and, in some instances, tragic. Consider the following anecdotes. "A party went on a two weeks' vacation. While they were gone, they wanted their house painted white, with green trimmings. When they returned from their trip, they found that the workmen had painted the vacant house next door! Naturally, the workers had to return and paint the right house. They lost money and the house owner was inconvenienced—all because the painters did not follow directions." Another example involved a woman who was cleaning some clothes on the back porch. "Suddenly a terrific blast shook the house. Flames leaped out. Splinters flew. Plaster fell. What had happened? Why, the cleaning fluid had exploded. On the bottle of cleaner there was a big warning not to use the fluid near an open flame, but the woman hadn't read the directions."

Reading Rate and Comprehension

Efficiency in reading comprehension is directly related to pupils' rate of reading. As they progress from grade to grade, their reading speed becomes a very significant factor in their overall efficiency. Usually, rapid readers are efficient readers because impressions are stronger when thought concepts are received in rapid sequence.

It is a mistake to assume, however, that speed per se automatically results in increased reading comprehension. The efficient reader is fluent, and his speed grows out of this fluency. The inefficient reader is not fluent, and his effort to cover the ground more quickly involves hurried reading rather than rapid reading. Hurried reading results in a quick loss of intellectual breath, and comprehension suffers.

Many pupils read slowly because they are inept at phrasing and read one word at a time. Word-by-word reading may be an outgrowth of over-analysis of words or the result of a meager sight vocabulary. If the situation continues for a length of time, the word-by-word pattern crystallizes into a habit and continues to persist even though word-perception difficulties cease to be a problem. It is important, therefore, for the teacher to determine whether the pupil's word-by-word reading pattern is an outgrowth of habituation or whether deficiencies in basic skills are involved. Oral reading tests and word-recognition tests can be employed to make this diagnosis.

Although many silent reading tests include estimates of reading rate, teachers may wish to make informal appraisals of their own. This can be done by asking pupils to read a selection silently while the teacher records the passing time on the blackboard in ten-second intervals. The readers are asked to record the largest number on the board immediately upon completion of the selection. Once this has been done, simple mathematical procedure (dividing the words read by the seconds involved and then multiplying the results by sixty) will give a words-per-minute score.

While silent reading is taking place, the teacher should scrutinize each pupil for habits that are known to be detrimental to reading speed. These include finger pointing, head wagging, and lip movements. The latter habit is manifest in many primary-grade pupils because of the instructional emphasis on oral reading. At these early stages, it is not of great concern since the majority of children read no faster silently than they do orally. In the intermediate grades, however, when silent reading speeds begin to exceed oral reading speeds, pupils are admonished if subvocalization is detected. At these grade levels pupils should be able to read two or three times faster silently than orally. Any movement of the vocal mechanism during silent reading can do nothing but impede a pupil's speed.

Flexibility and Reading Speed

Other things being equal, a child's speed of comprehension is dependent on the difficulty of the material read. Good readers are flexible readers who vary and adapt their rates to the nature of the content and the purposes for which they are reading. Poor readers are inept in this regard. A valuable index of efficiency on a silent reading test is the ratio of comprehension items answered correctly to those attempted. It is advisable for a teacher to express the results in fractional form. For example, a glance at the fraction 18/20 indicates that 20 comprehension items were attempted and 18 were answered correctly, resulting in an accuracy score of 90 percent. (A score of 80 percent is the usual minimum acceptable.) Such a procedure enables the teacher to categorize a child as a fast-accurate reader, a fast-inaccurate reader, an average-accurate reader, an average-inaccurate reader, a slow-accurate reader, or slow-inaccurate reader. This information is very important when making a diagnosis.

EXPLORING READING EXPECTANCY OR POTENTIAL

Intelligence Tests

Although scores from group intelligence tests lack the reliability and validity of individually administered intelligence tests, classroom teachers will find the scores that are available very helpful in their study of reading retardation cases.

Care must be exercised in selecting an intelligence test for a poor reader. Many group intelligence tests are largely verbal and therefore not valid for the retarded reader. These intelligence tests (in reality they are reading tests in disguise) should not be employed with poor readers if one wishes to use the results as a reading-expectancy criterion. Some group intelligence tests such as the *California Test of Mental Maturity, Pintner-Durost Elementary Test, Pintner Intermediate Test,* and the *Lorge-Thorndike* have nonverbal (quantitative) scores. A quantitative score is often used as an index of a pupil's potential while a verbal (language) score is an indication of how well the pupil is functioning scholastically. Usually, a retarded reader or a child from a bilingual home will score higher on the nonverbal section of an intelligence test.

Listening Comprehension Tests

The level at which a pupil can comprehend material read aloud to him (his auding level) is considered by some authorities the most valuable index of reading potential.[14] Commercial tests based on this premise are available and include the *Brown-Carlsen Listening Comprehension Test* (Harcourt Brace Jovanovich), *Diagnostic Reading Tests,* Section II, Comprehension: Silent and Auditory (The Committee on Diagnostic Reading Tests), *Durrell Reading-Listening Series* (Harcourt Brace Jovanovich), STEP tests—listening comprehension section (Educational Testing Service), the listening section of the *Spache Diagnostic Reading Scales* (California Test Bureau), the *Peabody Picture Vocabulary Test* (American Guidance Service), and the *Botel Listening Test* (Follett Co.)

IDENTIFYING NONEDUCATIONAL HAZARDS IN LEARNING

Screening Tests in Vision

Snellen Chart

All screening tests for vision used by the school have shortcomings. This is particularly true of the *Snellen Chart* which was designed by Herman Snellen in 1862.

The *Snellen Chart* is probably the most common screening test in use today. The chart consists of letters of various sizes arranged in rows with the larger letters at the top and letters in each succeeding row smaller in a measurable amount. Each letter is inscribed in a square whose sides are divided into five equal parts making twenty-five smaller squares. Each smaller square (representing one part of the letter) subtends a visual angle of one degree to the normal eye at the distance marked for that letter or line of letters.

The chart should be well illuminated, and the child should stand twenty feet from it. He is then asked to read without squinting the lowest line possible, first with both eyes, then with each eye separately. Visual acuity is expressed as a fraction. The numerator is always the distance in feet that he is from the chart, and the denominator is the number beside the lowest line that he is able to read. Thus, if the child is 20 feet from the chart and is able to read only the 200 letter with the right eye, his visual acuity is recorded R = 20/200. If he can read to the 30 line with the left eye, his acuity is recorded L = 20/30. Normal visual acuity is indicated when both numerator and denominator are the same, that is, 20/20.

Often the chart is administered in a way that permits a child to cheat. For example, some children simulate good vision by memorizing the chart; others squint, a practice helpful to the myope since the size of the pupil is reduced. It is important to recognize that the *Snellen Chart* checks vision only at far point and fails completely to detect severe cases of poor fusion and muscular imbalance. It also fails to detect most cases of astigmatism and farsightedness. Nearsightedness is the only defect adequately screened by the *Snellen Chart,* and this defect, ironically, is the one most often associated with good reading and good scholarship.

The *Snellen Chart* can be made more effective by employing a plus 1.00- or 1.50-diopter spherical lens for purposes of retesting (American Optical Co., Southbridge, Mass.). The farsighted child will see as well or better when the lens is used, but the child who has normal vision or who is myopic will be hindered by use of the lens. It is desirable to also have the child read the chart with both eyes after typical monocular testing has taken place. If the child sees less well with both eyes than he did when each eye was tested individually, a fusion problem may be suspected.

Stereoscopic Tests

There are a number of visual screening tests that are superior to the *Snellen Chart.* Probably the most popular screening instruments today are those of the Brewster-type stereotype such as the *Telebinocular* (part of the Keystone School Visual Survey Service), *Ortho-Rater,* and *Titmus School Vision Tester.* These are instruments which use lenses and prisms to obtain parallax, that is, the different view of an object experienced by the two retinas by reason of viewing it from two angles. These stereoscopic instruments allow the viewer to look simultaneously at two photographic pictures taken under a difference of angular view, corresponding to, or even greater than, the separation of the two eyes. Thus, as in ordinary binocular vision, the two images are fused by the brain, and the objects viewed are made to stand out in relief.

Sets of stereoscopic testing cards or slides for these instruments usually comprise a series to measure binocular acuity, monocular acuity, vertical and lateral distance phorias, fusion, depth perception, near phorias, near fusion, and near acuity. Record forms on which to note the findings may be obtained. Individual findings are checked either in or out of the expected columns. Thus, variations from a normal visual pattern can be indicated.

When the foregoing instruments are used, it must be remembered that they are screening devices and cannot be considered diagnostic. Care must be exercised with stereoscopic instruments since they all are not manufactured to the same specifications. If the identical stereoscopic cards are used with two stereoscopes of different make, the results will not be the same. Another factor which must be considered with the use of any stereoscopic device is this: The concept of nearness of the cards or slides viewed cannot be eliminated in the mind of the individual tested. This may alter the set of the eyes while they are being examined.

Walton Card

Of particular importance is the addition of the Walton card to the Mast/ Keystone battery which now is referred to as the Modified Telebinocular Technique. The Walton card measures acuity and detects the presence of astigmatism, amblyopia, and anisometropia (a difference in the refractice power of the eyes). Statistical analysis of data involved in a study comparing the Modified Telebinocular Technique with the Modified Clinical Technique *showed a significance of agreement greater than the .01 percent level of confidence that the two tests provide comparable results*.[15] At the present time the only method of vision screening used in our schools that is acceptable to optometrists and ophthalmologists is the Modified Clinical Technique.

Informal Visual Screening Tests

Several informal visual screening tests that require a minimum of equipment may be given by a teacher or reading specialist. These include the cover test, ocular motility test, the near point of convergence test, and the physiological diplopia test.

Cover Test (Unilateral and Alternate)

This test may be used to determine the presence of muscular imbalance of the two eyes both at distance and near point. The individual being examined is told to fixate the gaze at a specific target, keeping both eyes open at all times. When administering the unilateral cover test, a card or similar object is placed before one eye by the examiner. If the uncovered eye (both eyes should be checked) makes movement to gain fixation of the target, a tropia (strabismus) is manifest and immediate referral is called for.

The alternate cover test involves leaving the occluder in front of one eye for three to five seconds and then shifting it to the other eye. Any movement of the eye being uncovered is noted. The occluder is shifted from one eye to the other several times to make certain of the presence, or absence, of movement of the eye being uncovered. If movement is noted when shifting the occluder from one eye to the other, the presence (but not the degree) of fusion or binocularity is present. The quality of such fusional ability can be determined only by the vision specialist who is able to employ more specific and exacting testing procedures.

Ocular Motility Test

This test reveals weaknesses in the external muscles of the eyes. The individual being examined is directed to hold the head still and follow with the eyes an object held in the examiner's hand. A jeweled ornament is an excellent target when working with children. A vertically held penlight also can be used. The examiner rotates the target in a circle approximately two feet in diameter about twelve to eighteen inches in front of the child. He then moves the target through the cardinal directions, that is, right and left, up and down, up to the right and down to the left, and up to the left and down to the right. The examiner watches to see if the child's eyes both follow the target at all times. The examinee is told to report any experience of diplopia (seeing two targets) at any time during the test. Any jerkiness or unsteadiness in following the target should be noted and the test then repeated. If the same jerkiness appears on a repeat test, referral to a visual specialist is recommended.

Near Point of Convergence Test

The same target used for checking motilities can be used for this test. The child being examined is directed to watch the target as it is moved slowly by the examiner toward the tip of the child's nose. Most children are able to follow the target to the tip of the nose. The examiner should watch to see if one eye suddenly diverges as the target is brought close. The distance at which this happens should be noted. If there is any divergence, the subject should be asked whether he is aware of two targets. If he is not, it may be indication of suspension of vision in the diverging eye. A near-point convergence of four inches from the tip of the nose is generally considered sufficient. The child fails the test if this cannot be done. The examiner should record the distance at which one eye turned away from the target. He also should indicate whether it was the right or the left eye which deviated.

Physiological Diplopia Test

This is a relatively easy test to administer, and it indicates suppression or suspension of vision in one eye. The examiner, facing the subject, holds two targets (i.e., a pen and a pencil, preferably of different colors), one in each hand. One target is held approximately twelve inches from the subject's face and the other twenty-four inches away, both in line with the subject's nose. The individual being examined is directed to hold his fixation on one of the targets and report whether he is aware of one or two images of the target not being fixated. The process is then repeated with fixation being held on the other target. If the individual reports that he is aware of only one image of the nonfixated target (two are expected), it indicates that he is suspending or ignoring the image seen by one eye. When this is discovered, referral to a visual specialist is recommended.

Audiometer

The most valid test for measuring hearing is the pure tone audiometer. Recommended audiometers include Ambco, Beltone, Eckstein Brothers, and Zenith. A pure tone audiometric test yields far more information than any other hearing test. By studying the audiogram (a graphic representation of the measurements of hearing loss) it is possible to determine both the pattern and extent of a hearing loss. In addition, valuable information concerning the etiology of the loss is provided. For testing groups of children, the Western Electric Company's Model 4C and the Verbal Auditory Screen for Children (VASC) can be used.

When audiometric testing is not available, several informal screening tests may be used. These include the whisper test, watch tick test, and the coin click test.

Whisper Test

A series of unrelated words or two-digit numbers are whispered by the examiner with residual breath. A quiet room should be used for testing. The child being tested usually stands at a distance of twenty feet from the examiner, although this distance may be changed if the acoustical properties of the room warrant. (When this is done, it is necessary to determine the proper distance by noting how far the average person must be in order to hear the whisper.) The child who is being tested stands with one side toward the examiner and responds with one ear occluded, then the other. If the child does poorly, the examiner moves closer. Should the child fail to respond as well as a normal child would at the standardized distance, a hearing loss may be suspected.

Watch Tick Test

Ordinarily a loud-ticking watch which the average person can hear at a distance of forty-eight inches is used for this test. When other watches are employed, it is necessary to standardize them on a number of children. Any timepieces other than the watch being used by the examiner should be removed. The child then stands at right angles to the examiner with his finger in the ear not being tested. The youngster also should be required to hold a small card beside his head so he cannot see the watch when he is being tested. The examiner begins by placing the watch close to the child's ear. He withdraws it slowly until the child no longer hears it. He then moves the watch slowly toward the child until it is heard. An average of the two distances is taken. If a child fails to respond as a normal child would at the standardized distance, a hearing loss may be suspected.

Coin Click Test

The coin click test, like the watch tick test, is a test of high frequency. To the extent that it can be standardized for a given room and given coins, the coin click test is a useful supplement to the whisper test.

Some school systems do not provide adequate hearing testing. Instead of employing an audiometer periodically, they rely on the rough screening tests described. These tests will continue to have their place since they are easily given, and no expensive equipment or elaborate surroundings are required. The whisper test checks frequencies in the speech range extending from three hundred to three thousand cycles per second. The coin click and watch tick tests reach frequencies above this range. Since hearing loss often begins with high-frequency difficulties, the coin click and watch tick tests prove to be valuable supplementary tests.

There is no doubt that the whisper, watch tick, and coin click tests are better than no tests at all. But a word of warning. There are many hearing losses that may escape detection when these tests are used. It is essential, therefore, that teachers develop a seismographic sensitivity to any manifestations of auditory impairment so intelligent referrals to an otologist can be made.

Another significant aspect of hearing involves auditory discrimination. Deficiencies in auditory discrimination can be detected by reading aloud pairs of words that sound alike and pairs of words that sound different. The child is asked to distinguish between them. Commercial tests of auditory discrimination include the following: Boston University Speech-Sound Discrimination Test (Boston: W. Pronovost, Speech Department, Boston University); Goldman-Fristoe-Woodcock Test of Auditory Discrimination (Circle Pines, Minn.: American Guidance Service); Wepman Auditory Discrimination Test (Chicago: Language Research Associates); Lindamood Auditory Comprehension Test (Boston: Teaching Resources); Katz Kindergarten Screening Test (Chicago: Follett Publishing).

Diagnosis of Emotional Problems

One of the most simple and practical ways for classroom teachers to detect emotionally disturbed children is daily observation of the child's overt behavior. In this connection the teacher will find the following list of symptoms of emotional difficulty helpful. When employing such a list, however, teachers should realize that they are dealing with a whole child. Consequently, each symptom must be considered in light of the child's total personality.

1. Tics, twitchings
2. Psychosomatic illness (dizziness, nausea, or headaches).
3. Apathy, excessive daydreaming, fantasy.

4. Nailbiting, thumb-sucking.
5. Excitability, hyperactivity, uncontrolled emotionality.
6. Morbid fears or phobias.
7. Insomnia, nightmares, somnambulism.
8. Self-consciousness, stuttering.
9. Depression, guilt feelings.
10. Suspiciousness, tenseness, anxiety.
11. Fighting, stealing, bullying, and other antisocial behavior.

Psychologists are trained to employ a number of methods and techniques for studying personality. Most clinical psychologists give projective tests such a the *Rorschach Test* and the *Thematic Apperception Test.* Other tests that may be given include the *Michigan Picture Test, the Children's Apperception Test,* the *Fehrenbach Sentence Completion Test* and the *Rosenzweig Picture Frustration Study.*

Certain personality tests can be used by classroom teachers who wish to supplement their subjective judgment of children's personality patterns. One of these is the *California Test of Personality* (California Test Bureau/ McGraw-Hill). When employing such tests, teachers should realize that children often answer questions in a way they feel will be pleasing to parents or teachers. Teachers should also consider that poor readers may misinterpret questions. Reading the questions aloud for the child is not recommended either since tests are not standardized in this way, and the norms would be inapplicable.

A question employed by Paul Witty which frequently helps in uncovering the causes of an emotional problem is: If you had one wish which might come true, what would be your wish? Older students can be asked to write responses to questions such as What bothers you? and What things do you worry about?

A graduate student of Spache[16] learned a great deal of valuable information about children's personality by having them write stories based on a number of titles she provided. Some of these were: "What I Think Heaven Is Like," "The Way I Feel on Dark, Rainy Days," "The Reason I Like My Best Friend," "Why I Am Sad," "Ten Rules for Mother and Daddy," and "What Makes Me Bad." Teachers may be able to provide a number of other story-provoking titles that will encourage children's spontaneous verbalizations. The results can be very rewarding.

Determining The Best Method of Instruction

As stated by Schubert in an early publication, when the numerous methods of teaching words are pondered, many teachers are in a quandary. Each specialist (Gates, Monroe, Dolch, Fernald, all renowned in the reading field) advocates a different method. What is the answer? What should be used? Is there a best method?

Basically, there are three methods for teaching words to disabled readers: the visual, the phonic, and the kinesthetic. There is no best method per se. Only when a corrective program is based on individual needs can any method be cited as superior.

For example, Monroe and Rogers[17] tell of a seven-year-old boy who suffered from a severe reading disability of neurological origin. No matter how hard the child tried, he was unable to remember words when the usual sight method was employed. As soon as the cause was uncovered, he was taught by tracing large models of words while saying them out loud.[18] This was a kinesthetic approach. And it worked! Soon he was able to recognize words and began to show definite and competent progress.

Bonds' research shows that children suffering from hearing losses are at marked diadvantage in learning to read when a purely phonetic method is employed. On the other hand, he found that the look-and-say method does not penalize the child who has an auditory loss.[19] It is evident that if a child suffers from auditory or visual deficiencies, it is wise to choose a method of instruction that minimizes the handicap as much as possible.

It is also a mistake to assume that just because children are free from discernible sensory impairments they will learn just as easily with one method as with another. Any teacher can convince himself of the falsity of this belief by checking the auditory and visual memory spans of a group of children. Not infrequently does not find that students with fine visual memories have much poorer auditory memories or vice versa. For seemingly inexplicable reasons some children have great difficulty in making visual associations but show excellent phonic aptitude. In such cases, Monroe's phonetic approach of blending and forming word elements into whole words is to be recommended.

For the child who is adept at making visual associations but shows ineptitude when phonetic approaches are employed, Gates' method of stressing the general configuration of words as a basis for recognition is appropriate. Since it is not possible to tell which method will work best in an individual case, the teacher must be flexible and versatile. If Harry or Mary do not respond favorably to one method, another method must be tried.

In final analysis, if there is a best method, we are forced to term it eclectic. According to Harris and Sipay,[20] ". . . best results can be obtained by using a balanced, eclectic approach."

When an individual method is used to the exclusion of others, some children are doomed to failure regardless of how sincere, competent, and enthusiastic the teacher is. Today many teachers use the popular flash method. It is true that most children learn easily and quickly when this method is employed, but still there are needless fatalities. The number of failures could be reduced markedly if the teacher used several avenues of approach so the student could choose the particular method or combination of methods that seem to be best suited to his/her individual needs.

A simple yet ingenious test developed by Robert E. Mills provides a useful tool in studying this problem. *The Mills Learning Ability Test* (The Mills Center) introduces groups of words in four ways: visual, phonic, kinesthetic, and combined. It then checks retention after an interval of one day. By means of the test, an examiner can determine a particular approach for which a given child shows the most aptitude. It should be obvious that the test is a valuable tool in a reading diagnosis.

Other tests that are helpful in identifying a pupil's preferred mode of learning are as follows:

The *Wepman Auditory Discrimination Test* (Language Research Associates) involves having a pupil listen to word pairs. He responds by indicating whether each pair is the same or different. The pupil who scores poorly on this test is likely to experience difficulty with phonics.

The *Benton Visual Retention Test* (Psychological Corp.) requires a pupil to draw various designs from memory. The pupil who scores poorly on this test is likely to experience difficulty remembering word forms.

The *Illinois Test of Psycholinguistic Abilities* (ITPA) (University of Illinois Press) is designed to determine basic weaknesses in the areas of visual and auditory perception, association, and memory. Doing poorly on certain of the nine subtests involved may indicate a pupil's ineptitude for phonics, the kinesthetic approach, or the look-and-say method.

The *Marianne Frostig Development Test of Visual Perception* (DTVP) (Follett Publishing Co.) consists of five subtests. These measure various aspects of visual motor coordination, constancy of form, figure ground relationships, position in space, and spatial relationships. Scoring poorly on these tests indicate, it is thought, deficiencies that are basic to learning to read.

Robbins Speech Sound Discrimination and Verbal Imagery Type Tests (Expression Co.)are helpful in determining the specific sensory modality through which a pupil can learn most easily. The tests which are designed for children over four years of age require young children to point to pictures while older ones tell whether the three words they have listened to are alike, and if not, the one that is different.

Screening Tests for Identifying Children with Specific Language Disability (Educators Publishing Service) comprise a test designed for locating children who have or are likely to develop problems in reading, spelling, and handwriting. Its subjects include measures of visual copying, visual memory, visual discrimination, auditory perception, auditory memory, and auditory-visual association.

Some researchers have challenged the concept of modality preference. For example, Bateman employed the ITPA to divide her pupils into two groups: "visual learners" and "auditory learners."[21] These pupils were assigned randomly to two classes, one using a visual approach (Scott, Foresman & Co.) and the other using an auditory approach (Lippincott). She found no significant interaction between modal preference and method of instruction. She did find, however, that for both groups, the auditory approach was superior to the visual approach.

Blanton points out that it is virtually impossible to isolate any aspect of reading behavior where the auditory and visual modalities are not involved to a certain degree.[22] In other words, the visual learner may still visualize material even though it is presented auditorially.

SUMMARY OF THE DIAGNOSTIC PROCESS

A. At beginning of school year
  1. Objectives
    a. To determine readiness for reading
    b. To determine range of talent
    c. To discover handicaps in vision and hearing
  2. Procedures and materials
    a. Reading-readiness test
    b. Reading-readiness checklist
    c. Nonverbal intelligence test and/or listening test
    d. Screening tests in vision and hearing
B. Four to six weeks after opening of school
  1. Objectives
    a. To locate pupils in need of corrective instruction
    b. To determine instructional level for each pupil
    c. To determine nature and severity of individual reading problems
    d. To locate hazards to learning
    e. To determine difficulty of self-directed corrective material needed
    f. To discover learning potential of each pupil
    g. To select pupils in need of the services of a reading clinician
    h. To establish criteria for grouping
  2. Procedures and materials
    a. Observation
    b. Interviews
    c. Cumulative records
    d. Oral reading in class
    e. Oral reading test
    f. Survey silent reading test
    g. Diagnostic silent reading test
    h. Informal cloze testing
    i. Criterion-referenced assessments
    j. Word-recognition test

k. Word-analysis test
l. Group and individual intelligence tests
m. Listening tests
n. Screening tests in vision, hearing, and personality
C. At end of school year
1. Objectives (grades two to eight)
a. To determine individual level of achievement in reading
b. To ascertain individual growth in reading
2. Procedures and materials
a. Group survey test in reading or optional assessment
b. Scores to be entered on cumulative record

SUMMARY

A good reading diagnosis is basic to any program stressing individualized instruction. Informal tools and procedures that can be used by teachers for diagnostic purposes include studying cumulative records, observation, interviews, interest inventories, and reading inventories. Standardized oral and silent reading tests can be used to determine a pupil's weaknesses and strengths. Nonstandardized assessments such as the cloze procedure and criterion-referenced tests are also helpful. Special tests of both a formal and an informal nature are available for visual and auditory screening and personality maladjustment. A pupil's reading-expectancy level can be determined through the use of intelligence tests or by employing listening comprehension tests.

When classroom teachers accept responsibility for diagnosis and correction, learning is facilitated and pupils attain a higher level of achievement.

PROBLEMS FOR ORAL AND WRITTEN DISCUSSION

1. Discuss the uses of the cumulative record.
2. Administer the Dolch word list to an average reader and to a retarded reader in the same grade and interpret the results.
3. Administer the Wide Range Vocabulary Test to an average reader and to a retarded reader in the same grade and interpret the results.
4. Administer a survey test in silent reading to two or more pupils in the same grade. Score the tests, compute grade and age scores, and interpret the results.
5. Administer a diagnostic silent reading test to two or more pupils in the same grade. Score the tests, compute scores and interpret the results.

6. Administer an oral reading test to a pupil and record the performance on a tape recorder. Compute the errors and compare your results with two or more teachers listening to the same recording. Repeat until all agree on the number and types of errors.
7. Evaluate two or more diagnostic reading tests in terms of reliability.
8. Prepare a cloze procedure exercise by selecting a passage of appropriate length from unfamiliar prose. How many deletions are required? What level of difficulty is needed?

Notes

1. HOMER CARTER and DOROTHY McGINNIS, *Diagnosis and Treatment of the Disabled Reader* (New York: Macmillan Co., 1970), p. 78.
2. EMMETT BETTS, *Foundations of Reading Instruction* (New York: American Book Co., 1957), p. 455.
3. R. STRANG, C. McCULLOUGH, and A. TRAXLER, *The Improvement of Reading* (New York: McGraw-Hill Book Co., 1968), pp. 166-167.
4. KENNETH GOODMAN, "Dialect Barriers to Reading Comprehension," *Elementary English* (December 1965):853-860.
5. EARL F. RANKIN, "Grade Level Interpretation of Close Readability Scores." In Frank Greene (Ed.), *The Right to Participate*. (Milwaukee: National Reading Conference, 1971), pp. 30-37.
6. J. R. BORMUTH, ed., *Readability in 1968*. (Champaign, Ill.: National Council of Teachers of English, 1968), pp. 40-47.
7. R. P. CARVER, "Reading Tests in 1970 Versus 1980: Psychometric Versus Edumetric," *Reading Teacher* (December 1972):299-302.
8. W. OTTO et al., *Focused Reading Instruction* (Reading, Mass.: Addison-Wesley Publishing Co., 1974), pp. 105-107.
9. D. DURKIN, *Teaching Them to Read*, 2nd ed. (Boston: Allyn & Bacon, 1970), p. 507.
10. O. BURROS, ed., *Reading Tests and Reviews* (Highland Park, N. J.: Gryphon Press, 1968).
11. JOHN GILMORE and EUNICE GILMORE, *Gilmore Oral Reading Test* (New York, N.Y.: Harcourt, Brace, Jovanovich, 1968).
12. HAROLD NEWMAN, "Oral Reading Miscue Analysis is Good But Not Complete," *The Reading Teacher* (May, 1978), pp. 883-886.
13. WALTER BARBE, "Measuring Reading Comprehension," *Clearing House* (February 1958):343.
14. GEORGE SPACHE and EVELYN SPACHE, *Reading in the Elementary School* (Boston: Allyn & Bacon, 1973), pp. 83-84.
15. "Looking into Vision Schrrning," *California Optometrist* (August 1976).
16. GEORGE D. SPACHE, *Diagnosing and Correcting Reading Disabilities*. (Boston: Allyn & Bacon, Inc., 1976), pp. 104-105.
17. MARION MONROE and BERNICE ROGERS, *Foundations for Reading*. (Glenview, Ill.: Scott, Foresman and Company, 1951), pp. 168-169.
18. MARION MONROE, *Growing into Reading* (Chicago: Scott, Foresman & Co., 1951), pp. 63-65.

19. Guy Bond, *The Auditory and Speech Characteristics of Poor Readers*, Teachers College Contributions to Education, No. 657 (New York: Teachers College, Columbia University).
20. Albert J. Harris and Edward R. Sipay, *How to Teach Reading*. (New York: Longman, 1979), p. 117.
21. Barbara Bateman, "The Efficiency of an Auditory and a Visual Method of First Grade Reading Instruction with Auditory and Visual Learners," in *Perception and Reading*, ed. H. Smith (Newark, Del.: International Reading Association, 1968).
22. Bill Blanton, "Modalities and Reading," *Reading Teacher* (November 1971):210-212.

Selected Readings

Alexander, Estill J., ed. *Teaching Reading*. Boston: Little, Brown and Company, 1979, chap. 16.

Burmeister, Lou E. *Reading Strategies for Middle and Secondary School Teachers*. 2nd ed. Menlo Park, Calif.: Addison-Wesley Publishing Company, 1978, chap. 3.

Fry, Edward. *Elementary Reading Instruction*. New York: McGraw-Hill Book Co., 1977, chap. 11. :

Harris, Albert J. and Sipay, Edward R. *How to Increase Reading Ability*. 6th ed. New York: David McKay Co., 1975, chaps. 8, 9.

Harris, Albert J. and Sipay, Edward R. *How to Teach Reading*. New York: Longman, 1979, unit 6.

Kennedy, Eddie C., *Classroom Approaches to Remedial Reading*. 2nd ed. Itasca, Ill.: Peacock Publishers, Inc., 1977, chaps. 4, 5.

Lapp, Diane and Flood, James. *Teaching Reading to Every Child*. New York: Macmillan Publishing Co., Inc., 1978, chap. 4.

Michael J. Ritty. "Assessing and Alleviating Visual Problems in the Schools," *The Reading Teacher* (April 1979):796-802.

Schubert, Delwyn, and Torgerson, Theodore, eds. *Readings in Reading*. New York: Thomas Y. Crowell Co., 1968, selections 48-55.

Strang, Ruth. *Diagnostic Teaching of Reading*. 2nd ed. New York: McGraw-Hill Book Co., 1969.

9 The Diagnostic Process

THE DIAGNOSTIC STEPS

Locating and studying the types of errors a child makes on an oral reading test helps in the evaluation of a reading difficulty; converting scores on a silent reading test into grade scores provides a measure of a pupil's competence in reading; and determining a pupil's mental age through the use of a nonlanguage test or a grade score from a listening comprehension test provides an index of a child's potential or level of reading expectancy. Accomplishing all these things and arriving at an appropriate corrective program involves a series of systematic diagnostic steps and procedures. A guide to such an analysis follows:

STEP 1. Identify the retarded reader.
STEP 2. Determine the nature of the reading problem.
STEP 3. Determine the pupil's potential.
STEP 4. Determine the severity of the reading problem.
STEP 5. Identify hazards to learning and discover causal factors.
STEP 6. Summarize and record data.
STEP 7. Interpret data.
STEP 8. Institute the appropriate corrective program.

Identify the Retarded Reader

Before a teacher can identify pupils who are likely to profit from special help in reading (i.e., pupils whose reading level is below their potential), he/she must locate all pupils who are experiencing reading difficulty.

One of the simplest ways to locate poor readers in a classroom has been suggested by Dolch.[1] All pupils are told that the teacher wants to find out how hard a new book is. The book is opened to a specified page and each child reads aloud one sentence. Those who cannot read or who have difficulty are quickly brought to the teacher's attention. Since each child reads only one sentence, there is little embarrassment on the part of those pupils who do poorly.

Harris and Sipay are partial to the Dolch approach but recommend having each child read two or three sentences rather than one.[2] They also suggest administering a short-answer test to the class after pupils have read a short selection silently. By having each pupil close his/her book and look up as soon as he has finished reading the selection, the slowest readers can be spotted easily.

First-grade students can be given a readiness test and deficiencies can be noted. Their sight vocabulary (an excellent index of reading skill at the first-grade level) can be tested by drawing words from lists at the back of basal readers to which they have been exposed.

Pupils in the second grade and above can be given a silent reading test of the survey type at the beginning of the school year. By converting raw scores into grade scores the teacher can readily discover the poor readers. Those whose grade-placement scores are dubious should be subjected to further testing.

There are a large number of overt signs that reveal the presence of a reading problem. Some of these are as follows:

1. Dislike of school
2. Dislike of reading
3. Aversion to the library
4. Low scholarship
5. Behavioral difficulty
6. Irregular school attendance
7. Emotional disturbance
8. Slow, halting reading
9. Finger pointing
10. Lip movement
11. Inaccurate observation of punctuation
12. Inability to understand what is read
13. Inability to attack new words
14. Limited sight vocabulary.

Determine the Nature of the Reading Problem

Often the teacher can determine the general nature of a pupil's reading problem when an overall assessment of reading competence has been made. Later the teacher may want to delve more deeply into the nature of the reading problem. Informal and formal testing procedures are usually amenable to both survey and analytical treatment of data.

For example, the use of an informal reading inventory will quickly enable teachers to determine a pupil's independent, instructional, and frustration levels. If teachers wish to collect more data, they would note things such as enunciation, ability to recognize basic sight vocabulary words, phrasing ability, attention to punctuation, fluency, and word-attack skill. Should teachers wish to include comprehension questions, they can determine whether the pupil can discern main ideas and essential details.

A pupil's performance on an oral reading test will reveal faulty reading habits and mastery of the skills of word recognition and word analysis. A diagnostic silent reading test will bring to light strengths and weaknesses in comprehension, meaning vocabulary, and study skills. Entering these difficulties on a reading checklist (fig. 8.1) will provide a useful guide in pinpointing appropriate correction. Converting scores on oral and silent reading tests into grade scores will also prove helpful in highlighting a pupil's general level of competence.

Determine the Pupil's Potential

Mental ability as determined by intelligence tests is widely used as a measure of learning capacity. Other things being equal, an intelligent child has more reading potential than a child of limited intelligence.

Intelligence test scores can be expressed in terms of a mental age (M.A.) and an intelligence quotient (I.Q.). These scores mean different things, and it is helpful for a teacher to understand the difference. Mental age refers to mental maturity or the level of a child's mental development. Therefore, a mental age of 10.0 on a given test means that the child can accomplish intellectual tasks on a level of difficulty which an average ten-year-old child can cope with successfully. The M.A. is a valuable score because it can be compared with other age scores.

The I.Q. refers to the rate at which a child develops intellectually. A child with an I.Q. of 125 is growing 1.25 years mentally for each year of his chronological development; a child with an I.Q. of 75 advances 0.75 years mentally for each year of chronological age (C.A.). Since I.Q. is equal to MA/CA × 100, a ten-year-old child with an I.Q. of 125 has a mental age of 12.5 years, and a ten-year-old child with an I.Q. of 75 possesses a mental age of 7.5 years.

Group tests can be used to obtain mental maturity scores. Most primary tests use pictures and do not limit retarded readers. However, above the third grade, many group intelligence tests require reading. This is why a test such as the *California Test of Mental Maturity* is particularly valuable. It provides both verbal and nonverbal assessments. A pupil whose verbal score is markedly lower than his nonverbal score is usually being penalized by his lack of reading ability.

A factor that should be considered, particularly with group tests, is that poor readers are often completely discouraged because of continued failure and frustration. They develop a defeatist attitude which can easily invalidate intelligence test scores. Many disabled readers with this attitude take tests in a perfunctory manner. Therefore, pupils with intelligence quotients of 75 or lower and those showing a variability of ten or more points on successive administrations should be given an individual intelligence test by a trained examiner.

A number of individual intelligence tests are used by reading specialists and psychologists who work with retarded readers. Two of the most widely used are the *Stanford-Binet Intelligence Scale* and the *Wechsler Intelligence Scale for Children* (WISC). Another test that is popular is the *Peabody Picture Vocabulary Test* (PPVT).

Instruction required = I	Practice needed = P						Mastered the skill = M			
Difficulties	Correction									
	Instructional Periods									
	1	2	3	4	5	6	7	8	9	10
A. FAULTY READING HABITS										
1. Omits words										
2. Inserts words										
3. Substitutes words										
4. Repeats words										
5. Reverses words or word parts										
6. Reads word by word										
7. Vocalizes excessively										
8. Ignores punctuation										
9. Loses place										
10. Points to words										
11. Expressionless reading										
12. Faulty voice volume or pitch										
13. Poor book-body position										
14. Head movements										
15. Poor enunciation										
B. SIGHT VOCABULARY										
1. Faulty configuration clues										
2. Faulty contextual clues										
3. Faulty phonetic analysis using										
a. initial sounds										
b. initial blends										
c. medial sounds										
d. final sounds										
4. Structural analysis										
a. root words										
b. compound words										
c. syllabication										
d. prefixes										
e. suffixes										
f. endings										
C. MEANING VOCABULARY										
1. Oral vocabulary										
2. General vocabulary										
3. Technical vocabulary										
4. Dictionary skills										
D. COMPREHENSION AND STUDY SKILLS										
1. Reading in thought units (phrasing)										
2. Retelling a story										
3. Following a sequence of events										
4. Following directions										
5. Locating central thoughts of paragraphs										
6. Detecting related details										
7. Locating information										
8. Drawing conclusions										
9. Summarizing										
10. Outlining										
11. Reading maps, charts, tables, graphs										
12. Rate of comprehension										
13. Critical reading										

Figure 8.1 *Reading Checklist*

Unlike the *Stanford-Binet Scale*, the *Wechsler Intelligence Scale for Children* not only yields a verbal score, but also a performance score. This has the advantage of giving disabled readers who are obviously deficient in verbal skill an opportunity to demonstrate their potential. Understandably, poor readers are likely to score higher on the Wechsler Test than on the *Stanford-Binet Scale*. Both tests require about forty-five to sixty minutes to give, and it is necessary for the clinician to have special course work in administering and interpreting these tests.

Although more credence can be given to scores obtained from individual intelligence tests than from group tests, caution is still necessary. Bond and Fay report that retarded readers do considerably poorer on the *Stanford-Binet Scale* than do children of equal ability who have no reading problems.[3]

The *Peabody Picture Vocabulary Test* is a shorter and easier test to administer and interpret. In fifteen minutes a teacher can measure the size of a child's oral vocabulary. The resultant I.Q. score proves to be a good index of the child's listening comprehension or auding skill. Determining a child's listening or auding level is an index of potential that is considered valuable by many reading specialists.

Success in a nonlanguage area such as arithmetic is sometimes used as an index of reading potential. Terman has defined intelligence as the ability to deal with abstractions. Thus, there is some basis for believing that the poor reader who handles arithmetic fundamentals successfully has the mental ability needed for successful performance in reading. Sometimes, however, a poor reader with much potential does miserably in arithmetic because habitual frustration growing out of failure in reading results in hatred for school and all subjects associated with it.

Determining a child's reading potential is not a simple matter. Since each criterion has its advantages and disadvantages, its strengths and weaknesses, conscientious teachers will use a suitable combination of criteria to arrive at individual reading-expectancy levels.

Determine the Severity of the Reading Problem

How can one identify severe reading problems and select those pupils who are most likely to benefit from special help in reading? This is an important question which perennially plagues teachers. As Harris states it: "Attempting to serve all usually means giving the right kind of help to none. Lavishing time and energy on the wrong pupils also leads to disappointing results."[4]

A number of formulas and criteria are available for determining the expected reading achievement of pupils. But it is important for teachers to recognize that these will not yield identical levels of expected achievement for the same children. The criterion used most universally for determining the severity of a reading problem and for selecting poor readers for special help involves a comparison of reading and mental maturity. For example, if a child possesses a mental age of ten and reads as well as an eight-year-old, a retardation of two years is evidenced. Since reading scores are most often expressed as grade-placement scores, it is helpful to transmit a mental age into a grade-placement score. This can be done roughly by subtracting five from the mental age. (The assumption is that a child is six years of age in the first grade.) Thus a child with a mental age of twelve has the approximate mental level of an average seventh grader. Should he possess a reading grade-placement score of five, it is estimated that he is reading two grades below his mental level or potential reading level. Is this discrepancy sufficient to warrant concern? Harris suggests the following minima in this regard: ". . . six months in the first three grades, nine months for children in grades four and five, or a year for children above the fifth grade.[5]

The use of mental age as a reading expectancy index leads to an awkward situation when very bright or dull students are considered. Many studies show that bright students do not achieve academically on a level commensurate with their mental age. Dull students, on the other hand, overachieve in this regard. To handle such cases, and others as well, Bond and Tinker suggest calculating a reading expectancy score by the following method: Multiply the student's I.Q. by the number of years he has spent in school and then add 1.0.[6] For a student with an I.Q. of 150 halfway through the seventh grade, his reading expectancy score would be $6.5 \times 1.50 + 1.0$, or 10.75. Investigation has shown that calculations based on this formula are far more realistic than those using mental age alone.[7]

Some school systems use a combination of chronological age and mental age in arriving at an expectancy age.[8] Usually this is contingent on the belief that the older student has a greater apperceptive mass and should be expected, therefore, to read on a level above that of a younger one. Harris is of the opinion that the method is too complicated for school use and is of questionable value.[9]

Some reading authorities do not believe that subtracting reading scores from expectancy scores is the best way of arriving at the degree of retardation. They advocate the use of a ratio. To determine a ratio, the reading score is divided by the expectancy score and is then multiplied by 100 so as to eliminate the decimal point. When there is no difference between reading score and expectancy score, the ratio is 100. When the reading score exceeds the expectancy score, the ratio is above 100, indicating overachievement. And when the expectancy score exceeds the reading score, the ratio that results is below 100, indicating underachievement.

Monroe divides reading grade by expectancy grade and arrives at a Reading Index.[10] A sixth-grade pupil who reads as well as a fourth grader (4.0/6.0) would have a Reading Index of approximately 66. According to

Monroe, a Reading Index under 80 represents serious retardation in reading.

Johnson and Myklebust prefer age scores to grade scores in arriving at an index.[11] They divide reading age by mental age and refer to the resultant ratio as a Learning Quotient. Any learning quotient below 90 is considered serious.

Another method used to determine the severity or degree of reading retardation is to compare a child's level of listening comprehension with his reading achievement level. This can be accomplished by administering the *Sequential Tests of Educational Progress* (*STEP*) or the *Durrell Reading-Listening Series Tests* which have replaced the *Reading Capacity and Achievement Tests*. When the reading capacity score is higher than the reading achievement score, the examiner may conclude that the child involved is not measuring up to his potential in reading.

Teachers can develop their own oral comprehension test for determining the severity of a reading problem by utilizing duplicate forms of a suitable reading-comprehension test. One form should be given orally to the pupils, while the other is administered as a silent reading test. Poor readers with marked potential will score higher on the form they were given orally: the greater the discrepancy, the greater will be the promise of reading potential.

When using listening comprehension to judge the severity of a reading problem, the examiner should remember that the retarded reader's opportunity for acquiring a good vocabulary, as well as an understanding of written material, is usually poorer than that of the good reader. The language the underprivileged student may have heard seldom includes the unusual words encountered on vocabulary tests. What is more, written prose is often more complex structurally than that which is spoken. As a consequence, a poor reader may be bewildered by the unusual language and organization of paragraphs read aloud from a silent reading test.

Identify Hazards to Learning and Discover Causal Factors

Both educational and noneducational hazards to learning are usually present in various degrees of severity. While these hazards tend to interfere with learning, their influence upon individuals differs widely, both in form and intensity. If a corrective program of instruction is to succeed, individual hazards to learning must be discovered. Therefore, identifying the specific hazards that are operating as causal factors in retarding and inhibiting an individual's learning becomes a vital part of the diagnostic process.

A corrective program of instruction not only seeks to correct specific individual difficulties in reading whenever possible, but also eliminates or ameliorates causal factors, both primary and contributory. To locate the hazards which act as causal factors, an objective and impartial interpretation of all data is necessary. This involves a careful study and analysis of available information that has been gathered through observation, interviews, cumulative records, and formal and informal tests.

Summarize and Record Data

Enter all significant and relevant diagnostic data gathered in steps one through five on Part I of the Diagnostic Reading Summary, figure 8.2.

Enter the difficulties in oral and silent reading that were discovered in step 2 on the Reading Checklist, figure 8.1.

Interpret Data

The data gathered from informal and formal testing and school records must be analyzed carefully to determine a pupil's reading strengths and weaknesses, faulty habits, and other causes of failure. From this analysis a corrective program must be formulated and recorded on Part 2 of the Reading Summary.

Institute the Appropriate Corrective Program

On Part 3 of the Reading Summary enter the suitable corrective program, indicating skills to be corrected, types and difficulty of the instructional material to be employed, special methods recommended, and areas for recreational reading.

SUMMARY

All children who are severely retarded in reading and exhibit behavioral traits indicating frustration and aversion for learning reflect problems that are often difficult to diagnose and to correct. It now becomes imperative to determine the child's potential, existing hazards to learning, mental maturity, optimum instructional level, interests, and preferred methods of learning. Causal factors must be discovered and eliminated or ameliorated and the child's self-confidence restored. Screening tests, nonlanguage intelligence tests, listening comprehension tests, oral and silent reading tests, and personality tests are needed. In severe cases a thorough diagnosis is essential, one involving all seven steps described in this chapter. Records of the diagnosis and correction undertaken should be kept and made a part of the child's longitudinal history.

Utilization of self-directed corrective material described in chapters 12, 13, and 14 can be readily implemented for all retarded readers by classroom teachers within the framework of their scheduled activities. Recreational reading is a vital supplement to any corrective program. Children with severe psychological and emotional problems may require the services of a school psychologist and a special teacher of reading.

Pupil_____ School_____ Grade_____ Age_____

Teacher_____ Date_____

Attendance_____ Scholarship_____

Onset of Reading Problem_____

Part I   Diagnostic Data

Oral Reading Test_____ Silent Reading Test_____

Oral Reading Scores: Accuracy_____Comprehension_____Rate_____

Grade Equivalents: Accuracy_____ Comprehension _____Rate _____

Silent Reading Scores: Comprehension _____Meaning Vocabulary_____ Rate_____

Grade Equivalents: Comprehension _____Meaning Vocabulary_____ Rate_____

Group Intelligence Test_____

Date_____M.A. (Total)_____ Language M.A._____ Nonlanguage M.A._____

I.Q. (Total)_____Language I.Q. _____ Nonlanguage I.Q. _____

Auding Test _____ Auding Level _____

Part II   Interpretation

Oral Reading Retardation: From Grade_____From Nonlanguage M.A._____

From Auding Level_____

Silent Reading Retardation: From Grade_____ From Nonlanguage M.A._____

From Auding Level_____

Appropriate Instructional Level_____ Independent Reading Level_____

Potential Reading Level_____

Nature of the Reading Problem_____

_____

Severity of the Reading Problem_____

_____

Figure 8.2   *Diagnostic Reading Summary*

Noneducational Hazards to Learning

Health _____

Hearing _____

Vision _____

Personal Adjustment _____

Out of School Environment _____

Hazards to Learning in Need of Correction _____

Language Barrier _____

School Program Designed to Promote Improved Conditions for Learning

_____

_____

_____

_____

Specific Reading Difficulties

Prevalent Errors from Informal Oral Reading _____

_____

Prevalent Errors in Oral Reading Test _____

_____

_____

Difficulties in Silent Reading _____

_____

_____

Faulty Reading Habits _____

_____

Figure 8.2   (*continued*).

Part III Correction

Recommended Improvement Program in Reading

Reading Skills to Be Corrected and Mastered

Word Perception _____

_____

Word Analysis _____

_____

Meaning Vocabulary _____

_____

Comprehension _____

_____

Study Skills _____

Rate of Comprehension _____

_____

Corrective Material Recommended _____

_____

Difficulty of Material _____ Special Methods Recommended _____

_____

_____

Fields of Interest for Recreational Reading

_____

_____

Referral to Reading Specialist

_____

_____

Conference with Parents

_____

_____

Figure 8.2 (*continued*).

Diagnostic Steps	Problems to be Explored	Instruments	Procedures
1. Identify the retarded reader	Low scholarship No interest in school Textbooks too difficult Overage for grade Behavioral difficulty Reading difficulty	Observation Interviews Cumulative records Oral reading Group silent reading tests	Evaluate performance in oral and silent reading

2. Determine the nature of the reading problem	Instructional level
	Independent reading level
	Reading habits
	Reading skills
	  Sight vocabulary
	  Word analysis
	  Meaning vocabulary
	  Comprehension
	  Rate of comprehension
	  Study habits and skills
	Interest in reading
		Observation
		Reading Inventory
		Oral Reading Test
		Diagnostic Silent Reading Test
			Locate weaknesses in word recognition, word analysis, comprehension, and reading habits

3. Determine the pupil's potential	Level of mental maturity on nonlanguage intelligence tests Level of listening comprehension	Nonlanguage group intelligence tests Individual intelligence test Listening comprehension test	Convert scores on intelligence tests and listening comprehension test to grade and age scores
4. Determine the severity of the reading problem	Extent of retardation from grade and potential	Nonlanguage intelligence tests Listening comprehension test Oral and silent reading tests	Apply formulas described on page 211

Figure 8.3 *Summary of the Diagnostic Program*

Diagnostic Steps	Problems to be Explored	Instruments	Procedures
5. Identify hazards to learning and discover causal factors	Educational hazards Noneducational hazards	Observation Interviews Behavior Inventories Screening tests in vision and hearing Personality tests	Administer and interpret screening tests Determine preferred method of learning Locate factors that inhibit learning Consult special workers
6. Summarize and record data	Instructional level Independent reading level Reading difficulties Retardation in reading Specific hazards present	Diagnostic Reading Summary pages 217-219 Diagnostic Reading Checklist page 212	Enter data on Reading Summary Enter reading difficulties on Reading Checklist
7. Analyze Reading Checklist data; Reading Summary, Part I; and school records	Summarize findings	Reading Checklist; Reading Summary, Part I; School Records	Formulate corrective program
8. Summarize formulated corrective program based on Reading Summary, Parts I and II, and school records	How learning may be facilitated and how reading difficulties may be corrected	Reading Checklist; Reading Summary, Parts I and II; Observation, Interviews, and School Records	Record corrective program on Reading Summary, Part III

Figure 8.3   (*continued*)

PROBLEMS FOR ORAL AND WRITTEN DISCUSSION

1. Select two or more tests useful in evaluating a pupil's sight vocabulary. Describe and evaluate the tests.
2. Select two or more tests useful in evaluating a pupil's meaning vocabulary. Describe and evaluate the tests.
3. Select two or more tests useful in evaluating a pupil's competence in word analysis. Describe and evaluate the tests.
4. What is the significant difference between immediate recall and delayed recall in a word-recognition test?
5. Compute the language M.A.s and the nonlanguage M.A.s for four or more of your retarded readers and compare the results with their appropriate instructional level in reading. Interpret the results.
6. Administer a reading inventory to a retarded reader, an average reader, and an accelerated reader in a given grade and determine the instructional level, the independent reading level, and the frustration level for each pupil.
7. Select a retarded reader and apply all tests, procedures, and computations needed to complete the Reading Summary (fig. 8.2). Interpret the results.

Notes

1. EDWARD W. DOLCH, "How to Diagnose Children's Reading Difficulties by Informal Classroom Techniques," *Reading Teacher* 6 (1953):10-14.
2. ALBERT J. HARRIS and EDWARD SIPAY, *How to Increase Reading Ability*, 6th ed. (New York: David McKay Co., 1975), pp. 168-169.
3. GUY L. BOND and LEO C. FAY, "A Comparison of the Performance of Good and Poor Readers on the Individual Items of Stanford-Binet Scale, Forms L and M," *Journal of Educational Research* 43 (1950):475-479.
4. ALBERT J. HARRIS, *How to Increase Reading Ability*, 4th ed. (New York: David McKay Co., 1961), p. 299.
5. Ibid.
6. GUY L. BOND and MILES A. TINKER, *Reading Difficulties: Their Diagnosis and Correction*, 3rd ed. (New York: Appleton-Century-Crofts, 1973), p. 100-101.
7. Ibid.
8. HARRIS, *How to Increase Reading Ability*, p. 300.
9. Ibid., p. 301.
10. MARION MONROE, *Children Who Cannot Read* (Chicago: University of Chicago Press, 1932).
11. DORIS J. JOHNSON and HELMER R. MYKLEBUST, *Learning Disabilities: Educational Principles and Practices* (New York: Grune & Stratton, 1967).

10 The Corrective Program in Reading

CORRECTIVE INSTRUCTION IN READING

There is one question uppermost in the minds of conscientious teachers everywhere: How best can I teach boys and girls who are reading far above or below their grade placement?

This question is particularly pressing because the problem of variability in achievement is always with us. A retardation of 25 percent or more and an acceleration of a like amount in reading are prevalent in elementary classrooms everywhere. Third- and fourth-grade teachers encounter a range of talent covering five or more grades. And disconcerting though it may be, the situation becomes worse in this regard as one moves up the educational ladder. Fifth- and sixth-grade teachers are likely to find a still greater range. What is the answer to the chronic problem imposed by extreme heterogeneity in every grade?

Limitations of Group Instruction

With group instruction, the retarded reader is usually confronted with instructional material on a frustration level of difficulty in every subject throughout the school day.

The answer cannot be found in having all children use the same reader, cover the same pages, and answer the same questions. The school that prescribes or encourages a program for all children consisting of the same methods and the same curricular experiences breeds mediocrity. *Such a school is setting the stage for a human drama of failure and discouragement for some of its pupils and boredom for others. In such a system, scholarship difficulties and behavior problems are sure to flourish.*

Group instruction, the prevailing method used in present-day schools, consists of maximum teacher direction and minimum pupil motivation and participation. At its best, group instruction may provide differentiated assignments, individual projects, and special activities. Even then, however, it leaves much to be desired in terms of the systematic and sequential learning experiences required for developing better readers.

It is good to remember that instruction is not an end in itself. Learning is the end product, and instruction is but a means to this end. Learning, the goal of all instruction, engenders growth and total mastery.

Although learning is an individual experience, it should not be assumed that all instruction must be individualized. Group instruction proves quite effective when all the learners in a class have attained the necessary state of readiness. Children with good listening vocabularies and normal experiences in auding can acquire information and develop concepts just by listening to the teacher. Oral presentation by the teacher, then, proves an effective medium for imparting information. Similarly, when a teacher employs visual aids, all children are usually able to profit. Their learning is limited, of course, by the degree of their native intelligence, experiential background, attitudes, interests, and other conditioning factors.

The story is quite different, however, when a teacher requires all children to read the same material. Proficiency in reading skills is now the all-important factor. Those who are retarded in reading skills find the text too difficult and suffer confusion and frustration. They fail to profit from this kind of group instruction until they have attained a facility with written language (reading) that is comparable to their facility with spoken language.

It is recognized that as a phase of the developmental program, specific reading difficulties arise which require practice on specific skills in which a group is deficient. Group correction directed by the teacher can be effective in such instances if the difficulty of the material employed for corrective work is on an appropriate instructional level.

The most glaring deficiency of group instruction grows out of its failure to provide adequately for both retarded and accelerated readers. It also fails to provide for average readers who have special handicaps or disabilities.

Group instruction tends to be teacher directed, employing extrinsic rather than intrinsic methods of motivation. Frequently, children feel they are working for the teacher. With individualized correction they soon discover they are working for themselves at their own rate to overcome their own deficiencies.

Recitation during group instruction is frequently wasteful since each child actually participates for only a fractional part of the class period. Individualized instruction gives each child an opportunity to work independently and to function effectively every moment of the instructional period.

Tutoring has proved effective in clinical settings where a clinician is assigned one child. Unfortunately, classroom teachers do not enjoy the luxury of a one-to-one teacher-pupil ratio. With thirty or forty, or more, pupils in a classroom, it becomes impossible to implement an effective program of tutoring for the retarded readers. Working with a single pupil conceivably could consume a teacher's entire time.

Principles Underlying Corrective Instruction

The following practices and conditions are considered basic to a program of corrective instruction.

1. Learn all you can about the nature of each child and his specific reading problem. As part of the diagnosis, consult his cumulative folder, and catalog all important aspects of his growth. This involves valid measurements of his mental maturity, oral and silent reading levels, and proficiency in various subject matter fields. Other essentials entail awareness of the child's interests, hobbies, attitudes, and personality pattern. Work habits, too, should be scrutinized. General health and physical fitness with particular emphasis on vision and hearing must not be overlooked. Be alert to manifestations of sensory defects. In short, all facets of the child's reading readiness and hazards to learning must be considered.

2. Do not assume that an awareness of difficulties and hazards to a child's progress is enough. Appropriate ameliorative or corrective measures must be initiated if anything worthwhile is going to be accomplished. If, for example, a child with a physical defect is encountered, he should be referred to the proper specialist. Thus, a child with a visual problem would be brought to the attention of an optometrist or oculist for fitting of suitable corrective lenses. Only after correction is made can one be confident that this impediment to learning no longer exists.

3. Build a warm relationship with each pupil and recognize that this relationship is basic to his mental health and academic achievement. The child who likes his teacher is more highly motivated to overcome handicaps than the child who is indifferent to his teacher. One way to establish the kind of rapport essential to success is through personal conference. Convince the child by what you do and tell him you are his friend. Usually, a child who repeatedly has met failure in reading needs a sympathetic and understanding adult who can help him rebuild feelings of adequacy. Be optimistic about the possibilities of improvement by showing the child you have confidence in his ability to achieve. Help the child understand the nature of his reading problem and provide him with the tools that will enable him to improve.

4. Give the pupil insight into his strengths and weaknesses and indicate the goals toward which he is working. The child who has no idea where he is going is like a ship without a port. He may never reach a destination.

5. Begin by concentrating on a pupil's strengths. Then as he gains self-esteem and increased confidence gradually start working on areas of weakness.

6. Remember that pupils learn through doing. If the teacher does the doing, little pupil learning will result. By using materials that are self-directing and self-evaluating, pupils will become actively engaged in the process of teaching themselves.

7. Help a pupil discover and capitalize on his preferred mode or modes of learning. Some children learn faster when they see words, others when they hear them, and still others when they feel them. It is important, therefore, for a teacher to identify a pupil's preferred mode or modes of learning.

8. Recognize that overlearning is an essential part of mastery. However, repetition consisting of isolated drill is to be avoided since it usually is ineffective and at times can have a deadening effect on interest. If repetition is to be effective, it must consist of practice on meaningful material of appropriate difficulty.

9. Acquire and develop corrective instructional materials that allow children to work *independently* in overcoming their weaknesses and consolidating their strengths. Such materials provide simple directions for doing specific exercises and should be accompanied by answers. *Self-directed materials* which permit *individualized corrective instruction* include reading games, programmed learning materials, workbook exercise files, tape recordings, magic slates, electric boards, etc. These and many other self-directed approaches to learning are discussed in more detail in chapters 12, 13, and 14.

10. Encourage pupils to create instructional materials. Many children show considerable inventive power in creating new games and activities. Needless to say, pupil involvement of any kind is a spur to increased achievement.

11. Self-directed material, in and of itself, is not effective unless it relates to individual reading difficulties. The nature of a pupil's reading difficulties must be discovered by the teacher, and the self-directed material chosen to correct them must be appropriate in terms of difficulty, content, and interest.

12. Recognize that pupils differ in rate of learning just as they differ in maturity and level of achievement. If pupils are to attain personal goals, they must be permitted to progress at their own rate of learning. This can be achieved realistically through the use of self-directed instructional material of appropriate difficulty.

13. To facilitate individualized correction provide each child with a small activity notebook on which his name appears. All such notebooks are kept by the teacher and are made available to pupils during those periods when the group engages in corrective work. Each notebook lists by date corrective activity which the instructor feels is most appropriate for the child. A sample activity sheet from a notebook is given here.

> May _____, 19_____
>
> a. In SRA Laboratory 3a, read selection _____ and answer questions _____. Check your answers. If you miss more than three, read the selection again.
>
> b. Get Exercise 28 from the workbook file. Complete it and then check your answers.
>
> c. Work with Harry on card _____, level _____. (Durrell's Word Analysis Practice.) Ask your teacher for help if you get stuck on any of the words.
>
> d. Work with Flash-X level _____, card _____.
>
> e. On Table 2, you'll find many books on your reading level. Find one you like and start reading it.

14. Since we know that nothing succeeds like success, one must be sure to use instructional materials geared to the child's intellectual and educational levels. By beginning at the learner's level of accomplishment (with retarded readers it often is wise to begin slightly below this level), further failure, frustrations, and discouragement can be avoided. When in doubt as to the difficulty level of an ungraded book, it is very helpful to have the child "try it on for size" by having him read several passages orally.

15. Capitalize on each reader's interests by introducing or encouraging pupils to select books and materials through a recreational reading program which coincides with these interests. In this way, reading becomes a vital and worthwhile experience for the child. "Here is something," he says to himself, "that I really want to know about."

16. Implicit in the foregoing conditions is the need for a great variety of reading materials. These materials must vary not only in difficulty, but also in content and interest appeal. Helping the right books come in contact with the right children is foundational to an individualized reading program. In this connection, it is important for a teacher to provide guidance in the choice of books. Some children are prone to choose books that are too difficult. Remember that the ultimate goal of any reading program is to develop a love of reading in the child.

17. Corrective instructional material should be designed to unfold gradually and systematically a logical sequence of skills or concepts to be mastered. It must be of optimum difficulty for the learner. A child should not be introduced to more difficult material until he has thoroughly mastered all that is foundational or prerequisite to it.

18. Evaluate both developmental and corrective instruction at frequent intervals to determine their effectiveness. An inventory of individual

reading difficulties prepared by the teacher will serve as a useful guide. If what you are doing is not paying learning dividends, renovate your approach. Keep in mind that learning and not teacher-dominated instruction is the goal.

19. Help each pupil evolve charts of various types and descriptions as a means of recording achievement in a dramatic way. Such charts, particularly if constructed by the pupil rather than forced on him by the teacher, are valuable incentives to improvement in learning and useful guides for the teacher in planning individual instructional programs.

20. Do not make learning such a serious matter that it ceases to be rewarding. Use games to add spark to repetitive activity and do not overlook the value of humor in the classroom. Humor can do much to add spice to what may be deadening fare. Children who see humor in their errors and problems are less likely to experience frustration. What is more, children who enjoy their classroom and their teacher become satisfied customers who are eager to come back for more.[1]

21. Establish rapport with the parents of the child involved. Inform them about the child's status in reading ability and give a conservative estimate as to what progress may be expected. Whenever possible, give the parents something to do as part of the corrective program.

ADVANTAGES OF INDIVIDUALIZED SELF-DIRECTED CORRECTION

Since reading difficulties of specific pupils differ in number, type, and severity, correction should be individualized. If it is not, the unique array of problems peculiar to each individual cannot be met.

By utilizing *self-directed* material which provides practice in those skills and abilities each child has failed to master, corrective instruction can be *individualized* and made available to all who need it. When the instructional materials are of an appropriate level of difficulty, each pupil can work independently and successfully at his own rate. Consequently, pupils become motivated as they progress. As they become proficient at working independently, they gain skill in evaluating their own performance. Their teacher is relieved of the time-consuming activity of working individually with each child in need of corrective work and is able to direct group and individual projects simultaneously.

Severely retarded readers in the intermediate and upper grades usually are deficient in the basic reading skills of word perception. A reading difficulty at these levels can best be met through *individualized instruction* following a sound diagnosis. When the principles of this approach are understood and appropriate *self-directed* materials employed, reading problems will be minimized. As a result, scholarship problems will be resolved.

Corrective materials in reading tend to fall into two categories: teacher-made and commercial. Teacher-made instructional materials frequently consist of original games, while commercial or published materials encompass games, word lists, workbooks, multilevel materials, devices, and mechanical instruments. Most published materials are teacher-directed. However, in many instances these can be made self-instructive by simplifying directions and by providing answers which make self-evaluation possible.

IMPLEMENTING A SELF-DIRECTED PROGRAM

To implement a self-directed corrective program teachers begin by acquiring basal readers and supplementary books on several grade levels. These include a good classroom library of books for retarded, average, and superior readers. In addition teachers must have an array of teacher-made and commercial material that is multileveled in design. Included in this array may be kits, workbooks, programmed material, games, exercises, and mechanical devices of various types and descriptions. It is important that teachers design these materials to be self-directed. This will enable them to do developmental work with normal and accelerated readers, while the retarded readers are pursuing individualized self-directed activities independently without frustration or loss of attention to the tasks at hand. *Chapters 12, 13 and 14 contain lists of instructional materials that are in most instances self-directed or that can be made self-directed.*

After teachers have acquired a rich collection of self-directed corrective materials, they must locate pupils who can profit from their use. Helpful in this regard are reading inventories, informal and formal reading tests—both oral and silent—and critical observation. With these instruments the teacher soon knows his/her pupils' instructional levels as well as the specific difficulties with which they need help. At this juncture, all that remains is selecting the particular corrective material developed to help eliminate each child's specific reading difficulties. *In summary, a corrective program becomes a reality when the teacher sees through the child and then sees the child through.*

It must be remembered that self-directed materials will not prove effective unless they are used properly. One must keep in mind that we are seeking to correct learning and reading difficulties peculiar to each individual. If the same instructional material is assigned to a group of retarded readers, it will not prove effective even if the pupils are permitted to proceed at their own rate. While the instructional material may appear to be individualized, no provision would have been made for a diversity in individual instructional levels, variance in reading difficulties, preferred methods of learning, or variability in interests.

Assuming a 25 percent retardation in reading with a class of thirty pupils, a teacher will have seven or eight pupils in need of remediation. Individualized instruction for these pupils will vary from individual activities to group activities, depending on the skills to be mastered and the materials and techniques used by the teacher. If, for example, the entire group demonstrates a basic sight vocabulary deficiency of service words, a group game such as Look might be employed. On the other hand, if a single child in this group does not know the initial consonant sounds, specific pages from a workbook or specific exercises or games might be assigned individually to help overcome the deficiency.

Teachers should be reminded that an individualized corrective approach to reading is not in addition to but in place of a large portion of the time currently devoted to group instructional practices. The time previously devoted exclusively to teacher-directed group instruction now emphasizes early diagnosis to discover individual reading difficulties, followed by self-directed corrective instruction. Teachers will discover that while they are supervising the activities of the normal and accelerated readers retarded readers are successfully pursuing self-administering corrective material independently.

Nature of Self-Directed Instructional Materials

Little additional teacher time and effort are needed to make individualized reading materials and exercises self-directed. If a problem does arise, it is likely to center around two areas: (1) simplified directions which will enable pupils to work independently and (2) ways whereby materials can be made self-corrective.

Directions must be simple and specific and must be written on the pupil's independent or free reading level. If directions have a difficulty level that coincides with a pupil's instructional level, he will be unable to understand them without the aid of the teacher.

For example, directions reading "To reinforce your sentence comprehension select the most appropriate words from those offered and insert them in the sentences" are more understandable if they are changed to read: "Read the first sentence. Now look at the words at the bottom of the page. Choose the best word and write it in the blank. Do the same for the other sentences."

Pikulski and Jones[2] make the following suggestions to teachers who wish to write directions that can be easily read by children.

1. Employ syntactic structures that are similar to those the children use in their own speech.
   a. Adhere to the following pattern: subject, verb, direct object or complement.
   b. Use simple declarative or imperative sentences whenever possible.

2. Use the conjunctions "and, how, for," and "as," since they have been found to be the easiest for children to read and understand.
3. Substitute simple vocabulary for words that may not be understood. For example: *find out* for *determine* and *guess* for *predict*.
4. Discuss concept-related words that may be encountered in written directions so that they become a part of children's listening and speaking vocabularies. Writing the words on the blackboard as they are discussed is also helpful.
5. Construct a picture dictionary for children that will have illustrations to convey the meaning of concept-related words.
6. Number directions rather than using a story-like prose format.
7. Make sure directions are written legibly. Typewritten directions with generous use of open spaces are recommended.
8. Use color and underlining to highlight key words and to focus attention on important points.
9. Remember that children are more likely to struggle to follow directions if the activity involved is of interest to them. Careful selection of activities and the use of discussion to arouse children's interest are recommended.

Ways whereby materials can be made self-corrective are as follows:

1. Write answers on the backs of exercises.
2. Write answers upside down in a space somewhat removed from the focal point of attention.
3. Cover answers with a flap which can be folded back.
4. Write answers on a small card which can be inserted in a library card pocket.
5. Write answers on cards which can be filed in an answer box.
6. Write answers on sheets of acetate. These can be placed over exercises for purposes of evaluation.
7. Cut appropriately located holes in sheets of paper or oaktag to form an answer mask. These can be placed over exercises for purposes of evaluation.
8. Cut a picture into parts after pasting it on oaktag. Write answers on the backs of these parts. On another piece of oaktag, write matching problems. As the pupil locates answers, he begins to build a picture. Incorrect answers result in a jumbled picture.
9. Separate questions and answers by a jigsaw cut. If the pieces can be fitted together, the pupil is assured that a correct association has been made.
10. Cut five answer windows in an envelope. On each question card write five answers with only the correct answer positioned so that it will be exposed in an answer window when the card is slipped into the envelope.

Some teachers are concerned about making answers available to their pupils. "They'll cheat," the teachers say.

It is true that some pupils may cheat. However, cheating inhibits learning, and such activity will be minimal if teachers emphasize learning rather than grading of practice materials. And in spite of dishonesty, pupils who do find the correct answers are bound to make some valid associations so that learning will take place.

SUMMARY

When several pupils in a classroom are retarded in reading skills, the teacher has to cope with a diversity of individual difficulties. This makes undifferentiated group instruction highly ineffective. Individualized and self-directed corrective materials selected to provide remediation for known difficulties are needed. These self-instructive materials permit pupils to proceed at their own rate of learning while they are motivated by an awareness of personal goals.

A corrective program using self-directed corrective material involves a number of steps. (1) Collecting an array of multilevel reading materials—books, workbooks, exercises, kits, games, etc.; (2) Determining the reading status of each pupil in terms of his/her independent, instructional, and frustration levels and pinpointing specific undesirable habits and weaknesses; (3) Selecting the particular corrective material needed to eliminate each child's difficulties and to provide practice that is systematic and sequential in its development; (4) Encouraging recreational reading, which is needed to reinforce learning and to ensure mastery of basic skills.

PROBLEMS FOR ORAL AND WRITTEN DISCUSSION

1. Prepare a corrective program in reading for a pupil of average intelligence who is retarded two years in word analysis and three years in comprehension. Indicate the type of materials you would recommend.
2. Select a teacher-directed workbook in reading and make the necessary revision in the directions for five or more exercises in order to make them self-directed.
3. Select five principles of corrective instruction and discuss their implementation in a corrective reading program.
4. Evaluate the place of workbooks as self-corrective materials.
5. Procure several workbooks in reading on two or more levels of difficulty. Dissect, combine, and reassemble the workbooks to form a ready file of corrective material.

Notes

1. HAP GILLILAND and HARRIETT MAURITSEN, "Humor in the Classroom," *Reading Teacher* (May 1971):753-756.
2. JOHN J. PIKULSKI and MARGARET B. JONES, "Writing Directions Children Can Read," *The Reading Teacher* (March 1977), pp. 598-602.

Selected Readings

EKWALL, ELDON E., *Diagnosis and Remediation of the Disabled Reader.* Boston: Allyn and Bacon, Inc., 1976, chap. 10.

EKWALL, ELDON E., *Teacher's Handbook on Diagnosis and Remediation in Reading.* Rockleigh, New Jersey: Allyn and Bacon, Inc., 1979, chap. 9.

HARRIS, ALBERT, "Practical Suggestions for Remedial Teachers," in Diane J. Sawyer (ed.) *Disabled Readers: Insight Assessment, Instruction.* Newark, Delaware: International Reading Association, 1980.

HARRIS, ALBERT, and SIPAY, EDWARD R. *How to Increase Reading Ability.* 6th ed. New York: David McKay Co., 1975, chap. 13.

LAPP, DIANE and FLOOD, JAMES. *Teaching Reading to Every Child.* New York: Macmillan Publishing Co., Inc., 1978, chap. 15.

SCHUBERT, DELWYN, ed. *Readings in Reading: Practice-Theory-Research.* New York: Thomas Y. Crowell Co., 1968, selection 57.

11 Correcting Faulty Reading Habits

Pupils who are in need of corrective help in reading often show one or more faulty reading habits. This chapter is devoted to fourteen faulty reading habits accompanied by specific suggestions for their correction.

OMISSIONS

The following suggestions are helpful for pupils who habitually omit words as they read.

1. Have the pupil reread the sentence in which he has made an omission. In this way the examiner can determine if the word omitted was unknown or whether carelessness was involved. In the case of the former, instruction in word-attack skills is needed or easier material should be introduced.
2. Have the pupil undergo a visual examination. Sometimes muscular imbalance and even a blind spot may be responsible for the omission of words or parts of words when reading.
3. Have the pupil listen to a tape recording of his oral reading as he silently follows the printed version looking for omissions.
4. Ask specific questions which call for information dependent on words omitted by the pupil.
5. Provide a marker for the pupil who is a place-loser. Encourage him to keep his place by holding the marker above the line being read rather than below the line being read. When this is done, the marker is less likely to get in the way.

INSERTIONS

Many poor readers add words not found in the passages they are reading. These techniques are suggested to help such readers overcome this habit.

1. Have the pupil listen to a tape recording of his oral reading and ask him to audit the recording.

2. Type the sentence in which the pupil made a word addition in two ways: as it appeared in the text and as the pupil read it. Then have the pupil carefully read the two versions and discover the difference.
3. Read aloud with the pupil or have other pupils read with him in unison.
4. Make phrase and sentence cards involving misread material.
5. Have the pupil point to each word as it is read. Although pointing is an undesirable practice, it can be a helpful temporary expedient for eliminating the tendency to add words.
6. Design questions which bring word additions to the reader's attention. For example: Can you prove that the dog was big? Did the author say that Topsy was a "giant" dog?

SUBSTITUTION

For pupils who excessively substitute one word for another as they read the following practices are recommended.

1. Make sure the material being used is not beyond the comprehension of the pupil.
2. Evaluate the pupil's method of word analysis. Lack of word-analysis skill may be a reason for needless substitutions.
3. Show concern for meaningless substitutions such as *house* for *horse*. Ignore meaningful substitution such as *house* for *home*.
4. Record the pupil's reading and then ask him to audit the recording for substitutions.
5. Provide exercises requiring the pupil to select the proper word from several presented. For example: Jim's father *bit* on a racehorse.

bat

bet

but

6. Make flash cards of words likely to be substituted and play a rummy-type game with them.

REPETITION

A common fault of poor readers is to repeat words and phrases as they read. These suggestions are recommended for a pupil who makes repetitions.

1. Inform the pupil that he is making repetitions. If necessary, demonstrate the nature of the habit without embarrassing him.
2. Allow silent reading before oral reading on a similar passage. If the pupil makes no repetitions on this second exposure, the problem can be attributed to nervousness. Usually it can be disregarded.

3. Check the reading level of the material. Some repetitions are the result of material that is too difficult. A pupil who does not recognize a word may repeat preceding words as a stalling procedure.
4. Have the pupil read in unison with others. Choral reading is helpful in eliminating repetitions.
5. Emphasize reading in thought units.
6. Reassure the pupil. Sometimes repetitions are a manifestation of nervousness.
7. Use the Controlled Reader and other devices that make regression of projected material impossible.
8. Slide a small card in a left-to-right direction as the pupil reads, covering the words just read.
9. Record the pupil's reading and then ask him to audit the recording for repetitions.

REVERSAL

1. Have the pupil type words that are frequently reversed. Through typing, the pupil develops left-to-right orientation that facilitates accurate word perception.
2. Have the pupil categorize typed versions of words frequently confused. For example, *was* and *saw* may be typed in triple-spaced form a number of times and then cut into small squares for categorizing purposes.
3. Compose sentences with blanks in which only one of two readily confused words can logically fit. For example: The natives knelt before the statue of their sun_____." (dog, god).
4. Have the pupil trace troublesome words as he says them. This reinforces awareness of proper letter sequence.
5. Have the pupil write easily reversed words as they are read aloud by the teacher.
6. Draw arrows under troublesome words to highlight the left-to-right movement of the eyes.
7. Use stop-and-go cues by writing the first letter of the troublesome word in green and the final letter in red.
8. Cover the word with a card. Then slide the card to the right exposing the letters in left-to-right progression.

WORD-BY-WORD READING

Word-by-word readers have difficulty reading rapidly and meaningfully because ideas come in phrases, not too often in individual words. For example, the single word *a* carries no thought, no idea. The words *a small* are similarly devoid of meaning. But the three words *a small boy* prove quite meaningful. The word-by-word reader is supplying his mind with words that have little meaning when considered in isolation. Although he is aware of the trees, he misses the forest. The following suggestions are recommended to help the word-by-word reader.

1. Check the reading level of the material. If what is being read is too difficult, the pupil may be encountering many words that cannot be recognized without undue hesitation.
2. Place emphasis on the meaning of what is being read. Pupils who read aloud with little or no concern for meaning are likely to read with no regard for phrasing.
3. Use the tape recorder to provide the pupil with an opportunity to compare his spontaneous speech with his oral reading. Encourage him to read in the way that he speaks.
4. Have the pupil engage in choral reading with pupils who do a good job of phrasing.
5. Read aloud material which you phrase properly. Ask the pupil to imitate you.
6. Read aloud material which is phrased incorrectly. This often evokes laughter and the realization that without proper phrasing meaning is difficult to acquire.
7. Have the pupil listen to the reading of professional performers on radio or television.
8. Provide the pupil / with material / in which you / have drawn lines / (or used parentheses) (to emphasize) (proper phrasing).
9. Use a tachistoscope to provide practice in apprehending phrases.
10. Play phrase bingo with the pupil.

EXCESSIVE VOCALIZATION

Pupils who whisper or make slight movements of the tongue, lips, jaws, or vocal cords while reading silently are handicapped in reading rapidly. Above the third-grade level, most children should read two or three times faster silently than orally. The mind can grasp ideas more rapidly than it is possible to speak them. Any vocalization, no matter how slight, can do nothing but retard reading speed. The following practices are recommended to help a vocalizer.

1. Remind the child that he should discontinue vocalization.
2. Discourage temporarily all oral reading.
3. Provide the pupil with reminders such as holding a pencil or eraser between the teeth when reading silently.

4. Have the pupil chew gum rapidly while reading easy material. This makes articulation impossible because the speech mechanism is too preoccupied to permit it. However, once vocalization is eliminated, discontinue the gum chewing immediately. If you allow it to persist, the pupil may have to cope with another bad habit.

IGNORING PUNCTUATION

The pupil who fails to respond to punctuation marks finds comprehension difficult because he is likely not to separate sentences. Not pausing for commas also can lead to confusion. The following suggestions may help the pupil who ignores punctuation marks.

1. Explain to the pupil the value of punctuation marks.
2. Read aloud a selection in which punctuation marks have been displaced. This is a dramatic way to illustrate the importance of punctuation marks.
3. Ask the student to read aloud a selection in which all punctuation marks have been eliminated. Have him decide where they are to be inserted.
4. Have the pupil follow a passage as he listens to his recorded version of it. Errors are detected and insight is more quickly attained when the pupil acts as his own critic.
5. Color the first letter of each sentence in green, commas in yellow, and periods in red.
6. Condition the pupil to periods by having him lower his voice and pause each time you lower an upraised hand. The hand should be dropped just as the pupil reads the last word in each sentence. Doing this a few minutes daily will result in a conditioned response to periods.

POINTING

The habit of pointing at words when reading should be discouraged. The mind and the eyes can arrive at understanding far more rapidly when not paced by a finger, pencil, or pen. The following suggestions may help the pupil who is dependent on pointing when reading.

1. Have the pupil undergo a thorough visual examination. Muscular imbalance such as exophoria can cause a child to lose his place when reading. This, in turn, results in finger pointing.
2. Provide the pupil with a marker.
3. Have the pupil hold the book with both hands as he reads.
4. Have the pupil sit on his hands as he reads.
5. Have the pupil read material written on the blackboard or projected on a screen.

EXPRESSIONLESS READING

Some pupils read in a monotonous, expressionless voice. The following suggestions are recommended to help this problem.

1. Have the pupil read aloud a simple sentence several times. Each time he is to emphasize a different word. For example:
   a. HE kicked the ball down the stairs.
   b. He KICKED the ball down the stairs.
   c. He kicked the BALL down the stairs.
   d. He kicked the ball DOWN the stairs.
   e. He kicked the ball down the STAIRS.
2. Type a short selection in which certain words have been underlined for increased emphasis for the pupil to read aloud.
3. Offer suggestions to the pupil such as trying to read the scary part of the story so that it really scares the class.
4. Have the pupil practice making his voice happy, angry, fearful, demanding, and so forth.
5. Use plays and poetry to help overcome monotonous voice tones and rhythms.
6. Have the pupil listen to a recording of his voice.

FAULTY VOICE PITCH

Insecurity with resultant tenseness is frequently a cause of a high-pitched voice during oral reading. Teachers who wish to change a child's reading tone need not hesitate because modifications will not injure the vocal apparatus. The following suggestions are recommended to help the pupil with a high-pitched voice.

1. Choose reading material that is too difficult and allow the pupil to read the material silently before attempting to read it aloud.
2. Show the pupil how he sounds when reading in a high pitch but try not to embarrass him.
3. Compare the pitch of the pupil's reading voice with that of his speaking voice. This can be accomplished by having him sustain a long vowel sound while you locate its pitch on a piano keyboard.
4. Find the pupil's proper voice pitch. Begin by having the pupil sing the lowest note he can comfortably produce. Find the pitch on the piano. The pupil's proper voice pitch for reading and speaking is three or four notes above the lowest one he can sing easily.

POOR BOOK-BODY POSITION

Good posture is not only important for general hygiene, but also enhances perception of the printed page. The book or material read should be held 12 to 18 inches away at approximately a 90-degree angle to the eyes. The reader's back should be reasonably straight.

Holding the book at the proper angle encourages proper body position. It helps the pupil to sit up straight and not hunch over the book. Too many pupils bend their backs and hold their heads in a strained position when reading. Soon they experience muscular fatigue which almost empathetically results in mental fatigue that readily vitiates reading efficiency.

Holding the book up has the added advantage of increasing the readability of the text by making the print stand out with greater clarity. Seeing efficiency is increased markedly when material is held at the proper angle to the eyes.

Most stationery shops sell inexpensive book holders that are designed to hold a book at the proper reading angle. Those who are do-it-yourselfers can make their own book holder by screwing two hanger hooks into a board about 6 inches apart.

HEAD MOVEMENTS

Pendulum movements of the head during reading is an unnecessary habit which is not conducive to reading efficiency. Although not particularly harmful, head wagging does expend energy which should go into the reading process. The eyes are capable of moving across lines of print without any need to move the head. Having the pupil rest his chin firmly in the palm of his hand while his elbow is in contact with the desk or table is one way to provide a reminder that will help break the habit.

USING NEGATIVE PRACTICE TO BREAK FAULTY READING HABITS

We have experienced success in helping certain disabled readers through negative practice.[1] Jim, a ten-year-old child of normal intelligence, was an inaccurate reader who skipped words indiscriminatingly with alarming frequency. Positive practice proved ineffective. Diagnostic study of the situation revealed no logical reasons for the problem. In most instances, the words omitted were part of Jim's sight vocabulary. A careful appraisal of visual skills revealed no refractive or fusion difficulties at near point. Since a crystallized habit pattern seemed to be involved, negative practice was introduced in a somewhat disguised form.

Jim was told about a new game called Omission Detective. The teacher began by reading a page aloud, and it was Jim's job to follow the text, watching closely for omissions. Each time he detected an omission, his success was tabulated on a blank sheet of paper. Then it became Jim's turn to read aloud, while his teacher played the role of detective.

In the beginning, the clinician made omissions very obvious. Jim laughed as he checked the blank sheet of paper. "It sounds funny," he said. The clinician agreed, pointing out the bad effects the habit could have on comprehension and why it was advantageous to break the habit. When it was Jim's turn to read aloud, he became more serious. He cleverly tried to conceal the intentionally made omissions, hoping his teacher might not detect them. Usually, however, they were spotted and laughter ensued.

Approximately ten minutes were devoted to playing Omission Detective during each session. Jim was seen twice a week. At the end of four weeks, he rarely skipped words during regular oral reading.

Other successful detective games involving the elimination of substitutions, additions, repetitions, and reversals have been employed. Ingenious teachers can find many situations in the reading area and out of the reading area where negative practice might prove to be of value. The results certainly warrant more teachers' experimenting with the method. So when the usual approaches do not help, give negative practice a try.

Notes

1. KNIGHT DUNLAP, *Habits—Their Making and Unmaking* (New York: Liveright Publishing Corp., 1932).

Selected Readings

EKWALL, ELDON E. *Diagnosis and Remediation of the Disabled Reader.* Boston: Allyn and Bacon, Inc., 1976, pp. 280-285.
EKWALL, ELDON E. *Locating and Correcting Reading Difficulties.* Columbus, Ohio: Charles E. Merrill Publishing Co., 1970.
HARRIS, ALBERT J. and SIPAY, EDWARD R. *How to Increase Reading Ability,* 6th ed. New York: David McKay Co., 1975, chap. 15.
KENNEDY, EDDIE C. *Approaches to Remedial Reading.* Itasca, Illinois: F. E. Peacock Publishers, Inc., 1977, chap. 12.

12 Improving Word Recognition and Word Analysis

This chapter and the two which follow provide a classified and descriptive list of commercial and teacher-made material. Much of the material in these chapters is suitable for individual correction and is self-directed in nature. A sizable percentage of the material takes the form of games, the advantages and disadvantages of which are set forth on pages 291-292. Addresses of the publishers and manufacturers mentioned in this chapter are given in Appendix F.

Each set of materials is accompanied by a brief description of its nature and function as detailed by the publisher along with current prices. Although prices are subject to change, they have been included to give the reader an approximation of the cost of specific items and materials. With few exceptions, little attempt has been made to evaluate these materials. Prospective purchasers should evaluate them in terms of cost, appropriate difficulty, content, function, length, and skills to be corrected.

Pupils in the primary and intermediate grades who are deficient in word-recognition and word-analysis skills are in dire need of help. Teachers need more than basal readers to assist these pupils; they need supplementary intructional materials that will provide individualized practice to overcome specific reading difficulties. The following instructional techniques and materials provide a useful approach to the problem.

EMPHASIZING WIDE READING

Practice on common words and introduction to new words take place most naturally when children engage in easy, pleasurable reading. Individualizing and personalizing a child's reading program requires a knowledge of books and an understanding of the child and his interests. The teacher who is faced with the task of finding the right book for the right child should be guided by the following principles:

1. Utilize the child's present interests. No matter how immature his/her present interests are, it is essential to begin by introducing materials

which are related to them. If the child is given material which he/she sees as vital and functional, interest becomes spontaneous.

2. Provide reading materials which are on or slightly below the pupil's level of reading ability. Easy material is essential for success. And success generates interest.

3. Acquaint yourself with book lists and bibliographies of children's books. These materials simplify finding the right book for the right child. Two excellent books in this regard are *A Place to Start* and *Good Reading for Poor Readers.*[1, 2] Additional suggestions are provided in Appendix F.

UTILIZING WORD LISTS

The vocabulary lists described on pages 181-183 in connection with diagnostic procedures have considerable value in a corrective program for disabled readers. They help answer questions such as the following: What words are found most frequently in primary books? What words should be taught first when working with a disabled reader? What fourth-grade words should a pupil know on sight?

Although compilers of word lists have rendered a great service, certain points should be considered by those who wish to use them (DeBoer and Dallman provide an in-depth study of word lists[3]).

1. If a word list is based in part or in its entirety on the writing vocabulary of adults, it may not apply to the reading vocabulary of elementary school children.

2. Since a child's reading vocabulary is usually larger than his/her writing vocabulary, it is not wise to confine children's reading vocabulary to a list based on writing vocabulary.

3. Strict vocabulary control is likely to be debilitating to content. Content area subjects such as social studies and science will suffer if vocabulary control is too stringent. Remedial teachers should be cognizant of the fact that content field reading usually involves a heavier vocabulary burden.

4. Frequency of use, rather than word difficulty, is provided by vocabulary word lists.

When word lists are used for word study with pupils, meaningful contextual settings should be provided.[4] It is also advisable to employ a variety of approaches to help sustain interest. When possible, have the child evolve a progress chart that will highlight his/her vocabulary growth in a dramatic way.

COMMERCIAL MATERIALS FOR CORRECTING
DEFICIENCIES IN SIGHT VOCABULARY

Most of the following commercial material is designed to encourage the child to attend closely to a word while saying it or while having it said. This look-and-say method capitalizes on the general shape or configuration of words. Needless to say, pupils with reading problems tend to confuse words that have similar shape and that are met again and again in different settings before mastery is achieved.

Other materials such as Match present words with accompanying pictures. Children look at the picture cards and are told the correct words that go with the cards. Later, if a child forgets the words, he/she can check back and look at the pictures again.

1. *Autophonics*, Game 1: A phonetic alphabet game based on vehicles and vehicle driving. The bingolike game is composed of thirty-six different cards, a master card, call card, and markers. (For use with groups of children. $7.95. Warren's.)

2. *Basic Sight Vocabulary Cards*: Instructional materials are for use with slow readers. Included are 220 words which constitute more than 50 percent of all words encountered in ordinary reading. (For use with individual children or children working in pairs. $2.75. Garrard.)

3. *Boggle*: A game consisting of sixteen lettered wooden cubes that are scrambled on a tray. The players race to make words out of adjacent letters, backward, forward, and diagonally. When the time runs out, they compare lists and earn points for words no one else has. Designed for pupils in grade three through college. (For use with two or more players. $7.25. Warren's.)

4. *Build-It*: A word-recognition game for grades three to eight. It requires quick visual perception of the similarities and differences within words. Four decks of cards are involved. (For use with any number of children. $4.50 per deck. Remedial Education Press.)

5. *Context Clues Game*: A board game that asks players to draw a "story card" containing a brief story plus three definitions for an underlined word. Players must choose the correct definitions to advance their tokens on the board. (For use with two to four children. $11.95. Lakeshore.)

6. *Crossword Puzzles* (sixteen sets): Colorful crossword puzzles, 8½ by 11 inches in size. Each set contains eight different exercises. The plastic laminated surface permits easy removal of marking crayon. Difficulty levels vary from first through sixth grade. (For use with individual children or children working in pairs. $2.95 per set. Ideal.)

7. *Durrell's Hand Tachistoscope*: A simple tachistoscope (quick-exposure device) consisting of an oaktag cover, an aperture, a shutter,

and a series of word lists on strips of oaktag board. (For use with individual children or children working in pairs. $3.20. The Psychological Corp.)

8. *Educational Flash Words*: Instructional materials using cards consisting of two sets that help the primary-grade child learn words that are difficult to master through a picture approach. More than 200 sight words are included. (For use with individual children or with a group of children. $2.25 per set. Milton Bradley.)

9. *Educational Password Game*: A game based on a popular television show using basic sight and picture words found in primary and elementary readers. (For use with pairs of children or a group of children. $4.75. Milton Bradley.)

10. *Got a Minute*: A fast word game using a 3-inch clear cube that encases seven wooden lettered cubes and a one-minute timer. Upon flipping the cube, a player has 60 seconds to form as many words as he can. (For use with an individual child or a group of children. $2.98. Warren's.)

11. *Grab*: A sight vocabulary game for remedial or classroom teaching. Three levels are involved: Grab Junior (Sets I and II), Grab Senior (Sets III and IV), and Advanced Grab (Sets V and VI). (For use with two to four children; potentially self-directive. Two sets on any level $2.75. Teacher's Supplies.)

12. *Group Word Teaching Game*: A bingo-type game designed to teach the 220 basic sight words evolved by Dolch. (For use with two or more children; potentially self-directed. $3.00. Garrard.)

13. *Happy Bears Reading Game*: A game in which children learn common nouns by matching pictures with words under them. Since the pairs of pictures differ, attention is drawn to the word under each picture. (For use with individual children; potentially self-directed. $1.50. Garrard.)

14. *Heteronyms*: This set of materials includes 20 common pairs of heteronyms (40 cards in all) each illustrated and labeled at the bottom. Every card has a separate accompanying sentence strip showing the heteronym used in correct context. The cards measure 2¾" x 4½" and are printed on heavy tag. (For use with individual children or children working in pairs. $4.25. Incentives for Learning.)

15. *Homonym Cards*: This game activity helps students learn basic homonym patterns. Forty cards, 2⅛" x 4", are included. Twenty basic homonyms are represented. (For use with individual children or children working in pairs. $2.75. Developmental Learning Materials.)

16. *Homonym Slide Rule*: An ingenious slide rule designed to help students discover the difference between like-sounding words. An outer piece has one set of words printed on the surface. The student writes

homonyms on the erasable side and then verifies his work by sliding the rule. (For use with individual students or students working in pairs. $2.00. E-Z Grader.)

17. *Knock a Number*: This is a concentration game designed to help conquer words such as what, went, want, there, here, etc., as well as commonly reversed words such as saw-was, help-play, there-three, etc. Suggested for grades 1-4. (For use with any number of players. $6.95. Little Brown Bear.)

18. *Linguistic Drill Cards*: A Set of cards containing 240 words that are arranged by linguistic relationship, level of difficulty and numerical position on the Kucera-Francis high frequency word list. (For use with individual children, children working in pairs, or a small group of children under proper direction. $3.00. Kenworthy.)

19. *Make-a-Word Cards*: A set of eighteen 3 by 5 inch cards, accompanied by 240 letters on 1″ x 1″ yellow tag designed to aid in simple identification and formation of words. As an aid to individualized usage, the word cards are printed on both sides with a picture and name of the object included. (For use with an individual child or children working in pairs. $3.50. Developmental Learning Materials.)

20. *Match* (Sets I and II): A reading game consisting of two sets of cards, each set containing half of the ninety-five commonest nouns evolved by Dolch. (For use with one or two children; potentially self-directed. $2.45, per set. Garrard.)

21. *The Monkey Game*: An entertaining game which is designed to bridge the gap between sight vocabulary and phonics for beginning readers. (For two or three children. $3.25. Warren's.)

22. *My First Word Hunt*: A workbook for sight word recognition. Children develop their sight vocabularies by finding and encircling pictured words. (For use with individual children or children working in pairs. $3.95. Teaching Stuff.)

23. *New Linguistic Block Series, Set 1W*: A game consisting of thirty plastic blocks involving words. Also included as part of the set is a forty-eight-page teacher's instruction booklet. A workbook for children can also be purchased. (For use with individual children or with a small group of children. $16.17. Scott, Foresman.)

24. *Noun Puzzles*: Forty-eight noun puzzles are involved. The top section of each puzzle shows an object and the bottom (an interlocking section) provides its printed name. The puzzles are printed on 24 double-sided, 3″ x 4¾″ cards. (For use with individual children or children working in pairs. $5.00. Developmental Learning Materials.)

25. *Pairs Word Game*: A game consisting of three sets of 40 cards, 1¾″ x 2¾″ for matching picture to picture, word to picture, and word to rhyming word. (For use with 1 to 4 children. $2.50. Milton Bradley.)

26. *Perquackey*: A challenging word game in which a child spills out lettered cubes and forms as many single words as possible before the timer runs out. (For one child or a group of children. $3.95. Warren's.)

27. *Picture Words for Beginners*: A matching game which helps primary-grade children add over 100 words to their vocabulary. The child learns to associate pictures with words found in first reading books. (For individual children or with children working in pairs; potentially self-directed. $2.25. Milton Bradley.)

28. *Pictures for Peg Board Classification-Opposites*: A colorful set of 256 pictures and word cards printed on by 4-by-3¼ inch white tagboard for use with a pegboard or a flash cards. (For use with individual children or with a group of children. $7.50 per set. Ideal.)

29. *Popper Words* (Sets I and II): Sets of basic sight words. Popper Words Set I contains the easier one-half of the 220 Basic Sight Vocabulary evolved by Dolch. Popper Words Set II contains the harder one-half of this vocabulary group. (For use with individual children, children working in pairs, or a group of children under proper direction. $2.45 per set. Garrard.)

30. *Probe*: A provocative game in which each player selects a word of twelve or fewer letters which he keeps secret (dictionary may be used in making selections). Other players try to guess the word, letter by letter. Equipment includes four racks, four decks of letter cards, each of a different color and consisting of ninety-six cards, and four letter-card upright holders. The 384 cards in the game provide combinations for thousands of words. (For use with two to four children. $8.50. Parker.)

31. *Rhyming Word Puzzles*: Twenty-four puzzles that are designed to promote the discrimination of rhyming words are provided in this activity. Pictures of rhyming words appear on one side of 3″ x 4¼″ cards. The words themselves are printed on the other side of the cards. Each puzzle is cut into two interlocking pieces so that it is self-corrective. (For use with individual children or children working in pairs. $5.25. Developmental Learning Materials.)

32. *Rummy-Nyms*: A rummy-type game designed to develop a sight vocabulary of synonyms and antonyms. Each set contains one deck of word cards for pairs of synonyms and one deck for pairs of antonyms. (For use with two to six players. $4.95. Little Brown Bear Associates.)

33. *Same or Different Word Cards*: Colored cards, 1½″ by 4¾″, consisting of two sets. Set I contains word pairs differing in one letter only, such as *b/d*. Set II has word pairs that differ in letter arrangement, such as *states/tastes*. (For use with an individual child or children working in pairs. $2.75. Developmental Learning Materials.)

34. *Spello*: This is a word game that helps children develop spelling skills and learn to recognize basic sight words. Over 200 vocabulary words

are graded in difficulty. (For use with an individual child or a small group of children. $12.25. Lakeshore.)

35. *Spill & Spell*: A vocabulary-building game consisting of lettered cubes, shaker, and timer. The object of the game is to build as many words as possible from the letters appearing on the cubes before time runs out. A point system is used to record successes of the players. (For use with two children or a group of children; potentially self-directed. $4.75. Lakehore.)

36. *Synonym Puzzles*: This puzzle series contains 24 reversible puzzles, each introducing three synonyms. The puzzles are die-cut into three interconnecting pieces with one side showing two printed synonyms on either side of a matching color illustration while the reverse puzzle side shows the original two synonyms and introduces a third in sentence context. Each puzzle measures 8½" x 4". (For use with individual children or children working in pairs. $6.75. Incentives for Learning.)

37. *Vocab-Tracks*: This is a dominolike game which covers four areas of a student's basic vocabulary—colors, verbs, short sentences, and definitions. A total of 96 cards measuring 4" x 2⅛" are provided. There are 24 cards in each of the four areas. (For use with two or more children. $3.50. Developmental Learning Materials.)

38. *Word Cards*: Instructional materials consisting of 62 cards for developing instant recognition of high frequency words and for building rebus sentences. (For use with individual children or children working in pairs. $8.40. Houghton Mifflin.)

39. *Word Cover*: Game played like Bingo giving children motivating practice in learning fifteen high-frequency words like *it* and *the*. Each game contains enough cards for ten players. (For use with two to ten children. $3.15. Houghton Mifflin.)

40. *Word-Picture Dominoes* (Sight Words): This is a dominolike game in which seven words (horse, house, girl, bird, dog, boy, and car) are presented. Students match a picture with another one or its printed name. A total of 28 pieces, 1¾" x 3½", are provided. (For use with two or more children. $2.95. Developmental Learning Materials.)

41. *Word Power*: A word-definition game involving skill and luck in which players match synonyms and antonyms. The game consists of a playing board, 336 word cards, and a thirty-four-page vocabulary-building guide. It is designed for pupils in grades three through college. (For use with two or more children. $9.98. Warren's.)

42. *Word Puzzles*: Puzzles providing valuable practice in vocabulary building for kindergarten and first-grade children. Three sets are involved, and each set consists of three boards. (For use with individual children or children working in pairs. $7.83 per set. Scott, Foresman.)

TEACHER-MADE MATERIALS FOR CORRECTING
DEFICIENCIES IN SIGHT VOCABULARY

Although commercial material can be very helpful, there is a strong need for teacher-made materials which provide individualized practice. Teachers can design material to match the needs and interests of specific children. The following list is representative of suitable material.

1. *Bowling*: For this game make a bowling-pin tachistoscope (quick-exposure device) from tagboard by doing the following: Color and cut out the form of a bowling pin. At the center of the pin make an opening so words which have been printed on strips of oaktag and slipped behind the structure can be exposed quickly, one at a time. If the child who starts can name ten words, he has made a strike and can try a new strip of words. (For use with two or more children.)

2. *Build-a-Train*: For this game engines and railways cars are cut from oaktag. Each piece has a word printed or written on it. Children who pronounce the words correctly build a train which becomes longer and longer. The object of the game is to see who can build the longest train. (For use with two or more children.)

3. *Card Method*: Each pupil is equipped with a small pile of cards (3-by-5-inch cards cut in half are fine). When an unknown word is encountered, the pupil is instructed to write it on a card. The teacher, too, has cards in readiness at all times so that any child in the reading circle who misses a word can be given an immediate written record of it. Several times a week the children are allowed to get together in groups of three for the purpose of quizzing each other on their cards. The chances are good that at least one of the three children will know a word. When all are uninformed, the teacher or an especially appointed assistant can provide the help needed. (For use with a group of children; potentially self-directed.)

4. *Carpenter*: In making this game draw a picture of a house on a piece of heavy tagboard. Color all but the roof. Paste art corners on the roof, about 1½ inches apart in seven rows. On small cards about ½ inch by 1¼ inches print the words for drill. Each card is a shingle. If a child can say the word, he can put it in the art corner and add a shingle to the roof. If he does not know it, it falls to the ground. More than enough cards are given to the child so that he can have reasonable success in completing the house. (For use with children working in pairs.)

5. *Checkers*: For this game buy a cheap checkerboard. Cut squares from masking tape that coincide in size with the checkerboard squares and place these on the squares where the checkers are to be placed or moved. Words are then printed on the masking tape (Dolch words

frequently are used) right side up and upside down so that both players can read any word appearing on the board. The game proceeds like regular checkers, but a child must be able to read the word or words if he is to complete a move. If he fails to call the word correctly, he is told what the word is. He must wait, however, until his next turn before attempting the move again. (For use with two children; potentially self-directive.)

6. *Classification*: Print in color on individual cards two or more words that constitute categories such as *home* and *farm*. Place these in an envelope along with many other cards bearing words such as *kitchen, stove,* and *barn*. The latter must be categorized under the two words printed in color. By numbering the backs of the word cards, the exercise can be made self-corrective. (For use with individual children, potentially self-directed.

7. *Color Match*: Words pertaining to various colors are printed on pieces of oaktag. Clothespins that have been colored are placed in an accompanying envelope. The child engaged in color-match slows his understanding of the words by attaching the appropriately colored clothespins to the word cards. If the backs of the word cards are colored with the color named, this activity comes self-corrective. (For use with individual children; potentially self-directed.)

8. *Cookie-pan Magnet Match*: Paste pictures of various objects on the inside surface of a shallow cookie pan. Design matching word cards on the backs of which are glued small pieces of a bar magnet. The pupil engaged in this activity places words in proper position. The word cards are held in position by the pieces of bar magnet which adhere firmly to the metal of the cookie pan. Numbering the pictures and the backs of the word cards makes this activity self-corrective. (For use with individual pupils; potentially self-directed.)

9. *Fishing*: In this game word cards are cut from tagboard in the shape of fish. A paper clip is slipped over each word card. Fishermen are equipped with a pole (short stick),a fish line (20 inches of store string), and a fishhook (small magnet). Each child gets a turn trying to catch a fish. If he can read the word attracted to the magnet, he may keep the fish he caught. If he does not know it, he shows the word to the other children for the correct response and then returns it, face down, to the fishpond. (For use with two children or a group of children; potentially self-directed.)

10. *Jallopy Derby*: For this game make a five-car racetrack on as large a piece of cardboard as you can find. Divide the track into 3-inch spaces and mark a starting line. Let the children make little cars of paper or buy four little cars at a toy store.

On a small piece of tagboard print the words you want the children to learn. A die is tossed for order of beginning. Number One then tosses the die for his first move. He may move as many spaces as the number on the die if he can say the word on the card he draws. If he cannot say the word, he loses his turn, and the next child may use the same word or pick a new one. If he decides not to use the missed word, the next player may use it. If no one uses the missed word, it is put at the bottom of the pile. When the game is over, special help is given with the missed words at the bottom of the pile.

Each race is one lap. The winner is the one who first comes out even with the finish line. Should a potential winner throw a six and have only four or five spaces left, he may move just one space for the word he can say. Coming out even with the finish line adds excitement to the game. It gives each other child a chance to become a last-minute winner. (For use with one, two, three, or four children.)

11. *Match-A-Picture*: An ingeniously designed self-corrective exercise can be made by pasting a picture on a piece of oaktag on which two matched and parallel columns of synonyms or antonyms have been written. The left-hand column is numbered from top to bottom so that no difficulty can be experienced in arranging it properly at a later time. After this has been done, the oaktag is cut into individual word cards, and the pieces are placed in a stiff manila folder. The pupil who engages in this exercise begins by arranging the left-hand column as numbered. He then arranges in a parallel column the matching pieces. All the pieces involved are put in position inside the folder. When the pupil is ready to check his work, he closes the folder and flips it over. Upon opening the folder a complete picture appears. Any error is manifest by a jumbled picture. (For use with individual pupils; potentially self-directed.)

12. *Matching*: Print words that designate specific colors (*snow, fire engine, violets*, etc.) on a sheet of oaktag. Place small cards of different colors in an attached envelope. The child matches the colored cards with the words. Using an identification scheme on the backs of the color cards makes this activity self-corrective. (For use with individual children; potentially self-directed.)

13. *Old Maid*: To make this game print words on pieces of oaktag the size of playing cards. Complete twenty cards and then make a duplicate set so that twenty pairs of words result. Print one Old Maid card, or if you wish, one word alone may be used to designate the Old Maid card. Distribute the cards and begin with the person to the left of the dealer who starts the game by drawing a card from the person at his right. As pairs are formed, the words are called and placed on the table. This continues until all pairs are matched and one person holds the Old Maid. (For use with two to four children, potentially self-directed.)

14. *One Look Game*: Dolch cards are used with this game. Pupils work in pairs, with one child acting as helper. The pack of cards is placed before the learner who picks up one card at a time, calls the word, and then hands it to the helper. The helper retains those cards called correctly and segregates thos called incorrectly. Any marked hesitation constitutes an error. When all cards have been called, the number of words missed is calculated and recorded in chart form. The helper then calls each word for the player who repeats aloud each word he has failed. The entire pack is reshuffled and is made ready for another "one look" trial. (For use with children working in pairs.)

15. *Pairs*: Pairs (devised by Edward Fry, Rutgers University) is a game similar to rummy and can be played by two to five children. Twenty-five words, each of which appears twice on oaktag playing cards, make a fifty-card deck. The object of the game is to get as many pairs as possible. When the game is played, five cards are dealt to each player, and the remainder of the deck is placed face down on the table. The player to the right of the dealer begins by asking a fellow player for a specific card that will match one in his hand. If the latter has the card requested, he must give it up. If he does not have it, the asker draws one card from the pile and terminates his play. The player who gets the card for which he asks (should he not know the word, he may solicit help from anyone present), either from another player or from the pile, gets a second turn. As soon as a player has a pair, he places it on the table. The player with the most pair wins.

16. *Pick-A-Chip*: In this game divide Dolch's Basic Sight Vocabulary Words into four sections of fifty-five words each. Type or write the words on pieces of masking tape and place these on poker chips of four colors. Deposit the chips in four small boxes of matching colors. A pupil starts the game by choosing a color and then gives a spinner a whirl. He picks as many chips from his color section as the spinner indicates. If he fails to say one of the words, he is told what it is, but he must return the chip to the box and pass the spinner to the next player. The winner is the pupil who has acquired the most chips. (For use with two to four children.)

17. *Picture Checkerboard*: In this game the teacher writes sixteen nouns on the board in numbered order. The children fold a sheet of drawing paper into sixteen squares and number them correspondingly. They then draw pictures of the nouns on the numbered squares. Later, papers can be exchanged and corrected. (For use with individual children or a group of children.)

18. *Picture Dictionary Match*: Paste pictures cut from a dime-store dictionary in a row on a 9-by-12-inch card. Under each picture draw a space box 1½ inches by ½ inch. Prepare small word cards and put these

in an envelope which remains attached to the picture card. By numbering the pictures and the backs of the word cards, this activity becomes self-corrective. (For use with individual children; potentially self-directed.)

19. *Picture Riddle Matcho*: For this game children cut pictures from old magazines and place them in envelopes—five to an envelope. The teacher writes a riddle about one of the pictures and places it in the envelope with the pictures. The child who chooses the envelope selects the pictures which answer the riddle. A marking scheme can be devised to make this activity self-corrective. (For use with individual children; potentially self-directed.)

20. *Ring a Word*: For this game, use heavy plywood in constructing a board 2 by 3 feet in size. Space five nails on the board and paint numbers from one to five under the nails. Print words on small cards and hang them on the nails. (Easiest cards should be on Number One nail and hardest cards on Number five nail.) Equip children with a box of mason jar rubber rings. The directions for the game are: Ring a word and score the points if you can say it. (For use with two or more children.)

21. *Shoestring Matcho*: Two rows of mixed synonyms or an antonym and synonym row are written side by side. Shoestrings are attached to the right of the first row by knotting the ends on the reverse side. The child designates the correct answer by slipping the shoestring into the proper hole before words in the second column. A marking scheme can be devised on the reverse side to make this activity self-corrective. (For use with individual children; potentially self-directed.)

22. *Tachistoscope*: Let a child find a picture that interests him. Mount this picture on oaktag and cut two horizontal slits 1½ inches long and ⅜ inch apart. Words to be learned are printed or typed on strips of oaktag about 1½ inches wide. The strips are then inserted in the slits and pulled through so one word is exposed at a time. (For use with children working in pairs.)

23. *Word Authors*: In this game words are printed on corners of cards—four cards to a set. A set can consist of four colors, four animals, four synonyms, and the like. Each child is dealt four cards, and one child begins the game by calling for a word. If he gets the word, he may continue to call for words. When his opponent indicates that he does not have the card called for, the child draws from the deck of cards that is face down on the table. The child who acquires the most sets wins. (For use with two to four children; potentially self-directed.)

24. *Word Basket Ball*: To make this game remove the top and one of the long sides of a packing carton. Use green and white paint to give what remains the appearance of a basketball court. Baskets can be simulated by pasting two small paper bags on the outside ends of the box.

If a player can call correctly a word he has drawn from a word pile, he pushes the word card through a slot above his team's basket and his side gets two points. If he calls incorrectly someone on the other team tries. A referee will determine if the word is said correctly or not. The score can be kept by counting the number of cards in each bag. (For use with two children or two groups of children under proper direction.)

25. *Word File Pictures*: The name of an object is printed at the top of a card, and a picture or drawing is placed below to illustrate it. On the opposite side of the cards just the word is printed. The child tries to read the word and then checks his response by looking at the picture on the front side of the card. (For use with individual children; potentially self-directed.)

26. *Wordo*: In making the game the teacher with the help of the class prepares cardboard master cards 8 by 11 inches in size. These master cards are blocked off vertically and horizontally into twenty-five small squares. The middle space is marked *free*. Individual words that are troublesome are placed on the twenty-four squares that remain. Each cardboard master card must have the same words but in different positions. The twenty-four words are typed or printed on small cards and placed in an envelope. As individual words are drawn from the envelope and called aloud, the players find the words on their master cards and cover them with a marker of some sort. The marker may be a kernel of corn, a bean, or a small piece of cardboard. The first child to cover a row of words in a straight line, vertically, horizontally or diagonally, calls out "wordo." If he has not erred, he is declared the winner. (For use with two or more children; potentially self-directed.)

UTILIZING CONTEXT CLUES

As stated by Hildreth, "inferring the meaning of a word from what went before, and deliberately reading ahead for clues to meaning is an essential technique for word recognition."[5]

Because of its importance to word recognition, specific training and a variety of methods should be used in teaching pupils to use contextual clues. Some of these include the following.

1. Show the pupil who fails to use contextual clues how valuable they can be in identifying words.
   a. Read aloud a sentence, omitting the unknown word. Ask the pupil what he thinks the word is.
   b. Provide sample sentences which are designed to show that contextual clues may come before, after, or both before and after a strange word.

c. Provide samples which show that contextual clues may take the form of a phrase, a sentence, or a paragraph.

d. Provide sample sentences to show that the context may take the form of an appositive, a definition, or an example.

2. When a pupil encounters a strange word or is stymied by a word, suggest that he read on. Too often teachers are prone to encourage an immediate sound-it-out approach. It is more judicious to have a pupil skip an unknown word and read the entire sentence. At this point, the pupil might ask himself, for example, What word starting with *ch* would make sense in this sentence?

3. Use available commercial materials such as the following: *Using the Context,* levels 1 through 6. (Each workbook $1.75. Barnell Loft). *One Too Many,* Sets A and B ($6.95 per set. Barnell Loft). *We Read Sentences,* Sets 1 through 5 ($6.95 per set. Barnell Loft). *Using Context Clues* ($5.95. Lakeshore). *CGK: Context Clues* ($11.95. Comprehension Games Corp.).

4. Most workbooks contain exercises that are devoted to context clues, such as the following: *Word Enrichment Program* (Ginn & Co.); *Reading Systems* (Scott, Foresman); *Phonics We Use* (Lyons & Carnahan).

TEACHER-MADE MATERIALS FOR CORRECTING DEFICIENCIES IN CONTEXT SKILLS

When individual pupils or groups of pupils are deficient in use of context clues, corrective practice can be individualized by using teacher-made materials such as the following.

1. Present sentences in which words are missing. The pupils are instructed to read the sentences and decide which words fit the blanks most appropriately. Examples:

   a. They put the_____in the bank.
        paper, letter, money
   b. The day was bright and_____.
        sunny, dark cloudy
   c. Bill had to_____if he should_____the fort against attack.
        defend, decide

2. Present sentences in which a phonic clue is given to aid the pupil in providing missing words. Pupils are instructed to think of words which fit the blanks most appropriately. Examples:

   a. Betty said she would r   the ball on the floor.
   b. The cat dr   the milk.
   c. He was going to   ow his shoe at the barking dog.

3. Present sentences which contain unusual words whose meaning can be arrived at by using contextual clues. Pupils are instructed to read the sentences carefully before deciding on an answer. Examples:
   a. John will *deflate* the tire by opening the valve.
      Deflate means   (a) put air in   (b) let air out   (c) turn over (d) damage
   b. The *edifice* was of brick and covered a city block.
      Edifice means (a) bicycle (b) locomotive (c) building (d) ship
   c. The old trunk was *capacious* enough to hold all John's clothes.
      Capacious means (a) unclean   (b) colorful   (c) small   (d) large
4. Employ cloze exercises.

INSTRUCTIONAL MATERIALS FOR CORRECTING DEFICIENCIES IN DICTIONARY USAGE

Teachers who wish to help pupils use the dictionary effectively must begin by determining which of the major dictionary skills are in need of improvement. After this has been done, a planned sequence of instruction should be initiated.

The following exercises indicate the types of lessons that might be used to assist pupils in becoming more proficient at locating a word in the dictionary.

1. Put these letters in alphabetical order:
   a. *p, m, b, z, o, c, f, d*
   b. *s, n, x, d, c, t, l, h*
2. Fill in the blanks with letters that come before and after the letters listed:
   a._____ *l* _____
   b._____ *c* _____
   c._____ *k* _____
   d._____ *s* _____
   e._____ *b* _____
   f._____ *t* _____
   g._____ *m*_____
   h._____ *f* _____
3. Fill in the blanks with the in-between letter.
   a. *n*_____*p*
   b. *j*_____*l*
   c. *g*_____*i*
   d. *s*_____*u*
   e. *w*_____*y*
   f. *t*_____*v*
   g. *p*_____*r*
   h. *d*_____*f*

4. Encircle the letter which comes first in the alphabet.
   a. *g-h*
   b. *m-l*
   c. *d-f*
   d. *r-g*
   e. *n-l*
   f. *y-u*
   g. *w-x*
   h. *h-k*
5. Arrange these words in alphabetical order (word cards are recommended for this exercise).
   a. people
   b. elephants
   c. zebras
   d. bears
   e. cows
   f. ants

The foregoing exercise should be followed by others which include words to be placed in alphabetical order according to beginning two- and three-letter patterns.

6. The guide words *Joint-Judge* appear at the top of a given page in the dictionary. Encircle the words which could be found on the page.
   a. junk
   b. joist
   c. jigsaw
   d. jot
   e. join
   f. joy
   g. juice
   h. jubilee

After a pupil has located a word for which he has been looking, he must learn to pronounce it correctly. Teachers can help by explaining the various aids to pronunciation which are given by dictionaries. These include accent marks, syllabication, and respelling with diacritical marks or symbols. To profit from the latter, a pupil must learn how to use a pronunciation key.

Pupils need to be taught that the first definition of a word is not always the best one for their purpose. Often they must continue looking until they succeed in locating a definition that helps them understand the unknown word in the particular context involved. Teachers can acquaint pupils with the fact that words may have multiple meanings by having them look up a word such as *run*. An unabridged dictionary lists well over one hundred meanings for *run*. A beginning dictionary lists between thirty and forty.

One company publishes and distributes, free of charge, an enlargement of a dictionary page which is excellent for purposes of group instruction (Scott, Foresman & Co.). Other publishers issue free pamphlets from time to time which are valuable for dictionary study (Macmillan Co. and Holt, Rinehart & Winston). Particularly noteworthy are the teachers' manuals accompanying Merriam-Webster dictionaries for the elementary and secondary school levels.

Some of the widely available commercial materials for helping pupils develop dictionary skills includes the following: *Guide-Word Dictionary* ($1.50. Wordcrafters Guild). *Supporting Reading Skills: Learning to Alphabetize,* levels one through three; Using Guide Words, levels four through nine; Using an Index, levels three through nine ($12.50 each set. Barnell Loft). *Dictionary Games* ($29.95. Learnco Incorporated). *Dictionary Skills* ($4.50. The Teachers Market Place). *How to Use a Book Lab* ($29.95. Lakeshore). *Easy Dictionary Drills* ($4.50. Tarmac/tac Inc.). *Working with the Alphabet Activity Cards* ($4.95. Tarmac/tac Inc.). *Using the Dictionary Activity Cards* ($4.95. Tarmac/tac Inc.). *Quest* ($6.95. Creative Teaching Press). *Super Dictionary Unit* ($5.95. Lakeshore). *Dictionary Puzzles,* Sets 1-4. ($23.07. Scott, Foresman.)

UTILIZING PHONICS

Most teachers are in a quandary when it comes to phonics (phonics and related terminologies are defined in Appendix A). This is understandable. Research has shown that many experienced teachers lack knowledge in this area.[6, 7] Many have had little or no preparation in the teaching of phonics. In addition, the controversies that have raged and continue to rage over how reading should be taught add to the confusion. If the experts cannot agree, what should teachers do? What specific information do teachers need to identify a pupil's weakness or disability in the phonic area?

Opinions regarding phonics and phonic systems are diverse. Most authorities, however, would agree with the following generalizations.

1. *Auditory perception is basic to a phonic program.* Unless pupils can hear similarities and differences between sounds, they cannot be expected to associate sounds with printed letters. For pupils who lack auditory discrimination, a sequential program in ear training is recommended. It would include auditory perception of initial consonants, blends, rhymes, medial vowels, and syllables (for particulars see Scott and Thompson[8]).

2. *Phonics instruction should proceed from simple to complex.* It is unwise for a teacher to spend time on difficult principles that are limited in

applicability when simpler elements and generalizations could be employed. For example, a pupil should learn the sounds of initial consonants and digraphs before being introduced to diphthongs.

3. *Periods devoted to phonics should be brief and enjoyable.* There is nothing exciting about phonics. Exposing a child to too much work on sounds at any one time can be deadening. To minimize boredom many teachers employ a game approach to learning phonics.

4. *The phonics program for a given child should be individualized.* A teacher should determine what phonic knowledge a child does and does not possess and then tailor a program to meet these needs. The teacher should not cry phonics and proceed to give a child the entire treatment. Children vary in readiness for phonics and the degree of mastery attained at any grade level. Some learn quickly and need no additional practice with teacher-made or commercial materials, while others have to be taught and retaught many times before they can apply what they have learned.

5. *Pupils should be led to discover phonic principles rather than be taught rules.* When, for example, the silent-*e* rule is involved, a teacher should write on the blackboard several words exemplifying the principle. After each word is pronounced and attention is directed to the change from a short to a long vowel because of the final *e*, the children should be asked if they can make up a rule that applies. Children who discover for themselves the silent-*e* generalization are more likely to remember it. More important, they are likely to use it.

6. *To be most effective, phonics should not be used as an isolated word-attack skill.* Phonics proves far more valuable when used in collaboration with other word-attack skills such as contextual and structural analysis.

COMMERCIAL MATERIALS FOR CORRECTING DEFICIENCIES IN INITIAL CONSONANT SOUNDS

When individual pupils or groups of pupils are deficient in initial consonant sounds, corrective practice can be individualized by using available *commercial material* such as the following.

1. *Aims: Initial Consonants Kit*: Instructional material designed to further skills in auditory discrimination of initial consonant sounds and letter-sound association of initial consonants. A three-step pattern of instruction is used: (1) Matching picture to picture, (2) Matching picture to letter, and (3) Matching letter to picture. (For use with individual children or a group of children. $64.50. Continental Press, Inc.)

2. *Amos and His Friends*: This set of materials includes a fifteen-minute tape which allows children to listen to and then sing sounds they hear with Amos and His Friends. Twenty-six full-color, 8½-by-11-inch picture charts make listening more meaningful. Also included are twenty-four spirit duplicator masters of suitable activity sheets which correlate with the sounds learned. (For use with individual children or a group of children; potentially self-directed. $19.95; on cassettes. Imperial.)

3. *Animal Race*: Each game board is equipped with three or four race-tracks and an animal at each starting gate. The child chooses a race-track and using picture cards matches the beginning sound of the picture with the beginning sound of the name of the animal racer. (For use with two to four children. $14.25. Houghton Mifflin.)

4. *Breakthrough Filmstrips*: These silent filmstrips are designed to help teach 22 consonants and digraphs. Each filmstrip is in color, has 14 frames, and deals exclusively with one of the consonants or digraphs. (For use with an individual child or a group of children. $85.50. Houghton Mifflin.)

5. *Broken Letters*: Children locate the two or three pictures whose names begin with the same sound-consonants and consonant digraphs. The pieces fit together to form the letter or letters that stand for the sound. (For use with two to four children. $17.49. Houghton Mifflin.)

6. *Build It* (Decks 1 and 3): A game for practice in consonants and vowels. Deck 1 involves a phonetic card game that teaches single consonants and short vowels. Deck 3 teaches single consonants, long vowels, and the silent-*e* rule. (For use with any number of children. $4.50. Remedial Education Press.)

7. *Consonant Lotto*: A game consisting of eight lotto cards, each of which contains six pictures of familiar objects. Forty-eight picture cover cards have different pictures to be matched by the beginning sound of the word with the pictures on the lotto cards. (For use with a group of children; potentially self-directed. $3.00. Garrard.)

8. *Consonant Pictures for Pegboard*: These materials consist of 179 pictures in color and 30 symbols printed on 3¾-by-4-inch cards for use on pegboard or chalk tray or as flash cards. (For use with individual children, children working in pairs, or a group of children under proper direction. $6.50. Ideal.)

9. *Consonant Sounds*: An activity in which children listen to consonant sounds and hear them in word contexts. They manipulate a wheel card to form meaningful words. Pupils respond both verbally and in writing. Includes twenty lessons on five cassette tapes, five consonant wheels, and ten packs of seventy-two double-lesson response sheets. (For use with individual children or a small group of children; self-directed. $65. Milton Bradley.)

10. *Consonant Sounds*: A program including 20 lessons on five cassette tapes, five manipulative devices, and 10 packs of response sheets. The student hears the consonant sound, sees it in a word and manipulates teaching aids to form words. Finally, she/he writes the appropriate letters over pictures of objects on the response sheet. (For use with one or more children. $64.90. Dick Blick.)

11. *Cononant Wheels*: Five drill devices designed to help children learn initial and ending consonants. Each device present four consonants as they blend with other letters to form meaningful words. The consonants q, x, and z are excluded whereas soft g and c are included. (For use with individual children or children working in pairs. $5.50. Milton Bradley.)

12. *Dog House Game*: A phonetic game consisting of eighty-four assorted consonants and consonant blends along with thirty-five phonograms with which to build words. (For use with two or more children. $2.30. Kenworthy.)

13. *Dominoes*: A domino game in which children make consonant letter-sound associations. (For use with two to ten children. $16.29. Houghton Mifflin.)

14. *First Talking Alphabet,* Part I: A programmed instruction on consonants. Using records and cards, a child hears a sound, says it, sees the letter that represents it, and traces the flocked letter shape. (For use with individual children; potentially self-directed. $75.57. Scott, Foresman.)

15. *Go Fish* (Set I): A rummylike game designed to teach the sounds of initial consonants. (For use with two to four children; potentially self-directed. $4.50. Remedial Education Press.)

16. *Group Sounding Game*: A game which is a complete phonics course beginning with the recognition of initial consonants, blends, and vowels and ending with syllabication of three-syllable words. (For use with two or more children; potentially self-directed. $4.75. Garrard.)

17. *Highway Robbery* Game 3: An All-About-Consonants game consisting of three decks and involving words that are connected with cars, motorcycles, and obtaining a driver's license. (For use with groups of children. $5.95. Warren's.)

18. *Initial and Final Consonant Charts*: Instructional materials involving fifteen charts that are 23 by 36 inches in size. Each chart supplies a variety of consonant pictures headed by their consonant symbol and a key picture. A manual of directions is included. (For use with individual children or a group of children; potentially self-directed. $14.75. Ideal.)

19. *Letter-Picture Solitaire*: A game-in-a-book that is designed to reinforce consonant-sound associations. It consists of two ring binders, 44 letter

cards, and 176 picture cards. (For use with individual children and children working in pairs. $22.50. Houghton Mifflin.)

20. *Listen and Do* (Consonants): These instructional materials consist of cassettes and record which are designed to help pupils develop consonant-sound associations. They consist of 32 recorded lessons of 15 minutes duration. Each lesson is accompanied by a worksheet. $99.96, for cassettes, and $98.25 for records. Houghton Mifflin.)

21. *Magic Cards*: Instructional materials consisting of forty exercises printed on six 8½-by-11-inch cards. They are designed to stimulate learning of initial and final consonants. A transparent pocket in which the cards are inserted and on which answers are written with crayon is included. The pocket can be wiped clean to make it ready for the next exercise. (For use with individual children or children working in pairs. $4.50. Ideal.)

22. *The New Phonics We Use Learning Kits*: Two kits of 10 phonic games each, including the consonant games *Sound Off, Boo!, Countdown, Digraph Whirl, Road Race, Spin-A-Sound, Digraph Jungle*. These colorful card and/or board games are adaptable for two or more players. (Complete kits, $93.00 each. Rand McNally.)

23. *Phonetic Drill Cards*: Instructional material involving twenty-three cards for 345 word combinations. The lettering is one inch high and the cards are 8 by 11¼ inches in size. Consonants and letter combinations for complete words are hinged for the formation of fifteen words on each card. (For use with individual children, children working in pairs, or with a group of children under proper direction. $3.25. Milton Bradley.)

24. *Phonetic Factory*: A cassette-activity program that provides a basic foundation in forming and using consonant sounds. It consists of six cassettes which cover 34 lessons that coordinate with 34 duplicator worksheets. A lesson is devoted to each consonant sound and accompanied by vowel sounds. Each worksheet shows the letter symbol, corresponding picture, and a drawing of the human mouth forming the sound. (For use with one child or a group of children. $52.50. Lakeshore.)

25. *Phonetic Quizmo*: A lotto-type game consisting of thirty-eight Quizmo cards, teacher's word list, direction card, and markers. The game is designed to teach consonant sounds and consonant blends. (For use with two or more children; potentially self-directed. $3.25. Milton Bradley.)

26. *Phonics: Beginning and Ending Consonants*: Instructional material consisting of pictures of everyday objects which is designed for use with Charlie, the Teaching Robot. (For use with individual children or children working in pairs. $9.95. Tarmac/tac, Inc.)

27. *Phonics Learning Labs*: These self-directed and self-corrective laboratories employ cassettes and interest activity booklets. Each lab has 3 cassettes, 90 four-page activity booklets, 3 reproducible post-tests and a teacher's guide. Eight labs are involved. They include Initial Consonants (Labs 1 & 2), Consonant Blends (Labs 1 & 2), Short Vowel Sounds (Labs 1 & 2), Long Vowels (Labs 1 & 2), and Finishing Phonics Lab. (For individual children; potentially self-directed. $29.95 each. Lakeshore.)

28. *Phonics Skills Kit*: This kit presents interesting matching activities to promote word attack skill. Through the task of matching manipulaive cards with pictures and letters on Learning Folders, children receive desired practice. Skill areas are initial consonants, initial consonant digraphs, consonant substitution, final consonants, supplying missing consonants and vowel sound. The complete kit contains 30 Learning Folders and a package of manipulative cards to accompany each Learning Folder. (For use with individual children working in pairs. $64.50. The Continental Press, Inc.)

29. *Picture and Key Cards*: Instructional materials consisting of pictures and letters for teaching consonant-sound association. Twenty-two key picture cards, 22 letter cards, and 85 cards with pictures on both sides are included. (For use with individual children or children working in pairs. $9.69. Houghton Mifflin.)

30. *Reading Creatures and Reading Dinosaurs*: Workbooks in which children use crayons to show color-coded answers. Skills include consonants, consonant blends, rhyming, vowels and special sound. (For use with individual children or children working in pairs. $3.95. Teaching Stuff.)

31. *Silly Sounds*: A colorful game designed to teach consonants and help build vocabulary. Children learn to identify and practice using words beginning with consonants. The game requires the players to give two-word phrases in which both words have the same consonant sound. (For use with two or more children. $8.25. Ideal.)

32. *Sound Hunt* (Set I): A phonics game designed to teach initial consonants and consonant digraphs. The sixty cards in each deck are colored. (For use with two to eight children; potentially self-directed. $1.95. American Teaching Aids.)

33. *Speech-to-Print Phonics*: A kit of material initially designed as a readiness program which may also be used as supplementary material with any basal series. The kit contains a teacher's manual and specific lessons in relating phonemes to printed forms. It includes consonants and vowels and twenty-one consonant blends. Special response cards are used by pupils so that the teacher can detect any children who are experiencing difficulty. (For use with a group of children or an entire class. $50.00. Harcourt Brace Jovanovich.)

34. *Spelling/Language Learning Games Kits*: Two kits of 10 games each, including consonant games *Tiger Trail, End It,* and *Think.* These colorful card and/or board games are adaptable for two or more players. (Complete kits, $93.00 each. Rand McNally.)

35. *Spill & Spell*: A vocabulary-building game consisting of fifteen cubes and a sand timer. (For use with two children or a group of children; potentially self-directed. $4.75. Lakeshore.)

36. *Split Words*: A game consisting of wooden blocks involving consonants, consonant blends, and word endings. The latter are printed in red. A dictionary listing and defining some 500 words that can be built by combining the blocks in various ways is included. (For use with individual children, children working in pairs, or a small group of children; potentially self-directed. $3.25. American Teaching Aids.)

37. *Start Your Engines*: A word game for primary children that is designed to develop and reinforce recognition of initial consonant sounds and basic word families. (For use with two to four children. $3.45. Ideal.)

38. *Treasure Capture*: A game in which children capture treasure along with skills in distinguishing between consonant sounds, and associating consonant forms and sounds. (For use with two to four children. $14.25. Houghton Mifflin.)

39. *Turn 'N Learn Beginning Consonants*: One of ten colorful cards in which students write answers on their paper through holes in cards and then turn over the cards for the correct response. (For individual children or children working in pairs. $3.95 per set. Creative Teaching Press, Inc.)

40. *Webster Word Wheels*: Practice wheels consisting of twenty-five beginning blend wheels, twenty prefix wheels, and eighteen suffix wheels. (For use with individual children or children working in pairs. $39.00. Webster/McGraw-Hill.)

41. *What the Letters Say*: A beginning phonics game designed to teach letter names and letter sounds. (For use with individual children or a group of children; potentially self-directed. $2.50. Garrard.)

42. *Wipe-Clean Activity Books*: A series of eight books of write-on, wipe-off activity cards for individualized phonics learning. Each book is a binder with 12 removable cards. The series includes Initial Consonant Sounds, Final Consonant Sounds, Consonant Blends, Consonant Blends & Digraphs, Short Vowel Sounds, Long Vowel Sounds, and Rhyming Words. (For use with individual children; $3.50 each, Lakeshore.)

43. *Wipe-off Cards from Trend*: A set of twelve write-on, wipe-off cards that are 8 by 11 inches in size. Each card is devoted to a key initial sound. The child encircles the pictures having the proper sound. (For use with individual children or pairs of children. $3.95. Lakeshore.)

When individual pupils or groups of pupils are deficient in initial consonant sounds, individualized practice can be provided by using *teacher-or pupil-made materials* such as the following.

1. *Arrange-O*: Place in an envelope a large picture of an object starting with an initial consonant sound you are teaching. In another envelope, place small pictures of objects, some of which begin with the sound involved. The child arranges the appropriate pictures in a column under the master picture. Using an identification scheme on the back of the pictures makes this activity self-corrective. (For use with individual children; potentially self-directed.)

2. *Baseball*: For this game a baseball diamond is drawn on the blackboard or on cardboard. Two groups of children are chosen. The pitcher flashes a letter. If the batter calls a word beginning with the letter, he has made a hit and moves to first base. Should the next batter score a hit also, he moves to first base, and the first batter advances to second. Soon the run begin to come in. Teams change sides just as soon as three outs (wrong answers) have been given. The team with the most runs wins. (For use with groups of children.)

3. *Clothespin Wheel*: Cut out a circular piece of tagboard about 12 inches in diameter. Paste or draw pictures of common objects around the periphery of the oaktag. Equip the child with a box of clothespins on each of which is printed an initial consonant. The child then matches the clothespins with the proper pictures. For example, the *c* clothespin would be placed over the picture of a cat; the *p* clothespin over the picture of a pear. (For use with individual children; potentially self-directed.)

4. *Consonant Fishing*: For this game consonant cards are cut in the shape of a fish. A paper clip is slipped over each card. Fishermen are equipped with a pole (short stick), a fish line (20 inches of store string), and a fishhook (small magnet). Each child gets a turn trying to catch fish. If he can call a word that begins with the consonant sound on the fish he has caught, he may keep the fish. If he is unable to think of a suitable word, he returns the fish, face down, to the fishpond. (For use with two children or a group of children; potentially self-directed.)

5. *Consonant Lotto*: In making the game the teacher with the help of the class prepares cardboard master cards 8 by 11 inches in size. These master cards are blocked off vertically and horizontally into twenty-five mall squares. The middle space is marked *free*. Individual letters and digraphs are placed on the twenty-four spaces that remain. Each cardboard master card must have the same letters but in different

positions. Twenty-four words known by the children on sight that begin with the individual letters or consonant digraphs involved are placed in an envelope. As individual words drawn from the envelope are called, the players find the beginning letter or digraph on their master cards and cover it with a marker. The marker may be a kernel of corn, a bean, or a small piece of cardboard. The first child to cover row of letters in a straight line, vertically, horizontally, or diagonally, calls out Lotto. If he has not erred, he is declared the winner. (For use with two children or a group of children; potentially self-directed.)

6. *Matching Letters and Objects*: The teacher pastes a number of small pictures on a sheet of oaktag. (A flannel board, if available, might be used.) The pictures should be of things the children can recognize easily. An envelope containing a number of consonants is clipped to the sheet of oaktag. The child removes the consonant cards and places them on or below the appropriate pictures. An identification scheme on the backs of the cards makes this activity self-corrective. (For use with individual children; potentially self-directed.)

7. *Pockets*: Cut apart some cheap envelopes and mount them on a chart as pockets for 3-by-5-inch cards. A consonant is printed on each envelope. The 3-by-5-inch cards have pictures or drawings on them which are to be placed in the pockets beginning with the appropriate consonant sound. An identification scheme on the backs of the cards can be used to make this activity self-corrective. (For use with individual children; potentially self-directed.)

8. *Spin and Call*: For this game divide a large oaktag circle into eight sections. Place a consonant in each section. Attach a large pointer to the center of the circle so that it spins freely. The player spins the pointer and calls a word beginning with the particular consonant to which it points when coming to a stop. If a correct word is called, he scores a point. A record should be kept of the words called so that no repetitions take place. (For use with two children or a group of children.)

9. *Taxi*: To make the game, the teacher with the help of the class builds a little village of letters beside each of which is a small paper house. There can be several streets in Alphabet Village. Tall Street can consist of those letters which extend above the line (*b, d, f, h, k, l,* and *t*); Naughty Street can consist of those letters which extend below the line (*j, p,* and *g*); Coward Street, of those letters that go together to make a sound (*ch, sh, th,* and *wh*); Vowel Street, of the vowels; Main Street, of any letters left over.

One child acts as taxi driver. The other children ask the driver to take them to any word they want. The driver has to "drive" them to the house whose letter starts the word. (For use with a group of children.)

10. *Toss Game*: In his game using alphabet blocks or building blocks on which initial consonants have been painted, children can take turns rolling blocks and giving words beginning with the letters that come up. (For use with two or more children; potentially self-directed.)

11. *What Am I?*: For this game write on individual cards riddles which give initial sounds as clues. For example, "I am a tree-climbing animal. I have a long tail and like to swing from branches with it. I begin with the *m* sound. What am I?" Each child in the group has a chance at a riddle card. If he guesses the answer, he is given the card. The child with the largest number of cards is the winner. Placing the answers on the backs of the cards makes this activity self-corrective. (For use with a group of children; potentially self-directed.)

12. *Word Authors*: The game consists of words printed on corners of cards—four cards to a set. A set consists of four words beginning with the same consonant. Each child is dealt four cards. One child begins the game by calling for a card beginning with a certain initial consonant sound. If he gets the word, he may continue to call for words. When his opponent indicates that he does not have the card called, the child draws from the deck of cards that is face down on the table. The child who acquires the most sets wins. (For use with two to four children; potentially self-directed.)

COMMERCIAL MATERIALS FOR CORRECTING DEFICIENCIES IN CONSONANT BLENDS

When individual pupils or groups of pupils are deficient in knowledge of consonant blends, corrective practice can be individualized by using available *commercial material* such as the following:

1. *Amos and His Friends*: Instructional materials consisting of twenty-three colorful picture charts, a sound tape, and a set of twenty-three liquid duplicator masters. Children see Amos and his friends in situations involving blends, learn a song and poem about each blend, and follow up with an Amos coloring sheet for each blend. (For use with individual children or a small group of chidren. $19.95, on cassettes. Imperial.)

2. *Beginning Consonant Blends*: A twelve-card set that includes 24 initial consonant blends and displays a total of 144 words. The cards are numbered for easy reference. (For use with a group of children. $1.10. Kenworthy.)

3. *Blend Dominoes*: A domino game that encourages students to use blends and digraphs to build words. It consists of 108 domino cards and a spinner and timer. (For use with two children or a small group of children. $10.95. Lakeshore.)

4. *Blend-o-grams*: A word game designed to teach common blends and word endings by proper matching. (For use with two to four children. $2.00. American Teaching Aids.)

5. *Blends and Digraphs Pictures for Pegboard*: A set consisting of twenty-six consonant blends cards in full color printed on 3¾-by-4-inch white index cards for use on pegboard and chalk tray or as flash cards. (For use with individual children or a small group of children. $4.75 per set. Ideal.)

6. *Blends Puzzles*: This puzzle series consists of 10 reversible puzzles (20 in all), each die-cut into four interconnecting pieces. The one large piece represents a consonant blend sound in letters, and the other three pieces illustrate objects whose names contain that blend sound. To complete a puzzle, a child must match all three correct pictures with the appropriate blend. The puzzles measure 8½″ x 4″. (For use with individual children or children working in pairs. $5.25. Incentives for Learning.)

7. *Build It* (Decks 2 and 4): A game that provides practice in consonant blends and vowels. Deck 2 involves a phonetic card game that teaches consonant blends and short vowels. Deck 4 teaches consonant blends and long vowels and the silent-*e* rule. (For use with any number of children. $4.50. Remedial Education Press.)

8. *Clue of the Combining Letters (Consonant Blends)*: Consonant *Blends* consists of two parts. Each involves a filmstrip and a cassette. (For use with individual children or a group of children. $17.00 each part. Learning Tree Filmstrips.)

9. *Consonant Blends and Digraphs Charts*: A collection of four charts, 8½ by 11 inches, for teaching blends and digraphs. Each chart has three labeled illustrations. Charts are in full color. (For use with individual children or a group of children. $6.65. Warren's.)

10. *Consonant Pictures for Pegboard*: A set consisting of thirty consonant cards in full color printed on 3¾-by-4-inch white index cards for use on pegboard and chalk tray or as flash cards. (For use with individual children or a small group of children. $6.50, per set. Ideal.)

11. *Dog House*: A phonetic game consisting of thirty-five phonograms along with eighty-four assorted consonants and consonant blends with which to build words. (For use with a group of children. $2.30. Kenworthy.)

12. *Go Fish* (Set II): A rummylike game designed to teach the sounds of consonant blends. (For use with two to four children; potentially self-directed. $4.50. Remedial Education Press.)

13. *Group Sounding Game*: A game which is a complete phonics course beginning with the recognition of initial consonants, blends, and vowels and ending with syllabication of three-syllable words. (For use with two or more children; potentially self-directed. $4.75. Garrard.)

14. *Lumpy Looey*: This is an easy card game for teaching blending skills to beginning readers. Suggested for grade levels 1-4. (For use with three to six players. $4.95. Little Brown Bear.)

15. *Magic Cards-Blends and Digraphs*: Instructional materials consisting of eight exercises on six 8½-by-11-inch ply cards. They are designed to stimulate the learning of consonant blends and digraphs. The set includes a durable transparent pocket into which the cards are inserted and on which the answers can be marked with wax crayons. The pocket can be wiped clean easily to make it ready for the next exercise. (For use with individual children or a small group of children. $2.50. Ideal.)

16. *Monster Hunt*: A self-directing and self-correcting game designed to help children acquire basic word attack skills. Level 2 pertains to consonant clusters. (For two to four children, $59.95. Allied Education Press.)

17. *The New Phonics We Use Learning Kits*: Two kits of 10 phonic games each, including the consonant blend games *Road Race* and *Frustration*. These colorful card and/or board games are adaptable for two or more players. (Complete kits, $93.00 each. Rand McNally.)

18. *Phonetic Quizmo*: A lotto-type game consisting of thirty-eight phonetic Quizmo cards, teacher's word list, direction card, and markers. The game is designed to teach consonant sounds and consonant blends. (For use with two or more children; potentially self-directed. $3.25. Milton Bradley.)

19. *Phonic Game Mats Library*: The game library consists of six sets of colorful games that include a Consonant Blend Games Set. Other games involve Rhyming Games, Sets A and B; Short and Long Vowel Games, and a Consonant Digraph Game. (For use with individual children or a group of children; $9.95 per game. Lakeshore.)

20. *Phonics: Beginning and Ending Consonant Blends*: Instructional material consisting of pictures of everyday objects which is designed for use with Charlie, the Teaching Robot. (For use with individual children or children working in pairs. $9.95. Tarmac/tac, Inc.)

21. *Sound Hunt* (Set II): An exciting phonics game designed to teach consonant blends and trigraphs. The sixty cards in the deck are colored. (For use with two to eight children, potentially self-directed. $1.95. American Teaching Aids.)

22. *Speech-To-Print Phonics*: A kit of material initially designed as a readiness program which may also be used as supplementary material with any basal series and as a remedial activity. The kit contains a teacher's manual and specific lessons in relating phonemes to printed form. It includes consonants and vowels and twenty-one consonant blends. Special response cards are used by pupils so that the teacher

can detect any children who are experiencing difficulty. (For use with a group of children or an entire class. $60.00. Harcourt Brace Jovanovich.)

23. *Spelling/Language Learning Games Kits*: Two bits of 10 games each, including the consonant blend game *Start Smart*. These colorful card and/or board games are adaptable for two or more players. (Complete kits, $93.00 each. Rand McNally.)

24. *Super Stock*: A self-directing and self-correcting game designed to help children acquire basic word attack skills. Level 2 pertains to consonant clusters. (For two to four children. $59.95. Allied Education Press.)

25. *T-Scope Consonant Blends and Digraphs*: This T-Scope material has strips of consonant blends, digraphs, and consonants that slide through the scope to form words appearing in a slot. As the strip is advanced, answers appear for self-checking. (For individual children or children working in pairs. $3.95. Jane Ward, Co.)

26. *Turn 'N Learn Beginning Blends*: One of ten colorful cards in which students write answers on their paper through holes in cards and then turn over the cards for the correct response. (For individual children or children working in pairs. $3.95, per set. Creative Teaching Press, Inc.)

27. *Ugly Oogly*: This game consists of two decks of cards. The first deck provides practice in blending of consonants with common phonograms; the second deck is for practice in blending consonant blends with common phonograms. Suggested for grade levels 2-6. (For use with three to six children. $4.95. Little Brown Bear.)

28. *Word-Picture Dominoes* (Blends): A dominolike game which covers the blends *st, dr,* and *tr* and the short sounds of the vowels. The student matches one picture with another or with the printed name for the item. A total of 28 pieces, 1¾" x 3½", are provided. (For use with two or more children. $2.95. Developmental Learning Materials.)

29. *Word Trek*—Blends and Digraphs: This game features a 24" x 24" gameboard on which players "travel" while they build words by combining blends and digraphs with word endings. Word Trek consists of the gameboard, 40 blend-digraph cards, 85 word-ending pocket cards, four markers, and playing instructions. (For use with two to four children. $10.25. Developmental Learning Materials.)

TEACHER-MADE MATERIALS FOR CORRECTING DEFICIENCIES IN CONSONANT BLENDS

When individual pupils or groups of pupils are deficient in knowledge of consonant blends, individualized practice can be provided by using *teacher- or pupil-made materials* such as the following.

1. *Authors with Beginnings*: For this game words are printed on corners of cards—four words to a set. A set consists of four word that begin with the same consonant blend. This can be highlighted by underlining the first two letters or writing them in red. Each child is dealt four cards, and one child begins the game by calling for a word beginning with a given blend. If he gets the word, he may continue to call for words. When his opponent indicates that he does not have the blend called for, the child draws from the deck of cards that is face down on the table. The child who acquires the most sets wins. (For use with two to four children; potentially self-directed.)

2. *Authors with Blends*: Words are printed on corners of cards—four cards to a set. A set consists of four words beginning with the same consonant blend. Each child is dealt four cards, and one begins the game by calling for a card beginning with a certain consonant blend. If he gets the word, he may continue to call for words. When his opponent indicates that he does not have the card called for, the child draws from the deck of cards that is face down on the table. The child who acquires the most sets wins. (For use with two to four children; potentially self-directed.)

3. *Baseball*: For this game a baseball diamond is drawn on the blackboard or on cardboard. Two groups of children are chosen. The pitcher flashes a consonant blend. If the batter calls a word beginning with the blend, he has made a hit and moves to first base. Should the next batter score a hit also, he moves to first base and the previous batter advances to second. Soon the runs begin to come in. Teams change sides just as soon as three outs (wrong answers) have been given. The team with the most runs wins. (For use with groups of children.)

4. *Blend Fishing*: For this game consonant blend cards are cut in the shape of fish. A paper clip is slipped over each card. Fishermen are equipped with a pole (short stick), a fish line (20 inches of store string), and a fishhook (small magnet). Each child gets a turn trying to catch a fish. If he can call a word that begins with the consonant blend sound on the fish he has caught, he may keep the fish. If he is unable to think of a suitable word, he returns the fish, face down, to the fishpond. (For use with two children or a group of children; potentially self-directed.)

5. *Clothespin Wheel*: For this game cut out a circular piece of tagboard about 12 inches in diameter. Paste or draw pictures of common objects around the periphery of the oaktag. Equip the child with a box of clothespins on each of which is printed a consonant blend. He then matches the clothespins with the proper pictures. For example, the *fr* clothespin would be placed over the picture of a frog; the *pl* clothespin, over the picture of a plum. (For use with individual children; potentially self-directed.)

6. *Deezio*: For this game a set of twenty-five cards is constructed. Recommended card size is 2½ by 3 inches. An initial blend is written in two diagonal corners. A word beginning with this inital blend is written in the center of the card. It is necessary to have at least two cards with the same initial blend, but he word in the center should differ. The twenty-fifth card will have no duplicate. This card has a drawing of a funny face and is Deezio.

All cards are dealt to the players, and each player immediately looks for pairs of cards with the same blends. He places these pairs in front of him, saying the word on each card as he puts it down. If he cannot read the words, another player may tell him, but he must hold the pair until his next turn. Then the player to the left of the person with the most cards begins playing by drawing a card. He draws a card from the player holding the most cards. The drawer attempts to match the card with one in his hand. If he has a pair, he places it in front of him and reads the words. If no match is made, he retains the card in his hand. The playing continues clockwise around the table. The player who matches all his cards first wins. The rest continue to play until one person is left with Deezio; he is the Deezio. (For use with three to five children; potentially self-directed.) This game and the games *Happy Ending* and *Word Flight* were devised by Hildegard Ziegler and associates, teachers at the Madison, Wisconsin, public schools.

7. *Finding Partners*: Two types of cards are placed in an envelope—some involve word endings and others consonant blends. The cards are distributed to a group of children. Those children receiving cards with blends move around among the other children to see if they can form a word by combining their cards. When a word has been formed, the child says, "We made_____with our cards." Since there is the possibility that other blends may fit the ending, the teacher asks if anyone else can help make a word. The process continues until all pairing is exhausted. (For use with a group of children.)

8. *Lotto Blends*: To make the game with the help of the class, the teacher prepares cardboard master cards 8 by 11 inches in size. These master cards are blocked off vertically and horizontally into twenty-five small squares. The middle space is marked *free.* Individual consonant blends are placed on the twenty-four spaces that remain. Each master card must have the same blends on it but in different positions. Twenty-four words known by the children on sight that begin with the consonant blends are placed in an envelope. As individual words are drawn from the envelope and called, the players find the consonant blends on their master cards and cover them with a marker. The marker may be a kernel of corn, a bean, or a small piece of cardboard. The first child to cover a row of letters in a straight line, vertically, horizontally, or diagonally, calls out Lotto. If he has not erred, he is declared

the winner. (For use with a group of children; potentially self-directed.)

9. *Pockets*: Cut apart some cheap envelopes and mount them on a chart as pockets for 3-by-5-inch cards. A consonant blend is printed on each envelope. The cards which have pictures or drawings on them are to be placed in the pockets beginning with the appropriate consonant blend. Using an identification scheme on the backs of the cards makes this activity self-corrective. (For use with individual children; potentially self-directed.)

10. *Sound Box*: For this game choose a cardboard box with subdivisions—one that has been used to package bottles is ideal. By using common pins, label each subdivision with a small card on which a blend has been written. Players draw picture cards from a pile and attempt to place them in the spaces labeled with letters that represent the beginning blend sounds of the words pictured. Points can be given for correct choices. This activity can be made self-corrective by printing the correct letters on the backs of the picture cards. (For use with one or more children; potentially self-directed.)

11. *Spin and Call*: To make the game, divide a large oaktag circle into eight sections. Attach a large pointer to the center of the circle so that it spins freely. The player spins the pointer and calls a word beginning with the particular consonant blend to which it points when coming to a stop. If a correct word is called, he scores one point. A record should be kept of words called so that no repetitions take place. (For use with two children or a group of children.)

12. *What Am I?* For this game write on individual cards riddles which give initial consonant blends as clues. For example, "I grow in bunches on trees. I am good to eat. I begin with a *gr* sound. What am I?" Each child in the group has a chance at a riddle card. If he guesses the answer, he is given the card. The child with the largest number of cards is the winner. Placing the answers on the backs of the cards makes this activity self-corrective. (For use with a group of children; potentially self-directed.)

COMMERCIAL MATERIALS FOR CORRECTING DEFICIENCIES IN VOWEL SOUNDS, LETTER COMBINATIONS, AND PRINCIPLES

When individual pupils or groups of pupils are deficient in knowledge of vowel sounds, letter combinations, or principles, corrective practice can be individualized by using *commercial material* such as the following:

1. *Aims: Vowels Kit*: Instructional material designed to develop skills in the auditory discrimination of short and long vowel sounds and the letter-sound association of short and long vowels. Activities involve

three levels of difficulty: (1) Matching picture to picture, (2) Matching picture to letter, and (3) Matching letter to picture. (For use with individual children or a group of children. $64.50. Continental Press, Inc.)

2. *Astro Alley*: This game is designed for practice in auditory and visual recognition of short vowels in an initial position. One deck consists of illustrated cards with words such as elephant, octopus; the second deck consists of simple words such as ask, in, up, etc. Suggested for grades 1-4. (For use with two to six children. $4.95. Little Brown Bear.)

3. *Autophonics* Game 2: A vowel-review game based on vehicles and vehicle driving. The bingolike game is composed of thirty-six different cards, master card, call card, and markers. (For use with groups of children. $7.95. Warren's.)

4. *Autophonics* Game 4: A vowel-digraph-and-diphthong game based on vehicles and vehicle driving. The bingolike game is composed of thirty-six different cards, master card, call card, and markers. (For use with groups of children. $7.95. Warren's.)

5. *Blend and Build Games*, 1 & 2. Game 1 is devoted to short vowel instruction and Game 2 is devoted to long vowel instruction. Each game consists of 29 cubes. Green cubes are used for initial consonants and red cubes for word endings. (For use with individual children, children working in pairs, or a small group of children. $14.95 each. Lakeshore.)

6. *Bulletin Board of Basic Phonics*: A set of thirty-five 6-by-9-inch cards with large type and colored pictures introducing difficult consonants, vowel digraphs, and vowel sounds. In addition to a key word, six additional words employing the sound appear on each card. At the bottom of the card a key-word sentence is provided. (For use with individual children or a group of children. $3.00 per set. Educational Aids.)

7. *Case of the Long and Short Vowels*: These instructional materials consist of individual filmstrips and cassettes for each of the following: Long vowel, short a, short e, short i, short o, and shout u. (For use with individual children or a group of children. $17.00 each. Learning Tree Filmstrips.)

8. *End-in-E Game*: This game is designed to show how words change as *e* is added. There are fifteen word cards, each with a flap that turns in to add the letter *e*, changing the word. For example, *at* with an *e* is *ate*. There is a story to be used with the cards that adds fun to the learning. The letters on the cards involved are quite large. (For use with individual children, children working in pairs or with a group of children under proper direction. $1.25. Ideal.)

9. *First Talking Alphabet* Part 2: Programmed instruction on vowels. Using records and cards, a child hears a sound, says it, sees the letter that represents it, and traces the flocked letter shapes. Part 2 develops ability to discriminate among three sounds represented by each of the vowel letters—long, short, and r-controlled. (For use with individual children. $75.57. Scott, Foresman.)

10. *Group-Size Vowel Cards*: Instructional materials consisting of two cards each for all short and long vowels, digraphs, diphthongs, and other vowel combinations with consonants. Four phonetic rules are covered. (For use with individual children, children working in pairs, or a group of children under proper direction. $4.20. Garrard.)

11. *Group Sounding Game*: A game which is a complete phonics course beginning with the recognition of initial consonants, blends, and vowels and ending with syllabication of three-syllable words. (For use with two or more children; potentially self-directed. $4.75. Garrard.)

12. *Highway Robbery* Game 4: This digraphs-and-diphthongs game consists of two decks of cards and involves words that are connected with cars, motorcycles, and obtaining a driver's license. (For use with group of children. $5.95. Warren's.)

13. *Junior Phonic Rummy*: A game employing 110 most frequently occurring short vowel words from the most widely used first-grade basic reading books. A key picture is provided for each of the short vowel sounds. (For use with two or more children; potentially self-directed. $1.65. Kenworthy.)

14. *Listen and Do* (Vowels): These instructional materials consist of cassettes and records which are designed to help pupils develop vowel-sound associations. They consist of 22 recorded lessons of 20 minutes duration. Each lesson is accompanied by a worksheet. $74.97 for cassettes and $69.99 for records. (Houghton Mifflin.)

15. *Magical Silent E*: This game features an 18″ x 24″ gameboard on which short-vowel words appear. Players place an E tile at the end of one of the words and then read the newly formed long-vowel word. The 18″ x 24″ gameboard, four spirit masters, spinner, and six E tiles come boxed. (For use with two or more children. $7.75. Developmental Learning Materials.)

16. *Magic Cards-Vowels*: Instructional materials consisting of twenty-four exercises on six 8½-by-11-inch cards. Exercises can be reworked again and again because of a transparent plastic pocket into which cards are inserted and on which answers are marked with a wax crayon. The pocket is then wiped clean to make it ready for the next exercise. (For use with individual children or a group of children. $3.25. Ideal.)

17. *Magic Vowel*: A set of cards which carry silent-*e* words on one side and the same words without the silent *e* on the other side. (For use with individual children, children working in pairs, or a group of children. $2.50 per set. Educational Aids.)

18. *Match the Vowel*: A two-deck matching game designed to teach vowels and vowel combinations: digraphs and diphthongs. (For use with individual children, children working in pairs, or a group of children. $2.50. Educational Aids.)

19. *The New Phonics We Use Learning Kits*: Two kits of 10 phonic games each, including the vowel and diphthong games *Lucky Duck, Spin Out, Cover-up, Bone Zone, Spin-A-Sound, Vowel Dominoes, Pattern Match, Search, Full House,* and *Cross Words*. These colorful card and/or board games are adaptable for two or more players. (Complete kits, $93.00 each. Rand McNally.)

20. *Phonetic Word Wheel*: A device that gives a child varied practice in recognition of vowels, consonants, and phonetic blends. Countless variations of this game are possible, depending on the needs of the pupil. (For use with individual children or children working in pairs. $2.25. Milton Bradley.)

21. *Phonetics Factory*: A cassette-activity program that provides a basic foundation in forming and using vowel sounds. It consists of six cassettes which cover 34 lessons that coordinate with 34 duplicator worksheets. A lesson is devoted to each vowel sound and consonant sound as well. Each worksheet shows the letter symbol, correponding picture, and a drawing of the human mouth forming the sound. (For use with one child or a group of children. $52.50. Lakeshore.)

22. *Phonic Game Mats Library*: The game library consists of six sets of colorful games that include a Short Vowel Games Set and a Long Vowel Games Set. Other games involve Rhyming Games, Sets A and B, and a Consonant Digraph Game. (For use with individual children or a group of children; $9.95 per game. Lakeshore.)

23. *Phonic Rummy* (four sets): Games designed to teach short vowels and vowel principles. Each set contains two packs of sixty cards presenting words suitable for the grades on each set. (For use with two to four children; potentially self-directed. $1.70, per set. Kenworthy.)

24. *Phonics Learning Labs*: These self-directed and self-corrective laboratories employ cassettes and interest activity booklets. Each lab has 3 cassettes, 90 four-page activity booklets, 3 reproducible post-tests and a teacher's guide. Eight labs are involved. They include Short Vowel Sounds (Labs 1 & 2), Long Vowels (Labs 1 & 2), Initial Consonants (Labs 1 & 2), Consonant Blends (Labs 1 & 2), and Finishing Phonics Lab. (For individual children; potentially self-directed. $29.95 each. Lakeshore.)

25. *Programmed Reading Kit I*: A set of sixteen games including vowel games *Green Dozens, Half-Moons, Port-Holes*, and *Pattern Bingo*. In most instances, these games are adaptable for one or more players. (Complete kit of sixteen games, $30.90. Scott, Foresman.)

26. *Quiet Pal Game*: A game that builds words with silent letters in them. The word card has a flap that turns over to cover the end letter. The word is changed instantly to make a new word-one with a silent letter, as *ran* to *rain* with its silent *i*. The set includes fifteen story cards. (For use with individual children, children working in pairs, or a group of children under proper direction. $1.95. Warren's.)

27. *Say Its Name*: A long vowel game for pupils of all ages. (For use with one to six players. $5.00. Beaver Pond Learning Games.)

28. *Sea of Vowels*: A game designed to teach long and short vowels and help build vocabulary. The child travels by submarine in search of lost treasure, encountering adventures along the way. (For use with two to six children. $9.25. Ideal.)

29. *Short Vowel Drill*: A drill involving categorizing pictures of objects containing a short vowel sound. Each vowel is represented by a number of picture words. (For use with individual children or children working in pairs. $3.95. Remedial Educational Press.)

30. *Short Vowel Tic Tac Toe*: This game consists of one 12″ x 12″ cardboard game grid, five X's and O's and five game cards. The five game cards (A, E, I, O, U) have nine phonetically regular words on each side for a total of 90 words. Tic Tac Toe strategy and short vowel knowledge are needed to play the game. (For use with two or more children. $12.25. Developmental Learning Materials.)

31. *Skinny Winny*: A game which provides practice in easy short vowel patterns. One deck consists of three-letter short vowel words and the second deck consists of short vowel words with consonant blends. Suggested for grade levels 1-4. (For use with two to six children. $4.95. Little Brown Bear.)

32. *Spelling/Language Learning Games Kits*: Two kits of 10 games each, including the vowel games *Elephant Walk, Target, Train, Chance*, and *Match*. These colorful card and/or board games are adaptable for two or more players. (Complete kits, $93.00 each. Rand McNally.)

33. *Step Up To Reading Success*: A kit of sports game boards—Steeplechase, Race Track, Baseball, Football—that employs vowel cards and vowel pattern cards. Vowel Rummy also is available as an assortment of readiness and beginning reading activities. All are self-correcting. (For use with two children or a small group of children. $75.00. Educational Activities, Inc.)

34. *Tick-Tack-Go*: Board games for small groups of children engaged in the mastery of vowel sounds and patterns. ($12.95. Little Brown Bear Associates.)

35. *Turn'N Learn Short and Long Vowels:* One of ten colorful cards in which students write answers on their paper through holes in cards and then turn over the cards for the correct response. (For individual children or children working in pairs. $3.95 per set. Creative Teaching Press, Inc.)

36. *Vowel Bingo:* A game in which players identify underlined long and short vowels in the words on their cards. Thirty-six cards are included. Cards 1-18 have single syllable words; cards 19-36 include single and multiple syllable words. (For use with a group of chidren. $4.95. Trend Enterprises, Inc.)

37. *Vowel Charts:* A set of vowel charts in brilliant color showing vowel pictures, symbols, and rules. Each set contains ten 23-by-36-inch charts (nine vowel charts and one key chart) with metal eyelets to prevent tearing. A complete manual of directions is included. (For use with individual children or a group of children; potentially self-directed. $10.75. Ideal.)

38. *Vowel Lotto:* A game that gives practice in hearing and learning short vowels, long vowels, vowel digraphs, and diphthongs. Children match cover card pictures with those on the lotto cards having the same vowel sound. (For use with two or more children; potentially self-directed. $3.00. Garrard.)

39. *Vowel Pictures for Pegboard:* A set consists of twenty-four vowel cards, one hundred-three full color picture cards, and two hundred-twenty word cards, 3¾-by-4-inches in size. The cards can be used for pegboard or chalk tray or as flash cards. (For use with individual children or a small group of children. $8.50. Ideal.)

40. *Vowel Poster Cards:* These materials consist of twenty 11" x 14" cards each of which shows three words and pictures representing a vowel sound or a vowel combination. (For use with individual children or a group of children. $6.00. Lakeshore.)

41. *Vowel Solitaire:* A card game that reviews and reinforces knowledge of vowel sounds and the use of a pronunciation key. The set consists of three packs of cards, each pack to be used by one child for practice in the recognition of four vowel sounds and the letters that stand for them. A total of twelve vowel sounds is included. (For use with individual children. $8.76. Scott, Foresman.)

42. *Vowel Sounds:* In these materials students can hear vowel sounds, see vowels in word contexts, and manipulate a wheel card to form words. Includes ten lessons on five cassette tapes, five double-sided vowel wheel manipulatives and ten packs of seventy-two individual response sheets. (For use with individual children or a small group of children; self-directed. $64.90. Dick Blick.)

43. *Vowel Sounds Thinker Puzzles*: A set of two-piece self-correcting puzzles designed to teach the short vowels. (For use with individual children or pairs of children; self-directed. $5.50. Lakeshore.)

44. *Vowel Wheels*: Five drill devices designed to help children blend sounds and develop sound-symbol relationships. Each vowel is presented as an isolated sound in word settings and on the reverse side of the card in vowel-consonant combinations to form phonemes. Discs are moved to make meaningful words. (For use with individual children or children working in pairs. $5.50. Milton Bradley.)

45. *Wipe-Clean Activity Books*: A series of eight books of write-on, wipe-off activity cards for individualized phonics learning. Each book is a binder with 12 removable cards. The series includes Short Vowel Sounds and Long Vowel Sounds, Initial Consonant Sounds, Final Consonant Sounds, Consonant Blends, Consonant Blends & Digraphs, and Rhyming Words. (For use with individual children; $3.50 each. Lakeshore.)

46. *Word Games II*: A game covering the sounds *au/aw, oi/oy, ou/ow, oo* and the soft sounds of *c* and *g*. (For use with one to eight players. $6.00. Beaver Pond Learning Games.)

47. *Wow, Vowels*: A short vowel game for pupils of all ages. (For use with one to six players. $5.00. Beaver Pond Learning Games.)

48. *Zap*: Zap is designed for review in the recognition of long and short vowels. The game consists of one double deck of cards that includes most familiar long and short vowel patterns. Suggested for grades 2-6. For use with three to ten children. $4.95. Little Brown Bear.)

TEACHER-MADE MATERIALS FOR CORRECTING DEFICIENCIES IN VOWEL SOUNDS, LETTER COMBINATIONS, AND PRINCIPLES

When individual pupils or groups of pupils are deficient in knowledge of vowel sounds, letter combinations, and principles, individualized practice can be provided by using *teacher-* or *pupil-made materials* such as the following.

1. *Ask Me*: To make this game prepare about forty to fifty word cards on each of which is a word containing a vowel sound. Some cards should have duplicate vowel sounds, although the words themselves should differ. Four cards are dealt to each player, and the remainder are put in a pile on the table. The player to the left of the dealer reads one of his words. Other players holding cards with a similar vowel sound give their cards to the caller. The latter places any sets he acquires on the table. If the caller does not call his word correctly, he discards it but must draw another word from the pile. After drawing he waits until his

next turn before calling for another card. The winner is the player with the fewest cards. (For use with two to four children; potentially self-directive.)

2. *Baseball*: For this game a baseball diamond is drawn on the blackboard or on cardboard. Two groups of children are chosen. The pitcher flashes a word. If the batter can designate the short vowel sound in the word, he has made a hit and moves to first base. Should the next batter score a hit also, he moves to first base, and the first batter advances to second. Soon the runs begin to come in. Teams change sides just as soon as three outs (wrong answers) have been given. The team with the most runs wins. (For use with groups of children.)

3. *Matching Vowels and Objects*: The teacher pastes a number of small pictures on a sheet of oaktag. The pictures should be of things the children can recognize easily. An envelope containing a number of vowels (several of each kind) is clipped to the sheet of oaktag. The child removes the vowel cards and places them on or below the pictures whose names contain the vowel sounds. (For use with individual children.)

4. *Pockets*: Cut apart some cheap envelopes and mount them on a chart as pockets for 3-by-5-inch cards. A vowel is printed on each envelope. The cards which have pictures or drawings on them are to be placed in the pockets having the appropriate vowel sounds. An identification scheme on the backs of the cards will make this activity self-corrective. (For use with individual children; potentially self-directive.)

5. *Shoe-Box Match*: Paste pictures or drawings of objects beginning with a short-vowel sound on the fronts of shoe boxes. Players engaging in this activity attempt to sort small picture cards containing short vowel sounds. These are placed in the appropriate shoe boxes. The activity can be made self-corrective by numbering, correspondingly, the boxes and the backs of the small picture cards. (For use with individual children; potentially self-directive.)

6. *Spin and Call*: To make the game divide a large oaktag circle into eight sections. Place a vowel in each section. Attach a larger pointer to the center of the center so that it spins freely. The player spins the pointer and calls a word containing the short vowel to which it points when coming to a stop. If a correct word is called, he scores one point. A record should be kept of words called so that no repetitions take place. (For use with two children or a group of children; potentially self-directive.)

7. *Win-a-Row*: To make the game cut cards 7½ inches square. Rule five or more cards into 1½-inch squares so that there are twenty-five squares on the cards. Write or print selected words in the squares. Write the same word in a different position on all the cards so that no two cards are identical. However, each row must have one word with each of the short vowel sounds. Twenty-five different words with the short vowel

sounds will be written on a number of small cards. These will be numbered 1, 2, 3, 4, and 5. Numbers will represent rows on the playing card. Small paper circles can be made to be used as counters or markers to cover the words. The game is played very much like Bingo. The caller reads a row number and a word from the small cards. The players cover a word in the designated row which has the same vowel sound as the word read. The child who first covers five words vertically, diagonally, or horizontally reads his winning row. If he has not erred, he is declared the winner and may be the caller for the next game. (For use with more than two children; potentially self-directed.)

SUPPLMENTARY INSTRUCTIONAL ACTIVITIES FOR CORRECTING DEFICIENCIES IN VOWEL SOUNDS, LETTER COMBINATIONS, AND PRINCIPLES

When individual pupils or groups of pupils are deficient in knowledge of vowel sounds, letter combinations, or principles, provide individualized practice by employing activities such as the following. It should be noted that all these activities can be made self-directed by furnishing simple directions and accompanying answer keys.

1. The child is given a list of words. He underlines all the words that have the same vowel sound as that appearing in the first word.
2. The child is given a list of words containing long and short vowel sounds. He classifies the words into long and short vowels.
3. The child is given a list of words containing vowel blends or diphthongs. He classifies the words according to their vowel blends.
4. The child is given a list of words that have vowel combinations missing. He chooses that vowel combination from several given which will complete each word.
5. A series of pictures of objects are given to the child. He names each picture and tells whether the vowel in the name is long or short.
6. A list of words is given to the child. He checks the words in the list that have the same vowel sound.
7. The rules governing vowel sounds are given to the child along with a list of words. The child indicates the rule that governs the vowel sound of the words by writing the number of the rule before or after each word.
8. The child is given a list of words containing both the long and the short sounds of a given vowel. He checks the words that contain the long sound of the given vowel.
9. The child is given a list of words containing different long and short vowels. He draws a line under each word that contains a long vowel.
10. Lists of words containing long and short vowels are given to the child. He underlines each word that contains a short vowel.

COMMERCIAL MATERIALS FOR CORRECTING
DEFICIENCIES IN STRUCTURAL ANALYSIS

When individual pupils or groups of pupils are deficient in their knowledge of structural analysis, corrective practice can be individualized by using available *commercial material* such as the following.

1. *Advanced Prefix and Suffix Puzzles*: These materials consist of 38 three-piece puzzles. The puzzles are 9″ x 2⅝″ in size. Each puzzle involves matching a prefix and suffix with a word base. A jig-saw cut makes the puzzles self-corrective. (For individual children or children working in pairs. $6.50. Developmental Learning Materials.)

2. *Affixo*: A word-building game using roots, prefixes, and suffixes. (For use with two to five players. $4.00. Remedial Education Press.)

3. *Compound-A-Word*: This game consists of four 12″ square gameboards, 128 word cards, four spirit masters, and instructions. There are two sets of gameboards. In Set 1, a student matches the first half of a compound word with a picture that completes the compound. In Set 2, a student matches a card with the last half of a compound word with a picture that completes the compounds. (For use with two studens. $9.00. Developmental Learning Materials.)

4. *Compound Word Game*: This game consists of 50 word cards which are divided by color into three groups of 30 cards each. Card size is 3″ x 1″. The task is to form compound words within a given group and by mixing the groups. (For use with individual children or children working in pairs. $3.25. Developmental Learning Materials.)

5. *Freeze*: This game provides practice in the recognition of affixes and gives practice in decoding three-syllable words. One deck consists of three-syllable words with prefixes; the other deck consist of three-syllable words with suffixes. Suggested for grade levels 3 and up. (For use with two to six players. $4.95. Little Brown Bear.)

6. *Grab* (Set IV): A sight vocabulary game consisting of fifteen polysyllabic words which are subdivided into individual syllables. (For use with two to four children; potentially self-directed. Two sets on any level, $2.75. Teachers' Supplies.)

7. *Monster Hunt*: A self-directing and self-correcting game designed to help children acquire basic word attack skills. Levels 9 and 10 pertain to syllabication; level II, prefixes; and level 12, suffixes. (For two to four chidren. $59.95. Allied Education Press.)

8. *Mousetrap*: A game designed to provide practice in the analysis and synthesis of compound words and in the recognition of these words. One deck consists of easy compound words; and the second deck consists of more difficult compound words. Suggested for grade levels 2-6. (For use with three to six players. $4.95. Little Brown Bear.)

9. *The New Phonics We Use Learning Kits*: Two kits of 10 phonic games each, including the structural analysis game *Syllable Count*. These colorful card and/or board games are adaptable for two or more players. (Complete kits, $93.00 each. Rand McNally.)

10. *Prefix Puzzles*: These materials consist of 36 puzzles, 7" x 2¾" which are designed to expand a student's knowledge of prefix forms. Twelve prefixes are included. Each can be matched to three bases or forms of bases. A jig-saw cut makes the puzzles self-corrective. (For use with individual children or children working in pairs. $5.00. Developmental Learning Materials.)

11. *Roundup: Compound Words*: A cowboy and cowgirl game consisting of twelve activity cards which are illustrated around the theme of a roundup. Manipulatives, worksheets, record keeping and a direction card are included. Suggested for grades 2-4. (For use with two to four children. $9.95. S-T-E-P Ahead, Inc.)

12. *Spelling/Language Learning Games Kits*: Two kits of 10 games each, including the structural analysis games *A-Maze-Ment* and *Capture*. These colorful card and/or board games are adaptable for two or more players. (Complete kits, $93.00 each. Rand McNally.)

13. *Stop The Game*: This game consists of two decks of cards. The first deck provides practice in two-syllable words with vcv patterns. The second deck is for two-syllable words with vccv patterns. Suggested for grade levels 2-6. (For use with two to six players. $4.95. Little Brown Bear.)

14. *Student Word Set*: A set containing three hundred words drawn from the syllabication materials of William Kottmeyer. The cards are designed for use with the Student Syllabascope ($2) which is available from the same publisher. (For use with individual children. $2.50. Wordcrafters Guild.)

15. *Suffix Puzzles*: These materials consist of 33 puzzles, 7" x 2¾", which are designed to expand a student's knowledge of suffix forms. Eleven suffixes are included. Each can be matched to three bases or forms of bases. A jig-saw cut makes the puzzles self-corrective. (For use with individual children or children working in pairs. $5.00. Developmental Learning Materials.)

16. *Syllable Flip Cards*: A manipulative set that presents an effective aid for teaching reading through combining syllables to form words. (For use with individual children, children working in pairs, or a small group of children. $1.10, per set. Warren's.)

17. *Syllable Game*: A game containing three decks of cards. The words in the first two decks are of two syllables, and the player learns by sight the syllables in these words. The third deck has words up to four syllables in length. (For use with one student or two students playing solitaire; potentially self-directed. $3.80. Garrard.)

18. *Syllable Puzzles*: These 20 reversible puzzles (40 in all) consist of 10 two-syllable puzzles and 10 three-syllable puzzles. They measure 8½" x 4" and are made of heavy-duty puzzleboard with large print for aiding visually impaired pupils. (For use with individual children or children working in pairs. $6.75. Incentives for Learning.)

19. *Syllables*: A set of sixteen reversible flip cards that present 96 syllables and form 144 words as the flaps are manipulated. (For use with individual children, children working in pairs, or a group of children under proper direction. $1.10. Kenworthy.)

20. *Syllable Scoreboard*: This game features a basketball gameboard on which a student moves after drawing a word card from the "ball bin." He then moves one, two, or three spaces depending on the number of syllables making up the word. The 18" x 24" board, four spirit masters, 42 word and direction cards, and six markers come boxed. (For use with two or more children. $9.25. Developmental Learning Materials.)

21. *Take 5*: A game for teaching and reinforcing non-phonetic prefixes and suffixes such as *con, able,* and *ive* as well as giving practice in blending longer words. Each set contains one deck of two-syllable words and one deck of three-syllable words. (For use with three to four players. $4.95. Little Brown Bear Associates.)

22. *Teacher Syllabication Set*: A set of one hundred fifty words (on 3-by-14-inch cards) for the teacher who is introducing the concepts of syllable division. The cards are designed for use with the *Teacher Syllabascope* ($2.75) which is available from the same publisher. (For use with individual children or an entire class. $2.80. Wordcrafters Guild.)

23. *Third Syllable Game*: A set of cards that provides practice in attacking polysyllabic words one syllable at a time. (For use with individual children, chidren working in pairs, or a group of children; potentially self-directed. $2.25. Educational Aids.)

24. *Webster Word Wheels*: Practice wheels consisting of twenty-five beginning blend wheels, twenty prefix wheels, eighteen suffix wheels, and eight two-letter consonant wheels. The wheels are color-coded and numbered in order of difficulty. The set comes in a colorful cardboard file box. (For use with individual children or children working in pairs. $39.00. Webster/McGraw-Hill.)

25. *Word Building Slide Rule*: An ingenious slide rule that allows students to decode long words and learn how affixes modify meanings. A take-apart words section helps students discover prefixes, roots, and suffixes. (For use with individual student or students working in pairs. $2.00. E-Z Grader Co.)

26. *Word Parts*: *Word Parts* consists of individual filmstrips and cassettes for each of the following Prefixes, Suffixes and Roots I, Prefixes, Suffixes and Roots II, Syllables and Accents, and More About Syllables.

(For use with individual children or a group of children. $18.00, each. Learning Tree Filmstrips.)

27. *Word Prefixes*: A set of subdivided folding cards which highlight twenty-three prefixes that blend to form 216 words. The meaning of each prefix is given, and the words being shown are keyed on back of each card. (For use with individual children, children working in pairs, or a group of children. $1.10. Kenworthy.)

28. *Word Suffixes*: A set of subdivided folding cards that highlight twenty-four word endings. A total of 144 words are formed. The meaning of each suffix is given and words being shown are keyed in small type. (For use with individual children, children working in pairs, or a small group of children. $1.10. Kenworthy.)

TEACHER-MADE MATERIALS FOR CORRECTING DEFICIENCIES IN STRUCTURAL ANALYSIS

When individual pupils or groups of pupils are deficient in their knowledge of structural analysis, corrective practice can be provided by using *teacher- or pupil-made materials* such as the following.

1. *Author with Endings*: For this game words are printed on corners of cards—four cards to set. A set consists of four words that have the same ending. This can be highlighted by underlining the endings in red. Each child is dealt four cards, and one child begins the game by calling for a word with a given ending. If he gets the word, he may continue to call for words. When his opponent indicates that he does not have the ending called for, the child draws from the deck of cards that is face down on the table. The child who acquires the most sets wins. (For use with two to four children; potentially self-directed.)

2. *Baseball*: In this game two groups of children are chosen. The pitcher flashes a word. If the batter can tell the number of syllables in the word, he has made a hit and moves to first base. Should the next batter also score a hit, he moves to first base and the previous batter advances to second. Soon the runs begin to come in. Teams change sides just as soon as three outs (wrong answer) have been given. The team with the most runs wins. (For use with groups of children.)

3. *Happy Ending*: This is a structural analysis game consisting of one-hundred-eight playing cards divided into eleven units of eight cards, two units of four cards, and one unit of twelve cards. The first unit (twelve cards) is labeled *Perfect Fit. The second unit* (four cards) is labeled *Wait*, and four cards are labeled *Surprise*. The remaining eleven units make up the rest of the deck, and each of these units will have eight different words with the same ending. The ending is printed in

color. The cards are shuffled, and eleven cards are dealt to each player. The remaining cards are put into a pack in the center of the table. The top card is turned up next to the deck and starts the discard pile.

Anyone having a *Surprise* card in his hand places it on the table face up in front of him and immediately draws another card from the pack. The player to the left of the dealer begins playing. He will draw the card turned up or draw from the top of the deck. If he draws the turned up card, he must be able to use it immediately either in a triangle or on a triangle. (A triangle is three or more cards with the same ending put down face up in front of the player.) A player may add to any triangle that he has on the table. A triangle of three cards may have one *Perfect Fit* in it. *It is important that each card played on the table is read.* If a player cannot read the triangle or an individual card, his partner can attempt to read them. If neither can read the card or cards, a monitor may tell the player, but he must keep it or them in his hand until his next turn.

A player terminates his play by putting a card on the discard pile and reading it. If a player needs assistance in reading this card, he discards it. The playing continues clockwise around the table. One person in the partnership keeps the cards in front of him, and his partner plays on them or adds to the lay down. As the playing continues, the player who wants the top card of the discard pile for playing on a triangle or in a triangle must take all the cards in the pile and read and play the top one immediately.

Perfect Fit can be called any card and can help to make three or more of a kind. A *Wait* card on a discarded pile *Stops* the discard pile for the next player who then must draw from the unused pack. A *Happy Ending* is made when seven cards with the same ending have been played. This may include the *Perfect Fits;* however, only three *Perfect Fits* can be used in one *Happy Ending.*

The game is over when a player has a *Happy Ending* and is rid of all the cards in his hands. Each player will try to get as many *Happy Endings* as he can.

Scoring is as follows: A *Happy Ending* counts 100; going out counts 50; *Surprises* count 50; *Perfect Fits* count 10; every other card counts five. The score of all the cards left in the hands of the other players when a player goes out is subtracted from his score on the score. The remaining score for each couple is added and tallied. The couple who first attains a score of 1,000 is declared winner. (For use with two sets of partners.)

4. *Word Flight*: This is a structural analysis game consisting of fifty-two playing cards on each of which is a two-, three-, or four-syllable word. The difficulty of the game can be increased by having many multiple-syllable words.

The playing board is constructed by placing a mimeographed map of the United States on tagboard. A flight route should be drawn between major cities. Miniature airplanes of different colors should be made for use by each player.

To begin the playing, the deck of cards is placed in the center of the table near the playing board. Each player draws a first card from the center deck. The player who draws a word with the least number of syllables is the first to play. If he has a one-syllable word, he may travel to the first city on the route. If he has a two-syllable word, he travels to the second city, and so forth. Each player in turn draws a card, says the word on the card, tells how many syllables are in the word, and moves his airplane along the flight route. If he cannot say the word or determine the number of syllables in it, someone tells him, but he cannot move his airplane. The player who reaches the home field first wins the game. (For use with two to four children; potentially self-directed.)

SUPPLEMENTARY INSTRUCTURAL ACTIVITIES FOR CORRECTING DEFICIENCIES IN STRUCTURAL ANALYSIS

When individual pupils or groups of pupils are deficient in knowledge of structural analysis, corrective practice can be individualized by employing activities such as the following. Note that many of these activities can be made self-directed by\furnishing simple directions and accompanying answer keys.

1. Syllabication
   a. The child is given a list of common words. He divides the words into syllables.
   b. The child is given a list of words. He underlines words ending in a certain syllable such as -*ight* and -*ing*.
   c. The child is given a series of pictures. He names each object pictured and writes the number of syllables in the name under the picture.
   d. A list of words is given to the child. He indicates the number of syllables in each word.
   e. The child is given the rules governing syllabication together with a list of words. He divides the words into syllables and indicates which rule he used.
2. Suffixes
   a. A list of words containing suffixes is given to the child. He identifies the root word in each word.
   b. The child is given a list of words containing suffixes. He uses the root word in a sentence.

c. The child is given a list of unknown words. He separates the suffix from the word and pronounces both suffix and root word.
d. The child is given a list of words with definitions after each word. He adds one of a given group of suffixes to the words so that the newly formed word complies with the definition after the word.
e. The child is given a list of words. He makes new words by adding a given suffix to the words on the list.
3. Prefixes
a. The child is given a list of words. He writes a given prefix before the words and gives the meaning of the new words.
b. A series of sentences with one word missing in each is given to the child. He fills in the words using the correct prefixes.
c. A group of prefixes and a list of words with definitions are given to the child. He adds one of the prefixes from the group to each word so that it corresponds to the definition written after each word.
d. A list of words with prefixes is given to the child. He writes the words without the prefix and indicates how the meaning has been changed.
e. The child is given a list of unknown words with a known prefix. He finds the meaning of the new word.
f. The child is given a list of words with prefixes. He underlines the prefixes.
g. The child is given a list of words containing common prefixes. He underlines the root word.
4. Common Compound Words
a. A list of compound words is given to the child. He draws a line between the two words making up each compound word.
b. Two columns of words are given to the child. He makes compound words by matching the words in one column with the words in the other column.
c. The child is given a list of compound words. He writes the two short words that make up the compound beside each word.
d. The child is given two list of words. He combines words from the two lists to form single compound words.
5. Endings of Words
a. A series of phrases with accompanying pictures are given to the child. If a phrase refers to more than one, the child adds the plural to the subject of the phrases.
b. The child is given a group of pictures. The child names the objects in the pictures and gives the plural of the name if there is more than one object involved.
c. The child is given a list of singular words. He forms the plurals of each word in the list.
d. The child is given a list of words. He forms new words by adding endings to the words.

WORKBOOKS

In an effort to help pupils build their word-recognition and word-analysis skills, teachers should capitalize on the vast supply of practice material available in the form of workbooks (workbooks and their proper use are discussed more fully on pages 296-300). Some of these workbooks are designed to accompany basal series; others are supplemental skill-type workbooks. Both types can be used to advantage. Following is a representative sample of workbooks that are suitable.

Building Words by E. SAVAGE. Chicago: Beckley-Cardy Co. A first-grade workbook which provides ear and eye training in beginning, middle, and ending sounds of words with emphasis on vowel sounds. Suggestions are given for the teacher.

Building Word Power by D. D. DURRELL and H. B. SULLIVAN. New York: World Book. This workbook is accompanied by a teacher's manual and is devoted to exercises in auditory and visual discrimination on the primary level.

Building Reading Skills by L. ARMSTRONG and R. HARGRAVE. Wichita: McCormick-Mathers. These six workbooks are for elementary-grade children and are designed to build essential reading skills. Practice material is included to train children in phonetic and structural analysis, sight-vocabulary development, word meaning, phrase perception, paragraph comprehension, and the like. These workbooks can be used with any series of readers.

Eye and Ear Fun by C. STONE. New York: McGraw-Hill. A series of four books which can be used in connection with any series of readers. The workbooks are designed to provide a carefully organized course for developing fluency, accuracy, and independence in word recognition.

Fun with Words and Pictures by G. L. Garson. Chicago: Follett Publishing Co. A series of workbooks for the primary grades. Considerable space is devoted to coloring and pasting.

Functional Phonetic Books by A. D. CORDTS. Chicago: Benefic Press. A series of three phonics workbooks that employ a whole-word approach (words appear contextually, in sentences) that is compatible with the look-say method of teaching reading. A teacher's manual also is available.

Happy Times wih Sounds by L. M. THOMPSON. Boston: Allyn & Bacon. A series of three workbooks which give training in sounding for the primary grades. A teacher's handbook accompanies the series.

Iroquois Phonics Program by W. K. EATON and B. F. FAMES. Syracuse, N. Y.: Iroquois. These three workbooks with accompanying manuals stress letter phonics, combinations, and syllabication. Advanced sections include contextual reading.

Learning the Letters by M. A. STANGER and E. K. DONOHUE. London: Oxford University Press. A series of six workbooks for the primary grades which stress the sounds of consonants and vowels.

Learning for Letter Sounds by P. McKEE and L. M. HARRISON. Boston: Houghton Mifflin Co. A first-grade workbook for teaching initial consonant sounds.

Macmillan Reading Spectrum by M. W. SULLIVAN. Palo Alto, Calif.: Behavioral Research Laboratories. A self-checking series of workbooks that include letters and short regular words.

Primary Seatwork by J. McDADE. Chicago: Plymouth Press. Seatwork material designed to teach reading by the nonoral method.

Puzzle Pages by F. SHELTON and L. TATE. Wichita: McCormick-Mathers. These simple workbooks for primer and first-grade work involve pasting and cutting of words and sentences in connection with pictures.

Phonic Fun by G. N. EDWARDS et al. Chicago: Beckley-Cardy Co. Two workbooks for grades one and two presenting phonic elements (initial sounds, vowels, and endings) with word frequencies as contained in basic readers.

Phonics by S. HERR. Los Angeles: Educational Research Associates. A series of three phonic workbooks for the elementary grades designed to give a thorough understanding of basic phonic principles through the use of extensive materials. Liberal use is made of pictures and illustrations.

Phonics Skilltexts by M. McCRORY and P. WATTS. Columbus, Ohio: Charles E. Merrill Publishing Co. A series of four workbooks (A, B, C, D) for the elementary grades that give training in word-recognition skills through visual, auditory, and kinesthetic activities.

Phonics We Use, 1966 edition, by MARY MEIGHAN et al. Chicago: Lyons & Carnahan. A series of six workbooks which can be used in connection with any basic series of readers.

Phonics with Write and See by MARGARET BISHOP. New York: New Century. A series of four workbooks that are self-evaluating.

Phonogram Books by P. B. RADNER. Maplewood, N. J.: Hammond & Co. A series of four 6-by-8-inch workbooks that teach simple phonograms, vowel digraphs, and medial phonograms, initial digraphs, and terminal digraphs, respectively. Words employed are drawn from the speaking vocabulary of the beginner.

Programmed Reading by SULLIVAN ASSOCIATES, C. D. BUCHANAN, Program Director. New York: McGraw-Hill Book Co. This series is very much like the *Macmillan Reading Spectrum.*

Read Clues by LOUISE B. SCOTT. New York: Webster/McGraw-Hill Book Co. A workbook for the intermediate grades that is patterned after *Time for Phonics.*

Reading Essential Series, 1973 edition, by ULLIN W. LEAVELL et al. Austin, Texas: Steck-Vaughn. A series of eight workbooks and a remedial workbook for fifth to seventh graders functioning on third-to-fourth grade reading levels.

Reading with Phonics by JULIE HAY and CHARLES WINGO. Philadelphia, Penn.: Lippincott Co. A hard-cover book for the pupil, accompanied by three workbooks and a teacher's manual. Training involves isolated words, many of which are of the nonsense variety. Red ink is used to highlight phonic elements.

Remedial Reading Drills by T. G. HEGGE, S. A. KIRK, Ann Arbor: George Wahr. A booklet for primary or intermediate grades containing isolated words in list form. Teaching centers around letter-by-letter sounding with kinesthetic reinforcement.

Time for Phonics by LOUISE B. SCOTT and VIRGINIA A. PAVELKO. New York: Webster/McGraw-Hill Book Co. A series of workbooks for primary children that teach phonics via picture and context cues.

Words Are Important by H. C. HARDWICKE. Maplewood, N. J.: Hammond & Co. A series of meaning vocabulary workbooks for junior and senior high school. Graded words are based on frequency categories of *Thorndike and Lorge Teacher's Word Book of 30,000 Words.*

A World of Words by I. F. FORST, G. GOLDBERG, and A. L. BOCK. Philadelphia: Winston. This workbook has as its principal objective the building of vocabulary for junior high students. Its method is essentially the successful direct method used to teach foreign language.

EMPLOYING READING GAMES

In seeking material that will strengthen individual weaknesses, many teachers turn to reading games since they are or can be made self-directed. Although teachers have experienced varying degrees of success with reading games, they are in general agreement that the play technique does arouse interest and provides needed motivation. Articles appearing in the *Saturday Review of Literature* and the *Los Angeles Times* attest to the appeal of games at all age levels.[9, 10]

Reading games have advantages as effective instrumental devices, but they also have their limitations. Most reading games are designed to provide extra practice in word recognition, word analysis, and word meaning, but the material is limited to practice on words in isolation. Unless the games are supplemented by recreational reading and developmental instruction on meaningful content, their effectiveness in most cases will be of doubtful value. Especially valuable in this regard are the Dolch *Basic Vocabulary Series* (Garrard Publishing Co.) which are written almost entirely with the Dolch two hundred twenty basic sight words and ninety-five commonest nouns. Unfortunately, too many teachers use games as mere busywork with no follow-up to determine their effectiveness. These teachers fail to evaluate and reevaluate reading games by asking, when and for whom is this game valuable and useful?

Care must be taken that the reading game employed is not too juvenile and that it provides meaningful practice in terms of the individual's reading difficulty. Often too, meaningful practice can be assured only if the teacher or an able child provides some surveillance during the playing of the game. Certainly there is no need to continue a game for an individual or group when progress in the skill the game purports to develop comes to a halt. Once children fail to enjoy a game, they fail to profit from it, and it should be withdrawn.

Many commercial games such as monopoly can be turned into reading games if a teacher exercises a little ingenuity. As a matter of fact, any commercial game can be turned into a reading game if, before taking a turn, the student is required to identify a prefix or suffix, read a word, answer a question, and so forth.[11]

Reading games provide self-competition when the results are recorded by the pupil. Keeping a record of the number of successes per unit of playing time proves motivating for the child. It also enables the teacher to evaluate pupil progress and determine the effectiveness of the game for the learner.

In short, when reading games are selected carefully on the basis of appropriate content, difficulty, and pupil interest, and when the results are charted by the pupil and evaluated by the teacher, they serve as a useful individualized and self-directed instructional activity.

Many of the instructional aids presented in this chapter take the form of games.

MAKING READING GAMES

Some school districts enlist the help of parents in developing self-directed games for classroom teachers.

Teachers and interested parents meet in a room which provides ample table surface for working. All materials needed for the construction of games are made available including the following:

Crayons and colored pencils	Brads
Felt pens in a variety of colors	Staplers
Paints	Cards of various sizes
Paper of several types, sizes, and colors	Paper clips
	Library card pockets
Oaktag	Envelopes of varying sizes
Scissors	Transparent tape
Paper cutters	Masking tape
Sheets of acetate	Glue and paste

Of additional help are the booklets of *Reading Games that Teach*: Book 1: Readiness; Book II, Phonics; Book III, Word Recognition; Book IV Word Attack Skills; Book V, Comprehension. The step-by-step format and illustration makes the games easy to understand and use in the classroom. The follow-up form on the back of every page enables teachers to record for future reference their ideas and reactions. ($3.50 each. Creative Teaching Press.)

PROBLEMS FOR ORAL AND WRITTEN DISCUSSION

1. Why are the skills of word analysis important in reading?
2. What are the advantages and limitations of reading games?
3. Use an appropriate reading game with a group of pupils. Provide an objective method of recording results. Evaluate its effectiveness.
4. Construct an original reading game and have it evaluated by your colleagues.
5. Select three or more items from the list of corrective materials appearing in this chapter. Describe the nature and functions of these materials. Revise the directions for these materials in order to make them more self-directive.

6. Organize a self-corrective program in reading for a pupil who is deficient in word recognition or word analysis, indicating the pupil's grade placement, instructional level, intelligence, degree of retardation, reading expectancy, and nature of the difficulties in reading. Select the corrective materials to be used, indicating type and difficulty.

Notes

1. *A Place to Start: A Graded Bibliography for Children with Reading Difficulties* (Syracuse, N.Y.: Syracuse University).
2. George Spache, *Good Reading for Poor Readers,* rev. ed. Champaign, Ill.: Garrard Publishing Co., 1974).
3. John DeBoer and Martha Dallman, *The Teaching of Reading* (New York: Holt, Rinehart & Winston, 1964), pp. 105-106.
4. Joyce Hood, "Why We Burned Our Basic Sight Vocabulary Cards," *Reading Teacher* (March 1974):579-582.
5. Gertrude Hildreth, *Teaching Reading* (New York: Henry Holt & Co., 1959), p. 155.
6. Delwyn Schubert, "Teachers and Word Analysis Skills," *Journal of Developmental Reading* (Summer 1959):62-64.
7. Wallace Ramsey, "Will Tomorrow's Teachers Know and Teach Phonics?" *Reading Teacher* (January 1962):241, 245.
8. Louise Scott and James Thompson, *Phonics in Listening, in Speaking, in Reading, in Writing* (New York: Webster/McGraw-Hill Book Co., 1962), chap. 2.
9. Garry Shirts, "Games Students Play," *Saturday Review,* 16 May 1970, pp. 81-82.
10. "A Popularity Explosion in Adult Games," *Los Angeles Times,* 19 December 1970.
11. George F. Canney, "Making Games More Relevant for Reading," *Reading Teacher* (October 1978):10-14.

Selected Readings

Bond, Guy, and Tinker, Miles. *Reading Problems: Their Diagnosis and Correction.* 3rd ed. New York: Appleton-Century-Crofts, 1973, chap. 11.
Burns, Paul C., and Roe, Betty D. *Teaching Reading in Today's Elementary School.* Chicago: Rand McNally, 1980, ch. 3.
Carter, Homer, and McGinnis, Dorothy. *Diagnosis and Treatment of the Disabled Reader.* New York: Macmillan Co., 1970, chap. 12.
Chance, Larry. "Using a Learning Stations Approach to Vocabulary Practice." *Journal of Reading* (December 1974):244-246.
Dallmann, Martha et al. *The Teaching of Reading.* New York: Holt, Rinehart & Winston, 1974, chaps. 5A and 5B.
Durkin, Dolores. "Phonics Materials: A Big Seller." *Reading Teacher* (April 1967):610-614.
———. *Teaching Them to Read.* Boston: Allyn & Bacon, 1974, chaps. 10-13.
Glazer, Susan M. *Learning to Read Can Become Fun and Games.* Newark, Del.: International Reading Association, 1977.
Harris, Albert, and Sipay, Edward R. *How to Increase Reading Ability.* 6th ed. New York: David McKay Co., 1975, chaps. 14-15.

HARRIS, ALBERT, and SIPAY, EDWARD. *How to Teach Reading.* New York: Longman, 1979, Unit 7.

MANGRUM, CHARLES, and FORGAN, HARRY. *Developing Competencies in Teaching Reading.* Columbus, Ohio: Charles E. Merrill Publishing Company, 1979, Module 4.

MCNEIL, JOHN D.; DONANT, LISBETH; and ALKIN, MARVIN C. *How to Teach Reading Successfully.* Boston: Little, Brown and Company, 1980, ch. 4.

SPACHE, GEORGE, and SPACHE, EVELYN. *Reading in the Elementary School.* 3rd ed. Boston: Allyn & Bacon, 1973, chaps. 12-13.

THOMAS, ELLEN, and ROBINSON, ALAN. *Improving Reading in Every Class.* Boston: Allyn & Bacon, 1974, chap. 2.

THOMPSON, RICHARD. *Energizers for Reading Instruction.* West Nyack, N. Y.: Parker Publishing Co., 1973.

TIERNEY, ROBERT J.; READENCE, JOHN E.; and DISHNER, ERNEST K. *Reading Strategies and Practices.* Rockleigh, N. J.: Allyn and Bacon, Inc., 1980, part I.

13 Improving Comprehension and the Study Skills

This chapter is devoted to specific games, techniques, and materials that are of value in helping children overcome deficiencies in reading comperhension if properly used. The teacher who wishes to help pupils whose comprehension problems stem from limited sight and meaning vocabulary is referred to chapter 12. Addresses of the publishers and manufacturers mentioned in this chapter are given in Appendix F.

Cloze Procedure

Use of the cloze procedure for testing purposes was discussed on pages 183-184. But the cloze procedure can also be used very successfully to develop a pupil's comprehension ability. Pupils enjoy the informal cloze procedure and also seem to find commercial material such as Boning's *Using the Context* workbooks and the SRA *Reading for Understanding* kits (both use completion tests as a means of teaching comprehension) especially motivating.

When a cloze exercise for comprehension skills is constructed, a passage is selected from reading material that is appropriate for the classroom. The teacher then decides on an automatic word count which usually varies between five and ten. An every-tenth-word count is recommended for more difficult expository material, and a count as low as every fifth word may be employed with easy material such as fictional writing. Once a word count has been decided on, the teacher begins counting from the first word in the second sentence. (The first sentence and last sentence of the passage remain unmutilated.) Each time the teacher reaches the word coinciding with the predetermined count, that word is replaced by a blank space of uniform length. When finished, the passage looks like the following:

Finding one's way isn't always easy. Strangers are always getting
1._____and having to stop 2._____ask for directions. Usually
3._____drive into a gas 4. _____or stop someone on 5._____
street. You probably know 6._____your own experience how 7._____
such directions are to 8._____. Now, these directions may be hard to
follow for two reasons.

Answers: 1. lost, 2. and 3. they, 4. station, 5. the, 6. from, 7. hard, 8. follow.

Although only the exact words deleted are acceptable when the cloze
procedure is used for testing, any synonym may be accepted for instructional purposes.

When the selection is mounted on cardboard, it is possible to make cloze
exercises self-corrective by concealing the answers in a library card pocket
pasted on the back.

Workbooks

Workbooks which are widely used in developmental and corrective reading programs are of two types: those that accompany basal readers and
those that are independent of any series of readers. The former are designed for group instruction directed by the teacher. Their content usually
is divided into units paralleling the basal reader and is designed to provide
additional practice on those reading skills developed in the basal reader.

The content of independent workbooks does not parallel basal readers.
Some independent workbooks emphasize a single group of skills such as
word analysis or comprehension. Usually their difficulty is not expressed
in grade levels, and many of them provide simple directions written for
the pupils. Because of this, the teacher is able to utilize books on several
levels of difficulty in meeting class needs.

Independent workbooks are of particular value in meeting the needs of
pupils above the third grade who are retarded one to three years in their
reading skills. For these pupils, the regular basal reader and the accompanying workbooks are too difficult. In such cases, the teacher can turn
to an independent series of workbooks for the purpose of selecting those
of optimum difficulty for specific pupils. Such workbooks should have simple directions that have been written for the pupils so that they can pursue
the materials independently at their own rate.

An example of a paricularly popular independent workbook series is the
Readers Digest Reading Skill Builders (Reader's Digest Services). This
series contains short and highly motivating selections that have great appeal and are ideally suited to developmental and remedial work. Booklets are now available on each grade level from one to eight. A variety of
exercises for developing comprehension, rate, and vocabulary are included.
Audio Lesson Units on cassettes are available on each level.

Pupils who are retarded in any reading skills should be assigned only the skills or units they have not mastered. If the workbook does not provide enough practice, a second book should be provided in which the desired units are indicated. Answer sheets on which responses are to be written should be furnished so that the books are not consumed by one pupil but can be used over and over by many children.

Another method of providing flexibility with effectiveness in the use of workbooks is to secure two copies of two or three series of independent workbooks. Cut the pages apart and mount them on tagboard. Assemble and classify the material by units or skills according to the level of difficulty and then provide a file in which the pupil can readily locate the exercises he needs. Mounting paper of various colors can be employed to designate levels of difficulty, if desired. By combining materials from two or three workbooks, an adequate supply of self-directed practice material on several levels of difficulty is assured. Having the pupils write their responses on separate answer sheets ensures continued use of the workbook exercises.

When evolving an answer file, teachers will find it best to write the answers to single exercises on small cards. Exercises and cards must be marked to correspond. Letters or numbers can be used for this purpose.

Following is a representative list of workbooks that contains material suitable for developing pupils' comprehension and study skills.

Activities for Reading Improvement by Norman Schachter and John Whelan. Austin, Texas: Steck-Vaughn. A series of three books at the junior high school level. Each book contains exercises grouped in four units which include comprehension, vocabulary, skimming, and reading for enjoyment.

Be a Better Reader by Nila B. Smith. Englewood Cliffs, N.J.: Prentice-Hall, 1968. Workbooks for grades four through twelve that contain exercises to develop phonics, use and meaning of prefixes and suffixes, syllabication, rapid and critical reading, location of information, and vocabulary development. Special study skills in the content fields are emphasized.

Better Reading by J. C. Gainsburg and S. I. Spector. New York: Globe Book Co., 1962. A revised and modernized text for corrective work on the high school level. Exercises are provided on skimming, main ideas, outlining, and other reading areas.

Cowboy Sam Workbooks by E. W. Chandler. Chicago: Beckley-Cardy Co. A series of four workbooks which parallel the *Cowboy Sam Readers*. The workbooks range from primer to third-grade level and provide checks for reading vocabulary, understanding, following directions, and so forth. Space is provided for coloring.

Developing Reading Efficiency by Lyle L. Miller. Minneapolis: Burgess Publishing Co., 1965. A workbook for the junior high school. Exercises are devoted to word recognition, phrase and sentence reading, and timed reading of more lengthy selections.

Developmental Reading Text-Workbook Series by W. H. Burton et al. Indianapolis: Bobbs-Merrill Co., 1961. This series provides a complete developmental program in reading. Each workbook is organized into units with each unit consisting of a story followed by exercises in comprehension and word-analysis skills. The series can be used in conjunction with or supplementary to basal reading materials to reinforce learning. It also can be used independently of basal reading materials, as in programs emphasizing individualized or indepent reading.

Diagnostic Reading Workbooks by R. F. GREENWOOD and J. V. WILLIAM. Columbus, O.: Charles E. Merrill Publishing Co. This series of workbooks is designed to give elementary children practice in four important skills. These include (1) ability to comprehend facts, (2) ability to do independent things and to evaluate, (3) development of vocabulary and word mastery, and (4) ability to find the main ideas in a selection. Grade level is indicated by stars on the cover and the title page.

Diagnostic Tests and Exercises in Reading by L. J. BRUECKNER and W. D. LEWIS. Philadelphia: Winston Co., 1935. A workbook for retarded readers having fourth-grade reading ability. It contains tests and exercises in word recognition, vocabulary, phrasing, central thoughts, related details, and rate.

Mastery of Reading by M. BRADLEY and U. LEAVELL. New York: American Book Co. These three workbooks are for junior high school students and can be used independently of the three texts they parallel. Each chapter provides students with drills and exercises centered around a single reading skill.

Mother Hubbard's Seatwork Cupboard by D. E. KIBBE. Eau Claire, Wis.: E. M. Hale & Co. Two workbooks are involved. The first workbook is for first-grade children and concentrates on ninety-three words. Word-picture matching, coloring, and pasting are the predominant activities. The second workbook introduces sentence and paragraph reading.

My Work Book in Reading by E. M. ALDREDGE and J. F. McKEE. Chicago: Beckley-Cardy Co. These workbooks in reading for the primary grades contain a variety of reading and numbers materials. Considerable space is devoted to coloring and pasting.

New Reading Skill Builder Series. Pleasantville, N. Y.: A series of articles on levels one to nine which are followed by comprehension questions. Two or three booklets are available at each grade level.

Practice Exercises in Reading by A. I. GATES and C. C. PEARDON. New York: Bureau of Publication, Teachers College, Columbia University, 1963. A series of four workbooks which train students in the four types of reading corresponding to the types of ability measured by the Gates Silent Reading Tests. These involve (1) reading to appreciate the general significance of a selection, (2) reading to predict the outcome of given events, (3) reading to understand precise directions, and (4) reading to note details. These widely used booklets are provided for grades two to six.

Practice Readers by C. R. STONE and D. G. ANDERSON. New York: Webster/ McGraw-Hill Book Co., 1961. A series of seven workbooks consisting of short selections followed by exercises pertaining to direct details, implied details, meaning of the whole, correctness of a statement in relation to the selection, understanding the meaning of reference words, and perception of the truth or falseness of a statement. Cassettes accompany some of the work books.

Reading Comprehension by ADRIAN B. SANFORD et al. New York: Macmillan Co., 1964. Six programmed workbooks comprise this series. Difficulty levels vary from grades three to eight.

Reading for Concepts by WILLIAM LIDDLE. New York: Webster/McGraw-Hill Book Co. A series of eight workbooks involving stories related to subject matter areas such as social studies and science.

Reading Essential Series by U. W. Leavell et al. Austin, Texas: Steck-Vaughn Co., 1953. This series of workbooks which cover grades one through eight can be used to fit different reading levels in the various grades. Exercises include the development of phonetic skills, structural analysis, dictionary skills, and comprehension skills. The selections have high interest appeal and are carefully graded.

Reading for Meaning by W. S. Guiler and J. H. Coleman. Philadelphia: J. B. Lippincott Co., 1935. A series of nine workbooks designed to improve the following basic reading skills: (1) word meanings, (2) total meaning, (3) central thought, (4) detailed meanings, (5) organization, and (6) summarization.

Reading Skilltext by E. M. Johnson. Columbus, O.: Charles E. Merrill Publishing Co., 1956. A series of six workbooks that consist of illustrated stories followed by questions pertaining to comprehension, word meanings, and word-attack skills.

Reading Workbooks by A. L. McDonald. Austin, Texas: Steck-Vaughn Co. Three workbooks for grades one and two which provide readiness material and purposeful activities to develop reading skills.

Specific Skills Series by Richard A. Boning. Rockville Centre, N. Y.: Barnell Loft, 1962. These workbooks are available on levels one through six for each of the following: *Using the Context, Getting the Facts, Following Directions, Locating the Answer, Getting the Main Idea, Drawing Conclusions, and Detecting the Sequence.*

SRA Better Reading Books by E. A. Simpson. Chicago: Science Research Associates, 1962. A series of four workbooks for grades five to six, seven to eight, nine to ten, and eleven to twelve, respectively. The workbooks consist of timed reading selections followed by multiple-choice questions.

Standard Test Lessons in Reading by W. A. McCall and L. M. Crabbs. New York: Bureau of Publications, Teachers College, Columbia University, 1961. These widely used workbooks cover grades two to twelve. Five workbooks are involved, each of which contains short selections followed by questions and grade scores.

Step Up Your Reading Power by Jim Olson. St. Louis: Webster/McGraw-Hill Book Co., 1966. Five workbooks comprise this series. The workbooks are designed for use with remedial students on the secondary level. Each selection is followed by six fact questions and two thought questions.

Supportive Reading Skills by Richard Boning. Baldwin, N. Y.: Dexter & Westbrook, 1973. Multileveled workbooks which include *Reading Homonyms, Rhyme Time, Understanding Word Groups, Understanding Questions, Syllabication, Using a Table of Contents, Learning to Alphabetize, Using an Index, and Reading Homographs.* Forthcoming publications include *Reading Heteronyms, Reading Compound Words, Predicting Paragraph Content, Mastering Multiple Meanings, Interpreting Interjections, Reading Schedules, Interpreting Similes and Metaphors, Identifying Paragraph Patterns,* and *Reacting to Signal Words.*

Systems Studybooks by W. S. Gray, A. S. Artley, and M. Monroe. Chicago: Scott, Foresman & Co. A series of workbooks designed to accompany the Scott, Foresman basic readers. These workbooks cover grades one to eight and can be used independently of the series by pupils who need carefully planned practice.

Tactics in Reading and *Reading Skills for Young Adults* by OLIVE NILES, et al. Glenview, Ill.: Scott Foresman & Co. A series of paperback workbooks devoted to developing the reading skills of problem readers at the seventh- to twelfth-grade levels.

Your Reading Guide by N. F. RYAN. Chicago: Lyons & Carnahan, 1956. Two workbooks for junior-high level that pertain to reading and study skills.

Corrective Practice for Pupils Deficient in Word Meaning Vocabulary

Development of a meaning vocabulary is essential if a student is to understand what is read.[1] To acquire a large meaning vocabulary, one must read widely and must possess a curiosity about new words. (Note that some of the materials and techniques described in chapter 12 for developing sight vocabulary can also be used for meaning vocabulary development.) Helpful, too, is a system whereby new words can be recorded and reviewed until mastered.

A number of years ago the reading specialist Luella Cole evolved a vocabulary-building system for children that was completely individualized and self-directed. It is ideally suited for corrective work. She described it as follows:

> There is only one really efficient way of individualizing training in word study, and that is to have each pupil keep track of the words he does not know. The procedures involved are simple. The teacher first supplies each child with twenty-five or thirty slips of paper. If she can obtain 3-by-5-inch library cards and cut them in half, these small cards are better than paper slips because they can be handled more easily. She then instructs the pupils to copy each unknown word out of the books they read, writing one word on each card. The cards should be in readiness whenever the pupil is reading anything, no matter what the subject matter of the book may be. Since almost all the words thus recorded will be within a child's understanding as soon as they are pronounced, the teacher should let the pupils get together from time to time in groups of three, in which each one shows the others the words he does not know. Most of the words that have been collected by all three will be recognized by one child or another. Any remaining words may be looked up in the dictionary if the children are old enough or handed to the teacher for her to explain. After the words are identified, each pupil goes through his own cards, saying each word he can remember over to himself. The cards containing those words he can now identify he puts in one pile; the words he cannot remember he puts in another. Luella Cole, *The Improvement of Reading*, copyright 1938 by Holt, Rinehart & Winston, Inc., copyright 1966 by Luella Cole, pp. 142-143.

Cole suggests that the children continue quizzing each other until the pile of unknown words has disappeared. When pupils accumulate twenty to thirty cards, the reading period should be used for the drill described. Cards are to be kept and reviewed two or three times before they are discarded.

In 1973, more than thirty-five years after the introduction of Cole's vocabulary-building system, Quandt described an individualized word-bank approach to vocabulary development using cards.[2] He believed the method is highly motivating and advocated its use with any type of reading or language arts program. We are in complete agreement with Quandt. We know of many teachers who have had great success with the approach.

Facile use of the dictionary is a real asset to meaning vocabulary development. The various subskills involved in efficient dictionary usage should be cataloged, and pupils in the upper grades who show weaknesses should be given proper corrective instruction. (Dictionary skills are discussed on pages 256-258.)

Teachers are often in a quandary regarding which words pupils should learn. In making a decision as to the importance of specific words, the teacher should consult the following:

COLE, LUELLA. *The Teachers Handbook of Technical Vocabulary.* New York: Holt, Rinehart & Winston, 1938.

HERBER, HAROLD. *Success with Words.* New York: Scholastic Book Service, 1964.

THORNDIKE, EDWARD, and LORGE, IRVING. *The Teachers Word Book of 30,000 Words.* New York: Bureau of Publications, Teachers College, Columbia University, 1944.

The book by Thorndike and Lorge deals with general vocabulary, while the other two contain listings of words in various subject matter fields. The Herber book includes crossword puzzles, matching games, analogies, word puzzles, categorizing activities, and so forth, which are designed to make content field vocabulary development fun.

One of the most fascinating approaches to vocabulary enrichment involves a study of etymology, the origin or development of words. Pupils of all ages are intrigued by it. Since we have begged, borrowed, and stolen words, without compunction, from everyone—the Spanish, French, American Indians, and others—there is no dearth of words from which to choose.

All teachers ought to have a book in their professional library such as Wilfred Funk's *Word Origins and Their Romantic Stories* (Grosset & Dunlap). This book is an open sesame to many hours of enjoyment and personal enrichment. In addition, it proves a valuable source of instructional material for stimulating the vocabulary development of readers of all ages. Subject matter teachers will find a chapter devoted to word histories in their area of specialization. Among the chapter headings are the following: "Romance Behind Business Terms," "Political Terms and Their Origins," "War Words and Their Histories," "Terms of Science and the Professions," "Terms of Religion and Their Beginnings," "Origin of the Terms of Art, Music, and the Drama," and "Your Favorite Sports and Their Word Histories."

Since a large number of words in the English language start with pre-fixes, a knowledge of them is helpful when unfamiliar words are encountered. Some of the most common prefixes are as follows:[3]

ab (from)	*dis* (apart)	*ob, op, ov* (against)
ad, a, ap, at (to)	*en* (in)	*pre* (before)
be (by)	*ex, e* (out of)	*pro* (in front of)
com, con, col (with)	*in, en, im, em* (into)	*re* (back, again)
de (from)	*in* (not)	*sub* (under)
		un (not)

Suffixes are more difficult for children to learn than prefixes. Fortunately, suffixes are less valuable as clues than prefixes since they are less consistent in their meanings. Some of the more common suffixes are *ment, tion, able, ous, ly, er, ful, less, ness, ing, age, ed,* and *ance.*

Many words in the English language mean approximately the same thing. Children learn that such words are called synonyms. Words that are opposite in meaning are antonyms. Pupils enjoy and benefit from exercises dealing with synonyms and antonyms. An excellent source of synonyms and antonyms can be found in Fernald's *English Synonyms, Antonyms, and Prepositions* (Funk & Wagnalls). This book is far superior to other books of its kind because it not only lists synonyms and antonyms, but also employs them in sentences. In this way, fine differentiations between words are readily discernible. The words presented vary greatly in difficulty; therefore, teachers at all grade levels find it valuable for instructional purposes.

Scott, Foresman Company has published two student thesauri which are valuable. *In Other Words I . . . A Beginning Thesaurus* ($4.83) offers children over 1,000 substitute words for 100 they use and overuse. Pupils who read at third-grade level or above and who can use alphabetical order and interpret related sentences can use the book independently. *In Other Words II . . . A Junior Thesaurus* ($5.97) gives pupils reading at fifth-grade level or above the means whereby they can add 3,000 words to their working vocabulary. Three hundred commonly used entry words are involved. Exercise books accompanying the thesaurus are also available.

A widely used audiovisual tool for meaning vocabulary development is available in *Words! Words! Words!* (Encore Visual Education). This is a series of eight colorful filmstrips with accompanying records or cassettes that are designed to build the meaning and sight vocabularies of intermediate-grade students as well as of disabled readers on the junior and senior high school levels. Each filmstrip contains two lessons, with five words in each lesson—two verbs, two nouns, and one adjective. Individual words are shown in picture and sound. Each word is pronounced, spelled, illustrated by original art, used in a sentence, and defined. At the end of each

Numbered lists of words are followed by statements re-
[...] words. Pupils answer each statement Yes or No. Exam-

[...] (This is something that makes your eyes water.)
[...] er (Your father drives this to work.)
[...] (You do this in a bathtub.)
[...] swers can appear on the back of the exercise. (For use with
[...] pupils; potentially self-directed.)

[...]ctice for Pupils Deficient [...] omprehension

[...] xperience sentence comprehension difficulties and inability
[...] s into thought units may profit from use of the Dolch Phrase
[...] rd). Helpful, too, is the tachistoscope presentation of phrases
[...] ystone Overhead Projector and Flashmeter (Mast/Keystone)
[...] st-O-Flasher with accompanying phrase filmstrips (Learning
[...] ing).

[...] aloud several sentences in which words are incorrectly grouped
[...] the need for proper phrasing in an entertaining manner. The
[...] aragraph provides an example:

[...] /breakfast I have/   /jungle fruit, rice/   /and coffee
[...] at fresh/ /fish from a/ /stream or eggs/ /from a little jungle/
[...] ngs/ /are not so/ /very bad./

[...] inds of corrective practice for pupils who are deficient in ability
[...] ehend sentences can be individualized by using materials and
[...] s such as the following.

[...] bled Sentences: Disarrange sentences. Direct pupils to put the
[...] s in proper order. Examples:
[...] in an accident / Jane thought / were injured / that the boys.
[...] is true / you read / don't believe / that everything./
[...] rrectly arranged sentences can appear on the back of the exercise.
[...] or use with individual pupils; potentially self-directed.)
[...] issing Words: Numbered sentences containing missing words are
[...] epared. Pupils demonstrate comprehension of the sentences by
[...] oosing correct missing words. Examples:
[...] Many people have_____for family pets.
[...] Children learn many interesting things in_____.
_____are those times during the year when people should re-
lax and enjoy themselves.
(1) dogs
(2) vacations
(3) schools

---

five-word lesson, students may turn to the word practice booklets included
with the filmstrips and do the exercises which reinforce learning. Correct
answers are given at the end of each sound recording. The filmstrips, recordings, and word-practice booklets are designed so that the teacher may
use them with the class and for independent study by individuals and
groups. They are completely self-directed and self-corrective.

Additional kinds of corrective practice for pupils who are deficient in
meaning vocabulary can be individualized by using materals and techniques such as the following.

1. *Add On*: Lists of three words belonging to a category are followed by
   blank spaces. Pupils are encouraged to think of other words that fit
   the same classification. Examples:
   a. small, minute, little,_____, _____.
   b. coat, hat, shoes,_____,_____.
   c. dog, cat, horse,_____, _____.
   Probable answers can appear on the back of the exercise. (For use
   with individual pupils; potentially self-directed.)

2. *Classifying Words*: Present lists of words which pupils must classify
   under three or more headings. Examples:

	Vegetables	Fruits	Meats

   a. carrots   d. celery
   b. apples   e. oranges
   c. pork   f. lamb
   Correct answers can appear on the back of the exercise. (For use with
   individual pupils; potentially self-directed.)

3. *Cross It Out*: Lists of words which belong to a specific classification
   are presented along with one word which is completely foreign to the
   group. Pupils are told to cross out the word which does not belong
   with the others. Examples:
   a. run, jump, walk, sleep, crawl
   b. cold, hot, windy, chilly, torrid
   c. milk, turpentine, cocoa, coffee, tea
   Correct answers can appear on the back of the exercise. (For use with
   individual pupils; potentially self-directed.)

4. *Label Me*: On a piece of tagboard paste a large picture of any scene
   relating to the unit being taught. Provide small word cards and put
   these in an accompanying envelope. Pupils are directed to place the
   word cards on or near the proper items in the picture. Correct answers
   in the form of pictures can appear on the back of the individual word
   cards. (For use with individual pupils; potentially self-directed.)

5. *Matching*: Prepare parallel columns of synonyms or antonyms and direct pupils to match the two. Examples:

    a. strong   a. gigantic
    b. large   b. powerful
    c. fast   c. rapid

    Correct answers can appear on the back of the exercise. (For use with individual pupils; potentially self-directed)

6. *Picture Dictionaries*: Pupils are instructed to build a dictionary of words they have encountered in their reading. Old books, magazines, workbooks, and newspapers can be furnished to provide pictures for illustrating the words. Pictures can also be drawn by the children for illustrative purposes. A shoe box that has been painted with tempera colors is fine for housing the materials. Dividers can be cut from tagboard and labeled with letters of the alphabet. (For use with individual children; potentially self-directed.)

7. *Prefixes, Suffixes, and Word Stems*: Devise exercises consisting of three prefixes, suffixes, or word stems for which examples of usage are given. Pupils will think of additional words. Examples:

    a. *pre* (before): preheat, preschool, _____, _____.
    b. *re* (again, back): repay, refill, _____, _____.
    c. *un* (not): unhappy, unhurt, _____, _____.

    Probable answers may appear on the back of the exercise. (For use with individual pupils; potentially self-directed.)

8. *Puzzle Words*: Furnish pupils with space blanks designed to accommodate words which are defined. The definitions should be in mixed order. Examples:

    a. The wife of an American Indian
       (squaw)
    b. A raccoon
       (coon)
    c. A weapon for shooting arrows
       (bow)

    Correct answers can appear on the back of the exercise. (For use with individual pupils; potentially self-directed.)

9. *Riddles*: Riddles can be used to stimulate dictionary usage and interest in new words. Example:

    a. There are many of us in Norway. We are frequently long and narrow. Steep, rocky banks come right down to the water of which we are made. We are called _____.

    Correct answers can appear on the back of the exercise. (For use with individual pupils; potentially self-directed.)

10. *See, Hear, or Smell?* Lis_
    categories. Pupils are exp_
    a. tulips
    b. clocks
    c. sunsets
    Correct answers can appear_
    individual pupils; potentially_

11. *Seeing Relationships*: Lists of_
    ship to each other are followe_
    pupils must find and underli_
    have the same relationships as t_
    a. baker, bread (sailor, tailor, n_
    b. cup, coffee (bookcase, table,_
    c. dog, barks (cat, snake, horse,_
    Correct answers can appear on th_
    individual pupils; potentially self-_

12. *Stick Me*: Paste pictures of objects_
    board. Type words on small squa_
    with a common pin. When a pupil_
    a picture which matches a given wor_
    ing the pin through the picture into t_
    with individual children or children w_

13. *Think of the Word*: Sentences contain_
    individual word can be substituted ar_
    the word needed and consults a diction_
    a. The man was *being very careful* be_
       thin. (cautious)
    b. The general was afraid the enemy wou_
       (defeat)
    c. The tiger was *going about slowly and s_*
       or steal. (prowling)
    Correct answers can appear on the back of t_
    individual pupils; potentially self-directed.)

14. *Which Is It?* Sentences are prepared with tw_
    entheses. The pupil chooses the one he consid_
    a. The man was (right, write) about the dista_
    b. The boy (road, rode) the horse home.
    c. The (pail, pale) was filled with water.
    Correct answers can appear on the back of the e_
    individual pupils; potentially self-directed.)

15. *Yes or No:*
    lating to th_
    ples:
    a. onion (_
    b. cucumb_
    c. bathe (_
    Correct an_
    individual_

Corrective Pra_
in Sentence C_

Pupils who e_
to group wor_
Cards (Garr_
using the Ke_
or the Tachi_
*Through Se_*

Reading _
dramatizes _
following p_
/For my_
when/ /I _
/town, thi_

Other k_
to compr_
techniqu_

1. Jum_
   par_
   a.
   b.
   Co_
   (F_

2. M_
   p_
   c_
   a_
   b_

Correct answers can appear on the back of the exercise. (For use with individual pupils; potentially self-directed.)

3. *Omit Two*: Mount a picture on an individual card together with three sentences that tell something about the picture. Print two extra sentences that do not relate to the picture. Pupils are instructed to find the two irrelevant sentences. Correct answers can appear on the back of the exercise. (For use with individual pupils; potentially self-directed.)

4. *Pictures and Sentences*: Two or three pictures are mounted on individual cards together with fifteen or twenty sentences which have been printed on separate cards. Pupils are instructed to read each sentence and match it with the picture to which it refers. A marking scheme can be devised on the reverse side of the cards to make this activity self-corrective. (For use with individual pupils; potentially self-directed.)

5. *Punctuate Me*: Type paragraphs in which all periods and capital letters have been omitted. Pupils are directed to designate the beginnings and endings of sentences by employing proper punctuation and capitalization. The correctly written paragraphs can appear on the back of the exercise. (For use with individual pupils; potentially self-directed.)

6. *Sentence Composition*: Have pupils study a picture carefully and then compose sentences that describe the picture.

7. *Sentence Detective*: Give directions which refer pupils to a picture appearing in a story previously read. Ask them to find all sentences on the page or pages that give more information than what is found in the picture. Correct sentences can appear on the back of the exercise. (For use with individual pupils; potentially self-directed.)

8. *Sentence Match*: Four sentences are prepared. Two of the four say approximately the same thing. Pupils are directed to find the synonymous sentences. Examples:
   a. The man went on and on until he became very tired.
   b. The man wandered about until he found what he was looking for.
   c. The man entered the wilderness looking for a place to build a cabin.
   d. The man continued walking for a great distance until he was exhausted.

Correct answers can appear on the back of the exercise. (For use with individual pupils; potentially self-directed.)

9. *Split Sentences*: Pupils are given two envelopes. One envelope contains cards with sentence beginnings and the other contains cards with sentence endings. Pupils are directed to match suitable parts to form sentences. Examples:

a. Jack and Jill went up the hill	1. lighter and warmer.
b. I ran and ran until I was	2. all out of breath.
c. As the sun began to rise it became	3. to fetch a pail of water.

Correct answers can appear on the back of the exercise. (For use with individual pupils; potentially self-directed.)

10. *True or False*: True-or-false statements that are related or unrelated to the reading lesson can be used to help develop sentence comprehension. Since many such statements are humorous, children enjoy these exercises immensely. Examples:
   a. A twelve-year-old boy can run 100 miles an hour.
   b. This sentence has more than seven words in it.
   c. A wild tiger would make a fine house pet.
   Correct answers can appear on the back of the exercise. (For use with individual pupils; potentially self-directed.)

11. *When, What, Where?* Sentences which tell when, what, or where are prepared. Pupils read each sentence and categorize it according to these designations. Examples:
   a. The Jones family spent their summer in the country.
   b. A slender piece of metal that is driven into two blocks of wood can hold them together.
   c. He said the world would come to an end last week.
   Correct answers can appear on the back of the exercise. (For use with individual pupils; potentially self-directed.)

12. *Where's the Joker?* Sentences pertaining to a given subject are presented together with a sentence that does not belong. Pupils are directed to find the foreign sentence. Examples:
   a. The car is a Ford. b. The body is red and the wheels are black. c. The sky became dark and cloudy. d. The top speed is 100 miles an hour.
   Correct answers can appear on the back of the exercise. (For use with individual pupils; potentially self-directed.)

Corrective Material for Deficiencies in Following Directions

When individual pupils or groups of pupils are deficient in ability to follow directions, corrective practice can be individualized by using materials and techniques such as the following.

1. *Can You Eat Me?* Pupils are given a list of simple words with these directions—Find things you can eat. Examples:
   a. orange
   b. window
   c. door
   d. crayon
   e. butter
   f. cookie

   Correct answers can appear on the back of the exercise. (For use with individual pupils; potentially self-directed.)

2. *Do This*: Pupils are given a list of simple words with these directions: Draw a circle around all words you can make pictures of. Examples:
   a. go
   b. dog
   c. squirrel
   d. chicken
   e. see
   f. with

   Correct answers can appear on the back of the exercise. (For use with individual pupils; potentially self-directed.)

3. *Following Directions*: Provide pupils with a number of statements such as the following:
   a. If the fifth letter in the alphabet is *E*, write that letter in this space _____.
   b. Draw a circle around all words in this sentence that have four letters.
   c. If March comes after June, write your last name backwards in this space_____.

   Correct answers can appear on the back of the exercise. (For use with individual pupils; potentially self-directed.)

4. *Read and Do*: Pupils are given a number of directions to carry out:
   a. Draw a house.
   b. Put three windows in the house.
   c. Put two panes of glass in each window.
   d. Draw a chimney on the right-hand side of the roof.
   e. Color the chimney brown.
   f. Color the house red.
   g. Draw a circle on the bottom right-hand side of your paper.
   h. Now draw a square around the circle.

   (For use with individual pupils; potentially self-directed.)

5. *What's Cooking?* Provide directions for preparing different foods (French toast, pancakes, pies, etc.) and require pupils to identify the particular dish or food involved. Correct answers can appear on the back of the exercise. (For use with individual pupils; potentially self-directed.)

6. *What's Wrong?* Provide directions for making or assembling model airplanes, mixing paint, repairing flat tires, and so forth, and for various cooking recipes. Reverse some of the directions. Pupils are expected to indicate what is wrong. Correct answers can appear on the back of the exercise. (For use with individual pupils; potentially self-directed.)

Corrective Material for Deficiencies in Locating Central Thoughts

When individual pupils or groups of pupils are deficient in ability to find central thoughts of paragraphs, corrective practice can be individualized by using materials and techniques as the following.

1. *Best Central Thought*: Select short paragraphs and have them followed by several statements. Pupils are directed to read each paragraph and then choose the particular statement they feel is the most adequate expression of the central thought. Correct answers can appear on the back of the exercise. (For use with individual pupils; potentially self-directed.)

2. *Composing Topic Sentences*: Furnish pupils with paragraphs consisting of details (the key sentences must be removed) and direct them to write their own key sentences. Later they compare their efforts with the original key sentences found on the back of the exercise. (For use with individual pupils; potentially self-directed.)

3. *Decapitated Headings*: Cut headings from three or four short articles. Place the headings in one envelope and the articles in another. Pupils are directed to match the headings with the proper articles. A marking scheme appearing on the back of the headings and articles can be used to make the exercises self-corrective. (For use with individual pupils; potentially self-directed.)
   A more difficult version of exercises using the decapitated-heading technique involves having pupils compose their own headings. Later they compare their efforts with those of the journalists who wrote the articles.

4. *Find the Paragraph*: Designate a story or articles in a book to which pupils have access. Provide a series of key sentences. Pupils are instructed to find the paragraph from which each was taken. Key paragraphs can appear on the back of the exercise. (For use with individual pupils; potentially self-directed.)

5. *Picture Summary*: Instruct a pupil or group of pupils to draw a picture expressing the main idea of the story or other material read. (For use with individual pupils; potentially self-directed.)

6. *What's the Number?* Number the sentences in paragraphs and direct pupils to find the number of the key sentence. Correct answers can appear on the back of the exercise. (For use with individual pupils; potentially self-directed.)

7. *What's the Question?* Furnish students with a paragraph and direct them to write a question which the entire paragraph answers. (For use with individual pupils; potentially self-directed.)

Corrective Practice Material for Deficiencies in Detecting and Remembering Details

When individual pupils or groups of pupils are deficient in ability to read for details, corrective practice can be individualized by using materials and techniques such as the following.

1. *Answering Questions:* Provide pupils with paragraphs followed by questions (true-false or multiple-choice) which are designed to test understanding of the details in each paragraph. Correct answers can appear on the back of each exercise. (For use with individual pupils; potentially self-directed.)

2. *Describing Pictures:* Have pupils design for each other draw-a-picture exercises consisting of details which describe a picture to be drawn. The picture described can be pasted on the back of the exercise. (For use with individual pupils; potentially self-directed.)

3. *Finding Irrelevant Details:* Provide pupils with paragraphs in which the sentences have been numbered. One of the sentences carries an irrelevant detail. Pupils are directed to read each paragraph carefully and detect the irrelevant sentence. Correct answers can appear on the back of the exercise. (For use with individual pupils; potentially self-directed.)

4. *Finding Nonsense Phrases:* Provide pupils with a series of paragraphs in each of which a nonsensical phrase has been inserted. Pupils are directed to read each paragraph carefully and detect the absurd phrase. Correct answers can appear on the back of the exercise. (For use with individual pupils; potentially self-directed.)

5. *Skeletal Outlines:* Provide pupils with an outline of a selection which presents main ideas but no details. Pupils are instructed to read the selection and complete the outline. The complete outline can appear on the back of the exercise. (For use with individual pupils; potentially self-directed.)

6. *Which Paragraph Is Best?* Mount a detailed picture on a piece of cardboard. In an accompanying envelope, provide pupils with three-by-five-inch cards on which individual paragraphs about the picture have been typed and numbered. Pupils are directed to find the paragraph which gives the most accurate details about the picture. Correct answers can appear on the back of the exercise. (For use with individual pupils; potentially self-directed.)

7. *Writing Details:* Provide pupils with a main idea and direct them to compose a paragraph by adding related details. (For use with individual pupils.)

In addition to the foregoing, it is helpful to point out to pupils the value of cue words in spotting important details. Some of these words are *specifically, namely, for example, for instance,* and the like. In providing additional illustrations of a main idea, authors often use words such as *moreover, then, in addition, further,* and so forth. These, too, can prove helpful. On occasions authors will highlight important details by using letters or numbers.

Corrective Material for Deficiencies in Following a Sequence of Events or Anticipating Outcomes

When individual pupils or groups of pupils are deficient in ability to follow a sequence of events, corrective practice can be individualized by using materials and techniques such as the following.

1. *Drawing Endings*: Mount a series of pictures that tell a sequential story on cardboard. Omit the last picture and place it in an accompanying envelope. Pupils are directed to draw the last picture. After the drawing, pupils may compare their efforts with the picture in the envelope. (For use with individual children; potentially self-directed.)
2. *End the Play*: Have pupils read the first two acts of a three-act play and then predict the ending. (For use with individual pupils; potentially self-directed.)
3. *How Does It End?* Present unfinished stories which stop at a critical point. Pupils are directed to make up suitable endings. The story ending can appear on the back of the exercise. (For use with individual pupils; potentially self-directed.)
4. *Paragraph Shuffle*: Prepare stories in which the numbered paragraphs are out of order. Pupils are directed to rearrange the paragraphs so that the sequence is proper. Correct answers can appear on the back of the exercise. (For use with individual pupils; potentially self-directed.)
5. *Problem Solution*: Have students read about a community problem and then predict what they think will happen. At a later date they can check the accuracy of their prediction. (For use with individual pupils; potentially self-directed.)
6. *Sentence Shuffle*: Prepare short stories in which the numbered sentences are out of order. Pupils are directed to rearrange the sentences so that the sequence is proper. Example:
   a. The strange man walked to the door and rapped.
   b. The man was invited into the house.
   c. The dog barked when he heard the sound.
   d. The lady of the house went to the door and opened it.
   Correct answers can appear on the back of the exercise. (For use with individual pupils; potentially self-directed.)

7. *Two Minute Mystery:* Have pupils read a short incomplete mystery story and then solve the crime. See *Two Minute Mysteries* (Scholastic Book Services). (For use with individual pupils; potentially self-directed.)

8. *Weather Guess:* Have pupils study the day's weather map and predict the weather. The following day they can check the accuracy of their prediction. (For use with individual pupils; potentially self-directed.)

Corrective Practice for Pupils Deficient in Critical Reading Ability

Teachers will find the following suggestions helpful in working with pupils who do not critically evaluate the material they read.

1. *Ask questions which stimulate students to analyze and evaluate what they have read.* Teachers will find it profitable to tape-record several class sessions so that they can compare the number of inferential questions asked as opposed to the number of literal questions.

2. *Encourage students to talk back to a book.* Have them evaluate statements in the light of their previous knowledge and beliefs. The good reader is always on guard, asking himself/herself questions such as Does that make good sense? Is that possible?

3. *Encourage pupils to check copyright dates.* Indicate the rapid advance that has taken place in many fields during the last few years. What may have been true a few years ago does not always hold today. The following serve as examples:

   a. "The top speed for all fighter craft does not exceed 500 miles per hour." Copyright 1941.

   b. "The population of the United States total 130,000,000." Copyright 1947.

4. *Give pupils training is distinguishing between statements of fact and opinion.* Show that opinions are merely beliefs which cannot be supported by objective evidence and that facts, on the contrary, are capable of being proved through objective evidence. Use statements such as the four listed:

   a. Men make better legislators than women. (Opinion)

   b. The majority of legislators are men. (Fact)

   c. California oranges are better than Florida oranges. (Opinion)

   d. Oranges contain vitamin C. (Fact)

5. *Have pupils compare several sources of information.* Select from a given field different authorities who contradict each other, or bring to class two newspapers or magazines of opposed political complexions and compare them. Strike up a discussion as to why discrepancies exist. Exercises such as these will indicate to pupils that a critical reader does not accept as final the viewpoint of any one author.

6. *Have pupils investigate an author's competence and possible prejudice.*
    Students should learn to look at the title page or book cover for informa-
    tion pertaining to an author's background and experience. Checking
    the appropriate *Who's Who* and sampling the opinions of other author-
    ities are also helpful in determining the reliability of an author. Fre-
    quently, the preface is of value in giving a clue as to an author's pur-
    pose in writing. Bringing to class for study a number of advertisements
    or political speeches is an excellent way to train students to recognize
    prejudiced writings.
7. *Encourage students to test statements for possible exceptions.* Many
    authors make dogmatic and sweeping statement which do not hold un-
    der all circumstances. The following are suggestive for suitable drill:
    a. An apple a day keeps the doctor away.
    b. You can't teach an old dog new tricks.
    c. He who hesitates is lost.
8. *Train students to identify and be on the alert for various advertising
    and propaganda devices that are commonly used to influence people.*
    Students should be made aware of the needs to which writers of this
    kind appeal. Some of the most common are (a) social need: the desire
    to be accepted by the group by doing what it does; (b) ego need: the
    desire to feel important; (c) physical need: comfort, food, rest; (d)
    desire for social and economic security; (e) desire for excitement.
    Paragraphs like the following might be used to sensitize students to
    how advertisers capitalize on these needs:
    Rideway is the car of tomorrow. It's faster, it's smoother, and more
    economical than any other car manufactured. Sales are mounting by
    leaps and bounds. People from all walks of life are choosing this upper-
    class car. Be smart. Stay out in front. Buy the beautiful and economical
    adventure car of the future. Rideway.
9. *Have students be alert to words which evoke emotional reaction.* The
    semanticist Hayakawa has labeled words such as *communism* and *total-
    itarianism* growl words; others such as *freedom* and *statesman* are
    categorized purr words. Students can be asked to underline all emo-
    tionally loaded words in a selection.

Corrective Practice for Pupils Deficient in the Ability to Remember What They Have Read

It has been stated by some authors that "material is remembered in proportion to the degree that it is understood."[4] It is patently true that a pupil's
ability to remember what he/she has read has little value unless understanding accompanies it. On the other hand, understanding what one has
read is of questionable value if nothing can be retained.

Usually, as pupils improve in ability to sustain attention and become more adept at spotting main ideas and related details, retention is enhanced. For pupils who are chronically inattentive to the meaning of what they read, the following procedure is suggested.

Start with a short sentence and direct the pupil to read it to himself. When he finishes, cover the sentence with a small card or close the book and ask, What did it say? If the pupil is unable to respond satisfactorily, allow him to reread the sentence and then query him again. Continue this on various occasions until he is able to tell, after a single reading, what a short sentence says. At this point, move on to more complex sentences.

The foregoing method is effective for the following reason. When a pupil realizes that as inevitably as death and taxes he has to tell you what he has read, he begins to pay closer attention. Greater concentration spells better retention.

Dallman and associates believe that one cause of inadequate retention stems from poor habits of attentiveness which should be attended to during the readiness period.[5] Some of the suggestions they give for increasing a pupil's memory span include the following:

1. Provide a reason for paying attention by making the work interesting.
2. Provide work that coincides with the pupil's level.
3. Provide variety in activities.
4. Encourage pupils to remain with an activity until it is completed. Let each pupil see how wasteful it is to discontinue something before he/she has completed it.
5. Keep things orderly so as to enhance good attention.
6. Require pupils to remain with the topic under discussion.
7. Hold pupils responsible for remembering the answer to a question that was asked of a community worker when on a trip outside school.

Corrective Practice for Pupils Who Have Difficulty in Concentrating

Concentration difficulties are often associated with emotional disturbances. The teacher, therefore, should do what she can to uncover any causes of emotional disturbances. If the services of a school psychologist are available, his/her help should be enlisted.

Practical suggestions which a teacher can give to pupils who have difficulty concentrating are as follows.

1. *Assume a questioning attitude.* Instruct pupils to immediately turn all headings into questions so that they are seeking something when reading takes place. The words *how, what, when, where,* and *why* are helpful in this regard. For example, the section heading "Causes of Tooth

Decay" should become "What are the causes of tooth decay?" By assuming a questioning attitude children become active readers rather than passive readers. Active readers have little trouble concentrating.

2. *Reduce distracting influences.* Pupils would not think of playing tennis while trying to memorize a poem. Yet at home they frequently read while listening to a radio or watching television. No wonder concentration is difficult!

   For maximum concentration at home, pupils should study by themselves, away from family and all distracting influences. Pictures, banners, and souvenirs should be removed from view. If possible, their desk should face a blank wall. Blank walls offer books little competition.

   When studying in a library, pupils should seat themselves in a place where they will not be disturbed. Sitting near friends who will tempt them to visit is not recommended. It is also advisable for pupils to sit with their back toward the library entrance. This will discourage their looking up to check on the identity of newcomers.

3. *Sit in a straight-backed chair.* Soft chairs and reclining davenports are not conducive to maximum concentration. Through years of conditioning they have become associated with rest and relaxation. The slight muscular tension that accompanies sitting up in a straight chair keeps students alert and makes concentration easier.

4. *Work rapidly.* The auto racer driving to win has to attain a maximum speed and hold it. The greater his speed, the greater will be his need to concentrate on steering. To divert any part of his full attention from the task at hand would be to lose the race. Similarly, readers who force themselves to work as fast as they can to accomplish their purpose have no time for mind wandering.

5. *Adopt a study schedule.* Pupils should plan and adhere to a schedule which will require them to study the same subject in the same place at the same time each day. It is easier to get down to business and concentrate on those things which have become routine and habitual.

6. *Provide proper lighting.* Reading makes heavy demands on the eyes. Frequently, improper lighting in the home causes visual fatigue which quickly hinders concentration. To reduce eyestrain, pupils should read under lights that are sufficiently strong. Desk lamps should be equipped with a minimum wattage of 75 and floor lamps should have 150 watts. In addition to direct lighting on the book a pupil is reading, the entire room should be dimly lighted. This reduces extreme contrasts which the eyes cannot tolerate. Glare should be guarded against by covering shiny surfaces or shifting lamps slightly to avoid reflections. Finally, students should be told not to read on and on without respite. Occasionally, they should rest their eyes by closing them or by looking at a distant object across the room or through a window.

A method of study that can aid concentration and boost retention tremendously was evolved by Francis Robinson.[6] It is particularly effective with content field material and can be introduced most profitably as early as the fourth-grade level (A simplified version of this valuable method of study is given on pages 114-115.)

Mechanical Devices for Improving Rate of Comprehension

Manufacturers wish to convince us that mechanical devices have great value in helping pupils overcome reading difficulties. Magazines have popularized mechanical gadgets and often give the impression that they constitute a panacea for ills. Much of this, of course, is an outgrowth of a tremendous emphasis on "speed reading."

Controlled readers, tachistoscopes, and pacers of many types are found in schools throughout the country. How valuable are these machines?

Spache in his discussion of the machine approach to reading rate indicates the following concerns:

1. Does a pupil's accomplishment achieved while using machines transfer to the act of book reading?
2. What dangers to vision does the machine approach pose?
3. What are the effects of after-image on recall following tachistoscopic presentation?
4. Do machines that expose material in a constant fixed span introduce an element of artificiality that should be given consideration? George Spache, *Toward Better Reading* (Champaign, Ill.: Garrard Publishing Co., 1962), pp. 260-264.

In his review of research relevant to the use of mechanical devices in the teaching of reading, Karlin concludes the following:

From some of these studies it appears that gains in rate of reading can be achieved through the use of a mechanical device. To what extent credit may be given to such a device for such achievement is unknown. Few, if any, of these studies were sufficiently tight to minimize the influences of extraneous variables upon the outcomes.

A second conclusion may be reached: In eleven of the twelve investigations which measured natural reading against machine reading, the groups that received training in the former either equaled or surpassed the machine groups in rate of reading. From these data it can be said that outcomes in speed of reading similar to those achieved through the use of special instruments may be expected from suitable reading instruction which does not include these same instruments. Robert Karlin, "Machines and Reading: A Review of Research," *Clearing House* (February 1958):352.

Although studies of the future may prove to the contrary, available data seem to indicate that unless money is plentiful, a school would be wiser to invest in good books and efficient teachers than in machines.

A description of some of the mechanical devices available for improving rate of comprehension follows.

Tachistoscopes

1. *Adjustable Lens Barrel Tachistoscope*: This model retains all the features of the standard Lens-Type Tachistoscope and is attachable to any projector with lens barrel size 1⅞ inches to 2½ inches O.D. Placement onto the projector lens barrel is easy and quick. The shutter is activated remotely from a hand switch and from the included power supply. Exposure times are 1/150, 1/100, 1/50, 1/25, 1/10, 1/2, 1 and 2 second intervals. (Lafayette Instrument. $325.00.)

2. *All-Purpose Electric Tachistoscope*: This is a more advanced version of the standard All-Purpose Tachistoscope. This unit is to be controlled remotely by a hand switch and included power source. Shutter speeds are 1/150, 1/100, 1/50, 1/25, 1/10, 1/2, 1, and 2 second intervals. (Lafayette Instrument. $325.00.)

3. *All-Purpose Tachistoscope*: This tachistoscope can be used for presentation to an entire classroom or for individual training. It is usable with any make projector. Exposure times of the shutter are 1/125, 1/60, 1/30, 1/15, 1/8, 1/4, 1/2, and 1 second. (Lafayette Instrument. $125; carrying case $15.00.)

4. *Attachable Lens Barrel Tachistoscope*: This tachistoscope is adaptable to any projector having a lens barrel size of 1⅞ inches to 2½ inches O.D., and it is mounted directly to the lens barrel of the projector. It slides on easily and is tightened securely by means of three thumbscrews. Shutter exposure times are 1/150, 1/100, 1/50, 1/25, 1/10, 1/2, 1, and 2 second intervals. (Lafayette Instrument. $150.00, carrying case $15.00.)

5. *Automatic Projection Tachistoscope*: All operations of this projection tachistoscope are completely automatic. Slides can be presented automatically at 5-, 8-, and 15-second intervals as the shutter is triggered automatically when the slide changes. Shutter exposure times are 1/150, 1/100, 1/50, 1/25, 1/10, 1/2, 1, and 2 second intervals. Forward and reversing of slides, focusing of lens, and changing of slides may be accomplished by remote control. Switching is also provided on the remote control to skip slides or to repeat slides. (Lafayette Instrument. $595.00.)

6. *Craig Reader*: This device is a combination tachistoscope and controlled reader using filmstrips mounted on plastic. One to three individuals can use the device simultaneously. (Creative Curriculum, Inc. $349.00.)

7. *EDL Combo-8 Projector*: This device is a combination tachistoscope and controlled reader. Its tachistoscope training speeds are 1/100, 1/10, 1/4 and 1/2 second. (EDL/McGraw-Hill. $395.00.)

9. *Split Sentences*: Pupils are given two envelopes. One envelope contains cards with sentence beginnings and the other contains cards with sentence endings. Pupils are directed to match suitable parts to form sentences. Examples:

a. Jack and Jill went up the hill
b. I ran and ran until I was
c. As the sun began to rise it became

1. lighter and warmer.
2. all out of breath.
3. to fetch a pail of water.

(For use with individual pupils; potentially self-directed.)

Correct answers can appear on the back of the exercise.

10. *True or False*: True-or-false statements that are related or unrelated to the reading lesson can be used to help develop sentence comprehension. Since many such statements are humorous, children enjoy these exercises immensely. Examples:

a. A twelve-year-old boy can run 100 miles an hour.
b. This sentence has more than seven words in it.
c. A wild tiger would make a fine house pet.

(For use with individual pupils; potentially self-directed.)

Correct answers can appear on the back of the exercise.

11. *When, What, Where?* Sentences which tell when, what, or where are prepared. Pupils read each sentence and categorize it according to these designations. Examples:

a. The Jones family spent their summer in the country.
b. A slender piece of metal that is driven into two blocks of wood can hold them together.
c. He said the world would come to an end last week.

(For use with individual pupils; potentially self-directed.)

Correct answers can appear on the back of the exercise.

12. *Where's the Joker?* Sentences pertaining to a given subject are presented together with a sentence that does not belong. Pupils are directed to find the foreign sentence. Examples:

a. The car is a Ford. b. The body is red and the wheels are black. c. The sky became dark and cloudy. d. The top speed is 100 miles an hour.

(For use with individual pupils; potentially self-directed.)

Correct answers can appear on the back of the exercise.

Corrective Material for Deficiencies in Following Directions

When individual pupils or groups of pupils are deficient in ability to follow directions, corrective practice can be individualized by using materials and techniques such as the following.

-Tach: This is a tachistoscope for individual use. It employs an ...nic flash unit and has shutter speeds of 1/100, 1/50, 1/25, 1/10, ...econd. Five hundred targets accompany purchase of the ma-...Lafayette Instrument. $195.00.)

Eye Span Trainer: This simple hand-operated tachistoscope ...inyl plastic requires no electric power. It has variable shut-...of 1/25, 1/50, or 1/100 of a second. Available slides are ...No. 3-elementary and junior high; No. 1-senior high and ...No. 2-advanced. (Audio-Visual Research. $9.95 with No. ...des; $13.75 with No. 1, No. 2, or No. 3 slides; blank slides

... is a hand tachistoscope for individual training using ...(Educational Development Laboratories. $10.50.)

...: This hand-operated tachistoscopic device trains stu-...n meaningful phrases. Included are cards containing ...of varying widths, beginning with simple words and ...nating in complete paragraphs. (Reading Laboratory.

...combination tachistoscope, accelerator, and pacer, ...witch, functions as a tach flasher and illuminates ...part or 5 picas apart. (Ken-A-Vision. $209.00.)

...his light, portable tachistoscope employs circular ...res per reel. The interval of exposure varies from ...ond. (Rheem Califone. $135.)

...ndividual near-point tachistoscope. Electronic ...xposure times of 1/100, 1/50, 1/25, 1/10, and 1 ...(Lafayette Instrument. $310.00.)

Slide Tachistoscope: This standard tachisto-...projector. This particular projector projects ...The standard shutter is attached to the lens ...tions are 1/125, 1/60, 1/30, 1/8, 1/4, 1/2, and ...rument. $296.00.)

...chistoscope projects single-frame filmstrips ...ning. (Learning Through Seeing. $34.50.)

...using filmstrips with an exposure interval ...tional Communications Technology, Inc.

...ses filmstrips which permits varying the ...conds to 1/100 of a second. (Education-...$285.00.)

...rated four-speed tachistoscopic device ...(Learning Through Seeing. $99.00.)

...stoscope that flashes card material at ...ond. (Instructional Communications

Controlled Readers and Pacers

1. *AVR Reading Rateometer*: An inexpensive device designed for individual use. It consists of an electrically driven plastic bar which descends over the page at a speed determined by the user. (Audio-Visual Research. $47.85.)

2. *Combo-8 Projector*: This device is a combination controlled reader and tachistoscope. Controlled reading speeds vary between 40 to 800 words per minute. (Educational Developmental Laboratories/McGraw-Hill. $395.00.)

3. *Controlled Reader*: A machine designed for group work (individual pupils can use it, however). It employs a filmstrip projector which exposes printed material on a screen at varying rates of speed as determined by the operator. The material can be exposed one line at a time in a left-to-right manner by employing a moving slot. (Educational Developmental Laboratories. $355.00; smaller model, the Controlled Reader Junior, $305.00.)

4. *Guided Reader Projector*: A controlled reading machine that uses filmstrips capable of providing projection rates between 40 and 1,050 words per minute. It can be used by individuals and by small groups. (Instructional Communications Technology. $139.95.)

5. *Shadowscope Reading Pacer*: A device designed for individual use. It employs a 1-inch-wide beam of light to pace the user's reading speed. The horizontal beam gradually descends over the page at a speed controlled by the user. (Psychotechnics. $99.50.)

6. *Skill Builder*: A 35mm controlled reader with super-slow scanning action. (EDL/McGraw-Hill. $395.00.)

7. *Skill Mate*: An individual training version of the Skill Builder. (EDL/McGraw-Hill. $345.00.)

8. *SRA Reading Accelerator, Model III*: A device designed for individual use. It is constructed of metal and employs a mechanically operated shutter which descends over the page of a book at a speed determined by the user. (Science Research Associates. $120.95.)

9. *SRA Reading Accelerator, Model IV*: A lightweight plastic version of the foregoing device. It weighs 1½ pounds. (Science Research Associates. $86.90.)

10. *SRA Reading Accelerator, Model V*: A lightweight plastic device weighing 19 ounces. Reading exposure speeds range from 16 to 2,200 words per minute. (Science Research Associates. $41.00.)

11. *Tachomatic 500*: A device designed for group work (individuals or small groups can use it, too). It is specifically designed for the presentation of Tachomatic film essays, in single line, two or three fixations per line, at rates from 100 to 1,200 words per minute. (Psychotechnics. $375.00.)

answers can appear on the back of the exercise. (For use with
al pupils; potentially self-directed.)

: Mount a picture on an individual card together with three
that tell something about the picture. Print two extra sen-
do not relate to the picture. Pupils are instructed to find
elevant sentences. Correct answers can appear on the back
ise. (For use with individual pupils; potentially self-di-

Sentences: Two or three pictures are mounted on in-
together with fifteen or twenty sentences which have
on separate cards. Pupils are instructed to read each
atch it with the picture to which it refers. A marking
devised on the reverse side of the cards to make this
ective. (For use with individual pupils; potentially

ype paragraphs in which all periods and capital let-
itted. Pupils are directed to designate the begin-
of sentences by employing proper punctuation and
correctly written paragraphs can appear on the
(For use with individual pupils; potentially self-

: Have pupils study a picture carefully and then
t describe the picture.

ive directions which refer pupils to a picture
eviously read. Ask them to find all sentences
at give more information than what is found
entences can appear on the back of the exer-
dual pupils; potentially self-directed.)
ntences are prepared. Two of the four say
ing. Pupils are directed to find the synony-

until he became very tired.
t until he found what he was looking for.
lderness looking for a place to build a

g for a great distance until he was ex-

the back of the exercise. (For use with
f-directed.)

CORRECTIVE MATERIAL FOR IMPROVING RATE OF COMPREHENSION

When individual pupils or groups of pupils are deficient in rate of comprehension, corrective practices can be individualized by using *teacher-made material* such as follows.

1. Magazine articles that are fairly easy and interesting for the grade being taught are ideally suited for practice in improving rate of comprehension. It is suggested that expository articles, 500 to 1,000 words in length, be mounted on cardboard. On the back of the cardboard, ten questions pertaining to the article should appear. A library card pocket can be used to conceal a slip of paper on which the answers to the questions are written. A file of similar articles should be evolved so that pupils can be given periodic practice in improving their comprehension rate. Each pupil is encouraged to keep his/her own progress chart and to enter into vigorous self competition. (See pages 194-195 for information on giving informal speed tests.)

2. Provide pupils with 3-by-5-inch cards. Show them how to expose a line of print very briefly by means of a quick pull-push movement with the fingers. Encourage pupils to practice in this manner so that they broaden the recognition span. (For use with individual pupils; potentially self-directed.)

3. Provide pupils with paragraphs in which they are instructed to underline key words. The selection with key words underlined can appear on the back of the exercise. (For use with individual pupils; potentially self-directed.)

4. Provide pupils with selections in which they are instructed to insert vertical lines between words to highlight the phrasing. The selection with lines inserted to show proper phrasing can appear on the back of the exercise. (For use with individual pupils; potentially self-directed.)

5. Provide a variety of easy, interesting reading materials and encourage pupils to do a large amount of pleasurable reading. When pupils read interesting materials, they become eager to learn what is going to happen. This results in a natural increase in reading rate.

Corrective Practice Material for Improving Deficiencies in Locating Information

When individual pupils or groups of pupils are deficient in ability to locate information, corrective practice can be individualized by using materials and techniques such as the following.

1. Provide pupils with a pack of cards on each of which a topic appears. Pupils are directed to place the cards in alphabetical order. Numbers can be written on the backs of the cards to indicate correct sequence. (For use with individual pupils; potentially self-directed.)

2. Provide pupils with a list of words and instruct them to place these in alphabetical order. The correct sequence can appear on the back of the exercise. (For use with individual pupils; potentially self-directed.)

3. Remove a page from the table of contents of a discarded book and mount it on cardboard. Follow the selection by specific questions such as How many topics are listed? On what page would you first find information about_____? What kind of book do you think this was? Correct answers can appear on the back of the exercise. (For use with individual pupils; potentially self-directed.)

4. The index of the want ads from a daily paper can be cut out and mounted on a piece of cardboard. Pupils are asked questions such as In what section would you look if you wished to buy a violin? Where would you look if you were interested in used furniture? Correct answers can appear on the back of the exercise. (For use with individual pupils, potentially self-directed.)

5. The index of the features from the Sunday paper can be cut out and mounted on a piece of cardboard. Pupils are asked questions such as On what page would you find an article about space travel? If you wish to go to the movies, where would you find the theaters listed? Correct answers can appear on the back of the exercise. (For use with individual pupils; potentially self-directed.)

6. Provide pupils with a series of questions based on an indexed book to which they have access. Pupils are directed to indicate the key word in the question which appears in the index. For example: How much *iron ore* is mined yearly in the United States? Correct answers can appear on the back of the exercise. (For use with individual pupils; potentially self-directed.)

7. Ask pupils which of four numbered words or phrases, if looked up in an index, would *not* be likely to lead to the answer of a given question. For example: What water routes in America are considered important? 1. rivers 2. lakes 3. canals 4. rainstorms. Correct answers can appear on the back of the exercise. (For use with individual pupils; potentially self-directed.)

8. Provide pupils with a question and instruct them to think of headings under which the information might be found if an index were consulted. Possible correct answers can appear on the back of the exercise. (For use with individual pupils; potentially self-directed.)

9. Provide pupils with a list of reference books to which they have had access. Follow this by a series of questions. Pupils are instructed to indicate which reference books would be consulted to answer the questions involved. Correct answers can appear on the back of the exercise. (For use with individual pupils; potentially self-directed.)

Corrective Practice Material for Improving Deficiencies in Reading Maps, Charts, Tables, and Graphs

When individual pupils or groups of pupils are deficient in ability to read maps, charts, tables, and graphs, corrective practice can be individualized by using materials and techniques such as the following.

1. Provide pupils with exercises consisting of mounted maps, charts, tables, and graphs that have been taken from discarded books or magazines. Write a series of questions which pertain to the interpretation and use of each. For example, a bar graph pertaining to the annual oil production of Texas, California, Louisiana, Oklahoma, and Kansas might be followed by true-and-false statements such as Oklahoma produces more oil than California and The state that produces the most oil is Texas. A map of Sweden might be followed by questions such as What is the name of the river passing through Goteburg? and What city is located farthest south in Sweden? Correct answers to questions can appear on the back of the exercises. (For use with individual pupils; potentially self-directed.)
2. Provide pupils with data of various kinds. Direct them to prepare their own charts, graphs, and tables to represent these data. Correct representations can appear on the back of the exercises. (For use with individual pupils; potentially self-directed.)
3. Provide pupils with a graph, chart, or table and direct them to list ten questions or more which any of the foregoing sources of data can answer.
4. Provide pupils with a table, chart, or graph and ask them to write a paragraph or two that presents the same information as any of the foregoing sources of data.

Corrective Material for Improving Deficiencies in Outlining Skill

When individual pupils or groups of pupils are deficient in ability to outline (since outlining skill is dependent on the ability to detect main ideas and related details, exercises designed to develop these subskills should be reviewed), corrective practice can be individualized by using the following materials and techniques.

1. Provide pupils with paragraphs followed by a simplified outline of the main ideas and related details. Follow this by comparable paragraphs and a skeletal outline. Pupils are instructed to complete the skeletal outline. The correct outline can appear on the back of the exercise. (For use with individual pupils; potentially self-directed.)

2. List main ideas and related details in sequential order but do not indicate any degree of subordination. Pupils are directed to show subordination by numbering, lettering, and indenting properly. The correct form can appear on the back of the exercise. (For use with individual pupils; potentially self-directed.)
3. Provide pupils with a number of main ideas and related details in mixed order. Pupils are directed to straighten out the sequence and show subordination by numbering, lettering, and indenting properly. The correct outline can appear on the back of the exercise. (For use with individual pupils; potentially self-directed.)
4. Provide pupils with a number of paragraphs. Pupils are directed to discern the main ideas and related details and put them into proper outline form. The correct outline can appear on the back of the exercise. (For use with individual pupils; potentially self-directed.)
5. Ask pupils to prepare an outline for a particular subject which they then use in giving an oral report to the class.

Corrective Practice Material for Improving Deficiencies in Summarizing

When individual pupils or groups of pupils are deficient in ability to summarize what they have read, corrective practice can be individualized by using the following materials and techniques.

1. Refer pupils to a story in a book to which they have access. Place pictures which depict the story in an envelope together with some which are unrelated to the story. Instruct pupils to find the pictures that depict the story and to place these in proper sequence. A numbering scheme on the backs of the proper pictures can make this exercise self-corrective. (For use with individual pupils; potentially self-directed.)
2. Refer pupils to a story in a book to which they have access. Pupils are instructed to read the selection and then draw a series of pictures which tell the story. (For use with individual pupils; potentially self-directed.)
3. Provide pupils with a selection consisting of several paragraphs which is followed by a summary. Pupils are instructed to read the selection and then evaluate the summary in light of the following questions.
   a. Does the summary include all main ideas?
      (1) List any omitted.
   b. Does the summary include all related details?
      (1) List any omitted.
   c. Does the summary include any unnecessary details?
      (1) List these.
   d. Does the summary keep ideas in proper order?
   e. Does the summary use complete sentences?

Correct answers can appear on the back of the exercise. (For use with individual pupils; potentially self-directed.)

4. Provide pupils with a selection consisting of several paragraphs which is followed by several summaries. Pupils are instructed to read the selection and then decide which summary is best. The correct answer can appear on the back of the exercise. (For use with individual pupils; potentially self-directed.)

PROBLEMS FOR ORAL AND WRITTEN DISCUSSION

1. Select five principles of corrective instruction from the following list and discuss how they could be implemented in a school reading program.
   a. Correction must be based on a diagnosis of reading difficulties.
   b. A variety of materials should be provided.
   c. Materials used should be self-directive.
   d. Materials must be of optimum difficulty.
   e. Materials must be ample for each type of difficulty.
   f. Materials must sustain the child's interest.
   g. Materials must not carry a grade level and should have an appealing format.
   h. The teacher should be enthusiastic and reassuring.
   i. The teacher should be alert to manifestations of sensory defects.
   j. The teacher should be acquainted with the child's home environment.
   k. The teacher's relationship with the child should be wholesome.
   l. Hazards to the child's learning should be ameliorated whenever possible.
   m. The teacher must employ a variety of techniques.
   n. The child should be made aware of his/her reading difficulties.
   o. The child should be made aware of his/her progress and keep a record of it.
   p. The child should progress at his/her own rate.
   q. The program must not interfere with other enjoyable school activities.
   r. The program must foster a child's self-confidence.
   s. Recreational reading under supervision must become an integral part of the program.
   t. The program should engender in the child a love of reading.
2. Evaluate the place of workbooks as self-corrective materials.
3. Obtain a workbook in reading. Set up criteria for its evaluation and apply the criteria.

4. Procure several workbooks in reading on two or more levels of difficulty. Dissect, combine, and assemble the workbooks to form a ready file of corrective reading material as described in this chapter.
5. Obtain a completed cumulative record for a pupil with a reading problem and record all pertinent data on the Diagnostic Reading Summary appearing in chapter 9. What additional data are needed in order to provide a more complete diagnosis?
6. Select a pupil with a reading problem. Apply and consult all available and appropriate diagnostic techniques needed to analyze his problem. Utilize the Reading Checklist and the Reading Summary (see chapter 9).
7. Organize a self-corrective program in reading for a pupil who is deficient in reading comprehension, indicating the pupil's grade placement, instructional level, intelligence, degree of retardation, reading expectancy, and specific difficulties to be corrected. Select the corrective materials to be used, indicating type and difficulty.

Notes

1. PAUL BURNS and BETTY RUE, Reading Activities for Today's Elementary Schools (Chicago: Rand McNally, 1979), p. 78.
2. I. QUANDT, "Investing in Word Banks—A Practice for Any Approach," Reading Teacher (November 1973):171-173.
3. RUSSELL STAUFFER, "A Study of Prefixes in the Thorndike List to Establish a List of Prefixes That Should Be Taught in the Elementary Schools," Journal of Educational Research (1942):453-458.
4. ALBERT HARRIS and EDWARD SIPAY. How to Teach Reading. (New York: Longman, 1979), pp. 343-344.
5. MARTHA DALLMAN et al., The Teaching of Reading, 4th ed. (New York: Holt, Rinehart & Winston, 1974), p. 90.
6. FRANCIS ROBINSON, Effective Study (New York: Harper & Row, 1946), p. 28.

Selected Readings

BADER, LOIS A. Reading Diagnosis and Remediation in Classroom and Clinic. New York: Macmillan Publishing Co., Inc., 1980, ch. 8.
BERGER, ALLEN, and PEEBLES, JAMES, "Rates of Comprehension," Newark, Del.: International Reading Association, 1976.
BOND, GUY, and TINKER, MILES. Reading Problems: Their Diagnosis and Correction 3rd ed. New York: Appleton-Century-Crofts, 1973, chaps. 13, 16.
COMBS, WARREN E., "Sentence Combining Practice Aids Reading Comprehension," in Diane J. Sawyer (ed.) Disabled Readers: Insight, Assessment, Instruction. Newark, Delaware: International Reading Association, 1980.
HARRIS, ALBERT. How to Increase Reading Ability. 6th ed. New York: David McKay Co., 1975, chaps. 16, 17.
HARRIS, ALBERT, and SIPAY, EDWARD. How to Teach Reading. New York: Longman, 1979, Unit 8.

HARRIS, LARRY A. and SMITH, CARL B. *Reading Instruction.* 2nd ed. New York: Holt, Rinehart and Winston, 1976, chap. 12.

GIBSON, E., and LEVIN, H. *The Psychology of Reading.* Cambridge: MIT Press, 1975.

GRIESE, ARNOLD. *Do You Read Me? Practical Approaches to Teaching Reading Comprehension.* Santa Monica, Calif.: Goodyear Publishing Company, Inc., 1977.

KARLIN, ROBERT, *Teaching Elementary Reading,* 3rd ed. (New York: Harcourt Brace Jovanovich, Inc., 1980), ch. 7.

MAGRUM, CHARLES, and FORGAN, HARRY. *Developing Competencies in Teaching Reading.* Columbus, Ohio: Charles E. Merrill Publishing Company, 1979, Module 5.

OTTO, WAYNE, and SMITH, RICHARD J. *Corrective and Remedial Teaching.* Boston: Houghton Mifflin Co., 1980, ch. 9.

ROBECK, MILDRED, and WILSON, JOHN. *Psychology of Reading: Foundations of Instruction.* New York: John Wiley & Sons, 1974, chap. 14.

SILVAROLI, NICHOLAS J., and WHEELOCK, WARREN H. *Teaching Reading.* Dubuque, Iowa: Wm. C. Brown Company Publishers, 1980, ch. 2.

SMITH, BROOKS E., GOODMAN, KENNETH S., and MEREDITH, ROBERT. *Language and Thinking in School.* 2nd ed. New York: Holt, Rinehart and Winston, 1976, chap. 16.

SPACHE, GEORGE D. *Diagnosing and Correcting Reading Disabilities.* Boston: Allyn and Bacon, Inc., 1976, chap. 11.

SPACHE, GEORGE, and SPACHE, EVELYN. *Reading in the Elementary School.* 3rd ed. Boston: Allyn & Bacon, 1973, chap. 14.

THORNDYKE, P. "Cognitive Structures in Comprehension and Memory of Narrative Discourse," *Cognitive Psychology* (January 1977):77-110.

14 Multilevel Materials and Devices

Chapters 12 and 13 were devoted to descriptions of materials, methods, and devices that were designed rather specifically to meet individual deficiencies in word perception, word analysis, comprehension, study skills and rate of comprehension. The content of this chapter is devoted to descriptions of commercial and teacher-made materials and devices applicable to the improvement of several kinds of reading and/or study skills on various levels of difficulty. These materials are designed for use with individuals or groups. Addresses of the publishers and manufacturers mentioned in this chapter are given in Appendix F.

MAGIC SLATES

Some heavy cardboard and a sheet of acetate can be turned into a magic slate. After the acetate is placed over the cardboard, the sides are taped, leaving the top and bottom open. With a magic slate of the proper size (9 inches by 12 inches is recommended) individual exercises can be slipped between the cardboard and the sheet of acetate and marked with crayon. Crayon marks will rub off very easily with a dry cloth or cleansing tissue. With five or six magic slates on hand, it is not difficult to keep a sizable number of children working independently with a variety of materials of an individualized nature.

Many teachers provide children with answer files so that they can carry on independently with a minimum amount of supervision. There is, however, an ingenious way of making an acetate-covered exercise of alternate-choice items immediately self-corrective. To do this, the teacher should encircle the correct answers on the surface of a second sheet of transparent acetate which is hinged to the one on which the pupil will record his responses. The acetate sheet carrying the answers is then folded under the cardboard. When a pupil completes the exercise, he swings the hinged sheet of acetate over the one on which he has written his answers. If the superimposed key does not coincide with his answers, the pupil knows he has erred.

THE ELECTRIC BOARD

A relatively inexpensive and versatile teaching device which intrigues pupils of all ages is the electric board. It is entirely self-instructive and can be used to teach many things. Through its use pupils can learn to match synonyms, antonyms, and blends, as well as questions and answers of all sorts.

In constructing an electric board the first item needed is a wooden board. Pegboard is highly recommended because of the ready-made holes. The board may be of any desired dimensions, but twenty-four by thirty inches seems to be an optimum size.

In addition to the board, the following materials are needed: stove bolts (about ½ inch in length), small pegboard hooks, No. 25 copper wire, a radio battery (about 4½ volts), a flashlight bulb, some three-by-five-inch cards. The entire set of equipment needed should not cost more than $5.

Two-thirds of the board (from left to right) can be devoted to spaced stove bolts that are placed so sufficient room remains directly under each for a hook on which will hang a three-by-five-inch card. Questions for which an answer must be found are written on these cards.

The answer column is set up at the right of the board. It consists of a series of bolts placed in a single vertical row. Sufficient space between the bolts or to the right of the bolts is provided for small hooks on which answer cards will hang.

On the reverse side of the board, pieces of insulated wire are used to connect a bolt at the left of the board with one of the bolts in the answer column to the right. The battery is fastened to the base of the board on the back. A small hole is made in the board for inserting the bulb.

One of the battery terminals is now connected with one of the lamp-socket terminals. On the other battery terminal, a piece of free wire is connected. This wire should be long enough to reach completely around the board to the bolts in the answer column at the right. Another free wire is connected to the remaining lamp-socket terminal. This wire should be long enough to reach the remaining bolts (questions are under these) on the front of the board.

When the ends of both of the free wires are in contact with two bolts that have been connected behind the board, the light goes on. The pupil knows he has made a correct association.

TEACHER-MADE FILED MATERIAL

Teachers can evolve their own files of material by cutting up old copies of children's magazines or newspapers. Typewritten copies of children's own stories can be kept in notebooks for easy, interesting reading. Sometimes, too, copies of discarded readers can be obtained, dissected, and accompanied by comprehension, vocabulary, and word-attack exercises of a self-directive nature. Workbooks of different types can be cut up and incorporated into a valuable file of self-corrective exercises.

Stiff-paper folders of different colors can be used to house separate numbers of *My Weekly Reader*. Upper grades can be provided with articles drawn from back issues of *Scholastic Scope* magazine and the *Reader's Digest*. These can be mounted in stiff-paper covers and placed in a subject file.

Children can be encouraged to assist in the cutting, pasting, and mounting of materials. They can make attractive illustrated covers for certain stories and can classify them under headings like "Rocket Travel," "Airplanes," "The Wild West," and so forth.

COMMERCIALLY MADE KITS AND PROGRAMS

Many commercially made materials are accompanied by self-directed or potentially self-directed exercises which pertain to practically all areas of reading improvement and study skills. These materials are extremely valuable in any program that stress individualization. A number of such programs are described on the pages that follow. They are arranged alphabetically according to the names of the publishers involved.

The Reading Achievement Program

This program is designed to help under-achieving students who are reading at the third, fourth, and fifth grade levels. It consists of ten units, comprising one-hundred exercises. Each exercise includes an instructional full-color filmstrip with an accompanying audio cassette; a printed essay corresponding to the audio cassette; and student answer sheets. The exercises are color-coded for quick identification. Correct answers are provided for all questions. ($247.50. ACT Publishing Corporation.) Addison-Wesley Reading Development Kits. This three-kit program teaches essential word-attack and comprehension skills from early reading level through grade ten. It is designed for the disabled reader in the teens and adult years. Within five subject matter areas—health, law, safety, science, and the world of words—topics of concern to the student (drug abuse, mail fraud, looking for a job, income tax, etc.) are presented.

To build student confidence in their abilities to "go it alone," the authors have carefully constructed each lesson to follow a carefully plotted sequence. Each lesson has three distinct but interrelated and interdependent parts: (1) Getting Ready-vocabulary building exercises, presentation of the new word-attack and/or comprehension skills to be mastered in the lesson; (2) Reading the Selection-a short (350 to 500 words) selection of high interest in which the student practices the skills presented in Getting Ready; (3) Follow-Up-questions to test comprehension and recall, checks on skill mastery, and open-end questions and activities to extend interests and experiences. (Addison-Wesley.)

Description	Price
Kit A: (early reading level) is a learning laboratory designed to aid disabled readers and older children and may also be used in junior and senior high school or in adult education courses.	$ 93.09
Kit B: (reading levels 4 to 6) contains materials at grade levels of approximately 4 through 6 and may be used in reading improvement program at the junior or senior high school level.	93.09
Kit C: (reading levels 7 to 10) is designed for adolescents and adults reading at grade levels 7 through 10 plus and provides secondary school and college reading instructors with a program that provides reading class materials and meets individual interests as well.	130.02

Sesame Street/Electric Company Reading Kits

This program consists of two kits: The Sesame Street Prereading Kit and the Electric Company Sentence Comprehension Kit.

The Sesame Street Prereading Kit uses characters from the "Sesame Street" television show and is designed for kindergarten and first-grade students. It consists of ten sound-filmstrips (accompanied by ten cassettes), sixteen audiocassettes containing thirty-two different audioactivities, and ten games. Included also are three different activity books that contain the pages for the thirty-two audioactivities and the three minibooks. A Teacher's Resource Book is furnished.

The Electric Company Sentence Comprehension Kit emphasizes a different aspect of comprehension. This material concentrates on comprehension at the sentence level to show how certain words can change the meaning of a sentence, provide a cue as to what the sentence conveys, or give an indication of the logical relationships implied. The kit includes eight sound-filmstrips (with eight accompanying audiocassettes), twelve audiocassettes containing twenty-four audioactivities, and eight games. (Addison-Wesley.)

Description	Price
Sesame Street Prereading Kit	$609.90
Electric Company Sentence Comprehension Kit	561.75

Target Reading Skills Program

This program provides students with extended practice in basic skills at all grade levels. The *Target Reading Skills Program* consists of six audio-tape kits. They have been designed on the basis of behavioral objectives to provide sequential training in skills to supplement any classroom reading program. The practice exercises in the Target kits can be used with any reading program. Each kit can be used by one student or by a group of students. Since the Target kits are self-instructional, minimal teacher supervision is required.

Each kit includes a series of duplicating masters for pretests and lessons called target sheets, a cassette recording for each target sheet, duplicating masters for progress charts, file labels to be attached to standard file folders for storing quantities of target sheets, a cassette containing directions for the teacher, and a teacher's manual. (Addison-Wesley.)

Description	Price
Target Red Auditory-Visual Discrimination Kit: The lessons in this kit help build basic discrimination skills important to the development of phonetic and structural analysis skills. Ten lessons and one pretest are for practice in auditory discrimination; twenty-two lessons and two pretests are provided for developing visual discrimination. Each lesson is based on a single behavioral objective, and the tasks within each objective have been carefully sequenced on a scale from simple to complex.	$237.00
Target Yellow Phonetic Analysis Kit: The exercises in this kit allow students to approach phonetic analysis through vision, hearing, and kinesthetic responses. The following skills are covered in the thirty lessons and four pretests: identifying consonants, identifying short and long vowel sounds, identifying initial and terminal consonant blends, and identifying consonant digraphs, vowel digraphs, and diphthongs.	237.00
Target Blue Structural Analysis Kit: The exercises in Target Blue teach skills for systematically attacking new words through visual analysis of known parts of words. The thirty-two lessons and three pretests cover roots, compounds, plurals, inflectional endings, prefixes, suffixes, contractions, possessiveness, and syllabication.	237.00
Target Green Vocabulary Development Kit: This kit introduces word functions through three classifications: naming words, action words, and describing words. Thirty-two lessons and three pretests cover word function, context clues, homonyms, homographs, synonyms, antonyms, root words,	
Target Orange Vocabulary Development Kit: This kit helps students expand their vocabulary in an organized way studying words that occur frequently in various content fields. The thirty-four lessons and two pretests cover homonyms, homographs, synonyms, antonyms, context clues, prefixes, suffixes, and roots.	237.00
Target Purple and Copper Study Skills Kits: The lessons in these kits are designed to help students develop strategies for improving their reference skills. Lessons and pretests cover the following skills: alphabetizing; using a textbook; locating information in encyclopedias, newspapers, and library and catalog; and reading and interpreting graphs, tables, charts, and diagrams.	243.00

Supportive Reading Skills

Supportive Reading Skills are sold only in sets. Single title sets contain a total of eight booklets unless otherwise specified. Also provided are a teacher's manual, pretests and posttests, spirit masters for duplicating work sheets, a class record sheet, and a display container. Complete sets contain only one copy of each booklet in the series. (Barnell Loft.)

Description	Price
Reading Homonyms	
Booklets A to F (levels 1 to 6)	$12.50
Advanced (levels 7 to 9)	20.50
Complete set (1 copy each of 42 different booklets)	64.50
Rhyme Time	
Booklets A1 to A4 (level 1)	12.50
Booklet B (level 2)	12.50
Complete set (2 copies each of 5 different booklets)	15.50
Understanding Word Groups	
Booklets A to F (levels 1 to 6)	12.50
Advanced (levels 7 to 9)	12.50
Complete set	12.50
Understanding Questions	
Booklets A to F (levels 1 to 6)	12.50
Advanced (levels 7 to 9)	12.50
Complete set (1 copy each of 8 different booklets)	12.50
Syllabication	
Booklets B1, B2, C1, C2, C3, D1, D2, D3, E1, E2, E3, F1, F2, and F3 (levels 2 to 6)	14.50
Advanced 1 (levels 7 to 9)	14.50
Advanced 2 (levels 7 to 9)	14.50
Advanced 3 (levels 7 to 9)	14.50
Complete set	26.50
Using a Table of Contents	
Booklets C to F (levels 3 to 6)	12.50
Advanced (levels 7 to 9)	12.50
Complete set	12.50
Learning to Alphabetize	
Booklets A to C (levels 1 to 3)	12.50
Using Guide Words	
Booklets D and F (levels 4 to 6)	12.50
Using an Index	
Booklets C to F (levels 3 to 6)	12.50
Advanced (levels 7 to 9)	12.50
Complete set	15.50
Reading Homographs	
Booklets A and B (levels 1 and 2)	12.50
Using An Index	
Booklets C to F (levels 3 to 6)	12.50
Advanced (levels 7 to 9)	12.50

Instructional Aid Kits

Individual Instructional Aid Kits are priced at $6.95 each. A complete set of Instructional Aid Kits consisting of one each of a total of twenty-two priced at $152.95. (Barnell Loft.)

Description

Time for Sounds (grades 1 and 2) Kits A and B deal with consonant sounds, blends, and digraphs.

One Too Many (grades 1 and 2) Kits A and B deal with context clues and sentence comprehension.

Riddle Riddle Rhyme Time (grades 1 and 2) Kits A and B deal with practicing auditory rhyme.

We Read Sentences (grade 1) Kits A1, A2, A3, A4, and A5 deal with sentence comprehension.

Pronoun Parade (grades 1 to 5) Kits A, B, C, D, and E deal with understanding the function of referral words.

Fun with Words (grades 1 to 6) Kits A, B, C, D, E, and F deal with word meanings and vocabulary growth.

Comprehension Games Kits:

These game kits are written to appeal to any age level although they are written for specific reading abilities. Word lists from basal readers were used and readability formulas were employed to assure appropriate difficulty levels. (Comprehension Games Corporation)

Description	Price
Context Clues: A game on the third grade reading level for two to six students. It contains a game board, one die, 110 story cards, golden treasure chips, six colored markers, an answer key, direction sheet, and a storage box.	$11.96
Main Idea Travel Game (*Primary* Edition): A game on the second grade reading level for two to six students. It contains a playing board, one die, six colored markers, 110 story cards, an answer key, direction sheet, and a storage box.	11.95
Main Idea Travel Game: A game on the fourth grade reading level for two to six students. It contains a playing board, one die, six colored markers, 110 story cards, an answer key, direction sheet, and a storage box.	15.95
Drawing Conclusions: A game on the third grade reading level for two to five students. It contains five bingo cards, one spinner, 80 plastic markers, 110 story cards, an answer key, direction sheet, and a storage box.	9.95
Fact or Opinion: A game on the 3.5 to 4.5 reading grade level for two to six students. It contains a playing board, one die, six colored markers, 110 story cards, 25 package pieces, an answer key, direction sheet, and a storage box.	11.95
Reading for Detail: A game on the 3.5 to 4.5 reading grade level for two to six students. It contains a playing board, two spinners, six plastic horses, 72 story cards, an answer key, direction sheet, and a storage box.	11.95

Spiral II Reading Kit

Spiral II Reading Kit consists of 36 paperback books that contain A Selections written on a 3.0 grade level of difficulty, B on a 3.5 level, C on a 4.0 level, and D on a 4.5 level. Eight major themes are presented: teen-age problems and choices, mystery-supernatural, sports, biography, true adventure, vocational guidance, and future. Thirty-six job cards accompany the paperbacks and are designed to help pupils improve in the following skill areas: finding main ideas, factual and inferential comprehension, sequence, vocabulary, and word analysis. Through the use of a Progress Chart each pupil is able to keep a record of his/her performance in the various skill areas. ($49.50. Continental Press, Inc.)

Reading Quick Skills

Reading Quick Skills is a multimedia reading competency program that teaches eight essential comprehension skills at four levels. The specific skills involved include: Using Details, Finding the Main Thought, Organizing and Sequencing, Vocabulary in Context, Drawing Inferences/Conclusions, Story Components, Critical Reading, and Following Directions/Test Taking Techniques. (Coronet.)

Each Reading Quick Skills Learning Unit includes one 13" x 17" Action Poster, one filmstrip with a cassette, 30 Quick Skills (8 page work booklets) and one Unit Guide for teachers.

Description	Price*
Level A Reading Quick Skills (Reading Level: 1.6-2.5)	$179.95
Level B Reading Quick Skills (Reading Level: 3.0-3.5)	179.95
Level C Reading Quick Skills (Reading Level: 4.0-4.5)	179.95
Level D Reading Quick Skills (Reading Level: 5.0-5.5)	179.95

*The complete Reading Quick Skills Program is available for $649.50.

Counterpoint Reading Program

Counterpoint Reading Program is a multimedia program that builds 120 basic skills involving comprehension, vocabulary and study. Each unit consists of four color-and-sound filmstrips, 25 copies of the unit reader with four different stories, 25 copies of the unit Skill Power Builder Workbooks, a unit program guide, and a unit Skill Achievement Chart. (Coronet)

Description	Price*
Unit 1 Comprehension Skills (Reading Level: 4.8-5.4)	$319.60
Unit 2 Vocabulary Skills (Reading Level: 5.1-5.3)	319.60
Unit 3 Study Skills (Reading Level 4.4-5.1)	319.60

*The complete Counterpoint Reading Program is available for $475.00.

EDL Study-Skills Library

The Study-Skills Library consists of a series of kits containing graded and sequential exercises for grade levels three through nine. On each grade level, there are three kits: one each in the areas of science, social studies, and reference skills. A total of twenty-one kits are available.

The major study skills developed include interpretation (detecting author's purpose, drawing conclusions, making comparisons, making inferences, visualizing); evaluation (judging relevancy, noting significance, recognizing validity, verifying accuracy); organization (finding main ideas, selecting details to support main ideas, outlining, classifying, determining sequential order); and reference (using alphabetical order, using parts of a book, using reference material, using library facilities).

A new version of the EDL Study Skills library combines Science, Social Science and Reference Lessons into one kit for each level. This has reduced the cost (the materials in these complete kits are non-consumable) and, for many, will increase the usefulness of the kits. (EDL/McGraw-Hill)

Description	Price
Science Kits C, D, E, F, (G, H, I) Levels 3-9	$24.95 ea.
Social Science Kits C, D, E, F, (G, H, I) Levels 3-9	24.95 ea.
Reference Kits C, D, E, F, (G, H, I) Levels 3-9	24.95 ea.
The New Complete Study Skills Kits C, D, E, F, (G, H, I) Levels 3-9	89.00
Teachers Guide	1.50

Language Experiences in Reading

This program values the oral language each child brings to school and uses it as the basis for developing his or her competency as a reader and a writer. Materials for decoding and word-attack skills are included as an integral part of the program. It offers an abundance of activities from which a teacher can choose those that best meet the interests and learning styles of each child.

Basic among the teacher materials are the daily lesson plan guides—one for each of the six units—which contain day-by-day suggestions for establishing classroom learning centers and for the activities in each. Other materials include a language study teacher's guide, a class record sheet, a teacher's resource guide, and resource cards for the learning center.

Among the student materials are motivating filmstrip experiences, listening experiences and listening skill lessons, reading experiences, and other materials. Components for a total decoding and word-attack program are also included. A cardboard kit is furnished for permanent storage. (Encyclopaedia Britannica.)

Description	Price
Kit (level I)	$289.00
Kit (level II)	289.00
Kit (level III)	289.00

Tutorgram Teaching System (grades K through 6)

The Tutorgram Teaching System employs a vast number of programs, each of which consists of 54 question cards. The cards are used in connection with a battery-operated device called the Tutorgram Teaching Unit. When a question card is placed on the Tutorgram Teaching Unit, the child places the pointer into a hole next to an answer. If it is the correct answer a light and buzzer are activated. A switch on the Unit is provided to deactivate the buzzer when it is not needed. (Enrichment Reading Corporation of America)

Description	Price
Tutorgram Teaching Unit, Carrying Case, and Educators Handbook	$39.95
Matching Upper and Lower Case Letters (Program 1D)	10.95
Language Arts Readiness (Program 2B)	10.95
Alphabet Recognition and Sequencing (Program 2C)	10.95
Basic Word Recognition (Program 3A)	10.95
Consonant Sounds (Program 4A)	10.95
Vowels (Program 4C)	10.95
Syllabication (Program 5J)	10.95
Synonyms 1 (Program 5K)	10.95
Synonyms 11 (Program 5L)	10.95
Antonyms (Program 5M)	10.95
Homonyms (Program 5N)	10.95
Word Completion II (Program 7A)	10.95
Primary Suffixes (Program 7C)	10.95
Prefix Meanings Intermediate Level (Program 8C)	10.95

Reading Attainment System

The *Reading Attainment System* consists of two kits. Kit 1 covers reading levels three and four; kit 2 covers reading levels five and six. Each kit contains 120 individual Reading Selections arranged in six color-keyed groups. The reading level gradually increases from group to group, allowing the student to move forward at his own pace.

Each kit has 120 Skill Cards, one for each Reading Selection, color-and-content-matched. These cards contain glossaries of difficult words used in the corresponding Reading Selection, word-attack exercises, and vocabulary-building aids. Also included in each kit are thirty Reader Record Books. Answer keys for the Reading Selections and Skills Cards are included so that students can monitor their own progress. The instructor is provided with a sixty-page guide containing full information on methods of administration, suggested student activities, and bibliography. (Grolier Educational Corp.)

Description	Price
Reading Attainment System (Kit 1)	$149.00
Reading Attainment System (Kit 2)	149.00

Careers: A Supplemental Reading Program

This supplemental reading program for grades 4-8 is based on 128 career fields that are categorized as "goods producing industries" or "major service producing industries." Emphasis is on the careers within these industries and development of reading skills. Each box includes two copies each of thirty-two story folders, two copies each of one activity card for each story, one full-color sound-filmstrip, one cassette, one activity poster, thirty student management folders, and a teacher's manual. The student management folder is the only consumable item in each box. (Harcourt Brace Jovanovich.)

Description	Price
Levels A, B, C and D (grades 4, 5, and 6)	$96.00 each
Student Management Folders	0.66 each
Teacher's Manual	1.50

Reading Practice Program

This program kit uses criterion-referenced tests for diagnostic purposes. Lessons are prescribed to coincide with problem areas. Both tests and lessons are printed on cards that can be used by individual pupils. Lessons are self-pacing and self-correcting and can be completed by most pupils in less than fifteen minutes. The program can be used in either regular or remedial classrooms by an individual child, by children working in pairs, and by a group of children. The basic skills of decoding, vocabulary, and sentence study and comprehension are covered. Each lesson has specific and measurable behavioral objectives. (Harcourt Brace Jovanovich.)

Description	Price
70 Decoding Lesson Cards (8½ by 11 inches)	Complete Program $90
66 Vocabulary Lesson Cards	
97 Sentence Study Lesson Cards	
13 Pretest Cards, one per unit	
13 Posttest Cards, one per unit	
3 Answer Key Booklets	
Student Profile Duplicating Masters	
Teacher's Manual	

Try This

Try This Too

Now Try This

These materials consist of three boxes of self-directing and self-correcting activity cards. They provide follow-up activities to review and reinforce decoding, comprehension, study skills, and vocabulary; and give pupils an early opportunity to work on their own.

The reusable cards are color coded so children can select and replace cards independently. To complete the activities in *Try This* and *Try This Too,* pupils write their answers with an ordinary crayon on transparent erasable plastic overlays which pupils place on the cards. Children check the correct answer on the back of each card, record completion, and tissue off their responses, leaving the card and overlay ready for reuse. Pupils using *Now Try This* activity cards write their responses on a separate piece of paper and then check their answers on the back of each card. (Harcourt Brace Jovanovich.)

Description	Price
Try This (Grade 1)	$84.00
Try This Too (Grade 2)	84.00
Now Try This (Grade 3)	84.00

Vocabulary Improvement Practice

This kit of materials consists of 10 nonconsumable cards (8½″ x 5½″) that are grouped into four graduated levels for grades 4, 5, 6 and above. (A, B, C, and Challenge.) Over 5,700 words are presented. Each level includes 40 cards and each card has a lesson on the front and answers on the back. A lesson consists of words which pupils who work individually or in teams are asked to classify. Three classification categories are involved. (Lessons are ideally suited for individual pupils or pupils working in pairs; completely self-directed and self-corrective. $27.00 per box. Harcourt Brace Jovanovich, Inc.)

Individualized Reading Skills Program
(Intermediate and Junior High Levels)

The Individualized Reading Skills Program (it replaces the old Reading Skills Lab) can be used as a self-contained skills program or a skills supplement. Each level consists of 30 booklets which provide instruction in the areas of decoding, comprehension, reference and study skills. Pre-assessment and post-assessment testing are an integral part of the program. (Houghton Mifflin)

Description	Price
Level A, Box 1: Pre-Assessment Tests (35 copies of the test booklet, 35 copies of the pupil's individual record card, a manual, a class record chart, and a scope and sequence chart)	$40.50
Level A, Blx 2: Reading Skill Booklets (10 copies each of 30 skill booklets, 2 copies each of 32 answer cards for booklet practice pages, a teacher's guide with annotated post-assessment tests, and a scope and sequence chart)	99.99
Level B, Box 1: Pre-Assessment Tests (35 copies of the test booklet, 35 copies of the pupil's individual record card, a manual, a class record chart, and a scope and sequence chart)	40.50
Level B, Box 2: Reading Skill Booklets (10 copies each of 30 skill booklets, 2 copies each of 32 answer cards for booklet practice pages, a teacher's guide with annotated post-assessment tests, and a scope and sequence chart)	99.99
Level C, Box 1: Pre-Assessment Tests (35 copies of the test booklet, 35 copies of the pupil's individual record card, a manual, a class record chart, and a scope and sequence chart)	40.50
Level C, Box 2: Reading Skill Booklets (10 copies each of 30 skill booklets, 2 copies each of 32 answer cards for booklet practice pages, a teacher's guide with annotated post-assessment tests, and a scope and sequence chart)	99.99

Any level complete (Box 1 and Box 2) sells for a special price of $129.15.

Imperial Games 'n Frames

Games 'n Frames consists of ten sound filmstrips, twenty spirit masters for duplicating activity sheets, eleven learning games, and ten teacher's guides. Each lesson is packaged individually in a colorful storage box. The material is suitable for use in grades four through six. (Imperial International)

Description

Cooking with Consonants, Vincent Van Bleep (consonant blends), The Strange Case of the Vanishing Vowels, Dr. Digraphs Hocus-Pocus, Al's Pit Stop (contractions, possessives), Word News Roundup (prefixes, roots), Strengthening Your Suffixes, The House of Fortune (syllabication), Soul Trip (accents), and Getting to Know the Unknown (silent letters).

(Filmstrips can be used with individual children or with groups of children; reading games can be used with two to four students; potentially self-directive. One lesson $19.95; complete program $210.00.)

Phonics Crossword Puzzles

These puzzles are designed to develop skill in phonetic analysis, to enrich vocabulary, to provide practice in spelling, and to improve reading comprehension. They constitute a completely individualized phonics program that will enhance any basic reading, spelling, or phonics text. The emphasis in each puzzle is on a single sound, sound pattern, or phonetic principle. (Imperial International)

Description	Price
Early Phonics Word Puzzles (Readiness)	$1.20
Teacher's Annotated Edition	2.25
Phonics Crossword Puzzles, Book A (Grades 1-2)	1.20
Teacher's Annotated Edition	2.25
Phonics Crossword Puzzles, Book B (Grades 3-4)	1.20
Teacher's Annotated Edition	2.25
Phonics Crossword Puzzles, Book C (Grades 5-6)	1.20
Teacher's Annotated Edition	2.25

Early to Read—Early to Rise

This supplemental reading series is designed to build competency in the comprehension, word analysis, study and vocabulary skills necessary in the first critical steps toward literacy. The complete series consists of eight units. Each unit contains five lessons. A lesson consists of a cassette tape, a four-page story card, and the skill-building pages of the unit activity book. Eight copies of the story card are included for each lesson and eight activity books accompany each unit. Reading levels increase throughout the program from readiness to a level of 3.9. The self-directing lessons in this series are designed to be used independently by children or in small special help groups. (Imperial International)

Description	Price
Part I (Units 1-4)	$219.00
Part II (Units 5-8)	219.00
Complete set of parts I and II	415.00
Additional activity books	.90

CBR Curriculum Based Reading

CBR is intended to give children in grades 3 through 6 reading experiences in the content areas of social studies, science and mathematics. The program focuses on helping students to see the relevancy of what they study in school to real life situations. All vocabulary, comprehension and word skills are developed within the specialized contexts of the CBR content area reading selections. Each CBR unit has 12 lessons on six cassettes, 8 copies each of 12 different story cards, 24 spirit masters and a teacher's guide. (Imperial International)

Description	Price
Readings in Social Studies (grade 3)	$ 74.95
Readings in Science (grade 3)	$74.95
Readings in Math (grade 3)	74.95
Complete Set (Units A, B, and C)	219.00
Readings in Social Studies (grade 4)	74.95
Readings in Science (grade 4)	74.95
Readings in Math (grade 3)	74.95
Complete Set (Units A, B, and C)	219.00
Readings in Social Studies (grade 5)	74.95
Readings in Science (grade 5)	74.95
Readings in Math (grade 5)	74.95
Complete Set (Units A, B, and C)	219.00
Readings in Social Studies (grade 6)	74.95
Readings in Science (grade 6)	74.95
Readings in Math (grade 6)	74.95
Complete Set (Units A, B, and C)	219.00

Early to Read—Early to Rise

This supplemental reading series is designed to build competency in the comprehension, word analysis, study and vocabulary skills necessary in the first critical steps toward literacy. The complete series consists of eight units. Each unit contains five lessons. A lesson consists of a cassette tape, a four-page story card, and the skill-building pages of the unit activity book. Eight copies of the story card are included for each lesson and eight activity books accompany each unit. Reading levels increase throughout the program from readiness to a level of 3.9. The self-directing lessons in this series are designed to be used independently by children or in small special help groups. (Imperial International)

Description	Price
Part I (Units 1-4)	$219.00
Part II (Units 5-8)	219.00
Complete set of Parts I and II	415.00
Additional activity books	.90

CBR Curriculum Based Reading

CBR is intended to give children in grades 3 through 6 reading experiences in the content areas of social studies, science and mathematics. The program focuses on helping students to see the relevancy of what they study in school to real life situations. All vocabulary, comprehension and word skills are developed within the specialized contexts of the CBR content area reading selections. Each CBR unit has 12 lessons on six cassettes, 8 copies each of 12 different story cards, 24 spirit masters and a teacher's guide. (Imperial International)

Description	Price
Readings in Social Studies (grade 3)	$ 74.95
Readings in Science (grade 3)	74.95
Readings in Math (grade 3)	74.95
Complete Set (Units A, B, and C)	219.00
Readings in Social Studies (grade 4)	74.95
Readings in Science (grade 4)	74.95
Readings in Math (grade 3)	74.95
Complete Set (Units A, B, and C)	219.00
Readings in Social Studies (grade 5)	74.95
Readings in Science (grade 5)	74.95
Readings in Math (grade 5)	74.95
Complete Set (Units A, B, and C)	219.00
Readings in Social Studies (grade 6)	74.95
Readings in Science (grade 6)	74.95
Readings in Math (grade 6)	74.95
Complete Set (Units A, B, and C)	219.00

Reading Around Words Program (grades 4-12)

This program consists of nine sets. On each level, a student Activity Book and cassette set present context clue activities with vocabulary drawn from a special Study Guide. The Study Guide includes words selected from graded vocabulary lists. Two hundred and forty words are presented on each reading level. Activity Book exercises utilize four avenues of analysis. These are: Synonym, Definition, Comparison/Contrast, and Interpretation/Application. (Instructional/Communications Technology, Inc.)

Reading Around Words Program procedures center around six steps: (1) Target words in an oral context are pronounced by the narrator via cassette recordings; (2) Students read short paragraphs containing the target words; (3) Exercises are given which reflect students' sensitivity to the use and meaning of each target word; (4) The narrator provides the correct answers; (5) Dictionary exercises are given which focus on multiple meanings of selected lesson words; (6) (Optional) Vu-Mate or Tach-Mate materials are employed for reinforcement.

Description

Reading Around Words Set D (4th reading level)
Reading Around Words Set E (5th reading level)
Reading Around Words Set F (6th reading level)
Reading Around Words Set G (7th reading level)
Reading Around Words Set H (8th reading level)
Reading Around Words Set I (9th reading level)
Reading Around Words Set J (10th reading level)
Reading Around Words Set K (11th reading level)
Reading Around Words Set L (12th reading level)

Each of the foregoing sets is accompanied by Activity Books (20 lessons) at $2.00; Cassette Sets (10 cassettes, 20 lessons) at $80.00; Vu-Mate Word Recognition Sets (12 cards) at $4.00; Tach-Mate Filmstrip Sets

(5 filmstrips) at $20.00; and Tach-Mate or Vu-Mate Words Activity Books at $2.00. Vu-Mate is available at a cost of $10.00 and Tach-Mate is priced at $153.00.

Readmaster Program Materials

These materials are designed for use with the Readmaster, a machine that is a combination tachistoscope, accelerator, and pacer. When used as an accelerator for any level of student progress, the Readmaster program sheets, teacher-created lessons, or even newspaper columns are inserted into the machine. Activating a switch sets the Readmaster's tachistoscopic flasher to function. Inserting a unique T-shaped vinyl screen into the machine turns the Readmaster into a pacer that can utilize the student's own reading materials. By means of a dial setting, the speed of the pacer is adjusted. (Ken-A-Vision.)

Description	Price
Readmaster	$209.00
Perception Set A (K to grade 3)	16.50
Perception Set B (K to grade 3)	16.50
Phonics Set A (K to grade 3)	16.50
Phonics Set B (K to grade 3)	16.50
Vocabulary Set A (K to grade 3)	16.50
Vocabulary Set B (K to grade 3)	16.50
Root Words Set A (K to grade 3)	16.50
Root Words Set B (K to grade 3)	16.50

Reading Skills Practice Kit

This kit is designed as a supplemental program that will fit easily with any elementary or middle grade reading series. It is composed of 160 reusable activity cards that are divided into six categories. These include: Reading Comprehension, Word Meaning, Story Analysis, Structural Analysis, Reading Analysis, and Research Skills. (Learnco Incorporated.)

Students can work individually, in pairs or in groups with minimal teacher supervision. Many of the cards are self-directive, with answers on the backs. Other cards ask concrete, practical questions that refer to on-going classroom reading.

Description	Price
Reading Skills Practice Kit: 160 Reusable activity cards, teacher's guide, sturdy classroom box.	$29.95

Reading and Classifying Words

Reading and Classifying Words is a multi-set package of self-directing and self-correcting activity cards that focus on classification exercises. The material directs attention to four areas: Reasoning from available facts, Determining categories, Analyzing word structure, and Interpreting word meanings. It is designed for children in elementary and/or middle school. (Learnco Incorporated).

Description	Price*
Reading and Classifying Words—Level A (This level covers short vowel words, consonant blends and digraphs, and one syllable and polysyllable words.)	$6.95
Reading and Classifying Words—Level B (This level covers words containing suffixes, vowel digraphs and long vowel combinations.)	6.95
Reading and Classifying Words—Level C (This level contains words with vowel combinations including th schwa, final silent "e," and open syllables.)	6.95
Reading and Classifying Words—Level D (This level covers all vowel combinations of regular and irregular spelling patterns and consonant variations, such as soft "c," soft "g," and silent letters.)	6.95

*All four levels can be purchased for $26.95.

Word Wizard

Word Wizard provides four levels of activities (riddles, mazes, crossword puzzles, etc.) designed to develop 45 basic word skills. For each skill there are five activity sheets—35 copies of each sheet bound into a tablet. Each skill box contains a teacher reference sheet, summaries of the activities, and answer keys. (NCS-Word Wizard)

Description		Price
Level A Kit (Rhyming Words; Rhyming Phrases; Shapes; Letters; Numbers; Word; Phrases; Colors; Initial Consonants)		
	Entire Kit	$ 65.00
	Each Skill	9.50
Level B Kit (Sight Vocabulary; Left-Right Sequence; Beginning Consonants; Ending Consonants; Consonant Blends; Rhyming Elements; Short Vowels; Consonant Digraphs; Compound Words; Contractions; Base Words; Plurals; Possessives)		
	Entire Kit	120.00
	Each Skill	9.50
Level C Kit (Sight Vocabulary; Consonant Variants; Consonant Blends; Long Vowels; Diphthongs; Long and Short oo; Middle Vowel; Two Vowels Separated; Two Vowels Together; Final Vowel and Vowel Generalizations; Consonant Digraphs; Base Words; Plurals; Homonyms; Synonyms; Independent Application; Multiple Meanings)		
	Entire Kit	175.00
	Each Skill	9.50
Level D (Sight Vocabulary; Consonant Blends; Silent Letters; Syllabication; Accent; Unaccented Schwa; Possessives)		
	Entire Kit	65.00
	Each Skill	9.50

Phonics Kits

This phonics kit is designed to help review, maintain, and reinforce decoding skills taught in the early grades. The primary phonics kit is especially designed for children who have had little or no phonic instruction. The upper-level kit provides the same instruction in a more mature context and can be used at intermediate or junior-high levels. (Open Court Publishing Company)

Description	Price
Primary Phonics Kit: Teacher's Guide to the Phonics Kit; Phonics Session Teacher's Cards; Stand Word Recognition Cards; Wall Sound Cards (Primary): Individual Sound Cards (Primary); Sound Flash Cards; Response Cards; Phonics Cassette 2; Phonics Progress Charts.	$110.31
Upper-Level Phonics Kit; Teacher's Guide to the Upper-level Phonics Kit; Phonics Session Teacher's Cards (Upper-level); Standard Word Recognition Cards; Wall Sound Cards (Upper-level); Individual Sound Cards (Upper-level); Sound Flash Cards; Response Cards; Phonics Cassette 2; Phonics Progress Charts.	104.50

The Quizzer Programs

The Quizzer Programs consist of printed cards that can be inserted into the throat of a device called the Quizzer. (The Quizzer is battery operated and has four multiple-choice touch buttons with illuminated right/wrong response.) The user reads the question on one of the cards, studies four possible numbered answers, depresses the numbered touch-button she/he thinks is correct and receives his illuminated right or wrong answer. (Ore Press, Inc.)

Description	Price
Quizzer unit with battery	$30.00
Reading Readiness (100 cards)	11.00
Picture Recognition, Sets 1 and 2 (100 cards)	11.00 each
Initial Sounds, Sets 1 and 2 (100 cards)	11.00 each
Long and Short Vowels (100 cards)	11.00
Irregular Vowels (100 cards)	11.00
Sounds of c, g, s, x	11.00
Vocabulary Builders Series	
Level 4-12 (100 cards each)	11.00 each

Peek-A-Boo Pocket Kit

This game kit contains materials for 18 games, with levels of difficulty from K-8. Children insert a skill card into the durable vinyl pocket and complete each game by inserting the correct "answer stick." The child then flips the pocket to the reverse side and it self-corrects by the use of corresponding numbers on the card and sticks. The 12 preprinted cards cover consonant blends and digraphs as well as color words, beginning sounds, ending sounds, long and short vowels, variant vowels, context clues, classification, sequence, root words and critical reading. Each kit contains 12 preprinted game cards, 6 open-ended game cards, 1 reinforced vinyl plastic pocket, 60 wooden playing sticks and complete instructions. ($6.95. Reading Joy, Inc.)

Double Peek-A-Boo Pocket Kit

This game kit contains materials for 18 games. Children insert a skill card into the durable vinyl pocket and complete each game by inserting the correct "answer sticks." The child then flips the pocket to the reverse side and it self-corrects by the use of corresponding numbers on the card and sticks. The 12 preprinted cards cover sight vocabulary, synonyms and antonyms, multiple word meanings, number words contractions, compound words, affixed words, syllabication, and other vocabulary related skills. Each kit contains 12 preprinted game cards, 6 open-ended game cards, 1 reinforced vinyl plastic pocket, 100 wooden playing sticks, and complete instructions. ($8.95. Reading Joy, Inc.)

Shape-Ups

Shape-Ups are delightful, multi-colored puzzles in the round. The cardboard on which they are mounted measures 16″ x 18″. Each time a child makes a response it is immediately self-corrected. (Reading Joy, Inc.)

Description	Price
Beginning Sounds (K-2)	$4.95
Ending Sounds (K-2)	4.95
Short Vowels (1-3)	4.95
Long Vowels (1-3)	4.95
Consonant Blends (2-3)	4.95
Consonant Digraphs (1-3)	4.95
"S" Consonant Blends (2-3)	4.95
Variant Consonants (2-4)	4.95
Silent Consonants (2-4)	4.95
"R" Controlled Vowels (2-4)	4.95
Variant Vowels (2-4)	4.95
Compound Words (2-4)	4.95
Syllabication (2-5)	4.95
Synonyms (3-5)	4.95
Antonyms (3-5)	4.95
Detail Questions (3-5)	4.95
Related Pairs (3-5)	4.95
Classification (4-6)	4.95
All 18 of the above puzzles	80.00

Puzzler Kits

These kits are designed to teach 30 different K-8 readiness, word attack and comprehension skill games by printing, drawing, or gluing desired skill information in each puzzle space. Children play by placing "answer" puzzler pieces picture-side-up over corresponding items or questions on the puzzler board building a "turn-me-around" cartoon. The puzzle automatically self-corrects itself. (Reading Joy, Inc.)

Description	Price
Puzzler Kit, Primary (K-2)	$3.95
Puzzler Kit, Intermediate (3-8)	3.95

Game Board Kits

These multi-leveled reading games are designed for children to play independently or in small groups. Self-correcting playing cards are included with each kit. Kits contain 17" x 22" inch game boards, playing cards, and simple instructions. The games are self-correcting. (Reading Joy, Inc.)

Description	Price
Kit F—(K-1-2) *Readiness—Auditory and Visual Skills*	$7.95
Jelly Bean Jar—visual discrimination	
Bug Hug—rhyming words	
The Monkeys—shapes and colors	
Echo-Copter—listening and recall	
Ginger Bear Twins—auditory skills	
Kit G—(K-1-2) *Readiness—Letters and Sounds*	7.95
Giralphabet—capital & lower case letters	
Color-Shape-Alphabet Mixer—naming	
Patchworm—letter sounds	
Byron Bear—beginning sounds	
Ouch!—same or different sounds	
Kit A—(K-1-2) *Levels: Pre-Primer, Primer, Grade 1*	7.95
Sound Spot—letter sounds	
Mice on Ice—rhyming	
Word Whale—short vowel words	
Pair-It—common sounds	
Kit B—(2-3-4) *Levels: Grades 2-4*	7.95
Compound Hound—compound words	
Zig-Zag-Zoo-following directions	
What's the Main Idea?—main ideas	
Word Factory—constructing words	
Kit C—(4-5-6) *Levels: Grades 2-6*	7.95
Detail Detective—detail questions	
Cat-Egory-Cat—word categories	
Word to Meaning Match—vocabulary synonyms	
Point Partners—word synthesis	
Kit D—(6-7-8) *Levels: Grades 4-8*	7.95
Comprehension Concentration—recall details	
Duo Duel—prefixes, roots, suffixes	
Multiconformity—affix meanings	
Great "Onym" Monster Hunt—synonyms, antonyms, homonyms	

Wordcraft Vocabulary Programs

These are multimedia programs that are designed to aid students in the rapid development of their reading vocabulary. Key words are introduced in a series of short, easily understood sentences which join to form meaningful stories. After the student hears and sees the sentence once and guesses at the meaning of the word involved, it is repeated, substituting simple definitions that clarify and reinforce understanding of the new word. (The Reading Laboratory, Inc.)

Description	Price
The Wordcraft/1 Vocabulary Program: Three hundred core words in thirty separate lessons. A student manual is included. The word list is for grades 4 through 6.	
Six Filmstrips, Three Cassettes, Student Manual	$74.95
Three Cassettes with Student Manual	29.95
Additional Student Manuals, 24 or less	2.50 each
The Wordcraft/2 Vocabulary Program: Two hundred core words in twenty separate lessons. A student manual is included. The word list is for grades 6 through 8.	
Four Filmstrips, Two Cassettes, Student Manual	49.90
Two Cassettes only with Student Manual	19.95
Additional Student Manuals, 24 or less	2.00 each
The Wordcraft/3 Vocabulary Program: Two hundred core words in twenty separate lessons. A student manual is included. The word list is for grades 6 through 8.	
Four Filmstrips, Two Cassettes, Student Manual	49.90
Two Cassettes only with Student Manual	19.95
Additional Student Manuals, 24 or less	2.00 each

Study Cards

These materials consist of three sets of forty-eight cards that can be used for independent review and reading development. The pupils read a selection, answer questions, and then check their answers. The cards maintain or extend the following skills: main ideas, context cues, relationships, critical thinking, reading purposes, vocabulary development, use of maps and graphs, and reference skills. (Scott, Foresman.)

Description	Price
Study Cards Set 1 (grade 4)	$18.03
Study Cards Set 2 (grade 5)	18.03
Study Cards Set 3 (grade 6)	18.03

SRA* Reading Laboratory 1A, 1B, and 1C (grades 1, 2, and 3)

These self-corrective materials are written on seven to ten graded reading levels varying from 1.2 and 3.5 (kit 1A) 1.4 to 4.5 (kit 1B), and 1.6 to 5.5 (kit 1C). They are designed to accommodate the range of individual differences found in first grade (kit 1A), second grade (kit 1B), and

*Science Research Associates.

third grade (kit 1C). Skills provided for include basic sight vocabulary, word attack, vocabulary development, reading comprehension, and listening comprehension. A color scheme is employed to designate difficulty levels. Additional materials for the individual pupil, class, and teacher are included also. Replacement materials can be purchased. (Kits 1A and 1B $135.00; kit 1C $135.00; student books, $1.19.)

SRA Reading Laboratory 1—Word Games (grades 1 to 6)

This box contains the phonics portion of the reading laboratory program. It is a separate laboratory designed to supplement laboratories 1A, 1B, and 1C in grades one, two, and three. It can also be used successfully in grades four, five, and six. It consists of forty-four color-coded, word-building games that help students develop their reading vocabulary to match their listening vocabulary. (Kit $208.75; student book, $.38.)

SRA Reading Laboratory Series (grades 4 to 6)

Each laboratory kit contains Power Builders with key cards; Rate Builders with key booklets; a Teacher's Handbook containing Listening Skill Builders; a Student Record Book; and colored pencils with which students chart their progress.

Power Builders are illustrated four-page reading selections. These are accompanied by exercises designed to help students develop vocabulary, comprehension, and language skills. Fifteen Power Builders are provided at each of the ten reading levels.

Rate Builders are short timed reading selections designed to develop reading speed and concentration. Each selection is followed by comprehension questions. Fifteen Rate Builders are provided at each of the ten reading levels.

Listening Skill Builders are selections that are read to the students to develop their ability to understand, retain, and analyze what they hear. The Listening Skill Builders are included in the Teacher's Handbook. After hearing each selection, the students test their comprehension by answering questions in the Student Record Book.

Description	Price
Reading Laboratory 2A for grade 4 (reading levels 2.0, 2.5, 3.0, 3.5, 4.0, 4.5, 5.0, 5.5, 6.0, 7.0)	$135.00
Reading Laboratory 2B for grade 5 (reading levels 2.5, 3.0, 3.5, 4.0, 4.5, 5.0, 5.5, 6.0, 7.0, 8.0)	135.00
Reading Laboratory 2C for grade 6 (reading levels 3.0, 3.5, 4.0, 4.5, 5.0, 5.5, 6.0, 7.0, 8.0, 9.0)	135.00
Student Record Books for Laboratories 2A, 2B, and 2C	.92

SRA Dimension Series

Each dimensions kit focuses on a different interest area. The reading selections explore the major theme, presenting a wide range of information, viewpoints, and writing styles. The stories, selected for their high interest level, are designed to make students want to read.

Countries and Cultures explores the world, presenting stories about life as others live it. The 120 selections include stories about the fire-walking natives of the South Seas, the flea markets of Europe, going to school in Ghana, security measures at Monte Carlo, life on an Israel kibbutz, and other exciting vignettes. Each selection is followed by comprehension questions and questions that require critical thinking.

We Are Black, a program about black people for all students, contains 120 four-page reading selections about famous and unknown, contemporary and historical, American and non-American black people. The kit is designed to give today's student an opportunity to enjoy and improve his reading with stories about people he should know, people whose stories have been neglected in traditional textbooks. *We Are Black* is appropriate for use in all grades from elementary through high school. The selections vary in length from 300 to 900 words. Each selection is accompanied by a Skill Card. The student answers the Skill Card questions in his own Student Book.

Manpower and Natural Resources is for use in high school developmental reading, guidance, vocational, and technical courses, and all types of adult retraining programs. It is designed to enrich basic reading or special training programs with a wealth of reading material (300 selections) from popular books and magazines. Topics fall in three broad categories: (1) conservation and the skills involved; (2) related facts of natural history, geology, botany, zoology, weather, conservation, and mineralogy; (3) occupational skills such as those of the welder, carpenter, telephone repairman, soil scientist, and electrician. Comprehension questions follow each selection, and Key Booklets are used to check answers.

An American Album includes varied reading selections that constitute an anecdotal history of America's growth from Columbus's discovery to President Kennedy's assassination. It contains 300 four-page reading selections divided into six reading levels with fifty stories at each level. A comprehension check is provided at the end of each story. The wealth of subject matter can give the child insight into the origins and development of the American people and their institutions.

Description	Price
Countries and Cultures Kit (reading levels 4.5 to 9.5)	$91.50
Student Book	.54
We Are Black Kit (reading levels 2.0 to 6.0)	91.50
Student Book	.58
Manpower and Natural Resources Kit	130.00
An American Album	130.00

SRA Reading for Understanding (grades 3 to 12 and college)

This individualized reading program is designed to develop the student's ability to grasp the full meaning of what he reads by teaching him to analyze ideas and reach logical conclusions. It is available in three editions, each accommodating a number of grade levels.

Exercises consist of a card bearing ten short, provocative paragraphs in areas such as education, politics, history, art, science, business, sports, agriculture, and philosophy. The student reads the selection and chooses the best of four suggested conclusions, implied in the selection but not stated directly. Correct conclusions are provided in the Answer Key booklets.

Each of the three units in the series includes 400 lesson cards arranged in progressive levels of difficulty. A simple Placement Test indicates the level at which each student should begin. The student progresses to more difficult levels as he demonstrates proficiency.

Students work independently, recording their responses in their Student Record Book, checking their own work with answer keys provided, and charting their progress.

Description	Price
Reading for Understanding—2 (grades 3 through 7)	$69.50
Reading for Understanding—3 (grades 7 through 12)	69.50
Reading for Understanding—Senior Edition (grades 8 through college)	76.75
Student Record Book for any of the foregoing	.57

SRA Pilot Library Series (grades 4 to 9)

The Plot Library Series is designed to bridge the gap between reading training and independent reading with short excerpts from noted literature. Each Pilot Library set contains seventy-two selections from full-length books to whet the young reader's appetite and lead him to the original books. The selections, called Pilot Books, are excerpts of twenty-four or thirty-two pages carefully selected for their interest appeal and reading level.

Pilot Library Books are keyed to Power Builder selections in a particular Reading Laboratory kit so that a student who finds a selection interesting can go to the Pilot Library Books for further reading on the same topic and at his individual reading level. A short bibliography at the end of the Pilot Library Book leads him to other books of similar content and difficulty. Key Booklets permit him to check his own comprehension exercises, contained in the Student Record Book.

Description	Price
Pilot Library Set 1C for grade 3 (reading levels 2.0, 3.0, 4.0, 5.0, 6.0)	$116.50
Pilot Library Set 2A for grade 4 (reading levels 2.0, 3.0, 4.0, 5.0, 6.0, 7.0)	128.50
Pilot Library Set 2B for grade 5 (reading levels 3.0, 4.0, 5.0, 6.0, 7.0, 8.0)	128.50
Pilot Library Set 2C for grades 6 and 7 (reading levels 4.0, 5.0, 6.0, 7.0, 8.0, 9.0)	128.50
Pilot Library Set 3B for grades 8 and 9 (reading levels 5.0, 6.0, 7.0, 8.0, 9.0, 10.0, 11.0, 12.0)	116.50
Student Record Books for foregoing sets	.97

SRA Graph and Picture Study Skills Kit (grades 4 to 8)

This kit is designed to help students read and interpret illustrative materials such as photographs, editorial cartoons, graphic data, charts, and diagrams. These visual aids, which are common to texts, newspapers, and other media, are used to clarify various kinds of subject matter.

Description	Price
Graph and Picture Study Skills Kit	$164.50
Pupil Booklet	1.10
Additional Teacher's Guide	2.50

SRA Map and Globe Skills Kit (grades 4 to 8)

This kit is designed to help students develop skills that are essential to the effective use of maps and globes. By understanding the significance of facts shown on maps and globes, the student is able to draw logical conclusions and to make inferences from the data presented.

Description	Price
Map and Globe Skills Kit	$164.50
Pupil Booklet	1.10
Additional Teacher's Guide	2.50

SRA Organizing and Reporting Skills Kit (grades 4 to 8)

This kit focuses on basic elements of effective reporting, note taking, and outlining. Step by step, students progress through six skill units. These are: Form of the Report, Sticking to the Point, Order in the Paragraph, Quality in the Paragraph, Notetaking and Outlining, and Making an Outline.

Description	Price
Organizing and Reporting Skills Kit	$164.50
Pupil Booklet	.99
Additional Teacher's Guide	2.50

Distar Instructional System in Reading

The Distar Instructional System in Reading is a structured program designed to help children develop their reading skills. It employs a systematic approach that is accompanied by tests at critical points in the program to help monitor each student's progress. Motivational approaches include stars or points and "good work" letters which the student may take home. (Science Research Associates.)

Description	Price
Distar Reading I teaches the skills needed to decode words: sound-symbol identification, left-to-right sequence, and oral blending of sounds. Later, word and sentence reading are introduced. Teacher materials consist of three spiral-bound presentation books, a test book, a spelling book, a teacher's edition of the student Take-Home books, copies of the Story books, a cassette, a teacher's guide, an acetate page protector, and group-progress indicators. Student materials consist of three storybooks and three Take-Home books.	$125.00
Distar Reading II stresses comprehension and advanced reading skills. Emphasis is placed on reading and following directions. Teacher materials consist of four spiral-bound presentation books, acetate page protector, group-progress indicators, a teacher's guide, and three decks of colored cards for comprehension exercises. All student materials appear on Take-Home sheets.	125.00
Distar Reading III (Reading to Learn) is designed to teach children reading skills needed to learn from material that presents new concepts and concept applications. Factual content dealing with science and social studies is used. A total of 175 sequenced lessons are involved. Each lesson is divided into five levels. The teacher's material contains five teacher presentation books and five annotated workbooks, one for each level, and a teacher's guide. The student materials consist of five readers and five workbooks, one for each level.	99.50

New Mark II SRA Reading Laboratory 2A, 2B, and 2C (grades 4 to 6)*

This laboratory retains many of the features of the original SRA Reading Laboratory Series: Multi-level, color-coded format, Power Builders, Rate Builders, and Listening Skill Builders.

This kit contains new sections which are titled "How Well Did You Read?" These sections focus on eight comprehension skills: perceiving cause and effect, recognizing sequence, identifying problems and solutions,

*It is possible to order replacement components for the 1969 editions of Reading Laboratories 2A, 2B, and 2C.

identifying main idea, understanding character, identifying setting and mood, perceiving comparison and contrast, and understanding purpose and conclusion. "Learn About Words" sections help reinforce skills through phonics analysis, structural analysis, vocabulary building and sentence study activities. Study skills—dictionary usage, graph and map reading, card catalog usage and other skills—are presented.

Audio cassettes have been added to the "Listening Skills Builders" sections to help free teachers. There are 16 listening lessons in each kit. (Science Research Associates)

Description	Price
Mark II Reading Laboratory Kit 2A	$204.00
Student Operating Guide 2A (pkg. of 30)	10.25
Spirit Masters 2A	8.40
Mark II Reading Laboratory Kit 2B	204.00
Student Operating Guide 2B (Pkg. of 30)	10.25
Spirit Masters 2B	8.40
Mark II Reading Laboratory Kit 2C	204.00
Student Operating Guide 2C (Pkg. of 30)	10.25
Spirit Masters 2C	8.40

SRA Skills Series: Phonics

This kit is designed to help children in grades 1-3 to develop skills in letter/sound relationships. It consists of forty-eight lessons, each containing lesson plans, visuals, and cassette lessons for 155 phonics skills. Components include 48 Lesson Plan Cards, 48 Cassette Lessons, 96 Spirit Master Activity Sheets, Survey Test on Spirit Masters, 30 Student Progress Folders, 1 Teacher's Handbook and 1 Correlations Supplement. (Kit, $285; Teacher's Handbook, $1.95.)

SRA Skills Series: Structural Analysis

This kit employs magazines and is designed to help children in grades 3-7 to develop skills in word structure analysis including plural and possessive forms, roots and affixes, compound words, contractions, syllabication, and word origins. Components include 48 Lesson Plan Cards, 10 copies of the Student Magazine, 48 Cassette Lessons, 96 Spirit Master Activity Sheets, Survey Test on Spirit Master Activity Sheets, Survey Test on Spirit Masters, 30 Student Progress Folders, 1 Teacher's Handbook, and 1 Correlations Supplement. (Kit, $285; Teacher's Handbook, $1.95.)

SRA Skills Series: Comprehension

This kit employs magazines and is designed to help children in grades 4-8 to develop skills in literal, inferential, and critical areas that contribute to the comprehension process. Skills include main idea, supporting details, cause and effect, fact and opinion, literal and figurative language, and others. Components include 48 Lesson Plan Cards, 10 copies of the Student

Magazine, 48 Cassette Lessons, 96 Spirit Master Activity Sheets, Survey Test on Spirit Masters, 30 Student Progress Folders, 1 Teacher's Handbook, and 1 Correlations Supplement. (Kit, $285; Teacher's Handbook, $1.95.)

Spellbinder

Spellbinder presents a multi-leveled program involving cards and the use of one of three Spellbinder Consoles. The latter is a device consisting of six windows. As response cards are inserted into the windows of the console, only correct answers light up. At each step, correct responses are acknowledged and rewarded. The student builds toward successful completion of the exercise and the final lighted frame. (Spellbinder, Inc.)

Description	Price
Universal Console (Response windows light sequentially when correct answers are selected)	$72.00
Random Console (Any response randomly selected will light response windows.)	72.00
Senior Console (No lights are shown until all responses are correct.)	82.00
Readiness Skills Program	89.00
Letter-Sound Relationships	89.00
Long Vowels	89.00
Consonant Digraphs	89.00
Word Games and Puzzles	89.00
Consonant-Vowel Sounds	89.00
Two and Three-letter Blends	89.00
Advanced Reading-Comprehension Spelling	89.00

Reading Rx

Reading Rx is a boxed kit of 5″ x 8″ activity cards that provide hundreds of games and activities for the reinforcement of remediation of word attack, comprehension, and reference skills. It is designed to meet the needs of primary and intermediate grade children. ($9.95, each kit. Tarmac/tac, Inc.)

The Reading Box

The Reading Box consists of 4″ x 6″ cards that describe games and techniques in the areas of readiness, listening skill, phonics, vocabulary building, reading through writing, choral verse and dramatic play. The kit is designed to meet the needs of children in grades 1-6. ($6.95, each kit. Tarmac/tac, Inc.)

Reading Comprehension

Reading Comprehension consists of six kits, each of which contains 50 cards. The cards are arranged in order of difficulty. There are 10 cards for each reading level from grade 2 through grade 6. Comprehension check questions appear on the reverse side of each card. Answers are on separate cards. Teacher suggestions are included in each kit. (Tarmac/tac, Inc.)

Description	Price
Getting the Main Idea	$ 5.95
Noting and Recalling Details	5.95
Drawing Conclusions	5.95
Using Context Clues	5.95
Finding the Sequence	5.95
Understanding Sentences	5.95
Comprehension Series (Set of 6 boxes)	35.00

Pal Reading Games

Pal Reading Games for grades 5-12 consist of two kits (Rally 1 and 2). Each kit contains 20 games. Rally 1 has a word list difficulty of 2.5-5.0; Rally 2 has a word list difficulty of 3.0-5.5. The games are largely self-directed. A mini guide is included on each game board. (Xerox Education Publications)

Description	Price
Games 1-9: Super Van, Big Wig, Drag Strip, The Vette, Jukebox, Going Bananas, Big Foot, Dune Buggy, and Chopper (short vowel games)	$55.00
Games 10-17: Down the Tubes, Junkyard, The Iron Butterfly; Dirk Bike, Rally One, Skateboard, Traffic Jam (consonant blends, consonant digraphs, and short vowel games)	
Games 19-20: Knock It Off, This is Truckin' (soft c and g, ph, silent consonants and silent letters) (Rally 2)	55.00
Games 1-6 Dashboard, UFO, Rip Cord, Go-Cart Ten Speed, Wipeout (long vowel games)	
Game 7 Zombie (R-controlled vowels)	
Game 8 Zodia (Variations in pronouncing oo)	
Game 9 The Purple Pickup (Vowel diphthongs oy, ow)	
Game 10 Inside Out (Vowel diphthongs oi, oy)	
Game 11 Downstairs, Upstairs (Long vowels, simple or complex consonants)	
Game 12 Let's Glide (Letter a followed by 1, 11, u and w)	
Game 13 Motorcross (R-controlled vowels, oo variations, diphthongs)	
Game 14 The Fly (Plural endings -s, es, -ies)	
Game 15 Cobra (Sight words)	
Game 16 Clean Your Room (Contractions)	
Game 17 Get Off the Phone (Verb forms -s, ed, -ing.	
Game 18 The Bug (Root words and suffixes)	
Game 19 Roller Derby (prefixes un- and in-)	
Game 20 Jean Scene (Plurals -2, -es, -ies, contractions verb forms, suffixes, prefixes)	
Two of each kit	199.00

The Game Tree

The Game Tree games span reading levels 2 through 7 and come in four sequential kits—The Lime Tree, The Plum Tree, The Lemon Tree and The Apple Tree. Each kit includes 18 to 20 different games, complete with markers, cards, spinners, wax pencils and individual game boards with wipe-off surfaces. (Xerox Education Publications)

Description	Price
Apple Tree (grades 2-4)	$ 55.00
Covers consonant clusters (blends and graphs), vowels, basic sight words, single consonants, short and long vowels, vowel cues, inflectional endings, and compound words.)	
Plum Tree (grades 3-5)	55.00
Covers basic sight words, clusters (blends & digraphs), vowel cues, vowels, vowel plus "r," diphthongs, inflectional endings, compound words, possessives, contractions, prefixes, suffixes, syllabication, and homonyms.)	
Lemon Tree (grades 4-6)	55.00
Covers possessives, contractions, prefixes, suffixes, "y" to "i," double final consonant, dropping final "e," syllabication, homonyms, synonyms, antonyms, and roots.)	
Lime Tree (grades 5-7)	55.00
Covers prefixes, suffixes, "y" to "i," double final consonant, dropping final "e," syllabication, homonyms, synonyms, antonyms, and roots)	
All four of the above kits	199.00

MULTILEVEL BOOKS AND WORKBOOKS

A few of the many multilevel books and workbooks are described here. Additional workbooks are described in chapter 12.

The Story Teller

The Story Teller consists of 30 classic children's stories on cassettes with read-along books. The old favorites are narrated by professionals with background orchestral music. The tapes follow the books word-forward and are the same on both sides except that one side gives page turn signals. Spanish cassettes have English on the other side. The books are 5½" x 6¼" with hard covers and full-color illustrations through the 32 pages. The stories are written from K-4 pupils. (American Teaching Aids.)

	Description	Price
Cinderella	Beauty and the Beast	Book and Cassette
Sleeping Beauty	Bremen Town	in English, $3.00
Hansel and Gretel	Musicians	
Snow White	The Selfish Giant	
Tom Thumb	The Little Mermaid	Book only in English,
	Steadfast Tin Soldier	$1.15
Little Red Riding		
Hood	Puss in Boots	Book and Cassette
Jack and the		in Spanish/English,
Beanstalk	The Wizard of Oz	$3.00
Pinocchio	Gulliver's Travels	
Aladdin	Sinbad the Sailor	Book only in
The Ugly Duckling	Samson and Deliah	Spanish/English, $1.15
Rumpelstiltskin	Moses in Egypt	
Elves and the	Joshua and Battle	
Shoemaker	of Jericho	
Three Pigs and	Daniel in the Lion's Den	
Goldilocks		
Rapunzel and	Noah and the Ark	
Gingerbread Man		
Thumbelina	David and Goliath	

Specific Skill Series

This series consists of workbooks with accompanying worksheets. The worksheets permit optional self-correction. The series breakdown follows. All are for use on levels 1 through 6. A picture level and preparatory level also are available. (Barnell Loft.)

Books A to F: Detecting the Sequence
Books A to F (advanced): Using the Context
Books A to F (advanced): Working with Sounds
Books A to F (advanced): Following Directions
Books A to F (advanced): Locating the Answer
Books A to F: Getting the Facts
Books A to F: Drawing Conclusions
Books A to F: Getting the Main Idea
Price: Each workbook $1.75. Each Answer Key $0.25. Spirit masters for duplicating worksheets $2.25 per skill area.

Supportive Reading Skills

These multi-level workbooks constitute a diagnostic and prescriptive program that complements the Specific Skills Series described above. A number of areas are included. (Barnell Loft.)

Discovering Word Patterns (Levels 2-9)
Reorganizing Word Relationships (Levels 2-9)
Reading Schedules (Levels 1-9)
Reading Ads (Levels 1-9)

Phonic Analogies (Levels 1-3)
Rhyme Time (Levels 1-2)
Mastering Multiple Meanings (Levels 1-2)
Understanding Word Groups (Levels 1-9)
Understanding Questions (Levels 1-9)
Syllabication (Levels 2-9)
Reading Homographs (Levels 1-9)
Reading Homonyms (Levels 1-9)
Reading Heteronyms (Levels 3-9)
Interpreting Idioms (Levels 1-9)
Using a Table of Contents (Levels 1-9)
Using an Index (Levels 3-9)
Learning to Alphabetize (Levels 1-9)
Using Guide Word (Levels 1-9)
Word-O-Rama (Levels 5-9)
Price: Each workbook $1.55. Spirit masters for duplicating worksheets $2.25
per skill area. Teacher's manual $1.60.

Lessons for Self-Instruction in Basic Skills (Reading)

These programmed lessons consist of books with difficulty levels ranging
from grade levels 2.5 to 9 and above. Although designed primarily for intensive review, the materials are useful in strengthening the reading skills
of weaker students.

There are four levels of materials in the reading area. Titles include
Following Directions, Vocabulary Skills, Reference Skills, Reading Interpretations I and Reading Interpretations II.

Consumable record sheets for each book are provided in each LSI kit
or may be purchased separately. A short consumable Mastery Test is written for each LSI book. This test is designed to assess student understanding
of the material covered. Also included in each LSI kit are thirty Individual
Study Guides. (California Test Bureau/McGraw-Hill.)

Description	Price
Reading Assortment Kit: 55 Books, 275 Student Record Sheets, 30 Individual Study Guides, 1 Group Record Sheet, 1 Manual, 1 Display Box	$145.00

Basic Reading Units: Main Idea

This kit contains 36 booklets, 6 copies of each of six levels (A: 2.0-2.4
grades; B: 3.0-3.4 grades; D: 3.5-3.9 grades; E: 4.0-4.4 grades; F: 4.5-4.9
grades.) Skills covered involve locating and recognizing the main idea,
summarizing the main idea, recognizing a restatement of the main idea,
identifying details that support or prove the main idea, and visualizing the
main idea. The complete kit also contains 6 Main Idea Placement Inventory masters, 1 group introductory Trading Lesson master; 2 Answer Form
masters; 12 Answer Cards; 1 Class Record master; 2 Teachers' Guides and
5 Storage Folders. Price: $39.50. (The Continental Press, Inc.)

Basic Reading Units: Facts and Details

This kit contains 36 booklets, 6 copies of each of six levels (A: 2.0-2.4 grades; B: 3.0-3.4 grades; D: 3.5-3.9 grades; E: 4.0-4.4 grades; F: 4.5-4.9 grades). Skills covered involve comprehending details, recognizing translation of a detail, locating a detail that answers a specific question, and understanding questions. The complete kit also contains 6 Facts and Details Placement Inventory masters; 1 group Introductory Teaching Lesson master; 2 Answer Form masters; 12 Answer Cards; 1 Class Record master; 2 Teachers' Guides; and 5 file storage folders. Price $39.50. (The Continental Press, Inc.)

EDL Word Clues

The *EDL Word Clues* series is a multilevel program designed to help students develop and refine their vocabulary and to teach students a technique for unlocking the meaning of words through a study of context. The program consists of seven books for reading levels seven through thirteen. Placement tests are available so that each student may be assigned a book on an appropriate level.

Each Word Clues book consists of thirty lessons of ten words each with a total of 300 words per level. The words involved are taken from the EDL Core Vocabulary and are those judged to be of the highest frequency of usage at each level. A programmed format allows each student to work at his own pace. Use of the EDL Combo-8 or the Flash-X permits tachistoscopic presentation of the words involved. (EDL/McGraw-Hill.)

Description	Price
Word Clues Books G-M (Levels 7-13)	$3.25 each
Accompanying Flash-X Sets	4.75 each
Flash-X Tachistoscope	10.50

Reading Skills Lab

These boxed materials consist of workbooks developed for use in regular classroom situations to serve either basal or individualized reading programs. Each box of the *Reading Skills Lab* workbooks contains ten each of three ninety-six page consumable workbooks. The books have perforated pages (7 by 9½ inches) and are printed in two attractive colors. Also included are two Pupil's Answer Books and one Teacher's Edition for each workbook. The pages are perforated so that they can be removed and given to a number of students at the same time. They are designated Level 2 or Level 3 so that pupils of any grade can use whichever level they need.

In addition to the workbooks, sets of diagnostic tests are available. These can be administered at the beginning of the school year to help pinpoint each child's strengths and weaknesses.

The workbooks on Level 2 (fifth grade) include, "Overcoming Meaning Difficulties," "Reading for Different Purposes," and "Using Reference Aids." Workbooks on Level 3 (sixth grade) include, "Studying Informative Materials," "Using Reference Aids," and "Reading Critically." (Houghton Mifflin.)

Description	Price
Level 2 (grade 5)	
Box A Diagnostic Tests	$16.77
Box B Workbooks	38.88
Level 3 (grade 6)	
Box A Diagnostic Tests	16.77
Box B Workbooks	38.88

Controlled Reading Fluency Sets (Levels 1-14):
35mm. Filmstrips for levels 1-3, $165; Study Guides $2.45; Lesson Plans $2.50.
35mm. Filmstrips for levels 4-14, $165; Combo-8 Sets, $195; Study Guides, $3.25; Reading Efficiency Checks, $1.25.

Bookmark Reading Sound Filmstrips

Bookmark Reading Sound Filmstrips introduce basic reading skills and concepts by employing a cast of unusual and charming characters such as Sir Hilary Dragon, who teaches children the parts of a book (Grade 1); Montague the Magician, the master of compound words (Grade 2); and Wendy Wonder, the dictionary champion who races for words in the Dictionary Olympic (Grade 3). Bookmark Reading Sound Filmstrips are designed to adapt well to any reading program. Each box contains two full-color filmstrips, 2 cassettes and a teacher's manual. (Harcourt Brace Jovanovich.)

Description	Price
Level 1 (Blue)	
Box A: The Parts of a Book/Telling a Story in Order	$54.00
Box B: What's the Cause? What's the Effect? Words and Their Opposites	54.00
Box C: The Meaning Behind Words/What Will Happen Next?	54.00
Level 2 (Red)	
Box A: What's the Main Idea?/Contractions in Action	54.00
Box B: How Does the Character Feel?/New Words from Two Words	54.00
Box C: Reading Maps/Words with More Than One Meaning	54.00
Level 3 (Green)	
Box A: Word Parts/Following Written Directions	54.00
Box B: Finding Main Ideas and Details/Reading Between the Lines	54.00
Box C: Getting Pictures from Words/Using the Dictionary	54.00
Level 4 (Orange)	
Box A: Using Graphic Aids/The Case of Cause and Effect	54.00
Box B: Finding Time Clues/Is It Fact or Opinion?	54.00
Box C: Turning to the Dictionary/Context Clues in Orbit	54.00

Description	Price
Level 5 (Purple)	
Box A: The Structure of a Book/What/s What in the Library	54.00
Box B: Outlines That Work/Out West with Maps and Graphs	54.00
Box C: Looking for Comparison and Contrast/Topics, Main Ideas	54.00
Level 6 (Brown)	
Box A: Drawing Conclusions/Get the Study Habit	54.00
Box B: Following Those Directions/Spotting Slanted Writing	54.00
Box C: What's in the Newspaper/Taking Good Notes	54.00

Califone Perceptamatic Reading Series

The materials in this series are used in connection with a mechanical device called the Rheem T-Scope. The Rheem T-Scope is a light, portable tachistoscope which employs circular reels with forty-two exposures per reel. The interval of exposure varies from 1/10 to 1/100 of a second. The materials themselves are designed to correlate with existing reading programs in today's schools. Each of the eight reading levels includes three steps to improve reading skills: Step 1 (Digit Reels) to sharpen visual perception and eliminate transpositions and reversals; Step 2 (Vocabulary Reels) to reinforce grade-level vocabulary skills; Step 3 (Phrase Reels) to improve phrase perception. (Instructional Materials and Equipment Distributors.)

Description	Price
Rheem T-Scope	$145.00
Reading Level 1 (grade 1)	35.25
Reading Level 2 (grade 2)	35.25
Reading Level 3 (grade 3)	35.25
Reading Level 4 (grade 4)	35.25
Reading Level 5 (grade 5)	35.25
Reading Level 6 (grade 6)	35.25
Reading Level 7 (grade 7)	35.25
Reading Level 8 (grade 8)	35.25
Percepta-Phonics	46.00

Tachist-O-Filmstrips

These filmstrips are designed to improve attention, concentration, accuracy, and confidence; vocabulary development; phrase reading and unitary seeing; and retention, comprehension, and reading rate (Learning Through Seeing). The following are available:

Description	Price
Letter Form Training Program	$114.50
Writing, Spelling, and Reading Program	206.50
Reading Program One	206.50
Phonics: Basic and Intermediate Program	206.50
Problem Words Program	169.50

Description	Price
Reading Program Four	206.50
Vocabulary Program Four	206.50
Instant Words/Phrases Program	206.50
Reading Program Seven	206.50
Vocabulary Program Ten	206.50
Reading Program Ten	206.50
Adult Education Program	333.00
Wide Range Elementary Program	459.50
Wide Range Junior High Program	459.50
Wide Range Senior High Program	459.50

Let's Read Series, Level 3

Each filmstrip in this series is accompanied by cassette recordings. Stories are presented twice: First, as a silent reading exercise; then, as a fully illustrated sound filmstrip with accompanying type at the bottom of each frame. Students may read along or listen at this stage. Comprehension questions are included in each presentation. (Learning Tree Filmstrips.)

Description	Price
Stories of Mystery & Suspense	
A: The Toy Shop Mystery	$30.00
B: Buried Treasure	
C: The Secret of the Stone Tower	30.00
D: The Lost Locket	
Set of 4 filmstrips, 2 cassettes and a teacher's guide	55.00
Stories of Adventure & Heroism	
A: The Day I Was Invisible	30.00
B: The Girl Who Could Fly	
C: The Runaway	30.00
D: The Spinning Wheel	
Set of 4 filmstrips, 2 cassettes and a teacher's guide	55.00
Stories of Ghosts & Monsters	
A: The Greenhouse Horror	30.00
B: Something in the Attic	
C: A Visitor from Space	30.00
D: The Birthday Secret	
Set of 4 filmstrips, 2 cassettes and a teacher's guide	55.00

Reading Comprehension Skills

Reading Comprehension Skills consists of a series of filmstrips accompanied by individual cassettes. Reading levels vary between grades 3-5. (Learning Tree Filmstrips.)

Description	Price
Understanding What You Read	
A. Before You Begin	$18.00
B. Finding the Facts	18.00
C. Finding the Main Idea	18.00
D. Interpreting Facts and Ideas	18.00
Set of 4 filmstrips, 4 cassettes, and a teacher's guide.	62.00
Getting More from What You Read	
A. Words and Phrases	18.00
B. Types of Writing	18.00
C. Reading Between the Lines	18.00
D. Drawing Inferences	18.00
Set of 4 filmstrips, 4 cassettes, and a teacher's guide.	62.00
Using and Evaluating What You Read	
A. Practical Reading	18.00
B. Creative Reading	18.00
C. Critical Reading	18.00
D. Judgment and Taste	18.00
Set of 4 filmstrips, 4 cassettes, and a teacher's guide.	62.00

Psychotechnics Reading Programs

The filmstrip materials in the various series are used in connection with a mechanical device called the Tachomatic 500 Projector. This machine has fully automatic controls and offers a speed range from 100 to 1,200 words per minute. A flip of a switch holds an image on the screen indefinitely. With use of the filmstrips, two and three fixations per line or an entire line can be presented. Students progress from word-by-word to phrase-by-phrase reading. (Psychotechnics, Inc.)

Purdue Training Filmstrips

This filmstrip series is a reproduction of the Purdue Reading Films. The set includes an Instructor's Book with comprehension texts and vocabulary.

Description	Price
"Purdue Training Filmstrips" (grades 6 to 8; 20 filmstrips)	$85.00

Optimum Reading Achievement Series

This series consists of three sets of filmstrips designed for use with Optimum Reading Achievement Tests. Each text contains 20 essays together with corresponding vocabulary and comprehension checks.

Description	Price
Level 1 (grades 7 and 8; 20 filmstrips)	$85.00
Level 2 (grades 9 and 10; 20 filmstrips)	85.00
Level 3 (grades 11 and adult; 20 filmstrips)	85.00

T-Matic Films

T-Matic-Films feature 5,000 words and approximately 26,000 phrases. The films are designed to teach 25 words a week for 20 weeks. The words were selected after a study of twelve major basal publishers and Psychotechnics computerized dictionary of the most frequently used service words of the English language. (Psychotechnics, Inc.)

Description	Price
Words and Phrases Films, Grade 1 (20 films)	$90.00
Words and Phrases Films, Grade 2 (20 films)	90.00
Words and Phrases Films, Grade 3 (20 films)	90.00
Words and Phrases Films, Grade 4 (20 films)	90.00
Words and Phrases Films, Grade 5 (20 films)	90.00
Words and Phrases Films, Grade 6 (20 films)	90.00
Words and Phrases Films, Grade 7 (20 films)	90.00
Words and Phrases Films, Grade 8 (20 films)	90.00

Multi-Level Remedial Film Program

This is a multi-level film program (grades 3-adult) designed for students who have experienced difficulty in mastering the skills essential for efficient reading. The films can be used for supplemental reading in the classroom to reinforce a basal reading program at any elementary level. They also can be used as a remedial program for use with special reading groups formed within a classroom.

The films include contractions, word reversals, relation words, word opposites, word perception, silent consonants, word reversals 11, homophonous words, blends and digraphs, alphabet sequencing, word discrimination, "Look-A-Like" words, synonyms for "said," phonetic irregularities, contrasting word patterns, and which word is different. (Psychometrics, Inc.)

Description	Price
Multi-Level Remedial Reading Films (20 films)	$90.00
Teacher's Edition (extra copy)	1.50
Multi-Level Spirit Master Booklet and Answer Booklet	8.50
Basic Sight Words Films, Remedial Format (20 films)	90.00
Teacher's Edition (extra copy)	1.50
Spirit Master Booklet (35 exercises)	9.50

COMMERCIALLY MADE TAPE RECORDINGS

EDL Listen and Read Programs

The Listen and Read programs are available on four levels: intermediate, junior high school, senior high school, and college. Each lesson begins with an introductory sketch, dialogue, or sequence of sound effects designed to capture students' interest and attention. The narrator introduces the students to the skill or concept being dealt with and then guides them through listening and workbook exercises in which they gain practice in various phases of the skill or concept. The student workbook provides both visual reinforcement for the ideas being introduced and exercises in which the student applies what is learned at each step of the lesson. Each lesson lasts from twenty-five to thirty minutes including response time. Cassettes have replaced tapes, although the latter are still available. With the use of a connecting jack box for nine headsets, a number of students can work independently. (Educational Developmental Laboratories/McGraw-Hill.)

Listen and Read D (fourth-grade level listening and reading skills)

1. Visualizing
2. Identifying Main Ideas
3. Using Details
4. Recognizing Sequence
5. Comparing
6. Recognizing Cause and Effect
7. Using Maps and Graphs
8. Using PQR (Preview, Question, Read)
9. Outlining
10. Summarizing
11. Interpreting Figurative Language
12. Making Inferences
13. Interpreting Character
14. Predicting Outcomes
15. Interpreting Poetry

Listen and Read GHI album 1 (seventh- and eighth-grade reading and study skills)

1. Listening and Reading
2. Meeting New Words, Part 1
3. Meeting New Words, Part 2
4. Using Context Clues
5. Using Your Senses, Part 1
6. Using Your Senses, Part 2
7. Recognizing the Power of Words
8. Recognizing the Power of Words (continued)
9. Unlocking Sentences Meaning, Part 1
10. Unlocking Sentence Meaning, Part 2
11. Noticing Signs and Signals in Reading
12. Recognizing Main Ideas in Paragraphs
13. Understanding Paragraphs That Tell a Story
14. Understanding Paragraphs That Describe
15. Understanding Paragraphs That Explain

Listen and Read GHI album 2 (eighth- and ninth-grade reading and study skills)

1. Checking Your Study Habits
2. Making Remembering Easier
3. Using the Dictionary
4. Using Maps
5. Using Graphs
6. Reading Illustrations and Cartoons
7. Reading a Textbook, Part 1
8. Reading a Textbook, Part 2
9. Reading a Textbook, Part 3
10. Using Library References
11. Note-taking
12. Summarizing
13. Shifting Gears in Reading
14. Skimming and Scanning
15. Taking Examinations

Description	Price
Set LR-D, 15 cassettes (level 4)	$150.00
LR-D Lesson Book (level 4)	2.50
Listening Programs Teacher's Guide	2.50
Set LR-GHI Album 1, 15 cassettes (levels 7 to 9)	150.00
Set LR-GHI Album 2, 15 cassettes (levels 7 to 9)	150.00
LR-GHI Album 1, Lesson Book (levels 7 to 9)	2.25
LR-GHI Album 2, Lesson Book (levels 7 to 9)	2.25
Listening Programs Teacher's Guide	2.50

Listen and Think Program

The Listen and Think series develops listening comprehension and thinking skills. Each program provides a sequence of fifteen lessons that move the student from analytical skills (recognizing and organizing information, to interpretive skills (inferring, predicting, visualizing), to appreciative skills, to critical skills. Each lesson takes one sklll or aspect of a skill and develops it thoroughly. Each tape starts with an attention-getting situation demonstrating the specific skill. The skill is introduced. Then the student alternates between listening to the taped material and responding in the lesson book to taped instruction. Compressed speech is used during the latter portion of the tapes, challenging the student's attention, improving his/her concentration and thus his/her retention. Within the developmental organization of the series, programs AR (Auditory Readiness) for level 1 and B for level 2 develop listening and thinking skills that precede and facilitate reading the recognition of concepts of space and time, cause and effect, alike-different, and serial order. (Educational Developmental Laboratories/McGraw-Hill.)

Programs C through F (levels 3 to 6) develop and reinforce the listening and thinking skills most needed at these levels. The skills tested at levels C through F are as follows:

Identifying Main Ideas	Understanding Character
Recognizing Sequence	Understanding Setting
Summarizing	Recognizing Foreshadowing
Comparing	Sharing Feelings
Recognizing Cause and Effect	Enjoying Humor
Predicting Outcomes	Recognizing Speaker's Purpose
Using Our Senses	Fact and Opinion
Visualizing	Drawing Conclusions

Programs G, H, and I (levels 7 to 9) use works of acknowledged literary merit to develop the listening, thinking, and comprehension skill needed for effective response to literature. The skills introduced at levels G, H, and I are these:

Understanding Character
Understanding Setting
Recognizing Foreshadowing
and Climax

Understanding Theme
Understanding Conflict
Understanding Qualities of
Literature

Each Listen and Think set contains fifteen recordings. Each tape contains thirteen minutes of playing time. Teacher's handbooks are available for levels Auditory Readiness through F. Individual lesson books ($1.95 each) are provided for each of levels one through nine. They contain introductory material, exercises, and activity pages to be used during recorded lessons. A chart in the back of each lesson book permits the student to record his own progress.

Description	Price
Auditory Readiness Tapes (levels K to 1)	$150.00
B Tapes (level 2)	150.00
C Tapes (level 3)	150.00
D Tapes (level 4)	150.00
E Tapes (level 5)	150.00
F Tapes (level 6)	150.00
G Tapes (level 7)	150.00
H Tapes (level 8)	150.00
I Tapes (level 9)	150.00
Teacher's handbook $2.50 per book	150.00

The Reading Powertapes Program

This multi-media program for intermediate grades through senior high consists of 24 taped lessons to be used with a student's workbook. Each lesson includes a story, entirely on tape. During breaks in the story, reading and study skills are introduced and discussed by a teaching voice on the tape. Then the students turn off the tape and complete the practice exercises in their workbooks. The program is largely self-directing, and the students check their own work. (Globe Book Company, Inc.)

Description	Price
Reading Powertapes Program: Twelve cassettes in a binder with the Teacher's Manual and a package of ten workbooks.	$98.00
Packages of additional workbooks (ten per package)	22.50

Imperial Intermediate Reading Program

The *Imperial Intermediate Reading Program* is a tape-centered series of forty lessons specifically designed to help individualize and supplement reading instruction. Tapes and visual response materials provide motivation for the development of important reading skills. Self-direction and self-evaluation are built into the program.

An accompanying placement test helps determine the reading level at which each student will enter the program. From that point, the student proceeds at his own pace through succeeding units of increasing difficulty. Reading levels increase sequentially through the program from 2.0 to 9.0.

The program ($439.00) is accompanied by three copies of a comprehensive teacher's manual which contains a complete guide for each lesson. (Imperial International)

Minisystems in Reading (grades K-6)

Minisystems in Reading are self-teaching audio cassette lessons that explain, question, instruct, and entertain children with sound effects, music, and both male and female voices. Children write on activity sheets in response to what they hear. A teacher guide helps the teacher administer the program and lists the objectives to be achieved.

The following minisystems are representative of the 178 available. (Learning Systems Corporation.)

Description	Price
Left to Right Progression (K Level)	$9.95
Letter Recognition (K Level)	9.95
Listening to Rhymes (K Level)	9.95
Orientation to Letters (K Level)	9.95
Rhyming Words with Pictures (K Level)	9.95
Listening, Seeing, Writing B, P, D (Grade 1)	9.95
Listening, Seeing, Writing L, H, F (Grade 1)	9.95
Listening, Seeing, Writing, M, N, T (Grade 1)	9.95
Evaluation: Initial Consonants (Grade 1)	9.95
Evaluation: Final Consonants (Grade 1)	9.95
Short a (Grade 2)	9.95
Spelling with Short a (Grade 2)	9.95
Building Power Vocabulary a, e, i, o (Grade 2)	9.95
Long Vowels with Final e (Grade 2)	9.95
Medial Short to Long Vowel Plus e (Grade 2)	9.95
Review of Consonant Digraphs (Grade 3)	9.95
Vowels Controlled by r (Grade 3)	9.95
Contractions (Grade 3)	9.95
Hard and Soft c and g (Grade 3)	9.95
Roots, Prefixes and Suffixes (Grade 3)	9.95
Using Dictionary Guide Words (Grade 4)	9.95
Introduction to the Encyclopedia (Grade 4)	9.95
Interpreting Maps and Graphs (Grade 4)	9.95
Skimming for Specific Information (Grade 4)	9.95
Fact, Fiction, and Opinion (Grade 4)	9.95
Using Dictionaries and Glossaries (Grade 5)	9.95
Locating Key Words (Grade 5)	9.95
Using the Card Catalog (Grade 5)	9.95
Review: Reference Skills (Grade 5)	9.95
Reading Time Lines (Grade 5)	9.95

Description	Price
Taking Notes (Grade 6)	9.95
Preparing a Summary (Grade 6)	9.95
Preparing an Outline (Grade 6)	9.95
Using the Dictionary and Thesaurus (Grade 6)	9.95
Review: Reference Skills (Grade 6)	9.95

Radio Reading Series

Radio Reading tape cassettes feature a word-by-word reading of each story for a listening or read-along activity. A radio-style voice is used to establish a natural auditory pace and create a realistic meaning/understanding experience. After a story is read, a second voice guides the student through exercises that include comprehension, vocabulary, and discussion type questions. The student is able to correct his own work by following the directions supplied on the tape. Each level of the program contains five tape cassettes comprising ten stories, ten copies of each essay, a teacher's manual and lesson plans, and two copies of student booklets. (Tarmac/tac, Inc.)

Description	Price
Radio Reading Series 1 (3rd grade reading level)	$89.50
Radio Reading Series 2 (4th grade reading level)	89.50
Radio Reading Series 3 (5th grade reading level)	89.50
Radio Reading Series 4 (6th grade reading level)	89.50
Radio Reading Series 5 (7th grade reading level)	89.50
Radio Reading Series 6 (8th grade reading level)	89.50

VX Word Study Program

The VX Word Study Program is completely self-instructional and is designed to develop skills in the areas of visual memory, structural analysis, phonetic analysis, vocabulary in context, and dictionary usage. It can be used for individual, small group or full class work. Students work in their record booklets and correct their own answers. A placement test can be used to determine a student's entry level. (Tarmac/tac, Inc.)

Description	Price
VX Word Study Program including 2 sets of Lesson Cards, 15 Student Record Booklets, 5 answer books, 15 placement tests, and a teacher's manual	$99.50
Student record booklet (25/pkg.)	9.50
Answer book	.65
Placement test (50/pkg.)	9.50

Aesop's Fables Listening/Reading Program

This program features ten of Aesop's most popular fables. The stories average 500 to 600 words and appear in both tape cassette and story booklet form. The program comes boxed. The kit includes five tape cassettes, twenty essay booklets, seventy-five student record booklets, and a teacher's edition. The program is designed to help students improve listening skills, visualization, story sequencing, vocabulary, inferential thinking, and reading speed. (Tarmac/tac, Inc.)

Description	Price
Aesop's Fables Program	$89.50
Aesop's Fables Essay Booklet	1.10
Teacher's Edition	2.00

MULTIMODAL MACHINES AND DEVICES

Audiotronics Tutorette Systems

In this system a student-oriented self-pacing card reader provides individualized involvement in multisensory experiences. Programs are produced on sets of audiocards. There are both a visual presentation and a corresponding audio presentation on a strip of magnetic recording tape at the bottom of the card. To use the system, students insert an audiocard, observe the visual presentation, listen to the teacher audio portion, and then record their response on the student track. They next compare their response with the lesson material on the teacher track, and if they are dissatisfied with their response, they continue practicing, rerecording, and comparing until they are completely comfortable with their progress. (Audiotronics.)

There are five Tutorette cardreader models to choose from. Four models have both instructor and student record and playback capabilities, along with special features distinctive to each.

Description	Price
Model 822 is a "Double-Play Instructor and Student Record/ Playback Tutorette.	$164.95
Model 800SA is an Instructor and Student Record/Playback Tutorette with Electronic Programmed Stop.	179.95
Model 800A-H is an Instructor and Student Record/Playback Tutorette with Room-Mike Headphone.	172.95
Model 800A is an Instructor and Student Record/Playback Tutorette.	149.95
Model 810 is a Student Record/Playback and Instructor Playback-Only Tutorette.	99.95
Tutorette Blank Cards (box of 100 3-7/16-by-9-inch cards): Minimum order 6 boxes	8.00
Tutorette Blank Cards (box of 100 5½-by-11-inch cards): Minimum order 6 boxes	10.00
Tutorette Materials Development Kit: Instructor Guide, Precut Letters and Numbers, 4-color Art, and Blank Cards (300 3-7/16-by-9-inch cards and 75 5½-by-11-inch cards)	37.00
Alphabet Zoo (Audiocard Program: Prerecorded Audiocards, small quantity of Blank Cards, Experience Sheets and Program Guide (preschool and primary levels)	19.95

Description	Price
Visits to a Zoo, a City, and a Farm Audiocard Program: Prerecorded Cards, 4 Experience Sheets, and Program Guide (preschool and primary levels)	24.95
Sight Words for Beginning Readers Audiocard Program: Prerecorded Cards, 4 Experience Sheets, and Program Guide (primary level)	24.95
Structural Analysis: To help beginning readers develop sight vocabulary as well as decoding skills in analyzing compound words, plurals, roots, prefixes, suffixes, and contractions (primary level; remedial at intermediate levels)	24.95
Word Parts Audiocard Program: Prerecorded Cards, 4 Experience Sheets, and Program Guide (remedial at high school level)	24.95
Initial Consonants Audiocard Program (Part 1): Prerecorded Cards, 4 Experience Sheets, Answer Sheet, and Program Guide (preschool and primary levels)	19.95
Initial Consonants Audiocard Program (Part 2): Prerecorded Cards, 4 Experience Sheets, Answer Sheet, and Program Guide (preschool and primary levels)	19.95
Consonant Blends Audiocard Program: Prerecorded Cards, 4 Experience Sheets, Answer Sheet, and Program Guide (preschool and primary levels)	24.95
Short and Long Vowels Audiocard Program: Prerecorded Cards, 4 Experience Sheets, Answer Sheet, and Program Guide (preschool and primary levels)	19.95
Consonant Digraphs Audiocard Program: Prerecorded Cards, 4 Experience Sheets, Answer Sheet, and Program Guide (preschool and primary levels)	19.95
Vowel Digraphs/Diphthongs Audiocard Program: Prerecorded Cards, 4 Experience Sheets, Answer Sheet, and Program Guide (preschool and primary levels)	19.95
Three-Letter Consonant Blends Audiocard Program: Prerecorded Cards, 4 Experience Sheets, Answer Sheet, and Program Guide (preschool and primary levels)	19.95
Phonograms Audiocard Program: Prerecorded Cards, 4 Experience Sheets, Answer Sheet, and Program Guide (preschool and primary levels)	24.95
Silent Letters Audiocard Program: Prerecorded Cards, 4 Experience Sheets, Answer Sheet, and Program Guide (preschool and primary levels)	19.95
Syllables Audiocard Program: Prerecorded Cards, 4 Experience Sheets, Answer Sheet, and Program Guide (preschool and primary levels)	19.95
Tricky Words Audiocard Program: Prerecorded Cards, 4 Experience Sheets, and Program Guide (intermediate and junior high school levels; remedial at high school level)	24.95
Mispronounced Words Audiocard Program: Prerecorded Cards, 4 Experience Sheets, and Program Guide (intermediate and junior high school levels; remedial at high school level)	24.95

Borg-Warner System 80

System 80 consists of a boxlike device (16 inches wide, 14 inches high, and 14 inches deep) that provides simultaneous visual and auditory stimulation. Its television-like screen measures 8 by 4 inches. This audiovisual unit utilizes 12-inch vinyl records and a filmstrip encased in transparent plastic.

Computer-type markings on the filmstrip units make it possible for the instrument to move forward when a correct answer is given or repeat if an incorrect answer is given. A child responds to a recorded voice by pressing one of five selection buttons.

Each kit contains an average of twelve lessons with every fourth lesson serving as a review. In the review lesson, a branching technique is used. This means that a different contextual setting is presented if the pupil answers incorrectly. (Borg-Warner Educational Systems.)

Description	Price
Letter Names Through Sounds (12 kits)	$149.00 each
Reading Words in Context (17 kits)	160.00 each
Developing Spelling Skills (7 kits)	144.00 each
Improving Reading Skills (9 kits)	160.00 each
Learning Letter Sounds (12 kits)	144 to 208 each
Developing Structural Analysis Skills (3 kits)	144.00 each

EDL Aud-X Programs

The Aud-X programs provide motivating reading instruction for primary pupils and older students with limited reading ability. Aud-X instruction has unique features. It provides sight-sound synchronization or simultaneous visual and aural presentation of words. The use of aural context for sight-word presentation makes it possible to provide high-interest story content while building sight vocabulary. Student-controlled pacing allows students to respond at their own pace and to control the rate at which a lesson progresses. (Educational Developmental Laboratories/McGraw-Hill.)

The new EDL Aud-X not only plays EDL Aud-X programs but also will accommodate any standard 35mm filmstrip. A push-button panel gives complete control of the filmstrip projector and the audio cassette. (EDL/McGraw-Hill.)

Some of the programs designed for the EDL Aud-X include the following:

Description	Price
Aud-X Readiness Set A-X R-3	$300.00
Aud-X Readiness Book R-3	2.15
Aud-X Readiness Worksheet Pads (5 pads, 40 sheets each)	8.50
Word Study Skills, Lessons 1-30, Levels 1-2 (Aud-X Filmstrip—Cassette Box 1)	295.00

Description	Price
Lesson Cards, Box 1	85.00
Word Attack Tests for Box 1	18.30
Word Study Skills, Lessons 31-60, Levels 2-3 (Aud-X Filmstrip-Cassette Box 2)	295.00
Lesson Cards, Box 2	85.00
Word Attack Tests for Box 2	16.50
Word Study Skills, Lessons 61-85, Level 3-4 (Aud-X Film-strip—Cassette Box 3)	245.00
Lesson Cards, Box 3	70.00
Word Attack Skills Box 3	10.00
Reading Sampler Series, Level 3-6 (Aud-X Filmstrips and Cassettes)	275.00
Set of 25 Sampler Books	50.00
Lesson Book 1, Lessons 1-14	2.75
Lesson Book 2, Lessons 15-25	2.75
Teacher Aide	4.50
Aud-X Dictionary Skills Set, Level 4-6	240.00
Dictionary Skills Lesson Book	8.50
Dictionary Skills Test Masters	5.00
Teacher Information and Act-O-Masters Book	8.50
Aud-X Word and Skill Filmstrip/Cassette Set, AX-RA (Readiness)	205.00
AX-AA, Level 1	585.00
AX-BA, Level 2	585.00
AX-CA, Level 3	585.00

Hoffman Audiovisual Instructional System

The *Hoffman Audiovisual Instructional System* is centered around the Mark IV projector, an instrument which presents a simultaneous visual and audio signal. Its sound system and viewing screen are in one unit.

Study units consist of forty-minute lessons that are organized in ten-minute modules. Materials covering the primary and intermediate grades are available. These are presented on four filmstrips and two records which are packaged in colorful albums. (Primary study units consist of two filmstrips and one record in an album.) Each achievement unit consists of ten study units which are packaged in a durable file box. Workbooks accompany each achievement unit. Questions that are presented audiovisually are printed in answer books. By using headphones, students can work independently or in a small group. (Gould Inc. Educational Systems Division.)

Description	Price
Hoffman Mark IV projector	$389.00
Headset with air cushions	6.95
Jack box	24.48
Listening center	67.95
Speaker	16.33

Description			Price

Primary Language Arts and Phonics (60 study units)

Program	Price
100-0	125.00
101-0	125.00
102-0	125.00
103-0	125.00
104-0	125.00
105-0	125.00

Third Level Language Arts Reading Program

Program	Price	Answer Books	Price
02 1003	$198.00	03 1003	$ .68
02 1013	198.00	03 1013	.68
02 1023	198.00	03 1023	.68

Fourth Level Language Arts Reading Program

02 1004	198.00	03 1004	.68
02 1014	198.00	03 1014	.68
02 1024	198.00	03 1024	.68

Fifth Level Language Arts Reading Program

02 1005	198.00	03 1005	.68
02 1015	198.00	03 1015	.68
02 1025	198.00	03 1025	.68

Sixth Level Language Arts Reading Program

02 1006	198.00	03 1006	.68
02 1016	198.00	03 1016	.68
02 1026	198.00	03 1026	.68

Language Master

The Language Master is an instructional device that provides simultaneous auditory and visual stimulation. Nine inches of audio tape adhere to the bottom edge of instructional cards (standard size is 3½ by 9 inches). This feature allows the Language Master unit to function as a dual-channel audiorecorder and playback device with the following functions. Positioning of a concealed switch enables the instructor to record words, phrases, and sentences on the master track. After such recordings have been completed and the switch returned to its normal position, the master track cannot be accidentally erased by the learner. The student may listen to the master-track recording as a model when he views the material in printed form. He may then record his own version on the student track. At this time, the student listens to his responses and checks them with master-track recording. The student can rerecord his own efforts until he is satisfied that he has approximated the model recording. (Photo and Sound.)

The battery-operated Model 1727B is a lightweight portable the size of a textbook. The small unit is completely portable because it eliminates the need for AC power and a large working surface. The Model 1727B permits recording on the student track only, and playback of both the instructor and student tracks. With four "C" batteries, the machine weighs about three pounds. An automatic on/off switch extends battery life. Inserting a card turns on the unit. After the card is conveyed through the device, it automatically turns off. An AC adapter which is included converts the portable for use with wall current. (Photo and Sound.)

The portable unit is available in a Kit model, the 1727BK. The Kit's case has a luggage handle and safety catches. Inside is a 1727B unit, a lightweight headset, an AC adapter, an operating manual, and 60 blank cards. Instructions for the unit are mounted inside the case.

Description	Price
Portable Model with Instructor Playback and Student Record Playback (1727B)	$109.95
Portable Kit (1727BK)	139.95

The following are representative of the Pre-Recorded Programs:

Sound Blending and Beginning Phonetic Skills	49.50
Consonant Blends and Irregular Phonetic Elements	49.50
Word Building and Word Analysis Techniques	49.50
Reading Through Pictures—Set I	94.00
Reading Through Pictures—Set II	84.00
Practical Vocabulary & Expressions	49.50
Everyday Expressions	49.50
Everyday Words—Box 1	89.00
Everyday Words in Phrases—Box 2	89.00
Everyday Words in Action—Box 3	89.00
Everyday Words in Sentences—Box 4	89.00

RX Reading Program

The RX Reading Program is a self-intsructional and multisensory program that incorporates the senses of touch, hearing, and sight. It is considered ideal for kindergarten, grades one, two, three, and four, nongraded classes, special-education classes, and remedial classes from grades two through eight.

The program is self-correctional and is designed for use as either a teacher-directed activity or as a completely self-correctional teaching device. Its purpose is to provide actual teaching and/or reinforcement necessary for children to learn the skills of letter recognition, common nouns and pictures, basic sight words, and phonetic word analysis.

The complete RX Reading Program includes an Audio Tract Instructional Center with tape cassette module, an RX storage system, 160 single concept lessons (including eight skill cards and two checkstrips per lesson), 80 instructional tapes (160 lessons), four headsets, Teacher's Manual and Diagnostic Tests, Prescription Forms, a wall Progress Chart, and Record Sheets for 50 students. (Total cost $595. Psychotechnics, Inc.)

Voxcom, Mark II

Voxcom, Mark II is a combination card reader and cassette recorder. Programs consisting of ten-inch cards provide as much as 25 seconds playing time. The Voxcom Master Kit featuring Mark II is designed for innovative education teachers who wish to produce their own software for the individual needs of children. Included in the kit are the following: Voxcom Mark II, microphone, headphone, C batteries, scissors, color extender keys, hand eraser, 1000″ talk/tape, 220 assorted Tal/Cards, two cassettes, foam lined plastic carrying case and operating instructions. (Voxcom.)

Description	Price
Voxcom Master Kit (featuring Mark II	$225.00
Elementary Reading Skills Kit	150.00
Part I Phonetic Analysis (Consonants, Blends, Digraphs and Vowels); Part II Structural Analysis (Compound Words, Contractions, Prefixes, Suffixes, Synonyms and Antonyms.)	

PROGRAMMED LEARNING

The terms *teaching machine and programmed learning* are used interchangeably by many people. Actually, they are not the same. The program is the important thing. The machine merely acts as a vehicle for presenting the program.

A learning program consists of a carefully ordered and organized sequence of material to which a student responds. His response takes the form of filling in a space, selecting one of a number of multiple-choice answers, indicating agreement or disagreement, and so forth. Immediately after a student has made a choice or answered a question, he is permitted to see the correct answer so that he knows whether an error was made.

At the present time, programs are available on many grade levels and with a variety of subjects. Spelling, geography, arithmetic, algebra, biology, psychology, political science, logic, engineering, foreign languages, and reading are among the areas covered.

Some of the specific principles that characterize successful programs are as follows.

1. *Logical Sequence of Small Steps*: Subject matter is broken down into information fragments and is presented one step at a time so that it can be easily understood. No step is bypassed until mastery has been attained. The sequence is orderly, and the difficulty increment is narrow. This permits steady student progress uncomplicated by undue frustration.

2. *Immediate Feedback*: Since nothing succeeds like success, it is important that the program provide an immediate appraisal of each response. The theory of reinforcement emphasizes that students profit from the consequences of their responses. Since students are constantly appraised for how well they are doing, there is little danger they will go far astray.

3. *Self-pacing*: Students engaged in programmed learning activity can work at their own rate. They are not held back by other students who do not comprehend readily or who lack the drive to persist. On the other hand, students are not discouraged by others capable of working at a more rapid rate than they. The programmed learning process is completely individualized.

4. *Teacher Education*: The teacher can easily evaluate a student's progress by checking the nature of the responses made to the items involved. Thus the kind of special help a student needs is easy to pinpoint.

Capable children who are able to work independently achieve great success with programmed learning materials. But experience with disabled readers at the California State University Reading Clinic in Los Angeles leads us to the conclusion that programmed learning is no panacea. Children who lack adequate self-assurance and those who have a need for more attention than the average pupil find it difficult and often impossible to profit from programmed learning approaches.

15 Reading Improvement Program in Action

IN-SERVICE TRAINING

Many teachers enter service with minimal professional training in reading and are unable to cope with the problems they face in their classrooms. Other teachers received their training and teaching credentials so long ago that they feel the necessity of familiarizing themselves with more modern approaches to reading instruction. It is evident, therefore, that the principle of individual differences is as applicable to teachers as it is to the children they teach. Any in-service training program must take cognizance of this by being broad enough to meet the needs of the neophyte teacher as well as those of the veteran staff member who has had years of experience. The program must begin where each teacher is and move toward the goal of maximum teaching effectiveness for all. Such a program is most effective if centered around specific problems which both new and experienced teachers encounter. To be a genuine success, planning should grow out of a cooperative effort of both administration and staff. Teachers tend to reject an in-service training program imposed from above.

In discussing in-service programs, Nagle emphasizes the following:[1]

1. Nothing is more important to a successful in-service program than careful planning which gives rise to specific purposes that are clear to all involved.
2. In-service activities should not be scheduled after school. They should take place when teachers' energies are less likely to be at low ebb.
3. Resource personnel should be carefully selected and told exactly what is expected of them.
4. A consultant who has a program designed to meet teachers' needs should not be hired for one-day engagements. A four to eight day sustained service contract is more desirable.
5. The consultant or resource person should be flexible enough to modify the structure of the planned program if it is necessary.

Preschool and postschool workshops, orientation weeks, teacher institutes, and teachers' meetings are scheduled by many schools as part of an in-service training program. Criscuolo describes a number of other approaches to in-service reading programs.[2, 3] With most programs, consultants in reading from nearby colleges and universities may be used for these purposes, although on occasion individuals with little professional training in reading attempt to provide leadership. In any event, these one-shot attempts seldom provide any lasting benefits since more than momentary teacher enthusiasm is needed to sustain a program throughout the year. Harker states that "the success of the consultant depends upon the extent to which he answers the conscious needs of teachers and administrators for specific information and the extent to which he responds to their less conscious needs for moral support."[4]

A consultant can (1) help teachers determine the reading levels of pupils and assist them in instructional grouping, (2) aid in the selection of special methods and materials, (3) point out the latest trends in research, (4) assist in setting up teaching experiments, and (5) pinpoint strengths and weaknesses in the reading program.

More permanent benefits are achieved when school districts employ consultants who make classroom visits and carry out on-the-spot demonstrations of effective techniques and approaches for the teachers. Often such consultants give additional assistance to counselors, nurses, administrators, and parents.

Some schools have experienced success by initiating an intraschool visitation plan whereby new teachers are given opportunities to observe experienced teachers at work with children. Informal small group discussions according to grade level may continue throughout the year. These may be led by experienced teachers. The groups devote attention to the causes of reading retardation, classroom grouping techniques, methods that are helpful in overcoming specific weaknesses and problems, interpreting test scores, utilizing school records, and so forth.

Teachers should be encouraged to take advantage of extension courses, summer courses, and extended workshops in the reading area. Alert administrators should hold conferences with teachers and bring to their attention specific courses which will be of benefit to them and will strengthen the staff as a whole. Teachers availing themselves of prescribed opportunities for professional growth should be given opportunities to share their learnings with other interested teachers.

Larger districts can encourage teachers to contribute practical ideas for the publication of an inexpensive bulletin which might bear the title "It Worked for Me" and "Here's How I Did It."

Material centers which house the latest devices and materials can be organized for teacher use. A section of the school library or a shelf in the teacher's room may be set aside for books and magazines which constitute an up-to-date professional library in reading. Copies of reading and language arts bulletins which have been purchased with school funds may also be displayed. Teachers are invited to check out such materials for study away from school.

Some school districts encourage teachers to carry out individual and group research projects and experiments. These projects are of benefit not only to teachers who participate in them directly, but also to all teachers in the district with whom the results can be shared.

A few city school systems have developed reading clinics which are used as training centers for teachers who, after a semester's work in the clinic, go back into their classrooms bristling with new insights and competencies. Such a plan has been employed in the St. Louis schools for a number of years. A group of select teachers are trained in the clinic under close supervision. After a full year in the clinic, the teachers are returned to the classroom. Kottmeyer states, "Although the efficiency of the clinic program is no doubt curtailed, the values of the in-service training for many teachers justify the policy."[5]

THE SCHOOL LIBRARIAN

As stated earlier in this book, the degree to which a library is used in a school is a valid index of the success of the school's reading program. Nothing is more basic to a good school library than a good school librarian. And needless to say, a good librarian is of pivotal importance to the effectiveness of the school's reading program.

In developing a classroom library, all teachers look to the librarian for help in selecting books that vary in interest and level of difficulty. Junior and senior high school teachers who employ a multilevel unit approach in content areas need assistance in finding reading materials that will meet the varying levels of reading ability in their classes.

When pupils visit the library, the librarian can provide them with valuable guidance. She can help them become acquainted with such things as reference books, the card catalog, and the Dewey decimal system. Her own enthusiasm about books and her strong desire to help pupils find the right books can do much to develop in them a love of reading.

PROFESSIONAL LIBRARY

Teachers can build a library of professional books in reading which will enable them to keep abreast of current trends. A list of recommended books is given in Appendix E. Although teachers have access to public, university, and college libraries, they are not absolved of the responsibility of accumulating a personal library of authoritative books that deal with a process as important to learning as reading. Unfortunately, studies show that many teachers own few professional books in reading.[6] One would be suspicious of a medical doctor or a lawyer who practiced his profession without the fingertip accessibility of literature relating to his work. Functional books and manuals should be kept on the teacher's desk for ready reference.

Teachers should join professional organizations such as the International Reading Association or the National Council of Teachers of English, and subscribe to professional magazines which devote space to studies and articles in the area of reading. Periodicals particularly valuable in this respect are as follows:

Childhood Education. Association for Childhood Education International, 3615 Wisconsin Ave., NW, Washington, D.C. 20016

Education. Star News Publishing Company, 429 Third Avenue, Chula Vista, Calif. 92010

Education Digest. Prakken Publications, Inc., Ann Arbor, Mich. 48107

Elementary English. National Council of Teachers of English, Publisher, 1111 Keyon Rd., Urbana, Ill. 61801

English Journal. National Council of Teachers of English, Publisher, 1111 Keyon Rd., Urban, Ill. 61801

The Instructor. The Instructor Publications, Inc., 7 Bank Street, Dansville, N. Y. 14437

Journal of Education Psychology. American Psychological Association, 1200 17th St. NW, Washington, D.C. 20036

Journal of Educational Research. Heldref Publications, 4000 Albemarle St. NW, Suite 302, Washington, D.C. 20016

Journal of Reading. International Reading Association, 800 Barksdale Rd., Newark, Del. 19711

The New England Journal. University of Rhode Island, Kingston, Rhode Island 92881

Parents Magazine and Better Homemaking. Parents' Magazine Enterprises, Inc., 52 Vanderbilt Ave., New York, N.Y. 10017

Reading Horizons. Western Michigan University, Kalamazoo, Mich. 49008

Reading Improvement. Star News Publishing Company, 429 Third Avenue, Chula Vista, Calif. 92010

Reading Research Quarterly. International Reading Association, 800 Barksdale Rd., Newark, Del. 19711

Reading World. College Reading Association, One Lumb Memorial Drive, Rochester, N.Y. 14623

The Reading Clinic. Center for Applied Arts in Education, P.O. Box 130, West Nyack, N.Y. 10995

The Reading Teacher. International Reading Association, 800 Barksdale Rd., Newark, Del. 19711

Review of Educational Research. American Educational Research Association, 1126 16th St., NW, Washington, D.C. 20036

Teacher. Macmillan Magazine, Inc., 22 West Putman Ave., Greenwich, Conn. 06830

Today's Education. National Education Association, 1201 16th St. NW, Washington, D.C. 20036

Teachers can keep a file of advertising materials which lists the names and addresses of companies, along with the latest teaching aids available in the reading field. Another file can be devoted to free and inexpensive materials (booklets, charts, posters, filmstrips, etc.) which innumerable industrial, governmental, and business firms will send to any teacher who makes a request.

Teachers should not overlook but should exploit to the fullest all available school resources. For example, manuals accompanying basal and supplementary readers furnished by the school should be studied carefully to glean all value from them. Certainly, too, the counsel of any available reading consultants, psychologists, and other specialists should be sought in an effort to implement an instructional program in reading that is geared to individual needs.

RESEARCH

Teachers who are interested in research (reports, conference papers, etc.) should avail themselves of the Educational Resources Information Center (ERIC), a system providing abstracts and microfische of innumerable reading titles. Bibliographies on many reading topics are available through ERIC/NCTE, 1111 Kenyon Road, Urbana, Illinois 61801. Two publication of ERIC, Research in Education (RIE) and Current Index to Journals in Education (CIJE), list material appearing in education magazines.

Teachers can find a listing of articles devoted to reading in *Education Index, Reader's Guide to Periodical Literature,* and *Psychological Abstracts.* In addition to these reference works, most libraries have copies of *Textbooks in Print,* a volume which provides a complete list of reading texts.

CURTAILMENT OF SOCIAL PROMOTION

Social promotion relieves teachers from the responsibility of helping students achieve. Dedicated teachers who are well trained in the teaching of reading can succeed in salvaging most disabled readers. Parents of students who are retained because they do not meet achievement standards will readily support retentions when they are convinced that a corrective program can result in successful scholarship. Giving passing grades to disabled readers is misleading and fails to alert parents to the presence of a serious problem at a time when immediate action is needed to solve it.

ELIMINATION OF FUNCTIONAL ILLITERACY

The problem of immediate concern in connection with improving the reading program is to eliminate functional illiteracy at upper grade levels. To help solve this problem it is essential that a valid standardized test of reading be administered at the beginning of the school year in order to identify disabled readers. Such readers should then be assigned to a remedial class under the direction of a special teacher of reading. To provide an added opportunity for disabled readers to improve, summer school classes in reading should also be made available.

To eliminate functional illiteracy on the high school level it is necessary for all elementary pupils to achieve the status of reading independence. Permanent improvement in reading skills at all levels is largely dependent on mastery of these skills in the elementary school.

MASTERY OF THE BASIC SKILLS

In the previous chapters we indicated that complete mastery of the basic reading skills of word recognition and word analysis at each grade level is an essential prerequisite to independence in reading. While mastery of the skills of reading is but a means to the end, it is vital to the attainment of competence in reading comprehension. Pupils in the fourth grade who have not attained the status of an independent reader need appropriate corrective instruction. The importance of mastery of the basic reading skills of word recognition and word analysis before pupils enter the fourth grade must not be overlooked. At the fourth grade level, when emphasis is on content, independent reading habits are essential. Disabled readers already in the middle and upper grades should be studied for deficiencies in the basic skills of word recognition and word analysis. If these deficiencies exist they must be met before improvement of comprehension skills is undertaken. The basic reading skills are foundational to all high-level reading.

Considerable space and emphasis have been given to the need for individualized correction of reading difficulties through the use of self-directed material. The instructional material described in this book is designed for this purpose. Because the material is largely self-directed, it enables the teacher to meet individual needs with greater ease. The self-directed aids described in chapters 12, 13, and 14 are valuable to teachers who wish to employ individualized correction.

RECREATIONAL READING

The value of recreational reading for improving the reading status of normal and accelerated readers has been highlighted as important. Books properly selected and evaluated provide a valuable supplement to individualized practice for retarded readers as well. However, a recreational reading program which does not include recognition of hazards to learning, awareness of individual reading levels, specific reading difficulties, and individual interests is largely ineffective with retarded readers.

Other areas of emphasis have included the importance of wholesome teacher-parent relationships, a good home environment involving parents who are concerned about their child and the school, and a school promotion policy based on mastery.

ESSENTIALS OF A READING IMPROVEMENT PROGRAM

A successful reading improvement program as highlighted in this book is largely conditioned by the following factors:

1. Correcting individual hazards to learning.
2. Attaining mastery of the basic skills of word recognition and word analysis in the primary grades.
3. Attaining independent reading habits in the intermediate grades.
4. Eliminating functional illiteracy in the elementary school.
5. Making diagnosis and correction of reading problems as integral part of developmental instruction.
6. Making recreational reading an integral part of the reading program.
7. Employing formal and/or informal tests in reading, intelligence, vision
8. Using self-directed instructional material in the corrective program
9. Using instructional material of optimum difficulty in every subject.
10. Providing for in-service training of teachers.
11. Developing wholesome teacher-parent relationships.
12. Cooperating with parents in solving school problems.
13. Basing promotion on mastery.
14. Providing special teachers of reading.
15. Providing remedial instruction in reading for severely disabled readers

In implementing the foregoing elements of a reading program, priorities must be set in terms of greatest needs and in the nature of the community.

PROBLEMS FOR ORAL AND WRITTEN DISCUSSION

1. What criteria would you establish as a basis for an improved program in reading?
2. Why is it important for the school to establish cooperation with the home?
3. What can parents do to improve the reading skills of their children?
4. What can the school do to improve teacher-parent relationships?

Notes

1. JOHN E. NAGLE, "Staff Development: Do It Right," *Journal of Reading* (November 1972):124-127.
2. NICHOLAS P. CRISCUOLO, "Involving Principals in the Reading Program," *The New England Reading Association Journal* (1978) Vol. 13, No. 3, 6-11.
3. NICHOLAS P. CRISCUOLO, "Inservice Education: Design, Not Chance," *Reporting on Reading* (June 1979):1-3.
4. JOHN HARKER, "Get Your Money's Worth from the Reading Consultant," *Journal of Reading* (October 1973):29-31.
5. WILLIAM KOTTMEYER, *Teacher's Guide for Remedial Reading* (New York: Webster/McGraw-Hill Book Co., 1959), 243.
6. DELWYN G. SCHUBERT, "Do Teachers Read About Reading?" *California Journal of Educational Research* (March 1960):94-96.

Appendixes

APPENDIX A ELEMENTS AND PRINCIPLES OF PHONICS

A fluent reader will have mastered the skills of phonics along with under-lying principles.[1] Appendix A provides an outline of elements and prin-ciples involved in this area for ready reference. These are drawn from manuals accompanying widely used basal reader series.

PHONICS

Consonants

I. A consonant is a letter which is produced by stopping or interrupting the breath by a speech organ. Those consonants that are produced with no vocal-cord vibration are called voiceless consonants. Examples are *p*, *t*, and *s*. Consonants that involve vocal-cord vibration in their pro-duction are known as voiced consonants. Examples are *g*, *l*, and *m*. When consonants are sounded in isolation, teachers should do their best to minimize the *uh* sound which inescapably must be added to some of them.

Any material appearing in these appendixes may be reproduced by teachers for their own use.

1. Since Clymer's pioneer research on the utility of phonic generalization was pub-lished in 1963 (*Reading Teacher*, January 1963), many other studies have appeared in the literature. Some of these are as follows: C. Winkley, "Which Accent Generaliza-tions Are Worth Teaching?" *Reading Teacher* (December 1966); M. H. Bailey, "The Utility of Phonic Generalizations in Grades One Through Six," *Reading Teacher* (Feb-ruary 1967); R. Emans, "The Usefulness of Phonic Generalizations Above the Primary Grades," *Reading Teacher* (February 1967); L. E. Burmeister, "Usefulness of Phonic Generalizations," *Reading Teacher* (January 1968); L. E. Burmeister, "Phonics in a Word Attack Program—Place and Content," *Proceedings of the International Reading Association*, 1970; L. E. Burmeister, "Final Vowel-consonant-e," *Reading Teacher* (February 1971); D. C. McFeeley, "Syllabication Usefulness in a Basic and Social Studies Vocabulary," *Reading Teacher* (May 1974). In General, it has been shown that some of the so-called rules that have been taught as gospel for decades have too many exceptions to warrant their being taught to children in their present form.

A. Some consonants represent several sounds.
1. Most often *c* sounds like *k*: *cone, candy, cup.* Once children generalize this principle, the following rhyme can be employed.

When *c* comes before *o, u,* and *a*
It sounds exactly like a *k.*

a. When the letter *c* precedes the vowels *i, e,* or *y,* usually it has the sound of *s.* Examples are *cent, cigar, cyclone.* Once children generalize this principle, the following rhyme can be employed.

When *c* comes before an *i, y,* or *e,*
It makes a hissing sound for me.

2. Most often *g* has a hard sound: *go, game, gun.*
a. When the letter *g* precedes the vowels *i, e,* or *y,* usually it has the sound of the letter *j.* Examples: *gist, gem, gym.* (Exceptions to this rule are fairly prevalent.)
3. When *y* begins a word, it acts as a consonant. Examples are *yes, yard, yoke.*
a. When *y* ends a one-syllable word, it sounds like a long **i.** Examples: *by, cry, sly.*
4. The letter *x* usually has the sound of *ks.* Examples: *box, tax, six.*
a. When *x* begins a word it never has the *ks* sound. Examples: *X-ray, xylophone.*
5. The letter *s* usually has the sound of *s* when it follows a voiceless sound. Examples: *boats* (*t* is voiceless), *rips* (*p* is voiceless).
a. The letter *s* usually has the sound of *z* when it follows a voiced sound. Examples are *cars* (*r* is voiced), *hums* (*m* is voiced).
B. Consonant blends are combinations of two or three letters which when pronounced give credence to each letter. The first letter blends into the second: *gr*apes, *st*ick, *bl*ack. Blends may also appear in terminal position. Examples: fir*st,* cha*sm,* cla*sp.*
C. Consonant digraphs are two-letter sounds. Examples: *ch*icken, *sh*oe, *th*umb, *th*at, wi*ng,* *ph*one, *wh*ere, rou*gh.* (It is important for the child to learn that each letter loses its individual sound when the letters are working together to make a new sound.)
D. When two consonants appear together, one of them may be silent.
1. When *b* follows *m,* the *b* usually is silent: *lamb, comb.*
2. When *t* follows *b,* the *b* usually is silent: *doubt, debt.*
3. When a vowel follows *gh,* the *h* is usually silent: *ghost, ghastly.*
4. When a vowel precedes *gh,* the *gh* usually is silent: *taught, light, weigh.*

5. When *d, m,* or *k* follow *l,* the *l* is usually silent: *would, palm, talk.*
6. When *s* follows *p,* the *p* usually is silent: *psalm, psychic.*
7. When *r* follows *w,* the w usually is silent: *wrench, write.*
8. When *ch* follows *t,* the *t* usually is silent: *witch, watch.*

Vowels

I. A vowel is a sound which is produced with little or no narrowing or obstructing of the speech organs. Phonetically, single vowels are the most inconsistent letters in the English alphabet. Each vowel—*a, e, i, o,* and *u* (sometimes *y* and *w*)—has a number of sounds. Fortunately, however, these sounds seems to fall roughly into two broad categories. These are the long and short sounds. Examples of the long and short vowel sounds are *ate, at; even, elephant; iron, ink; old, ox; unicorn, uncle.*

A. As stated previously, when *y* begins a word, it acts like a consonant, but when *y* ends a one-syllable word, it has a long *i* sound.
  1. When *y* ends a two-syllable word, it may sound like a short *i* or a long *e.* A difference of opinion exists among lexicographers. Actually, the sound of the *y* in these instances seems to be somewhere between a short *i* and a long *e.* Examples: *slowly, lovely.*

B. In words like *crow, blow,* and *know,* the *w* acts as a vowel so the *o* says its name.

C. Vowel diphthongs involve a slurring of two vowels; that is, one vowel glides or slides into the other. Examples are b*oy, oil;* c*ow, house.* (It should be noted that the double vowel rule does not apply to diphthongs.)

D. Following are principles that aid in determining vowel sounds:
  1. When a word has one vowel and that vowel is at the end of the word, usually it has a long sound. Examples: *go, me.*
  2. When a word has one vowel and that vowel is *not* at the end of the word, usually it has the short vowel sound. Examples: *at, in, cut, hot, bet.*
  3. When there are two vowels together in a word, usually the first says its name and the second one is silent. Examples: *boat, feet, seal.* When children generalize this principle, it can be turned into the following rhyme.

        When two vowels go walking
        The first one does the talking

  4. When there are two vowels in a word, one of which is a final *e,* the first vowel says its name and the *e* is silent. Examples: *fine, home, tune.* Children like to call this principle the "Magic E Rule."

5. If a single vowel in a word is followed by an *r*, the sound of the vowel usually is controlled by the sound of *r*. Examples: *bird, hurt, work, hard.*
   a. When *r* follows *e*, *i*, or *u*, only the *r* sound is heard: *her, fur, sir.*
   b. When *r* follows *a* or *o*, the vowel and the *r* are pronounced. The *a* has an *ah* sound and the *o* sounds like *aw*: *far, car, order, north.*
6. When the only vowel in a word is an *a*, followed by *l* or *w*, the *a* usually has neither the long nor short vowel sound.

PRINCIPLES THAT AID IN UNDERSTANDING ACCENT

1. When two-syllable words end in a consonant followed by *y*, the first syllable is accented. Examples: *love'ly, slow'ly.*
2. When the first syllable of a word is *de, re, be, ex,* or in, the accent is on the last syllable. Examples: *de press', re press', re turn', be ware', ex pect', in spect'.*
3. When the final syllable of a word ends in *le*, the syllable preceding it is usually accented. Exampes: *ta'ble, lit'tle.*
4. When endings form syllables, they are usually unaccented. Examples: *fox'es, tall'est, test'ed.*
5. When a word ends in a suffix, the accent usually falls on the root word. Examples: *sneeze, sneez'ing; fool, fool'ish.*
6. When words end in *ity, ic, ical, ian, ial,* or *ious*, the primary accent usually involves the syllable preceding the suffix. Examples: *pub lic'ity, bombas'tic, mu si'cian, of fi'cial, re lig'ious.*
7. When words end in *ate*, the primary accent usually falls on the third syllable from the end. Examples: *in ter med'i-ate, de pre'ci-ate.*

GENERALIZATIONS THAT APPLY IN ATTACKING COMPOUND, INFLECTED, OR DERIVED FORMS

1. Root words, prefixes, and suffixes are meaning units in words.
2. Doubling the final consonant, changing a final *y* to *i*, or dropping a final *e* before an ending or suffix usually does not change the sound of the root word.
3. When an ending or a suffix is preceded by a single vowel letter followed by a single consonant, the root word usually ends in *e*.
4. When an ending or a suffix is preceded by the letter *i*, the root word usually ends in *e*.
5. Inflectional variants can be formed by adding an ending or suffix without changing the root word. Examples: *hunting, talked, foxes, shorter.*

6. When root words end in a single consonant, the consonant is usually doubled before an ending is added. Examples: *hitting, running.*
7. When root words end in *e*, the *e* is usually dropped before adding an ending that begins with a vowel. Examples: *wiping, strangest.*
8. When root words end in *y*, the *y* is usually changed to *i* before an ending or suffix is added. Examples: *fried, replied.*
9. When root words end in *f*, the *f* is usually changed to *v* before an ending is added. Examples: *wharves, calves.*

PRINCIPLES THAT AID IN DETERMINING SYLLABLES IN WORDS

1. When the first vowel in a word is followed by a double consonant, the word is divided between the consonants. Examples: *rab/bit, chip/munk.* (This is not true, however, when the digraphs *sh, ch, th, wh,* and *ph* are involved.)
2. When the first vowel in a word is followed by a single consonant, that consonant usually begins the second syllable. Examples: *a/bove, pu/pil.*
3. When a word ends in *le*, the consonant preceding the *le* begins the last syllable. Examples: *cir/cle, a/ble.*
4. When the ending *ed* is preceded by *d* or *t*, it usually forms a separate syllable. Examples: *pad/ded, fit/ted.*
5. When the various endings *less, ment, cion,* and *sion* appear, they usually form separate syllables. Examples: *care/less, gov/ern/ment, sus/pi/cion, de/ci/sion.*

APPENDIX B GLOSSARY

Ability: Power to perform a physical or mental act; proficiency in any type of behavior.

Acceleration: A rate of development of progress in excess of normal; a promotion rate of more than one grade per year.

Accent: The stress given a certain syllable of a word to make it stand out over the other syllables of the word.

Accent, Primary: The syllable receiving the main emphasis in the pronunciation of a given word.

Accent, Secondary: A stress weaker than the primary accent and one falling upon a different syllable of a given word.

Accommodation: Adjustment or changes in the shape of the lens of the eye as an individual focuses for varying distances.

From D. Schubert, *A Dictionary of Terms and Concepts in Reading*, 2d ed. (Springfield, Ill.: Charles C. Thomas, 1968).

Acuity, auditory: Hearing sensitivity; keenness of hearing. Syn. auditory threshold.

Acuity, visual: The sharpness, clarity, or acuteness of vision.

Adjustment: The process whereby an individual finds and adapts modes of behavior which bring about a more satisfactory relationship with his/her environment.

Affix: That which is added to a root of a word; a suffix or prefix.

Age, achievement: An individual's achievement test score expressed in terms of the chronological age for which his/her achievement is average. Also known as educational age or accomplishment age.

Age, mental (MA): An individual's mental maturity level; the chronological age for which a given score on an intelligence test is average.

Age, reading (RA): An expression of the level of reading ability in terms of age, based on norms from a reading test.

Agraphia: A type of asphasia resulting from a lesion of the central nervous system manifested by an inability to express thoughts in written language.

Alexia: Visual aphasia or word blindness; loss of power to grasp the meaning of written or printed words and sentences. Syn. word blindness.

Amblyopia: Reduced acuity or dimness of vision that is not refractive or dependent on visible changes in the eye.

Analysis, phonetic: A method of analyzing a printed word to determine its pronunciation through the use of consonant and vowel sounds, blends, syllables, etc.

Analysis, Structural: A method of analyzing a printed word to determine its pronunciation by identifying meaningful parts—roots, inflectional endings, syllables, prefixes, and suffixes—which in turn may be blended into the sound of the word.

Analysis, Word: Analyzing an unfamiliar printed word for clues to its sound and/or meaning. Synonym: word attack.

Aniseikonia: A defect of vision in which the retinal images do not fuse, due usually to their differing in size by more than four or five percent.

Anomaly: Devation from the common rule, type, or form; an irregularity or abnormality.

Anoxia: A deficiency of oxygen.

Antonym: A word which is directly opposite in meaning to another word.

Aphasia: A loss of the ability to use language symbols, e.g., alexia, agraphia.

Aptitudes: Abilities and other characteristics, whether native or acquired, known or believed to be indicative of an individual's ability to learn in some particular area.

Aqueous humor: The fluid which fills the anterior and posterior chambers of the eye.

Astigmatism: Refractive error due to abnormality of the corneal curvature or irregularity of the crystalline lens.

Atypical: Not typical; not conforming to type; irregular or abnormal.

Auding: A term used by J. I. Brown to encompass the process of hearing plus the interpretation of comprehension of spoken language.

Audiometer: An instrument used to measure the acuity and range of hearing.

Auditory discrimination: The ability to discern differences between sounds that are closely similar.

Behavior, overt: A term referring to the observable or manifest behavior of an individual.

Behavioral objectives: Observable and measurable goals a pupil is expected to attain after receiving appropriate instruction.

Bibliotherapy: The use of selective books for their therapeutic effect on children who are mentally or emotionally disturbed.

Bilingual: The ability to speak more than one language fluently.

Binocular vision: Relating to both eyes acting together.

Blend: The fusion of two or more letter sounds in a word without the identity of either sound being lost. A blend may consist of two or more consonant letters (*st, bl, st*) or one or more consonants and a vowel (*bi* as in *big*).

Blend, Consonant: See definition of blend.

Blend, Final: The fusion of two or more letter sounds at the end of a word with each sound maintaining its identity.

Blending, Sound: The fusion of two or more letter sounds without losing the identity of either sound, for example, *t* and *r* in *train*.

Breve: A curved mark placed over a vowel to indicate the short sound, for example, *big*.

Caldecott awards: Yearly awards for excellence which are given to the illustrators of children's books.

Capacity: The ultimate extent to which an individual can develop when given optimum training and opportunity.

Case study: An intensive diagnostic analysis of an individual's abilities and perceptions involving both formal and informal methods in an effort to discover the nature of a difficulty, its causal factors, and the remedial program to be applied.

Central tendency: A measure designed to represent a distribution of scores, e.g., a mean, median, or mode; the mean, median, or modal score in a frequency distribution; commonly known as "average."

Chart, Snellen: Square black letters printed on a card, employed in testing the acuteness of distance vision; the letters vary in size, the 20/20 letter subtends an angle of five minutes of arc at a distance of 20 feet.

Clue, Configuration: A clue to word analysis based on the general shape or pattern of a printed word.

Clue, Context: Utilizing surrounding words, phrases, or sentences as an approach to word recognition and meaning.

Clue, Picture: A picture related to a unit in reading that provides a useful clue to its meaning.

Cognition: The process of perceiving or knowing.

Concave: Having a curved, depressed surface; the opposite of convex.

Concept: A classification or systematic organization of the total meaning an individual has for any idea, person, place, thing, or word.

Configuration clue: A clue to word analysis based on the general shape or pattern of a printed word.

Congenital: Present in the individual at birth but not necessarily determined by heredity.

Consonant: A letter representing a speech sound characterized by a closure or very strongly modified narrowing of the mouth or throat, for instance, *b, t, s.*

Consonant, Final: A consonant which appears at the end of a word.

Consonant, Initial: A consonant appearing as the first letter of a word.

Consonant, Medial: A consonant appearing inside a word.

Consonant, Voiced: A consonant sound which when produced is accompanied by vocal-cord vibration, for instance, *b, d, g.*

Consonant, Voiceless: A consonant sound which when produced is not accompanied by vocal-cord vibration, for instance, *f, h, s.*

Context clue: Utilizing surrounding words, phrases, or sentences as an approach to word recognition and meaning.

Convergence: The turning inward of the visual axes which normally takes place when fixating on an object closer than infinity.

Convex: Having a surface that is curved and elevated like the outside of a sphere; opposite of concave.

Cornea: The outer, transparent membrane covering the front of the eyeball.

Criterion test: A test designed to assess a student's mastery of a particular unit of instruction.

Crystalline lens: The transparent, convex lens in the eye which is situated behind the pupil.

Curve, normal: A graphical representation of a normal distribution of scores or measures that has a distinctive bell-shaped appearance; scores or measures distributed symmetrically about the mean.

Decibel: Unit for expressing the intensity of sound on a logarithmic scale.

Derivative: A word composed of a root plus a prefix and/or suffix, for example, *unhappy, happiness, unhappiness.* Synonym-derived form.

Deviation, standard: A measure of variability expressed in terms of the extent of the deviations from the mean of the distributions.

Diacritical Mark: A symbol placed over a letter to indicate the pronunciation.

Diagnosis, reading: A scientific analysis and description of a reading disability designed: (a) to identify the nature of the difficulty such as reading errors, faulty reading habits, and levels of reading competence; (b) to locate underlying causes, and (c) to prescribe corrective or remedial treatment. The process encompasses both formal and informal techniques involving interviews, observations, oral reading, silent reading, and intelligence tests along with an assessment of personal and environmental factors conditioning learning.

Digraph, Consonant: Two consonants which lose their individual identity and go together to represent a single sound, for example, *ch* as in *chicken*.

Digraph, Vowel: Two vowels that together make one sound, for example, *oa* in *boat*.

Diopter: The unit of refracting power of lenses, denoting a lens which has a focal length of one meter.

Diphthong: A union of two vowels to make a gliding sound, as *oy* in *boy* or *ow* in *owl*.

Diplopia: Double vision; one object is seen as two.

Dominance, cerebral: The tendency of one hemisphere of the brain to be more involved in the control of body movements. Syn. hemispheric dominance.

Duction: Movement of the two eyes in opposite directions while binocular single vision is maintained.

Dyslexia: A controversial term considered by some as congenital word blindness that is hereditary in nature; used by many as synonymous with specific language disability or with reading disability.

Electroencephalogram (EEG): A graphic record of wave-like changes in the electrical potentials of the brain as derived from the use of electrodes placed on the scalp.

Emmetropia: The normal or ideal condition of the eye in refraction in which, without accommodation, an infinitely distant object is imaged sharply on the retina.

Encephalitis: A disease process involving inflammation of the brain substance and its coverings.

Esophoria: A type of heterophoria characterized by a tendency of the eyes to turn inward when fusion is broken.

Esotropia: A manifest convergence of the eyes; crossed eyes.

Etiology: Deals with the causes or origins of a disorder.

Etymology: The science which treats the origin and history of words.

Exophoria: A type of heterophoria characterized by a tendency of the eyes to turn outward when fusion is broken.

Exotropia: A manifest turning outward of one or the other eye.

Expectancy, reading: A term indicative of an individual's potential success in reading, ordinarily determined by his/her auditory comprehension and various combinations of mental and chronological age.

Expectancy, reading: A term indicative of an individual's potential success in reading, ordinarily determined by his/her auditory comprehension and various combinations of mental and chronological age.

Extrovert: An individual manifestating outwardly directed personality traits who is more interested in his/her environment and other people than in himself; opposed to introvert.

Eye movements, saccadic: The quick, jerky movements of the eye characteristic of shifting fixation points as in reading.

Eye-span: The amount of material which can be perceived in one fixation.

Eye-voice span: In oral reading the distance between the point to which the eyes have moved ahead in the line of print and the point which the voice has reached in pronouncing words.

Farpoint: A test distance normally considered optical infinity or twenty feet; usually associated with chart or blackboard reading.

Fixations: Brief pauses in eye movement during the reading act.

Formula, readability: A method of estimating the difficulty or readability of printed material usually based on vocabulary difficulty, sentence length and other factors.

Fovea: The area within the macula where the cones become thinner and more concentrated, providing the highest visual acuity.

Fusion: The process of blending the images from the two eyes into a single impression.

Genetic: Pertaining to the genes as determiners of hereditary traits.

Grapheme: A letter of the alphabet; the sum of all written letters and letter combinations that represent one phoneme.

Hawthorne Effect: A term which evolved as a result of a series of experiments at the Hawthorne Plant of the Western Electric Company and now pertains to any situation in which experimental conditions are such that the fact that an individual is participating in an experiment or is receiving special attention will improve his performance.

Heredty: Innate capacity of an individual to develop traits and characteristics transmitted by his ancestors.

Heteronym: A word spelled the same as another but having a different pronunciation and meaning, for example, *lead* (to conduct) and *lead* (a metal).

Heterophoria: A tendency of the eyes to deviate when fusion is broken.

Homograph: One of two or more identical in spelling but different in derivation and meaning, as *bow* (a tie) and *bow* (to bend).

Homonym: A word having the same pronunciation as another but differing from it in origin, meaning, and often, in spelling, for example, *bare* and *bear*; homophone.

Homophone: Words that are spelled differently but pronounced alike, for instance, *to, too, two*.

Humor, aqueous: The fluid which fills the anterior and posterior chambers of the eye.

Humor, vitreous: The semifluid, transparent substance inside the main part of the eyeball.

Hyperopia: The lack of refracting power, when accommodation is relaxed, to focus parallel rays of light on the retina. Syn. for far-sightedness, hypermetropia.

Hyperthyroidism: A condition due to excessive functional activity of the thyroid gland characterized by increased rate of basal metabolism.

Hypocusia: Impaired hearing.

Hypophoria: A type of heterophoria involving a downward deviation of the line of sight when fusion is broken.

Hypothyroidism: A condition resulting from a deficiency of thyroid secretion bringing about a lowered basal metabolism.

Illiterate: An individual, ten years of age or older, who has not learned to read or write.

Inflected Form: A word to which an inflectional ending has been added; for example, *s* may be added to the root word *fight*.

Inflectional Ending: Designating or pertaining to an affix used in inflection, for example, John*'s*, sing*s*, play*ed*, long*er*.

Initial Teaching Alphabet (ITA): A 44 letter alphabet evolved in England by Sir James Pitman which is designed to simplify learning to read. It employs all letters of our alphabet except x and q plus 20 new symbols, some of which are combinations or augmentations of conventional letters.

Intelligence, abstract: The ability to deal effectively with problems involving verbal, mathematical, and other abstract concepts.

Intelligence, nonverbal: The ability to work effectively with problems involving the use of abstract signs or symbols, e.g., performance and nonlanguage tests.

Introvert: An individual given to introspection; opposed to extrovert.

IQ (Intelligence quotient): A measure of a child's rate of development up to the age at which he is tested, computed by dividing the mental age (MA) as determined on a standardized test of intelligence by the chronological or life age (CA).

Joplin Plan: An interclass grouping plan in which children from several successive grades are grouped during the reading period according to reading ability and receive instruction from a teacher designated to work with a particular level.

Kinesthesis: The sense whose end organs lie in muscles, tendons, and joints and which is stimulated by bodily movements and tensions. Syn. kinesthesia.

Linguistics: The scientific study of the structure and sound signals within languages. Linguistics can be divided into three structural levels—phonemes, morphemes, and syntax.

Macron: A short, straight mark placed horizontally over a vowel to indicate that it has the long sound, e.g., ōver.

Macula lutea: The yellow spot on the retina about 1/12 inch in size, surrounding the fovea which comprises the area of acute or central vision.

Maddox Rod: A glass rod or series of parallel glass rods used with a small light source to test for a phoria or tropia.

Massachusetts Vision Test: Test of far-point acuity and eye-muscle balance; does not test near-point vision. Variations of this test include the American Optical School Vision Screening Test, King Sight Screeners, and the New York Vision Tester.

Maturation: Changes in the organism as a result of inner development—anatomical, physiological, and neurological.

Maturity: The state or quality of being fully developed in form, structure, and function with regard to a trait or number of traits.

Median (Md): The point on a distribution of test scores, or other measures, below which 50 percent of the cases occur.

Method, eclectic: The choosing of compatible features from two or more instructional methods that are best suited to bring about optimum learning.

Method, kinesthetic: A method of treating reading disability by having pupils trace the outlines of words.

Method, language-experience: A reading teaching method that is based upon the oral and written expression and identified needs of children.

Minus lens: A concave lens used in the correction of myopia.

Monocular: Pertaining to one eye.

Morpheme: The smallest meaningful unit in the structure of words (a root word, a prefix, a suffix, or an inflectional ending); for instance, *rainy* consists of two morphemes, the root *rain* and the suffix *y*.

Motivation: The incentives, both inherent and acquired, which initiate and sustain any given activity.

Multiple causation: The concept that a number of factors may contribute to the characteristics of an individual's behavior.

Myopia: Near-sightedness; a defect due to excessive refractitng power when accommodation is relaxed, resulting in parallel rays of light focusing in front of the retina.

Negativism: Behavior characterized by a tendency to resist suggestions or by adopting a contradictory mode of response.

Newberry awards: Yearly awards for excellence which are given to authors of children's books.

Norm: A standard, model, or criterion for judging individuals or groups; e.g., the mean or median score attained by representative age or grade groups on standardized tests.

Norm, age: Mean or median scores on standardized tests representative of successive chronological age groups; age equivalents for raw score values.

Nystagmus: Constant involuntary movements of the eyeballs.

Ophthalmograph: An instrument for photographing eye movements during reading; e.g., The Reading Eye-manufactured by the Educational Developmental Laboratories.

Ophthalmologist: A medical doctor who is concerned with medical and surgical care of the eye and its appendages and who has completed a residency in opthalmology.

Optician: A person who makes, fabricates, and often dispenses eye glasses or other optical instruments.

Optimum: Best, most favorable; often implying many factors to be considered.

Optometrist: A Doctor of Optometry (O.D.) is a person specifically educated, trained, and state licensed to examine the eyes and related structures to determine the presence of vision problems, eye diseases or other abnormalities. He prescribes and adapts lenses or other optical aids and utilizes visual training to preserve, restore and enhance efficiency of vision.

Orthoptics: The teaching and training process for the improvement of ocular perception and coordination of the two eyes for efficient and comfortable binocular vision.

Orthorater: Trade name for a stereoscopic visual screening instrument of the Brewster type with targets for measuring visual acuity, phorias, color perception, and stereopsis.

Otologist: A physician and/or surgeon who specializes in the branch of medicine dealing with the ear and its diseases.

Pacer: A machine employing a shutter, shadow, or line marker of some kind to guide the reader according to a predetermined rate.

Percentile: A point score in a distribution below which falls the percent of cases indicated by the given percentile. Thus the 20th percentile denotes the score or point below which 20 percent of the scores fall.

Perception: Awareness and interpretation of external objects as a result of impressions received through any one of the sense organs; a mental complex based upon sensory experiences.

Perception, haptic: Learning or recognizing words through tactual and kinesthetic clues.

Perception, kinesthetic: Recognition of words through stimulation of nerve ending in the muscles, tendons, and joints as a result of tracing or writing.

Perception, word: The act of meaningfully perceiving words in response to general configuration and sentence context without consciously noting individual letters or word parts.

Philology: The scientific and historic study of the origin, development, and relationships of language.

Phoneme: A speech sound or group of variants of one speech sound.

Phonetics: The science of speech sounds, including their pronunciation, the action of the larynx, tongue, and lips in sound production, and the symbolization of sounds.

Phonics:The study of sound-letter relationships in reading and spelling and the use of this knowledge in recognizing and pronouncing words.

Phonics, synthetic: Sounding words letter by letter, or in phonic units, and then blending the sounds together.

Phonics, whole word: Using words in which given phonemes are easily identified rather than sounding phonemes in isolation.

Phonogram: A letter or group of letters representing a speech sound.

Phoria: Syn. heterophoria.

Plus lens: A convex or magnifying lens used to correct far-sightedness.

Prefix: A letter, syllable, or group of syllables placed at the beginning of a word to modify or qualify its meaning.

Presbyopia: Impairment of vision due to loss of elasticity of the crystalline lens resulting in lack of accommodative power when reading.

Procedure, cloze: A technique introduced in 1953 by Wilson L. Taylor for the purpose of measuring comprehension and readability of materials. Cloze tests or practice exercises are constructed by deleting words in a regular manner from a passage. Underlined blank spaces are substituted for the word deleted. Individuals taking such tests or exercise attempt to fill in the paces with appropriate words.

Program, balanced reading: A program in which there is balance between study-type reading, recreational reading, oral reading and silent reading, etc., with no one aspect emphasized to the neglect of the other.

Psychologist, school: A member of the school staff (holding a M.A. or Ph.D. in psychology) with specialized training in psychological procedures, individual diagnosis, and testing, who assists teachers and parents in interpreting problems involving pupil behavior and learning.

Psychometrics: The science involving the administration and interpretation of psychological tests.

Quartile: One of the three points that divide the measures of a distribution into four equal groups. The lower quartile sets off the lowest fourth of the group.

Quoient, intelligence (IQ): A commonly used measure of the rate of mental growth; a measure of brightness expressed as the ratio of mental age to chronological age. $IQ = MA/CA \times 100$.

Quotient, reading: A quotient determined by dividing an individual's reading age by his mental age; considered an index of the reader's rate of learning to read.

Readability: An objective measure of the difficulty of a book usually in terms of average sentence length and vocabulary load.

Readiness, reading: The level of maturity a child must reach before he/she can succeed in formal reading under normal instruction. Factors considered include emotional and intellectual maturity, chronological age, vision, hearing, environmental experience, language development, and cognitive development.

Reading, corrective: Remedial activities carried on by a regular classroom teacher within the framework of regular class instruction.

Reading, remedial: Remedial activities taking place outside the framework of class instruction, usually conducted by a special teacher of reading.

Reading distance: The distance from the eyes to the point at which the eyes normally converge in reading; recommended working distance is that which is approximately equal to the distance between the middle knuckle of the child's clenched fist and elbow joint as measured on the outside of the arm; usually found to be between 14" and 16" among adults, and 10" and 13" among children.

Reading level, capacity: The level at which an individual's reading ability measures up to his/her expected potential.

Reading level, frustration: The lowest level at which an individual's reading skills break down; fluency disappears, word recognition errors are common, comprehension is defective, retention is poor, and evidence of emotional tension and discomfort manifests itself.

Reading level, independent: The highest reading level at which an individual can read easily and fluently, without help, with few word recognition errors and very good comprehension and retention.

Reading level, instructional: The highest level at which an individual reads satisfactorily provided he receives teacher preparation and supervision; word recognition errors are infrequent, and comprehension and retention are acceptable.

Records, cumulative: Pupils' individual records kept by the school which usually include educational, social, vocational, physical and health data.

Reliability: The extent to which a test is consistent in its measurements expressed by a reliability coeifficient or standard error of measurement.

Retention: Learning that permits later recognition and recall.

Root, Word: The basic form from which words are developed by the addition of prefixes, suffixes, and inflectional endings.

Scanning: A type of reading in which an individual attempts to locate specific information without reading the entire selection involved.

Schwa: A term borrowed from Hebrew phonetics designating an indistinct vowel, one represented by the letters, *a, e, i, o,* and *u* in unaccented syllables, for example, *April, problems*; represented in phonetic script by an inverted *e*.

Score, derived: A score that has been converted from a raw score into its equivalent on another scale, preferably one with a standard reference point and equal units; e.g., reading age, percentile rank, T-score, etc.

Score, grade placement: A derived or converted score on an achievement test that designates an individual's grade level for which the score is average. Syn. grade equivalent score.

Score, raw: The numerical score obtained by an individual on a test; usually stated in terms of items answered correctly.

Score, standard: A score based on the deviation of the raw score from the mean of the distribution expressed in terms of multiples of the standard deviation; e.g., T-score, z-score, stanine.

Score, T: A derived score obtained by converting raw scores to standard scores. The T score scale has a mean of 50 and a standard deviation of 10.

Sight word: A word recognized because of its shape or configuration, rather than by the blending of parts into the whole.

Skimming: Rapid reading to gain a general impression.

Squint: Strabismus.

Stereoscope: An instrument with two eye pieces through which slightly different views of the same picture are seen side by side, so that a three dimensional effect results.

Stereopsis: The ability to perceive visually objects in three dimensions because of a disparity in rentinal imagery.

Strabismus: The manifest condition of the eye in which the visual axes fail to maintain bi-fixation when looking at an object of regard. Syn. heterotropia.

Strephosymbolia: A term coined by Orton referring to the perception of words and letters as if they were reversed by a mirror (twisted symbols).

Structural analysis: A method of analyzing a printed word to determine its pronunciation by identifying meaningful parts—roots, inflectional endings, syllables, prefixes, and suffixes—which in turn may be blended into the sound of the word.

Suffix: A letter or syllable added at the end of a word or root to modify its meaning, such as the *ment* in *agreement*.

Suppression: Repression of vision in one eye or in specific retinal areas of either eye.

Syllabication: Synonym of syllabification.

Syllabification: The act of forming or separating words into syllables.

Syllable: A unit of pronunciation consisting of a vowel sound alone or with one or more consonant sounds and pronounced with one impulse of the voice.

Syllable, Closed: A syllable ending with a consonant, for example: *set*.

Syllable, Open: A syllable ending in a vowel, for example, *we*.

Syndrome: A complexus of symptoms and signs, which, when considered together, characterize a disorder or disease.

Synonym: A word that expresses the same idea as another word but usually differs from it in some shade of meaning.

Syntax: The branch of grammar dealing with sentence structure and the arrangement of words as elements in a sentence to show their relationship.

Tachistoscope: An instrument which exposes perceptual material for a brief period of time so as to permit a single glance; used in reading, spelling, and visual perception training.

Telebinocular: A trade name for a Brewster-type stereoscope for measuring acuity, phorias; color perception, and stereopsis.

Test, achievement: A test that measures an individual's mastery of information or skills taught in school; both teacher-made and published standardized tests are included.

Test, Eames Eye: An inexpensive, near-point visual screening test requiring the use of a simple stereoscope.

Tinnitus: A ringing or roaring sound in the ears.

Trigraph, Consonant: A combination of three consonants, for example, *str*.

Tropia: A manifest deviation of an eye from the normal position when both eyes are open and uncovered; strabismus or squint.

Underconvergence: The tendency of the eyes to turn out. See exophoria and exotropia.

Validity: The extent to which a test fulfills its purpose or use.

Vision, binocular: Relating to both eyes acting together.

Visual span: The number of letters, symbols, digits, or words that can be identified correctly in one fixation; perceptual span or recognition span.

Vocabulary, sight: The words which an individual need not sound out but recognizes immediately.

Vocalization: Movement of lips, tongue, or vocal apparatus during silent reading; articulation without speaking the words outloud during silent reading.

Vowel: A single, open vocal sound in which there is no audible frication or stoppage.

Word, Compound: A word composed of two or more elements, themselves usually words: *housetop, bluebird*.

Word, Monosyllabic: A one-syllable word.

Word, Polysyllabic: A word having two or more syllables.

Word-Attack Skills: Synonym of word analysis.

Reading Readiness: Group

Name of Test	Grade Level	Description	Number of Forms	Working Time Minutes	Publisher
American School Reading Readiness Test	1	Vocabulary, discrimination of letter forms, recognition of words, discrimination of geometric forms, following directions, memory for geometric shapes	1	45	Bobbs-Merrill Co.
Binson-Beck Reading Readiness Test	Kg-1	Picture vocabulary, visual discrimination, following directions, memory for story, motor control	1	40	Acorn Publishing Co.
Clymer-Barrett Prereading Battery	K-1	Visual discrimination, auditory discrimination, and visual-motor skills	2	90 30 (Short form)	Personnel Press
Gates-MacGinitie Reading Readiness Test	Kg-1	Listening comprehension, auditory discrimination, visual discrimination, following directions, letter recognition, visual-motor coordination, auditory blending	1	Untimed	Teachers College, Columbia University
Harrison-Stroud Reading Readiness Profiles	Kg-1	Using symbols, visual discrimination, using context, auditory discrimination, naming letters.	1	76	Houghton Mifflin

Name of Test	Grade Level	Description	Number of Forms	Working Time Minutes	Publisher
Lee-Clark Readiness Test	K-1	Discrimination of letter forms and word forms	1	20	California Test Bureau
Metropolitan Readiness Tests	K-1	Linguistic maturity, perceptual abilities, muscular coordination and motor skills, number and letter knowledge, ability to follow directions, and attention span	2	60	Harcourt Brace Jovanovich
Murphy-Durrell Diagnostic Reading Readiness Test	1	Auditory perception, visual perception, rate of learning	1	72	Harcourt Brace Jovanovich
Reading Readiness Test (M. J. Van Wagenen)	1	Information, perception of relations, vocabulary, memory span, word discrimination, word learning	2	30	U.S. Educational Test Bureau

Oral Reading: Individual

Name of Test	Grade Level	Description	Number of Forms	Working Time Minutes	Publisher
Diagnostic Reading Tests, Lower Level, Section IV, Oral Reading (Frances Triggs et al.)	4-6	Accuracy and comprehension of oral reading	2	20	Committee on Diagnostic Reading Tests

Test	Grades	Measures	Time (min.)	Publisher
Gilmore Oral Reading Test	1-8	Accuracy, comprehension, and rate of oral reading	20	Harcourt Brace Jovanovich
Gray's Oral Reading Paragraphs	1-12	Accuracy of oral reading	4	Untimed Psychological Corp.
Leavell Analytical Oral Reading Test	1-8	Accuracy and comprehension of oral reading	20	U.S. Educational Test Bureau

Word Recognition and Word Analysis

Test	Grades	Measures	Time (min.)	Publisher
Auditory Blending (Roswell-Chall)	2-6	Auditory blending	5	Essay Press
California Phonics Survey	7-Adult	Word analysis	40	California Test Bureau
Diagnostic Reading Test of Word Analysis Ross and Chall (Individual)	2-6	Word analysis	5	Essay Press
Diagnostic Silent Reading Test (Bond et al.)	3-8	Word recognition, auding	45	Lyons & Carnahan
Diagnostic Word Analysis Skills (Roswell and Chall)	1-4	Word analysis skills	5	Essay Press

Name of Test	Grade Level	Description	Number of Forms	Working Time Minutes	Publisher
Doren Diagnostic Reading Test	3-8	Eleven word-recognition skills	1	Untimed	American Guidance Service
Flash-X Sight Vocabulary	1-2	Word recognition	1	Untimed	Bausch & Lomb
Fry Group Phonic Analysis Test	1-3	Vowels, consonants, blends, syllabication	1	Untimed	Dreier Educational Systems
Fry Instant Word Recognition Test	1-4	Instant recognition of 600 words	2	Untimed	Dreier Educational Systems
Johnson Basic Sight Vocabulary	1-2	Sight vocabulary	2	45-60	Personnel Press
McCullough Word Analysis Test	4-8	Word analysis	1	Untimed	Teachers College, Columbia University
Phonics Knowledge Survey	1-6	Word analysis, phonics	1	30	Teachers College, Columbia University
Wide Range Vocabulary	3-Adult	Word recognition	2	Untimed	Psychological Corp.

Test	Grade	Skills	Forms	Time (min.)	Publisher
Gates-McKillop Reading Diagnostic Tests	1-6	Word recognition, word analysis	2	60-90	Bureau of Publications, Teachers College, Columbia

Silent Reading (Diagnostic)

Test	Grade	Skills	Forms	Time (min.)	Publisher
Learning Methods Test (Mills)	Kg-3	Learning proficiency visual-auditory, kinesthetic	1	80	Mills Center, Fort Lauderdale, Fla.
New Development Reading Tests. Bond et al. (Group)	1-2	Word recognition, comprehension	2	40	Lyons & Carnahan
Diagnostic Battery Section II (Triggs)	7-12	Five comprehension skills	4	Untimed	Committee on Diagnostic Reading Tests
Iowa Silent Reading, Elementary	4-8	Eight comprehension skills	4	49	Harcourt Brace Jovanovich
Stroud-Hieronymous Primary Reading Profile	1-2	Word recognition, word analysis, comprehension	1	six tests 6-18	Houghton Mifflin
Test of Study Skills	4-9	References, graphs, tables, maps	2	60	Steck-Vaughn

Silent Reading (Survey): Group

Name of Test	Grade Level	Description	Number of Forms	Working Time Minutes	Publisher
California Reading Tests		Meaning vocabulary comprehension	2	20-50	California Test Bureau
Elementary	4-6				
Junior High	7-9				
New Developmental Reading Tests					Lyons & Carnahan
Lower Primary	1-2.6	Basic reading vocabulary, comprehension	2	45	
Upper Primary	2.5-3.9		2	45	
Intermediate	4-6	Basic reading vocabulary, reading for information, relationships, interpretation, appreciation	2	45	
Iowa Test of Basic Skills Basic Skills Test B Work-Study Skills		Reading maps, graphs, charts and tables; use of references, index, and dictionary	4	Two 45-Minute Periods	Houghton Mifflin
Elementary	3-5				
Advanced	5-9				
Garvey Primary Reading Test	1-3	Recognition of form, sight vocabulary, and comprehension	2	40	California Test Bureau

Test	Grade	Skills			Publisher
Gates-MacGinitie Reading Tests					
Primary Survey D	1-3	Vocabulary, comprehension	2	47	Teachers College, Columbia University
	4-6	Vocabulary, comprehension, speed	3	45	
Survey E	7-9	Vocabulary, comprehension, speed	3	45	
Ingraham-Clark Diagnostic Reading Tests		Meaning vocabulary, comprehension, speed and accuracy of reading	2	40	California Test Bureau
Primary	1-3				
Intermediate	4-8				
Iowa Every-Pupil Tests of Basic Skills in Silent Reading Comprehension		Meaning vocabulary, comprehension; noting details, organization, total meaning			Houghton Mifflin
Elementary	3-5		4	46	
Advanced	5-9		4	68	
Iowa Silent Reading Test, Elementary	4-8	Rate of reading, meaning vocabulary, comprehension, work-study skills	4	49	Harcourt Brace Jovanovich
Nelson Silent Reading Test	3-9	Meaning vocabulary, comprehension; general significance, details, prediction of outcomes	3	30	Houghton Mifflin

Name of Test	Grade Level	Description	Number of Forms	Working Time Minutes	Publisher
Sangren-Woody Silent Reading Test	4-8	Word meaning, rate, fact material, total meaning, central thought, following directions, organization	2	27	Harcourt Brace Jovanovich
Stanford Diagnostic Reading Test	25-85	Vocabulary, comprehension, syllabication, auditory skills, phonic analysis, rate	2	Level I-37 Level II-93	Psychological Corporation
Traxler Silent Reading Test	7-10	Rate, story comprehension, word meaning, paragraph comprehension	4	46	Bobbs-Merrill Co.
(Additional tests contained in test batteries)					

Listening Tests (Oral and Silent)

Name of Test	Grade Level	Description	Number of Forms	Working Time Minutes	Publisher
Auditory Skills Test Battery (Woodcock et al.)	3-Adult	Auditory skills	1	10-15	American Guidance Service
Brown-Carlsen Listening Comprehension Test	9-12	Comprehension of spoken language	2	50	Harcourt Brace Jovanovich
Botel Reading Inventory (Group-Ind.)	1-12	Word recognition, word analysis, auding	1	Untimed	Follett

Test	Grade	Skills Measured	Forms	Time	Publisher
Classroom Reading Inventory	2-10	Oral reading, word list	1	Untimed	Wm. C. Brown
Diagnostic Reading Scales. Spache (Individual)	1-8	Vocabulary, comprehension word analysis, auding	1	60	California Test Bureau
Durrell Analysis of Reading Difficulty	1-6	Oral and silent reading, listening, word analysis, phonics	1	Untimed	Harcourt Brace Jovanovich
Durrell Reading Listening Series	1-9	Comprehension of spoken language	2	65	Harcourt Brace Jovanovich
Peabody Picture Vocabulary Test	Kg-12	Auding	2	15	American Guidance Service
Reading Placement Inventory	1-9	Oral reading, word recognition, instructional reading level	1	Untimed	Economy Co.
Step Listening Tests	4-9	Comprehension of spoken language	4	35	Cooperative Test Division
Test Auditory Discrimination (individual)	Kg-13	Auditory discrimination	1	15	American Guidance Service
Wepman Auditory Discrimination Test (individual)	1-6	Auditory discrimination	2	10	Language Research Associates

Group Intelligence Tests

Name of Test	Grade Level	Description	Number of Forms	Working Time Minutes	Publisher
California Test of Mental Maturity		Language and nonlanguage tests of memory, spatial relationships, logical reasoning, vocabulary			California Test Bureau
Preprimary Series	K-1		1	90	
Primary Series	1-3		1	90	
Elementary Series	4-8		1	90	
Intermediate Series	7-10		1	90	
California Short-Form Test of Mental Maturity		Language test of numerical quantity, inference, and vocabulary; nonlanguage tests of sensing right and left, manipulation of areas, similarities			California Test Bureau
Preprimary Series	K-1		1	45	
Primary Series	1-3		1	45	
Elementary Series	4-8		1	45	
Intermediate Series	7-10		1	45	
Chicago Non-Verbal Examination	1-12	Designed to measure the intelligence of deaf and foreign-born children and children who are handicapped in language area	1	25	Psychological Corp.

Test	Grade	Description	Forms	Time (min.)	Publisher
Davis-Eells Test of General Intelligence or Problem Solving Ability		Ability to solve problems common to all urban cultural groups			Harcourt Brace Jovanovich
Grade	1		1	60	
Grade	2		1	90	
Elementary	3-6		1	120	
Goodenough Intelligence Test	K-1	Based on spontaneous drawings of children	1		Harcourt Brace Jovanovich
Henmon-Nelson Tests of Mental Ability (self-marking)	3-8	Vocabulary, number completion, analogies	3	30	Psychological Corp.
Kuhlmann-Anderson Intelligence Tests	K-8	Separate booklet for each grade	1	30	Educational Test Bureau
Otis Quick-Scoring Test of Mental Ability		Revision of Otis Self-Administering Intelligence Test			Harcourt Brace Jovanovich
Alpha Test	1-4		2	25	
Beta Test	4-9		2	30	
Pintner General Ability Tests—Verbal Series		Seven tests composed entirely of pictures			Harcourt Brace Jovanovich
Primary	K-2		3	25	
Elementary	2-4	Scale 1, picture content Scale 2, reading content	2	45	
Intermediate	4-9	Verbal content; reasoning, vocabulary, logical selection, etc.	2	45	

Name of Test	Grade Level	Description	Number of Forms	Working Time Minutes	Publisher
Pintner General Ability Tests—Nonlanguage Series	4-9	Mental functions independent of word knowledge and facility	2	50	Harcourt Brace Jovanovich
SRA Primary Mental Abilities					Science Research Associates
Ages 5-7	K-2	Verbal meaning, quantitative, space, perceptual, speed, motor	1	35	
Ages 7-11	2-6	Verbal meaning, space, reasoning, perception, numbers	1	35	
Ages 11-17	6-12	Verbal meaning, space, reasoning, number, word fluency	1	26	

Screening Tests—Vision

Name of Test	Grade Level	Description	Number of Forms	Working Time Minutes	Publisher
Eames Eye Test		Near-point visual skills	1	5-10	Harcourt Brace Jovanovich
Keystone Telebinocular		Far- and near-point visual skills	1	10-15	Mast/Keystone
Massachusetts Vision Test		Far-point acuity, eye muscle balance at distance and near	1	5-10	American Optical Co.
Orthorater		Far- and near-point visual skills	1	10-15	Bausch and Lomb Optical Co.

Test	Purpose			Source
Pola-Mirror Test	Near-point binocularity, suppression	1	1	College Bookstore 950 W. Jefferson Blvd., Los Angeles, Calif. 90007
Reduced Snellen	Near-point acuity	1	2-4	Bausch & Lomb
Snellen Chart	Far-point acuity	1	2-4	American Optical Co.
Worth 4-Dot Test	Binocularity, near-point fusion, suppression	1	1-3	House of Vision

Developmental Tests

What Do Diagnostic Reading Tests Diagnose? Skills Included in Six Analytical Reading Measures*

DEVELOPMENTAL READING TESTS

	Botel Reading Inventory	Silent Reading Diagnostic Tests	Durrell Analysis of Reading Difficulty	Gilmore Oral Reading Test	Diagnostic Reading Scale	Gates-McKillop Reading Diagnostic Tests
Silent Reading Comprehension			X		X	
Oral Reading Comprehension			X	X	X	
Oral Reading Accuracy			X	X	X	X
Oral Reading Rate			X	X	X	
Listening Comprehension			X		X	
Word Recognition (oral)	X		X		X	X
Word Recognition (silent)		X				
Word Recognition in context (silent)	X					
Phrase Reading (oral)						X
Recognition of phonetic word elements (oral)	X	X			X	X
Recognition of phonetic word parts (silent and listening)			X			
Root Words (silent)		X				

418

Rhyming Words (listening or silent)	X	X				
Word Opposites (listening and/or silent)	X					
Word Blending (silent)		X				
Word Blending (oral)					X	X
Saying Syllables					X	X
Number and accent syllables (listening)	X					
Syllabication (silent)		X				
Identifying Letter Sounds (listening)		X	X			
Identifying Beginning Word Sounds (listening)	X	X	X			
Identifying Word Endings (listening)			X		X	
Saying Letter Sounds					X	
Identifying consonant blends and/or digraphs (listening)	X					X
Saying consonant blends and/or digraphs			X			
Identifying long and short vowels (oral)	X				X	X
Identifying long and short vowels (listening)					X	X
Naming capital and lowercase letters (oral)					X	
Spelling (listening)			X			
Spelling (oral)			X			
Reversible Words (silent)		X			X	
Visual memory of words (silent)			X			

*T. Trela, "What Do Diagnostic Reading Tests Diagnose? Skills Included in Six Analytical Reading Measures," *Elementary English Journal* 43 (April 1966): 370-372. Used by permission of author and the National Council of Teachers of English.

APPENDIX D BIBLIOGRAPHY

As an aid to teachers and administrators in selecting useful books for their personal library and for the school library as well, Appendix D has been prepared. Teachers as professional workers cannot afford to neglect their professional library if they are to maintain professional status. Appendix F provides lists of worthwhile professional books and materials and a list of sources of books adapted for retarded readers. An ample supply of these books is essential in every grade if retarded readers are to be provided with books for recreational reading that are of appropriate difficulty and interest.

SELECTED PROFESSIONAL BOOKS AND PAMPHLETS

BADER, LOIS A., *Reading Diagnosis and Remediation in Classroom and Clinic*. New York: Macmillan Publishing Co., Inc., 1980.

BOND, GUY L. and TINKER, MILES. *Reading Difficulties: Their Diagnosis and Correction*. 3rd ed. New York: Appleton-Century-Crofts, 1973.

BURMEISTER, LOU E. *Words from Print to Meaning*. Reading, Mass. Addison-Wesley Publishing Co., 1975.

BURNS, PAUL C. and ROE, BETTY D. *Reading Activities for Today's Elementary Schools*. Chicago: Rand McNally College Publishing Company, 1979.

CARRILLO, LAWRENCE. *Teaching Reading*. New York: St. Martin's Press, 1976.

DALLMAN, MARTHA, ROUCH, ROGER, CHANG, LYNETTE, and DeBOER, JOHN. *The Teaching of Reading*. 4th ed. New York: Holt, Rinehart & Winston, 1974.

DOWNING, JOHN, ed. *Comparative Reading: Cross-national Studies of Behavior and Processes in Reading and Writing*. New York: Macmillan Co., 1973.

DURKIN, DOLORES. *Teaching Them to Read*. 3rd ed. Boston: Allyn and Bacon, 1978.

DURKIN, DOLORES. *Teaching Young Children to Read*, 2nd ed. Boston: Allyn and Bacon, Inc., 1976.

EKWALL, ELDON E., *Diagnosis and Remediation of the Disabled Reader*. Boston: Allyn and Bacon, Inc., 1976.

EKWALL, ELDON E. *Locating and Correcting Reading Difficulties*, 2nd ed. Columbus, Ohio: Charles E. Merrill Publishing Co., 1977.

EKWALL, ELDON E. *Teacher's Handbook on Diagnosis and Remediation in Reading*. Rockleigh, N.J.: Allyn and Bacon, Inc., 1978.

GARLAND, COLDEN. *Developing Competence in Teaching Reading*. Dubuque, Iowa: Wm. C. Brown Company, Publishers, 1978.

GIBSON, ELEANOR and LEVIN, HARRY. *The Psychology of Reading*. Cambridge, Mass.: MIT Press, 1975.

GILLILAND, HAP. *A Practical Guide to Remedial Reading.* Columbus, Ohio: Charles E. Merrill Publishing Co., 1974.

GROFF, PATRICK. *Phonics: Why and How.* Morristown, N.J.: General Learning Press, 1977.

HARRIS, ALBERT J., and SIPAY, EDWARD R. *How to Increase Reading Ability.* 6th ed. New York: David McKay Co., 1975.

HARRIS, ALBERT J., and SIPAY, EDWARD R. *How to Teach Reading.* New York: Longman, 1979.

HARRIS, LARRY A. and SMITH, CARL B. *Reading Instruction.* 2nd ed. New York: Holt, Rinehart and Winston, 1976.

HASLAM, ROBERT and VALLETUTTI, PETER. *Medical Problems in the Classroom.* Baltimore: University Park Press, 1975.

HEILMAN, ARTHUR. *Phonics in Proper Perspective.* 3rd ed. Columbus, Ohio: Charles E. Merrill Publishing Co., 1976.

HEILMAN, ARTHUR. *Principles and Practices of Teaching Reading.* 3rd ed. Columbus, Ohio: Charles E. Merrill Publishing Co., 1972.

HITTLEMAN, DANIEL R. *Developmental Reading: A Psycholinguistic Perspective.* Chicago: Rand McNally Publishing Co., 1975.

IVES, JOSEPHINE P., BURSUK, LAURA Z., and IVES, SUMMER A. *Word Idenfication Techniques.* Chicago: Rand McNally College Publishing Company, 1979.

KARLIN, ROBERT, *Teaching Elementary Reading,* 3rd ed. New York: Harcourt Brace Jovanovich, Inc., 1980.

LUNDSTEEN, SARA W. *Children Learn to Communicate.* Englewood Cliffs, New Jersey: Prentice-Hall Inc., 1976.

McNEIL, JOHN D.; DONANT, LISBETH; and ALKIN, MARVIN. *How to Teach Reading Successfully.* Boston: Little, Brown and Co., 1980.

MONROE, MARION, and ROGERS, BERNICE. *Foundations for Reading.* Chicago: Scott, Foresman, & Co., 1964.

OLSON, JOANNE P. and DILLNER, MARTHA H. *Learning To Teach Reading in the Elementary School.* New York: Macmillan Publishing Co., Inc., 1976.

OLIVER, MARVIN E. *Making Readers of Everyone.* Dubuque, Iowa: Kendall/Hunt Publishing Co., 1976.

OTTO, WAYNE, CHESTER, ROBERT, McNEIL, JOHN, and MYERS, SHIRLEY. *Focused Reading Instruction.* Reading, Mass.: Addison-Wesley Publishing Co., 1974.

OTTO, WAYNE, and SMITH, RICHARD, J. *Corrective and Remedial Teaching.* Boston: Houghton Mifflin Co., 1980.

ROBECK, MILDRED, and WILSON, JOHN. *Psychology of Reading: Foundation of Instruction.* New York: John Wiley & Sons, 1974.

RUDDELL, ROBERT B. *Reading-Language Instruction: Innovative Practices.* Englewood Cliffs, N.J.: Prentice-Hall, 1974.

RUPLEY, WILLIAM H. and BLAIR, TIMOTHY R. *Reading Diagnosis and Remediation.* Chicago: Rand McNally College Publishing Company, 1979.

SCHUBERT, DELWYN G. *A Dictionary of Terms and Concepts in Reading.* Springfield, Ill.: Charles C. Thomas, 1968.

SCHUBERT, DELWYN. *Reading Games That Teach.* Monterey Park, Calif.: Creative Teaching Press, 1965.

SCHUBERT, DELWYN G., ed. *Readings in Reading: Practice-Theory-Research.* New York: Thomas Y. Crowell Company, 1968.

SMITH, BROOKS E., GOODMAN, KENNETH S., and MEREDITH, ROBERT. *Language and Thinking in School,* 2nd ed. New York: Holt, Rinehart and Winston, 1976.

SMITH, CARL B., and ELLIOTT, PEGGY G. *Reading Activities for Middle and Secondary Schools.* New York: Holt, Rinehart and Winston, 1979.

SMITH, NILA B. *American Reading Instruction.* Newark, Del.: International Reading Association, 1965.

SMITH, NILA B. *Reading Instruction for Today's Children.* Englewood Cliffs, N.J.: Prentice-Hall, 1963.

SMITH, RICHARD J., and JOHNSON, DALED D. *Teaching Children To Read.* Reading, Mass.: Addison Wesley Publishing Co., 1976.

SPACHE, EVELYN B. *Reading Activities for Child Involvement.* 2nd ed. Boston: Allyn and Bacon, Inc., 1979.

SPACHE, GEORGE. *Diagnosing and Correcting Reading Disabilities.* Boston: Allyn and Bacon, Inc., 1976.

SPACHE, GEORGE. *Good Reading for Poor Readers.* Rev. ed. Champaign, Ill.: Garrard Publishing Co., 1978.

SPACHE, GEORGE. *Reading in the Elementary School,* 4th ed. Boston: Allyn and Bacon, Inc., 1977.

SPACHE, GEORGE. *Toward Better Reading.* Champaign, Ill.: Garrard Publishing Co., 1963.

STAUFFER, RUSSELL G. *Directing the Reading-Thinking Process.* New York: Harper and Row, Publishers, 1975.

STRANG, RUTH. *Diagnostic Teaching of Reading.* 2nd ed. New York: McGraw-Hill Book Co., 1969.

TIERNEY, ROBERT J.; READENCE, JOHN E.; and DISHNER, ERNEST K. *Reading Strategies and Practices.* Rockleigh, N.J.: Allyn and Bacon, Inc., 1980.

WALCUTT, CHARLES C., LAMPORT, JOAN, and McCRACKEN, GLENN. *Teaching Reading.* New York: Macmillan Company, 1974.

WEAVER, CONSTANCE. *Psycholinguistics and Reading: From Process to Practice.* Cambridge: Winthrop Publishers, Inc., 1980.

ZINTZ, MILES V. *Corrective Reading,* 3rd ed. Dubque, Ia.: Wm. C. Brown Co., 1977.

Twentieth Yearbook, 1921, Part II—*Report of the Society's Committee on Silent Reading*, M. A. Burgess, et al.

Twenty-fourth Yearbook, 1925, Part I—*Report of the National Committee on Reading*, W. S. Gray, chairman.

Twenty-fourth Yearbook, 1925, Part II—*Adapting the Schools to Individual Differences.* Report of the Society's Committee, Carleton W. Washburne, chairman.

Thirty-sixth Yearbook, 1937, Part I—*The Teaching of Reading.* Prepared by the Society's Committee, W. S. Gray, chairman.

Forty-third Yearbook, 1944, Part II—*Teaching Language in the Elementary School.* Prepared by the Society's Committee, M. R. Trabue, chairman.

Forty-eighth Yearbook, 1949, Part II—*Reading in the Elementary School.* Prepared by the Society's Committee, Arthur I. Gates, chairman.

Sixtieth Yearbook, 1961, Part I—*Development In and Through Reading.* Prepared by the Society's Committee, Paul A. Witty, chairman.

Sixty-first Yearbook, 1962, Part I—*Individualizing Instruction.* Prepared by the Society's Committee, Fred T. Tyler, chairman.

Sixty-sixth Yearbook, 1967, Part I—*The Educationally Retarded and Disadvantaged.* Prepared by the Society's Committee, Paul A. Witty, editor.

Sixty-sixth Yearbook, 1967, Part II—*Programmed Instruction.* Prepared by the Society's Committee, Phil C. Lange, editor.

Sixty-seventh Yearbook, 1968, Part II—*Innovations and Change in Reading Instruction.* Prepared by the Society's Committee, Helen M. Robinson, editor.

Sixty-ninth Yearbook, 1970, Part II—*Linguistics in School Programs.* Prepared by the Society's Committee, Albert H. Marchwardt, editor.

INTERNATIONAL READING ASSOCIATION CONFERENCE PROCEEDINGS

Better Readers for Our Times, W. S. Gray and Nancy Larrick, editors, 1956.

Reading in Action, Nancy Larrick, editor, 1957.

Reading for Effective Living, J. Allen Figural, editor, 1958.

Reading in a Changing Society, J. Allen Figural, editor, 1959.

New Frontiers in Reading, J. Allen Figural, editor, 1960.

Changing Concepts of Reading Instruction, J. Allen Figural, editor, 1961.

Challenge and Experiment in Reading, J. Allen Figural, editor, 1962.

Reading as an Intellectual Activity, J. Allen Figura, editor, 1963.

Improvement of Reading Through Cassroom Practice, J. Allen Figural, editor, 1964.

Reading and Inquiry, J. Allen Figural, editor, 1965.

Vistas in Reading, J. Allen Figural, editor, 1966.

Forging Ahead in Reading, J. Allen Figural, editor, 1967.

Part I, *Forging Ahead in Reading,* J. Allen Figural, editor, 1968.
Part II, *Ivory, Apes, and Peacocks: The Literature Point of View,* Sam Deaton Sebesta, editor, 1968.
Part I, *Reading and Realism,* J. Allen Figural, editor, 1969.
Part II, *Current Issues in Reading,* Nila Banton Smith, editor, 1969.
Part III, *Reading Disability and Perception,* George D. Spache, editor, 1969.

SELECTED PUBLICATIONS OF THE INTERNATIONAL READING ASSOCIATION

Administrators and Reading, edited by Thorsten R. Carlson. 1972. 275 pp. (Members $8.50; nonmembers $8.50.)

Applied Linguistics and Reading, edited by Robert Shater. 1979. 174 pp. (Members $4.00; nonmembers $6.00.)

Attitudes and Reading, by J. Estill Alexander and Ronald C. Filler. 1976. 80 pp. (Members $2.50; nonmembers $3.50.)

Books about Children's Books, compiled by Virginia L. White and Emerita S. Schulte. 1979. 48 pp. (Members $1.50; nonmembers $2.00.)

The Cloze Procedure as a Teaching Technique, by Eugene Jongsma. 1971. 42 pp. (Members $1.50; nonmembers $2.25.)

Developing Active Readers: Ideas for Parents, Teachers, Librarians, edited by Dianne L. Monson and DayAnn K. McClenathan. 1979. 112 pp. (Members $3.00; nonmembers $4.50.)

Disabled Readers: Insight, Assessment, Instruction, edited by Diane Sawyer. 1980. 127 pp.

Evaluation of Teacher Education Programs in Reading, edited by Grayce A. Ransom. 1973. 60 pp. (Members $1.00; nonmembers $1.50.)

How Can I Help My Child Get Ready to Read? by Norma Rogers. 1972. 24 pp. (Members $0.35; nonmembers $0.50.)

Improving Reading in Science, by Judith Thelen. 1976. 60 pp. (Members $2.50; nonmembers $3.50.)

Improving Reading Research, edited by Roger Farr, Samuel Weintraub, and Bruce Tone. 1976. 125 pp. (Members $3.50; nonmembers $5.00.)

Inchworm, Inchworm: Persistent Problems in Reading Education, edited by Constance M. McCullough. 1980.

Individualized Reading, compiled by Harry W. Sartain. 1970. 19 pp. (Members $0.50; nonmembers $0.75.)

Inservice Education to Improve Reading Instruction, by Wayne Otto and Lawrence Erickson. 1973. 48 pp. (Members $1.75; nonmembers $2.00.)

Insights into Why and How to Read, edited by Robert T. Williams. 1976. 104 pp. (Members $3.50; nonmembers $5.00.)

Introduction to the Cloze Procedure, compiled by Richard D. Robinson. 1972. 12 pp. (Members $0.50; nonmembers $0.75.)

The Kindergarten Child and Reading, edited by Lloyd O. Olila. 1977. 88 pp. (Members $2.50; nonmembers $4.00.)

Linguistic Theory: What Can It Say About Reading? edited by Roger Shay. 195 pp. (Members $4.50; nonmembers $6.50.)

Linguistics, Psycholinguistics, and the Teaching of Reading, compiled by Yetta M. Goodman and Kenneth S. Goodman, 1971. 36 pp. (Members $0.50; nonmembers $0.75.)

Literacy for America's Spanish Speaking Children, by Eleanor W. Thonis. 1976. 78 pp. (Members $2.50; nonmembers $3.50.)

Meeting Individual Needs in Reading, edited by Helen K. Smith, 1971. 149 pp. (Members $3.50; nonmembers $4.50.)

Models of Efficient Reading, by Karen Cohen, Richard West, and George March. 1979. 78 pp. (Members $3.00; nonmembers $4.00.)

National Assessment of Educational Progress in Reading, edited by Robert Tierney and Diane Lapp. 1979. 48 pp. (Members $2.00; nonmembers $3.00.)

Reading and the Adult Learner, edited by Laura Johnson. 1979. 84 pp. (Members $2.50; nonmembers $4.00.)

Reading and the Bilingual Child, by Doris Ching. 1976. 48 pp. (Members $2.00; nonmembers $3.00.)

Reading and the Black English Speaking Child, compiled by Jean R. Harber and Jane N. Beatty. 1978. 48 pp. (Members $1.75; nonmembers $2.50.)

Reading and Writing Instruction in the United States: Historical Trends, edited by H. Alan Robinson. 1977. 91 pp. (Members $3.00; nonmembers $4.00.)

Reading, Children's Books, and Our Pluralistic Society, edited by Harold Tanyzer and Jean Karl. 1972. 90 pp. (Members $3.00; nonmembers $3.50.)

Reading for the Gifted and the Creative Student, edited by Paul A. Witty. 1971. 64 pp. (Members $2.00; nonmembers $2.50.)

Reading Interaction: The Teacher, The Pupil, The Materials, edited by Brother Leonard Courtney. 1976. 118 pp. (Members $3.50; nonmembers $5.00.)

Reading in the Content Fields, compiled by Leo Fay and Lee Ann Jared. 1975. 19 pp. (Members $1.00; nonmembers $1.25.)

Reading Readiness, by John Downing and D. V. Thackray. 1971. 128 pp. (Members $3.00; nonmembers $3.00.)

Reading Tests and Teachers: A Practical Guide, edited by Robert Schreiner. 1979. 92 pp. (Members $2.50; nonmembers $4.00.)

Recognition of Words, by Linnea C. Ehri, Roderick W. Barron, and Jeffrey M. Feldman. 1978. 70 pp. (Members $2.50; nonmembers $3.50.)

Research Within Reach: *A Research-Guided Response to Concerns of Reading Educators*, by Phylis Weaver and Fredi Shonkoff. 1978. 150 pp. (Members $4.50; nonmembers $4.50.)

Screening Vision in Schools, by Fred W. Jobe. 1976. 64 pp. (Members $2.50; nonmembers $3.75.)

Self-Concept and Reading by Ivan Quandt. 1972. 40 pp. (Members $2.00; nonmembers $3.00.)

Social Class and Ethnic Group Differences in Learning to Read, by Victoria Seitz. 1977. 44 pp. (Members $2.00; nonmembers $3.00.)

Teaching Reading and Mathematics, by Richard Earle. 1976. 95 pp. (Members $3.00; nonmembers $4.50.)

Teaching Reading in the Social Studies, by John Lundstrum and Bob Tayler. 1978. 92 pp. (Members $2.50; nonmembers $3.50.)

Teaching Reading Skills Through the Newspaper, by Arnold B. Cheyney. 1971. 50 pp. (Members $1.75; nonmembers $2.00.)

Teaching Word Recognition Skills, compiled by Mildred A. Dawson. 1970. 296 pp. (Members $3.00; nonmembers $4.00.)

Television and the Classroom Reading Program, by George J. Becker. 1973. 32 pp. (Members $1.75; nonmembers $2.00.)

The Torch Lighters Revisited, by Coleman Morrison and Mary C. Austin. 1977. 104 pp. (Members $3.50; nonmembers $4.50.)

Using Literature and Poetry Affectively, edited by Jon Shapiro. 1979. 128 pp. (Members $3.50; nonmembers $5.00.)

Views on Elementary Reading Instruction, edited by Thomas D. Barrett and Dale D. Johnson. 1973. 97 pp. (Members $2.00; nonmembers $3.00.)

Why Read Aloud To Children? by Julie M. T. Chan. 1974. 12 pp. (Members $0.35; nonmembers $0.50.)

PUBLICATIONS WHICH CONTAIN BIBLIOGRAPHIES OF BOOKS FOR RETARDED READERS

BERRIDGE, WAYNE, and SIEDROW, MARY. *Guide to Materials for Reading Instruction*. Bloomington, Ind.: ERIC Clearinghouse on Reading. Indiana University, 1971.

BOTEL, MORTON. *How to Teach Reading*. Chicago: Follett Publishing Co., 1962, pp. 117-120.

CARLSEN, G. ROBERT. *Books and the Teen-Age Reader: A Guide for Teachers, Librarians, and Parents*. New York: Harper & Row, 1967.

CARTER, HOMER, and McGINNIS, DOROTHY. *Learning to Read*. New York: McGraw-Hill Book Co., 1953, pp. 115-118.

DAWSON, MILDRED, and BAMMAN, HENRY. *Fundamentals of Basic Reading Instruction*, 2nd ed. New York: Longmans, Green & Co., 1963.

DECHANT, EMERALD. *Diagnosis and Remediation of Reading Disability*. West Nyack, N. Y.: Parker Publishing Co., 1968, pp. 174-175.

DELLA-PIANA, GABRIEL. *Reading Diagnosis and Prescription.* New York: Holt, Rinehart & Winston, 1968, App. E.

DUNN, ANITA, and JACKMAN, MABEL. *Fare for the Reluctant Reader,* 3rd ed. Albany: Capital Area School Development Association, State University of New York at Albany, 1964.

EAKIN, MARY. *Good Books for Children.* 3rd ed. Chicago: University of Chicago Press, 1966.

EAKIN, MARY. *Library Materials for Remedial Reading, Bibliography.* No. 4, Instructional Materials Bulletin, May, 1959, Cedar Falls, Iowa: Iowa State Teachers College Library.

EMERY, R. C. and HOUSHOWER, M. B. *High Interest Easy Reading for Junior and Senior High School Reluctant Readers.* Champaign, Ill.: National Council of Teachers of English, 1965.

GILLILAND, HAP. *Materials for Remedial Reading and Their Use.* Level 4. Billings, Mont.: Montana Reading Publication, 1972.

GUILFOILE, ELIZABETH. *Adventuring with Books.* Rev. ed. Champaign, Ill.: National Council of Teachers of English, 1966.

HARRIS, ALBERT J. and SIPAY, EDWARD R. *How to Increase Reading Ability.* 6th ed. New York: David McKay Co., 1975, app. B.

HARRIS, ALBERT J., and SIPAY, EDWARD R. *How To Teach Reading.* New York: Longman, 1979, pp. 453-455.

HART, J. A. *Books for the Retarded Reader: A Teacher's Guide to Books for Backward Children.* 3rd ed. Victoria, Australia: Australian Council for Educational Research, 1966.

JULITTA, SISTER MARY, and MICHAELLA, SISTER. "A List of Books for Retarded Readers," *Elementary English* 45 (1968):472-477.

KARLIN, ROBERT. *Teaching Reading in High School.* Indianapolis: Bobbs-Merrill Educational Publishing, 1977, p. 275.

KRESS, ROY. *A Place to Start: A Graded Bibliography for Children with Reading Difficulties.* Syracuse, N.Y.: Reading Center, Syracuse University, 1963.

LEIBERT, ROBERT, ED. *A Place to Start.* Lawrence, Kan.: University of Kansas Reading Center, 1971.

ORR, KENNETH. *Selected Materials for Remedial Reading.* Terre Haute, Ind.: Division of Special Education, Indiana State Teachers College.

ROSWELL, FLORENCE et al. *Selected Materials for Children with Reading Disabilities.* Rev. ed. New York: Remedial Reading Service, School of Education, The City College, 1966.

RUE, ELOISE. *America Past and Present.* New York: H. W. Wilson Co., 1948.

SHOR, RACHEL, and FIDEL, ESTELLE A. *Children's Catalog.* 11th ed. New York: H. W. Wilson Co., 1966.

SMITH, NILA BANTON. *Reading Instruction for Today's Children.* Englewood Cliffs, N.J.: Prentice-Hall, 1963.

SPACHE, GEORGE. *Good Reading for Poor Readers*. Rev. ed. Champaign, Ill.: Garrard Publishing Co., 1970.

STRANG, RUTH et al. *Gateway to Readable Books*. 4th ed. New York: H. W. Wilson Co., 1966.

WHITE, MARIAN. *High Interest-Easy Reading for Junior and Senior High School Students*. New York: Citation Press, 1972.

WILLARD, CHARLES B., and HELEN I. STAPP. *Your Reading*. Champaign, Ill.: National Council of Teachers of English, 1966.

WILSON, JEAN, ed. *Books for You*. Urbana, Ill.: National Teachers of English.

WITTY, PAUL A., FREELAND, ALMA M., and GROTBERG, EDITH H. *The Teaching of Reading*. Lexington, Mass.: D. C. Heath & Co., 1966, p. 66.

WRIGHT, JOSEPHINE. *Library Resources*. Salt Lake City, Utah: Exemplary Center for Reading Instruction, 1968.

APPENDIX E SURVEY OF HIGH-INTEREST, LOW-VOCABULARY BOOKS FOR DISABLED READERS

It is essential that teachers have an ample supply of these books to provide retarded readers with material at their level of interest and achievement.

Title	Difficulty Grade Level	Interest Grade Level
Spiral Book Series	3.0-4.9	7-12
Published by Continental Press, Inc.		
Awareness Pictorial Books	3-4	7-12
Published by Davco Publishers		
Dan Frontier Books Series (audio components available	pp-4	1-7
Cowboy Sam Books Series (audio components available)	pp-3	1-4
Button Books Series	pp13	1-5
Sailor Jack Books Series	pp-3	1-6
Space Age Books Series	1-3	2-6
What Is It Series	1-4	1-8
Tom Logan (audio components available)	1-3	1-6
Cowboys of Many Races (audio components available)	pp-5	1-7
Animal Adventure Series (audio components available)	pp-1	1-4
Moonbeam Series	1-3	1-6
Treat Truck Series	1-3	1-5
Sports Mystery Series	2-4	4-12
Space Science Fiction Series	2-6	4-12
Butternut Bill Series (audio components available)	pp-1	1-6
Inner City Series	1-3	1-5
Alley Alligator Series	1-3	1-6

Title	Difficulty Grade Level	Interest Grade Level
Target Today Series	1.9-4.9	4-12
Mystery Adventure Series	2-6	4-12
Racing Wheels Readers	2-4	4-12
Published by Benefic Press		
Childhood of Famous American Series	4-5	4-9
Published by Bobbs-Merrill Co.		
All About Books Series	2-4	2-8
True Books Series	2-3	2-8
Frontiers of America Series	3	3-8
Middle Grade Books Series	4	3-7
Fun to Read Classics	5-8	5-12
Rally Series	4-5	7-10
Published by Children's Book Centre		
Jim Forest Readers Series	1-3	2-7
Checkered Flag Series	2	5-12
Deep Sea Adventure Series	2-4	3-9
Morgan Bay Series	2-4	3-8
Wildlife Adventure Series	2-4	3-7
Americans All Series	4	4-7
The Top Flight Readers	2-3	7-12
The Time Machine Series	1-2	1-3
Published by Addison-Wesley		
Interesting Reading Series	2-3	4-11
Vocational Reading Series	4-6	9-12
Turner-Livingston Reading Series	4-6	7-9
Interesting Reading Series	2-3	4-11
Turner-Livingston Communications Series	5-6	8-10
Turner Career Guidance Series	5-6	11-12
Published by Follett Educational Corp.		
Junior Science Books Series	3-4	3-6
Pleasure Reading Books	4	3-6
Basic Vocabulary Series	1-3	2-4
Discovery Books Series	2-4	3-6
Folklore of the World Books Series	3	2-8
Pleasure Reading Series	3-4	3-5
Holidays	3	2-5
Creative People in the Arts and Sciences	5	4-7
Myths, Tales, and Legends	5	4-7
Rivers	5	4-7
Sports	4	3-6
Explorers	4	3-6
American Folktales	3-4	2-6
First Reading Books	1-2	1-4
Published by Garrard Publishing Co.		
Simplified Classics Series	4-6	4-10
Published by Globe Book Co.		
We Were There Books Series	4-5	5-9
Getting to Know Books Series	4-5	5-9

Title	Difficulty Grade Level	Interest Grade Level
How and Why Series	4-5	4-9
Published by E. M. Hale & Co.		
American Adventure Series	2-6	4-9
Modern Adventure Stories Series	4-6	4-11
Published by Harper & Row.		
Teen Age Tales	4-6	6-11
Strange Teen Age Tales Books	5-6	5-11
Published by D. C. Heath & Co.		
Beginner Books Series	1-2	1-2
Gateway Books	2-3	3-9
Step-Up Books Series	2-3	3-9
Allabout Books Series	4-6	5-11
Landmark Books Series	5-7	5-11
Published by Random House		
Boxcar Children Mysteries	2-3	3-8
Published by Albert Whitman & Co.		
Warner Mystery Series	3-6	4-6
Simplified Classics Series	4-5	4-10
Published by Scott, Foresman & Co.		
Junior Everyreaders Series	2-4	2-7
Everyreader Series	4-5	4-10
Published by Webster/McGraw-Hill Book Co.		
First Books	2-9	3-12
Published by Franklin Watts		

APPENDIX F PUBLISHERS AND MANUFACTURERS OF READING TESTS, TEXTBOOKS, MATERIALS, AND DEVICES

The following alphabetically arranged list contains the names and addresses of publishers and manufacturers of reading tests, textbook, material, and devices mentioned in this book. Because of the rapid change in publishers' names and addresses, some of these entries can be out of date.

Acoustifone Corporation, Box 3997, 7428 Bellaire Ave., North Hollywood, Calif. 91609

Addison-Wesley Publishing Co., Inc., Reading, Mass. 01876, and 2725 Sand Hill Rd., Menlo Park, Calif. 94025

Allied Education Council, Box 78, Galien, Mich. 49113

Allied Education Press, P.O. Box 78, Galien, Mich. 49113

Allyn & Bacon, Inc., 470 Atlantic Ave., Boston, Mass. 92210

American Book Company, 450 W. 33rd St., New York, N.Y. 10001

American Optical Co., 62 Mechanic Street, Southbridge, Mass. 01608

American Teaching Aids, Box 1652, Covina, Calif. 91722

Appleton-Century-Crofts, 292 Madison Ave., New York, N.Y. 10017

ATC Publishing Corporation, Box 5588, Lakeland, Fl. 33803

Audiotronics, 7428 Bellaire Ave., North Hollywood, Calif. 91605

Audio-Visual Research Co., 1317 8th St., S.E., Waseca, Minn. 56093

Barnell Loft, Ltd., 958 Church St., Baldwin, N.Y. 11510

Beaver Pond Learning, Box 5461, Hamden, Ct. 06518

Beckley-Cardy Co. (see Benefic Press)

Bell & Howell Co., Audio Visual Products Division, 7100 McCormick Rd., Chicago, Ill. 60645

Benefic Press, 10300 W. Roosevelt Rd., Westchester, Ill. 60153

BFA Educational Media, 2211 Michigan Ave., Santa Monica, Calif. 90025

Bobbs-Merrill Co., Inc., 4300 W. 62nd St., Indianapolis, Ind. 46206

Borg-Warner Educational Systems, 600 W. University Dr., Arlington Heights, Ill. 60004

Bowmar Publishing Corporation, 622 Rodier Dr., Glendale, Calif. 91201

Califone International, Inc., 5922 Bowcroft St., Los Angeles, Calif. 90016

California Test Bureau/McGraw-Hill Book Company Division, Del Monte Research Park, Monterey, Calif. 93940

Cenco Educational Aids, 2600 S. Kostner Ave., Chicago, Ill. 60623

Children's Book Centre, 140 Kensington Church St., London, W 8, England

Communacad, The Communications Academy, Box 541, Wilton, Conn. 06897

Comprehension Games Corporation, 63-110 Woodhaven Blvd., Rego Park, N.Y. 11374

Continental Press, Inc., Elizabethtown, Pa. 17022

Coronet, 65 East South Water St., Chicago, Ill. 60601

Creative Curriculum, Inc., 15681 Commerce Lane, Huntington Beach, Calif. 92649

Creative Teaching Press, 5305 Production Dr., Huntington Beach, Calif. 92649

Davco Publishers, 5425 Fargo, Skokie, Ill. 60076

Developmental Learning Materials, 7440 Natchez Ave., Niles, Ill. 60648

Dexter & Westbrook, Ltd., 958 Church St., Baldwin, N.Y. 11510

Dick Blick, P.O. Box 1267, Galesburg, Ill. 61401

Dreier Educational Systems, Inc., 320 Raritan Ave., Highland Park, N.J. 08904

Economy Company, Box 25308, 1901 W. Walnut St., Oklahoma City, Okla. 73125

EDL. See Educational Development Laboratories

Educational Aids, 845 Wisteria Dr., Fremont, Calif. 94538

Educational Development Laboratories/McGraw-Hill Book Company Division, 1221 Ave. of Americas, New York, N.Y. 10020

Educational Electronics, Inc., 284 Polaski Rd., Huntington, Long Island, N.Y. 11744

Educational Insights, 20435 S. Tillman Ave., Carson, Calif. 90746

Educational Progress Corporation, 4900 S. Lewis Ave., Tulsa, Okla. 74145

Educator's Publishing Service, Inc., 75 Moulton St., Cambridge, Mass. 02138

Encore Visual Education, Inc., 1235 South Victory Blvd., Burbank, Calif. 91502

Encyclopedia Britannica Education Corporation, 425 N. Michigan Ave., Chicago, Ill. 60611

Enrichment Reading Corporation of America, Iron Ridge, Wis. 53035

Essay Press, P.O. Box 2323, Lajolla, Calif. 92037

Follett Educational Corporation, 1010 W. Washington Blvd., Chicago, Ill. 60007

Garrard Publishing Company, 1607 N. Market St., Champaign, Ill. 61820

General Learning Corporation, Morristown, N.J. 07960

Ginn & Co., Division of Xerox, 191 Spring St., Lexington, Mass. 02173

Globe Book Company, Inc., 10010 50 W. 23rd St., New York, N.Y.

Gould, Inc., Educational Systems Division, 4423 Arden Dr., El Monte, Calif. 91731

Grolier Educational Corp., Instructional Systems Div., 845 Third Ave., New York, N.Y. 10022

E. M. Hale & Co., 1201 S. Hastings, Eau Claire, Wis. 54701

Harcourt Brace Jovanovich, Inc., 757 3rd Ave., New York, N.Y. 10017

Imperial International Learning Corporation, P.O. Box 548, Kankakee, Ill. 60901

Incentives for Learning, 600 West Van Buren St., Chicago, Ill. 60607

Instructional Communications Technology, Inc., Huntington Station, N.Y. 11746

Instructional Materials & Equipment Distributors, 1520 Cotner Ave., Los Angeles, Calif. 90025

Instructor Publications, Inc., 7 Bank St., Dansville, N.Y. 14437

International Reading Association, 800 Barksdale Rd., Newark, N.J. 19711

Ken-A-Vision, Inc., 5615 Raytown Rd., Kansas City, Mo. 64133

Kenworthy Educational Service, Inc., 138 Allen St., P.O. Box 60, Buffalo, N.Y. 14205

Lafayette Instrument Company, Box 1279, Lafayette, Ind. 47902

Lakeshore Curriculum Materials Co., 2695 E. Dominguez St., P.O. Box 6261, Carson, Calif. 90749

Language Research Associates, 175 E. Delaware Place, Chicago, Ill. 60611

Learnco Inc., Box L, Exeter, N.Y. 03833

Learning Dimensions, 2742 W. Orangethorpe Ave., Fullerton, Calif. 92633

Learning Systems Corp., 60 Connolly Parkway, Camden, Ct. 06514

Learning Tree Filmstrips, 934 Pearl St., Boulder, Colo. 80302

Learning Through Seeing, Inc., Box 368, Sunland, Calif. 91040

J. B. Lippincott Co., E. Washington Sq., Philadelphia, Pa. 19015

Little Brown Bear Learning Associates, Box 561167, Miami, Fla. 33156

Lyons & Carnahan, Division of Rand McNally & Company, Box 7600, Chicago, Ill. 60680

McCormick-Mathers Publishing Company, 7625 Empire Dr., Florence, Ky. 41042

McGraw-Hill Book Company, 1221 Ave. of Americas, New York, N.Y. 10020

Macmillan, Inc., 866 3rd Ave., New York, N.Y. 10022

Mast/Keystone, 2212 E. 12th St., Davenport, Iowa 52803

Media Materials, Inc., 2936 Remington Ave., Baltimore, Md. 21211

Charles E. Merrill Publishing Company, 1200 Alum Creek Dr., Columbus, Ohio 43216

The Mills Center, P.O. Box 597, Black Mountain, N.C. 28711

Milton Bradley Co., Springfield, Mass. 01101

NCS-Word Wizard, 4401 W. 76th St., Minneapolis, Minn. 55435

Open Court Publishing Company, Box 599, LaSalle, Ill. 61301

Ore Press, Inc., 5591 N.W. Broadway, West Linn, Or. 97068

Pendulum Press, Inc., Academic Bldg., Saw Mill Rd., West Haven, Conn. 06516

Perceptual Development Laboratories, 6767 Southwest Ave., St. Louis, Mo. 63117

Personnel Press, 191 Spring St., Lexington, Mass. 02173

Phonovisual Products, Inc., 12216 Parklawn Dr., Rockville, Md. 20852

Photo and Sound Company, 9956 Baldwin Place, El Monte, Calif. 91731

Prentice-Hall, Inc., Englewood Cliffs, N.J. 07632

The Psychological Corporation (see Harcourt Brace Jovanovich, Inc.)

Psychotechnics, Inc., 1900 Pickwick Ave., Glenview, Ill. 60025

Rand McNally & Company, Box 7600, Chicago, Ill. 60680

Random House, Inc., 201 E. 50th St., New York, N.Y. 10022

Reader's Digest Services, Inc., Educational Division, Pleasantville, N.Y. 10570
Reading Is Fun-Damental, Smithsonian Institute, Washington, D.C. 20560
Reading Joy, Inc., P.O. Box 404, Naperville, Ill. 60540
The Reading Laboratory, Inc., P.O. Box 681, South Norwalk, Conn. 06854
Remedial Education Press, Kingsbury Center, 2138 Bancroft Pl. NW, Washington, D.C. 20008
Right to Read, 400 Maryland Ave. S.W., Washington, D.C. 20202
Scholastic Magazines and Book Services, 50 W. 44th St., New York, N.Y. 10036
Science Research Associates, Inc., 155 N. Wacker Dr., Chicago, Ill. 60606
Scott, Foresman and Company, 1900 E. Lake Ave., Glenview, Ill. 60025
Singer Graphlex Division, 3750 Montrose Ave., Rochester, N.Y. 14603
Society for Visual Education, Inc., 1345 Diversey Pkway., Chicago, Ill. 60614
Spellbinder, Inc., 33 Bradford St., Concord, Mass. 01742
Steck-Vaughn Company, Box 2028, Austin, Texas 78767
S-T-E-P Ahead, Inc., Eugene, Oregon
Syracuse University Press, Box 8, University Station, Syracuse, N. Y. 13210
Tarmac/Tac, Inc., 8 Baird Mountain Road, Asheville, N.C. 28804
Teachers College Press, 1234 Amsterdam Ave., New York, N.Y. 10027
The Teachers Market Place, 16220 Orange Ave., Paramount, Calif. 90723
Teachers' Supplies, 6571 Beach Blvd., Buena Park, Calif. 90620
Teaching Stuff, P.O. Box 9366 Dept. K, Glendale, Calif. 91206
Trend Enterprises, Inc., P.O. Box 43073, St. Paul, Minn. 55164
University of Chicago Press, 1130 S. Langley Ave., Chicago, Ill. 60628
Visualcraft, Inc., 12842 S. Western Ave., Blue Island, Ill. 60406
Voxcom, 100 Clover Green, Peachtree City, Ga. 30269
Jane Ward Co., Box 978, Lakewood, Colo. 80228
Warren's Educational Supplies, 7715 Garvey Ave., Rosemead, Calif. 91770
Franklin Watts, Inc., 845 Third Ave., New York, N.Y. 10022
Webster/McGraw-Hill. See McGraw-Hill Book Company.
Western Psychological Services, 12031 Wilshire Blvd., Los Angeles, Calif. 90025
Albert Whitman & Company, 560 W. Lake St., Chicago, Ill. 60606
Wordcrafters Guild, St. Albans School, Massachusetts and Wisconsin Aves. NW, Washington, D.C. 20016
Xerox Educational Publications, 191 Spring St., Lexington, Mass. 92173
Richard L. Zweig Associates, 20800 Beach Blvd., Huntington Beach, Calif. 92648

Author Index

Subject Index

Implementing the Reading Program, 350–387
Incentives to learning, 64
Independent reading, 8, 385
Independent reading habits, 8, 385
Individual differences, 138–139
  and correction, 138–139
  and frustration, 21–22
  and group instruction, 123–124
  and instructional level, 175
Individualized correction, 202–210, 223–232
  advantages, 228–229
  implementing, 229–230
  instructional material, 230–232
  principles, 225–228
Individualized reading, 104–105
Individual reading needs, 138
Initial Teaching Alphabet, 203
In-service education, 24, 380–382
Instructional material, 242–379
  commercial, 242–379
  corrective, 242–379
  multilevel, 328–386
  reading games, 291–292
Instructional practices, 6–28
Intelligence, 53–54
  and potential, 211
  and reading, 53–56
  tests, 54–55, 414–416
Interests, 125–135
  and free reading, 242–243
  and instructional level, 175
  and learning, 125–135
  and motivation, 125–135
Interviewing, 171–172
Inventories, 165–170
  pupil behavior, 168–169
  of reading difficulties, 217–221
  of the reading skills, 212

Kindergarten, 84–85
Kinesthetic method, 98–100

Language-experience method, 100–101
Learning
  centers, 153–154
  and correction, 4, 223–231
  emotional problems, 48–49
  and experiential background, 71–72
  and frustration, 9, 175
  gifted, 147–148
  goals of instruction, 2
  hazards, 6–62
  and instruction, 3–4
  and mastery, 7–8, 11, 385–386
  methods, 97–107
  neurological impairment, 45–48, 168
  potential, 195–196, 211–213

programmed, 378–379
tenets of, 2–3
versus teaching, 2
Letter names, 85
Letter to parents, 75–78
Levels of reading, 175
  frustration, 175
  independent, 175
  instructional, 175
  potential, 175
Library, 25, 382–384
Lighting, 26–27
Linguistics, 101–102
Listening
  comprehension, 196
  and reading potential, 213
  tests, 412

Machines. See mechanical devices
Mastery
  importance, 7–8, 385–386
  levels, 175
  of skills, 385–386
Meaning vocabulary, 300–306
Mechanical devices, 317–320
Minimal competence, 64
Motivation, 125–135
  and comic books, 130
  extrinsic, 125–126
  instructional material, 125–135
  and interest, 125–135
  intrinsic, 125–126
  law of effect, 126
  Sustained Silent Reading (SSR), 151–152
  use of paperbacks, 128–129
Multilevel reading material, 328–378

Negative practice, 240–241
Neurological impairment, 45–48
Norms, 17–18
Nutrition, 71

Observation, 163–165
  and behavior inventories, 165–174
  of child behavior, 168–169
  of oral reading, 174–177
  of reading habits, 212
  of silent reading, 212
Oral reading, 93–96, 178–180
  analysis of, 178–183
  checklist, 212
  errors, 178–180
  habits, 234–241
  informal analysis, 93–96
  instruction, 94–95
  and round-robin reading, 93–94
  and tape recorder, 95
  tests, 406–407

Paperbacks, 128–129
Parental involvement, 64–67
Parent-child relationships, 67–68
Parents as models, 68–69
Parent-teaching pool, 74–75
Perceptual training, 85–87
Phonics, 87–91
  analysis of, 88–89
  corrective materials, 258–281
  principles of, 388–392
Potential, 16, 195–196, 211–213
Preschool period, 82–83
Prevention, 19, 21–22
  and parent-child relationships, 67–68
Professional books, 420–430
Professional library, 420–421
Publishers, 430–433

Reading
  and book reports, 132–133
  checklist, 212
  and content fields, 108–110
  correction, 223–233
  developmental, 80–124
  disabilities, 72
  and disadvantaged, 14
  expectancy, 214–215
  and experiential background, 71–72
  games, 291–292
  goals, 11, 17
  group instruction, 248–251
  illiteracy, 1–2, 385
  importance of, 1–2
  improvement program, 380–386
  individualized, 104–105
  and instructional materials, 242–378
  and interests, 125–137
  inventory, 174–179, 212
  levels of difficulty, 175
  and library, 25, 382–384
  mastery, 7, 21
  and materials, 242–378
  and motivation, 125–136
  oral, 8, 93–96, 178–181
  oral reading difficulties, 180
  oral reading tests, 406–407
  and phonics, 87–92
  potential, 195–196, 211–213
  prevention, 19–20
  recreational reading, 11
  school practices, 6–29
  and self-directed material, 242–378
  silent reading tests, 409–412
  skills, 111–120
  sustained silent reading, 131–132
  and vision, 31–37
  and word analysis, 19–20, 92, 107–108
  word-by-word, 236–237
  workbooks, 87, 296–299

Reading disabilities
  and brain injury, 45–47
  causal factors, 30–62
  corrective material, 242–378
  cultural deprivation, 52–53
  and dominance, 42–44
  and emotional factors, 48–51
  hazards to learning, 6–62
  prevalence, 1–2
  severity, 213–215
  signs of, 209–210
Reading improvement program
  essential elements, 386
  implementing, 386
  in-service program, 380–382
  school library, 25, 382
  teacher library, 382–385
  teacher training, 23–24, 380–382
Reading is fundamental (RIF), 129
Reading readiness
  and beginning reading, 83–85
  checklist, 173–174
  defined, 83
  developing, 84–85
  evaluating, 87, 173–174
  in every grade, 83
  in first grade, 83
  and kindergarten, 84
  maturities in, 83
  tests, 172–173
  workbooks, 87
Reading skills
  comprehension, 111–114
  outlining, 118, 323–324
  rate of comprehension, 115, 317–321
  skimming, 117–118
  SQ3R Method, 114–115, 117
  summarizing, 119, 324–325
  word analysis, 19, 107, 242–292
  word recognition, 7–8, 96–97, 244–254
Reading tests
  diagnostic, 406–412
  group, 186–189, 410–412
  informal, 174–177
  list, 406–413
  listening, 412–413
  oral, 406–407
  reading readiness, 405–406
  silent, 409–412
  survey, 410–412
Reading to children, 69
Recreational reading, 11, 69, 242
  and independent reading level, 175
  and interests, 126, 242–243
Remedial reading. See corrective reading.

School calendar, 64
School practices
  and hazards to learning, 6–27
  and learning, 6–27

Self-directed correction, 228–232
Self-directed instructional material, 230–231
  advantages, 228–229
  teacher-made, 229
Sleep, 71
Slow learners, 146–147
Snellen chart, 196–197
Speech, 40–41, 170
Speed of reading, 115, 317–321
Strephosymbolia, 43
Sustained Silent Reading (SSR), 131–132
Survey Q3R Method, 114–115, 117

Tachistoscopes, 318–319
Tape recorder, 179
Teacher-parent relationships, 67
Teacher-pupil relationships, 13
Teacher training, 23
Telebinocular, 197–198
Television viewing, 73–74
Testing program, 17–18
Tutoring, 224

Vandalism, 70
Vision
  errors of refraction, 31–32
  fusion difficulties, 32–35
  immaturity, 35
  informal tests, 198–199
  symptoms of difficulty, 167

Vocabulary
  corrective practice, 242–293
  lists, 243
  meaning, 300–306
  sight, 7–8, 96–97, 244–254
  workbooks, 289–290, 296–300
Vocalization, 233–238

Walton card, 198
Word analysis, 19, 107, 242–292
  corrective materials, 285–288
  glossary, 392–404
  importance, 19–20
Word-by-word reading, 236–237
Word lists, 181–183
Word meaning, 300–306
  corrective materials, 300–306
Word recognition, 7–8, 96–97, 244–254
  corrective material, 242–293
  importance, 7–8
  and independent reading, 7–8
  instructional program, 96
  and phonics, 87–92, 258–285
Words in color, 104
Workbooks
  for comprehension, 296–300
  for readiness, 87
  for vocabulary development, 289–290